Shot in America

Television, the State,
and the Rise of Chicano Cinema

Chon A. Noriega

University of Minnesota Press
Minneapolis
London

Published by the University of Minnesota Press
111 Third Avenue South, Suite 290
Minneapolis, MN 55401-2520
http://www.upress.umn.edu

Printed in the United States of America on acid-free paper

Library of Congress Cataloging-in-Publication Data

Noriega, Chon A., 1961-
    Shot in America : television, the state, and the rise of Chicano cinema / Chon A. Noriega.
        p. cm.
    Includes filmography.
    Includes bibliographical references and index.
    ISBN 0-8166-2930-7 (HC : alk. paper) -- ISBN 0-8166-2931-5 (PB : alk. paper)
    1. Mexican Americans in motion pictures. 2. Mexican Americans on television. 3.
Mexican Americans in the motion picture industry. I. Title.

PN1995.9.M49 N69 2000
791.43'652036872073--dc21

                                                                                    99-088112

11 10 09 08 07 06 05 04 03 02   10 9 8 7 6 5 4 3 2

Lights, camera, cultural infraction! . . .
As Hollywood continues to shoot Chicanos,
Chicanos will have to shoot right back.
                    —*Harry Gamboa Jr., 1978*

Contents

Preface

I did not intend to write a history about television, social movements, and the state, but my research would not let me do otherwise, since it is in that nexus that I discovered the origins of Chicano cinema. My study of Chicano-directed feature films and experimental works must be the subject of another book. Needless to say, I find this change of direction both ironic and instructive with respect to the fields within which I work, a subject I cover in the first part of this book.

In the introduction and chapters 1 and 2, I consider the historiographic implications of combining ethnic studies, cinema studies, and television studies in the broadest sense—that is, to such an extent that each field could claim the object of study. Is it possible to write a history of cinema that is also a history of television, or a history of cultural formations that is also a history of the state? And is it possible to do so using the example of a political generation of Chicano filmmakers? Conversely, can a Chicano history speak these other histories, too? My concern is to bridge two divides: the nation and the minority group, and the aesthetic and the sociological. In the first part, then, I consider "Chicano cinema" vis-à-vis nationalism, social movements, telecommunications, and the state, providing a critical template for the remainder of the book.

In the second part of this book, chapters 3 through 8, I provide a history of Chicano cinema through the institutional frames of U.S. broadcast television and state regulation. I start with the protests against the Frito Bandito commercials in the 1960s, then consider the subsequent media reform movement, the rise and fall of Chicano public affairs programming, and the development of Chicano professionalism within the independent sector. I end with a brief overview of the impact of the digital revolution and the rise of global media.

Here I would like to add a few words about my primary field—cinema studies—and the major influences on this book. In my career, I have followed a path that pretty much reflects that of cinema studies itself: an unexamined bias toward feature films, the theoretical centrality of feminism, and a strong belief in the redemptive powers of close textual analysis. I started my research looking at the dozen or so Chicano feature films. Since none of these were produced by women, I also looked at the documentaries and short narratives directed by Lourdes Portillo and Sylvia Morales. When I was asked to curate programs for museums and festivals, I expanded my search for documentaries and short narratives, finding many of them through public affairs series, media arts centers, and social service agencies. I quickly realized the need to know more about television and the avant-garde, both of which were outside the purview of my initial training in cinema studies. But if the realization was quick, it took time to understand these seemingly discrete practices.

I have been fortunate to be able to draw from what at first appeared to be an eclectic set of influences. David James's *Allegories of Cinema* (1989) provided an important example of pulling together diverse film practices in a breathtaking attempt to understand a significant period of American cinema. Similarly, Thomas Streeter's *Selling the Air* (1996) provided an interdisciplinary critique of the laws and policies that define commercial broadcasting in the United States, something that I realized needed to be incorporated into cultural and aesthetic analyses. Finally, Francisco J. Lewels Jr.'s *The Uses of the Media by the Chicano Movement* (1974) and Jo Freeman's *The Politics of Women's Liberation* (1975) made me see that social movements have often generated their own best histories and theoretical paradigms, speaking quite astutely to their location within the imagined community and administrative apparatus of the nation-state.

No matter how tenuous, informal, and short lived, social movements have had a profound impact on the history of the "culture industry" (James) and "corporate liberalism" (Streeter), not to mention a history that James and Streeter generally do not address: the emergence of minority identities as the product of the state's efforts to contain social movements in the name of corporate capitalism. Indeed, this configuration should serve as a cautionary note to both the critics and the proponents of identity scholarship, who in very different ways nonetheless accept identity as an autonomous category. There is no identity that is not also juridical and corporate and, as such, also already part of the totality it names itself against, challenges, and even changes.

In having written a cinema history by way of television, a cultural critique by way of the state, I find some explanation and confirmation in Rudolf Arnheim's "The Film Critic of Tomorrow" (1935):

> Film is one of the most characteristic means of expression, and one of the most effective means of influence in our time. Not just individuals, but also peoples, classes, and forms of government play a part in it. The film critic of tomorrow will have to take this into account.

Earlier in the essay he offers a telling qualification: "perhaps he [sic] will even be called a 'television critic.'" Indeed. Sometimes the past understands us better than we understand the past. But we qualify each other.

Acknowledgments

If knowledge begins with negation, it must necessarily end with recognition. Tomás Ybarra-Frausto, by example and encouragement, taught me that one needs to make a life as well as a living. I am fortunate to have had him as a mentor, for he troubled my dead certainties with good humor, a sense of the impossible, and an unerring humanity. Where I sought film "texts" he turned me toward the many and diverse people who made community.

In their own way, Saturnino Noriega and Charlotte Roach inspired me to learn as if my life were at stake. I am their son. Reni Celeste has been a true inspiration and my sister. Gabrielle James Forman saw me through the first part of this project and the first part of my adulthood; and, in the end, we were kind to each other. Sandra Sarnoff has helped me put it all together.

I am quite fortunate to have been able to know and befriend many of the filmmakers, artists, programmers, and media advocates whose experiences inform this book: Laura Aguilar, Isaac Artenstein, Carlos Avila, Aida Barrera, Francisco X. Camplis, Luz Castillo, Henry Cisneros, Osa Hidalgo de la Riva, Nancy de los Santos, Eduardo Diaz, Robert Diaz LeRoy, Alberto Dominguez, Armando Durón, Frances Salomé España, Moctesuma Esparza, Paul Espinosa, Evelina Fernández, Harry Gamboa Jr., Juan Garza, Luis Garza, A. P. González, Rita González, Gronk, Efraín Gutiérrez, Sandra P. Hahn, Gina Hernandez, Lillian Jiménez, Rick Leal, Jesse Lerner, Richard "Cheech" Marin, Beni Matias, Jim Mendiola, Luis Meza, Sylvia Morales, Eduardo Moreno, Mylene Moreno, Gregory Nava, Ray Navarro, Frances Negrón-Muntaner, Yvette Nieves-Cruz, Alex Nogales, Edward James Olmos, Antonio Parra, Sandra "Pocha" Peña, Severo Pérez, Lourdes Portillo,

Cheryl Quintana Leder, Susan Racho, Esther Renteria, Luis Reyes, Cathy Rivera, Eugene Rodríguez, José Luis Ruiz, Graciela Sanchez, Ray Santisteban, John Phillip Santos, Laura Angélica Simón, Jennifer Maytorena Taylor, Rick Tejada-Flores, Ray Telles, Jesús Salvador Treviño, Ela Troyano, John Valadez, Armando Valdez, Jeff Valdez, Luis Valdez, Rosalia Valencia, José Luis Valenzuela, Ethan van Thillo, Willie Varela, Gustavo Vazquez, Carmen Vega, Edit Villarreal, and Robert M. Young. Thank you for your insights, stories, and generous support along the way.

But to a few others I am especially indebted. José Luis Ruiz and Jesús Salvador Treviño took the time to help me understand Chicano cinema, and Ruiz always encouraged me to speak to more and more people and get other points of view, often quite different from his own. Your words were always like music to my ears. Sylvia Morales and Lourdes Portillo let me know that if I could not sing—and I cannot— I could at least laugh. Harry Gamboa Jr. and Frances Negrón-Muntaner showed me how beautiful such laughter could be in the face of an absurdly cruel world. In the final months of this project, as discussed in chapter 8, I joined nearly one hundred producers and advocates fighting to maintain Latino programming on public television. They have taught me more in the past few months than I could have ever learned in the archive. It seemed like a good time to end this history and enter the untimely present and its need for actions.

Numerous people have helped shape both my research and my career over the years. Virginia Wright Wexman, Linda Williams, and Henry Breitrose introduced me to cinema studies, Estelle Freedman to historical research, and Mary Louise Pratt and Tomás Ybarra-Frausto to interdisciplinarity. Early on I gained a clearer sense of my project in numerous and endless conversations with several colleagues: Charles Ramírez Berg, Carlos Cortés, Rosa Linda Fregoso, Christine List, David Maciel, and especially Kathleen Newman. John Hess, Chuck Kleinhans, and Julia Lesage *(Jump Cut),* Marsha Kinder *(Spectator),* and the UCLA Film and Television Archive provided early and rewarding opportunities for my editorial inclinations. Ever since Roberto Trujillo hired me to conduct bibliographic research on my own dissertation topic, I have carried with me the mission and secret fear of becoming an archivist. Roberto has obliged these inclinations by allowing me to place various filmmakers' and artists' papers in the Mexican American Collection at Stanford University Libraries. The UCLA Film and Television

Archive did the rest. I owe special thanks to Steven Ricci, Geoffrey Gilmore, Andrea Alsberg, Andrea Callas, Edward Richmond, and Charles Hopkins. More than any other person, Ana M. López introduced me to the fine points of academia, provided considerable advice and reassurance, and then let me know when my accomplishments had become clichéd. Lillian Jiménez and Amalia Mesa-Bains helped keep my feet on the ground with their unmatched example as community-based intellectuals. They also taught me a lot about the media and visual arts. So did Tania Blanich, Tim Gunn, Richard Herskowitz, Yvette Nieves-Cruz, David Schwartz, Joan Shigekawa, Janet Sternberg, John Stout, and Maria Christina Villaseñor. But it is John G. Hanhardt who first introduced me to public exhibition, allowing me to follow various paths of my own making: as cultural nationalist, coalition builder, and perhaps the last and greatest lover of the avant-garde. In short, he helped me learn what it means to program work for a public audience; but more important, he helped me understand my own scholarship in a more expansive and honest way. Thank you all. You have made my life a wonderful surprise and I hope that this book returns the favor.

UCLA has provided an ideal environment within which to work and grow as a scholar. I am grateful to a number of colleagues for their contribution to my research, my thinking, and my career. Candy Candelaria and Wendy Belcher have been good friends and fabulous editors. Guillermo Hernández has convinced me time and again that we are the only two people who know the true meaning of Chicano studies—and he paid for lunch, too. Raymund Paredes has provided invaluable support, encouragement, and advice, helping me to do the right thing, in large part by placing my ideas and travails in a larger context. Sandra Harding, James Schultz, Theresa Dawson-Muñoz, Carol Peterson, and Howard Gadlin have involved me in that larger context on campus. In my department, Robert Rosen and Vivian Sobchack have been a constant source of inspiration. My sense of film studies would be greatly diminished if it were not for their example, their support, and their ability to see past conventional boundaries. I am especially grateful to my colleagues in the Critical Studies Program: Peter Wollen, Steven Mamber, Teshome Gabriel, John Caldwell, Nicholas Browne, and Janet Bergstrom. But it is without a doubt our students who have taught me the most.

Over the years, I have been fortunate to work with a number of research assistants who have helped with library research and the dreaded

task of transcribing audiotaped interviews: Eddie Tafoya, Annette Pa-
laez, L. S. Kim, Gilberto Blasini, Monica Hulsbus, Marc Siegel, Jignasa
Patel, Cathy Rivera, Carmen Vega, Rebecca Epstein, Jesse Zigelstein, Jin-
soo An, Beth Kluender, and Azadeh Farahmand. Marc and Rebecca de-
serve a special note of thanks for their extraordinary efforts as well as
their combined creativity and diligence in getting the job done.

I was able to complete the research on this project during 1996–97
thanks to a Getty Postdoctoral Fellowship in the History of Art and the
University of California President's Fellowship in the Humanities. Over
the years, I have been fortunate to have been awarded various grants to
pursue research on or related to this project. These include project grants
from the American Council of Learned Societies (1992); the Center
for Regional Studies and Southwest Hispanic Research Institute at the
University of New Mexico (1991–92); the Institute of American Cultures (1994–95, 1995–96), Chicano Studies Research Center (1995),
Academic Senate (1992–93, 1998–99), and Office of the Chancellor
(1996–97) at the University of California, Los Angeles; and the University of California Institute for Mexico and the United States (1997–
98, 1998–99).

Finally, I owe thanks to my unofficial sponsor, the Coffee Bean, and
its Mocha Iced Blended, which has always filled me with deep feelings
of love for humanity and a compulsion to copyedit.

The University of Minnesota Press has provided constant encouragement throughout the process of researching and writing this book.
I am grateful to Lisa Freeman and Douglas Armato for the opportunity
to be involved with the press on a number of levels over the years. I have
been fortunate to work with three editors with a keen sense of the field,
of where it meets other disciplines, and of humor: Janaki Bakhle first
sent my dissertation out for review as a prelude to extending that study;
Micah Kleit saw the project become something else altogether, chanting "sociology, sociology, sociology" as I restructured the manuscript
three times; and Jennifer Moore performed the Solomonesque task of
cutting the baby into two books. I want to thank everyone involved
in bringing this book into print: Alison Aten, Kathryn Grimes, Barbara
Norton, Mark Smith, Amy Unger, Linda Webster, and Laura Westlund.
Finally, I am extremely grateful for the insights and suggestions offered
by the readers: Ana M. López, Marvin D'Lugo, John Hess, Chuck
Kleinhans, and Ellen Seiter. The following people read portions of the
final manuscript: Charles Ramírez Berg, Lisa Cartwright, John G. Han-

hardt, David James, Roberto Trujillo, Virginia Wright Wexman, and Bryan Wolf. Thanks for helping me go to the next step.

When all is said and done, however, this book represents an entirely new direction in my work and was written and completed in relative isolation. With one extraordinary exception. Kathleen McHugh has gone through the manuscript with me word by word over the past two years. From the start, she articulated a clearer sense of its purpose than I could muster, and her unflagging support, critical interventions, and repeated insistence that I take breaks and reward myself along the way—an unheard-of idea for me at the time!—made it possible for me to finish. She has given me a new sense of my work and of myself. My father once claimed that a man's wealth is determined by the number of books he owns. But surely one's wisdom can only be judged by the number of friends. In that respect, I have been blessed. But I have been especially blessed in meeting Kathleen McHugh. She saw something in my work that I could not see at the time: me. And that has made all the difference.

Acronyms and Abbreviations

AFI	American Film Institute
AMPTP	Association of Motion Picture and Television Producers
BBC	Bilingual Bicultural Coalition on Mass Media
BEST	Black Efforts for Soul in Television
CARISSMA	Council to Advance and Restore the Image of Spanish-Speaking and Mexican Americans
CCC	Citizens Communications Center
CORE	Congress on Racial Equality
CPB	Corporation for Public Broadcasting
CRS	Community Relations Service (Department of Justice)
EEOC	Equal Employment Opportunity Commission
ETC	El Teatro Campesino
FAMA	Federation for the Advancement of Mexican-Americans
FCC	Federal Communications Commission
HAMAS	Hispanic Academy of Media Arts and Sciences
IATSE	International Alliance of Theatrical and Stage Employees
IMAGE	Involvement of Mexican-Americans in Gainful Endeavors
ITVS	Independent Television Service
Justicia	Justice for Chicanos in the Motion Picture and Television Industry
LULAC	League of United Latin American Citizens
MALDEF	Mexican American Legal Defense and Education Fund
MAPA	Mexican American Political Association
MAYO	Mexican American Youth Organization

MEChA	Movimiento Estudiantil Chicano de Aztlán (Chicano Student Movement of Aztlán)
NAACP	National Association for the Advancement of Colored People
NCLR	National Council of La Raza
NEH	National Endowment for the Humanities
NLCC	National Latino Communications Center
NMAADC	National Mexican-American Anti-Defamation Committee
NOW	National Organization for Women
PBS	Public Broadcasting Service
PTAR	Prime Time Access Rule
TACOMA	Television Advisory Committee of Mexican-Americans
UCC	United Church of Christ
UFW	United Farm Workers
UMAS	United Mexican American Students

Introduction

> When causes cannot be reproduced, there is nothing to do but to
> deduce them from their effects.
> —*Carlo Ginzburg, 1989*

> ¡Que viva la causa! (Long live the cause!)
> —*Chicano movement slogan*

They've told me their stories, again and again. Their words wash over
me like water, cleansing me to the soul; but I can never quite remember
them. So I bring a tape recorder, take notes, photocopy documents, dub
videotapes, and place their artifacts into the archive. I listen, again and
again, each time fulfilled, but when *I* speak another story emerges, one
filled with paradox, irony, and ambivalence. Even if I believe in the political poetics of their story—because it does speak against the historical and ongoing subjugation of the Mexican-descent population in the
United States—my own story resists such oppositional narration. I was
not there. These events did not form me, nor I them, and so I see things
differently, trying to take other perspectives into account.

Chicano studies locates its origins in Américo Paredes's *"With His
Pistol in His Hand": A Border Ballad and Its Hero* (1958), then finds its
redemption in Gloria Anzaldúa's *Borderlands/La Frontera: The New
Mestiza* (1987).[1] Paredes documents the *corrido* tradition of Greater
Mexico, providing an extended analysis of "The Ballad of Gregorio Cortez."[2] The corrido or border ballad represents a masculine oral folk narrative that Chicano scholars have argued is the "master poem" for all
Chicano literature.[3] "In the symbolic sphere," Ramón Saldívar writes,
"the *corrido* became the preeminent form of action and resistance
against the ever-increasing political and cultural hegemony of Anglo-

American society. . . . Residing as a repressed element of the political unconscious, thereafter the *corrido* exerts symbolic force in the spheres of alternative narrative arts."[4] For Anzaldúa, writing as a Chicana lesbian and against a "tradition of silence" for women exemplified by the corrido, "there are more subtle ways that we internalize identification," not the least of which is a "border tongue" that mixes languages, dialects, and slangs.[5] If the corrido is formal, public, and masculine, a border tongue is informal, private, and gender neutral.[6]

For both Paredes and Anzaldúa, however, these oral forms express an oppositional cultural identity that emerges along a "border" placing Chicanos outside the U.S. national imaginary. As Anzaldúa writes, "The coming together of two self-consistent but habitually incompatible frames of reference causes *un choque,* a cultural collision."[7] Thus, while Anzaldúa questions a politics based on a reactive "counterstance" to the dominant side of a cultural collision, she nonetheless juxtaposes her call for an all-inclusive "new consciousness" against a repressively "self-consistent" Western culture.[8] For his part, Paredes identifies this cultural collision as a historical point of origin against which he reads an ironic expression of the future conditional that ends his book: "Transcending national boundaries, the Border heroic *corrido* belongs to Texas as much as to Mexico. A product of past conflicts, it may eventually serve as one of the factors in a better understanding."[9] In this respect, Paredes and Anzaldúa mirror each other: Paredes uses subtle irony to undercut resistance to his study about resistance, especially insofar as it critiques the still-prevalent Texas Rangers, while Anzaldúa is unequivocally sincere about the indeterminacy of Chicano language and mestiza identity. In the end, despite their catholic impulses to look beyond the borders they describe, Paredes and Anzaldúa locate Chicano redemption in premodern isomorphic social groups, whether in the folk culture of Greater Mexico or the ostensible preduality of the indigenous.

I want to propose another direction for understanding cultural collision, one that questions the "self-consistent" claims of "incompatible" cultures. Before telling the history of Chicano cinema, therefore, I want to consider two modalities for Chicano intellectual discourse: mythopoetic and political. In chapter 1, I will delineate the consequent poetic tradition that not only generates a canon within Chicano cinema and other expressive forms, but provides the identity-based contours for Chicano historiography itself.[10] My goal, however, is not to reconcile these modalities with each other in an attempt to pursue, *pace* Cherríe

Moraga, the re-formation of the Chicano tribe.[11] Instead, I will look at these modalities as they are imbricated in the dominant discourses and practices they challenge. For Chicano cinema, these include the federal regulatory arena, commercial broadcasting practices, and print discourses. In short, I will place my story in the present—among institutions, social movements, and the various publics that determine its overall "discursive fact"—and not in the transcendent impulse of an unencumbered past, where, before conquest, before duality, before capital, something existed that was then repressed and now, as an act of resistance, "speaks verbosely of its own silence."[12]

Perhaps don Américo was wrong, men should *not* sing with their heads thrown back, with their mouths wide open, and their eyes shut.[13] In the pasture's farther end, another story echoes, and neither we nor our enemies can quite hear its promise. Perhaps only with the irony of knowing more than your own story—what Anzaldúa calls a "tolerance for ambiguity"[14]—will we rise and push everything up with us as we go. To do otherwise would be to forsake hope for the old way.[15]

Mythopoetic Discourse

It is important to place a Chicano mythopoetics in the context of all nationalisms, since what is at stake is not so much the truth claims of a myth of origins, but rather the poetics such a myth mobilizes in the present. Whether tied to a state apparatus or to the bonds of ethnicity or sexuality, nations are "imagined communities" because their large membership requires that any sense of belonging must be a mediated one. For Benedict Anderson, such imaginings give rise to three paradoxes, which are worth quoting in their entirety:

> (1) The objective modernity of nations to the historian's eye vs. their subjective antiquity in the eyes of nationalists. (2) The formal universality of nationality as a socio-cultural concept—in the modern world everyone can, should, will "have" a nationality, as he or she "has" a gender—vs. the irremediable particularity of its concrete manifestations, such that, by definition, "Greek" nationality is sui generis. (3) The "political" power of nationalisms vs. their philosophical poverty and even incoherence.[16]

For Chicanos, then, it is a simple story, really, even if *mestizaje* blurs the racial boundaries between the social actors, oppressor and oppressed, thereby making history into family melodrama. There is the period of myth, the prehistory of the Americas, the source of our redemption, followed by conquest and *mestizaje* (the racial mixture between Spaniard and Indian), until the *hijos de la chingada* (the sons of the violated mother) won their independence from Spain. Then Manifest Destiny motivated another conquest that turned the northern half of Mexico into the American Southwest. Mexican subjects became American citizens but existed more or less as an "internal colony" that resisted, accommodated, then made moderate demands, until the 1960s, when their children, calling themselves Chicanos, said, "¡Ya basta!" Enough was enough. Then a people became what they had always already been.[17]

If the story is simple, starting it has been a problem, since few are familiar with the context of its telling. And nothing hampers a good story—not to mention its social function—like having to stop and provide context. Did it begin in 1492 or 1942?[18] Upon whose body do we enact the sacrifice that creates a people? As René Girard writes in *Violence and the Sacred,* "[A]ll man's religious, familial, economic, and social institutions grew out of the body of an original victim."[19] If we look back to 1492, that body belongs to the Aztec warriors betrayed by La Malinche, the Aztec woman—of noble birth and sold into slavery—who translated for the Spaniards and became Cortés's mistress (*I Am Joaquin,* 1969). Or perhaps it belongs to La Malinche herself (*Chicana,* 1979). If we look back to 1942, that body belongs to the pachuco zoot-suiters who resisted the state and produced the Chicano generation (*Zoot Suit,* 1981). Or perhaps it belongs to those zoot-suiters who succumbed to the state and whose children, the Chicanos, are the result of hetero- and homosexual rape—another conquest (*American Me,* 1992). In any case, the Chicano body politic partakes of a particularly ambivalent genealogy. Drawing from Mexican nationalism, Chicanos become the product of violence between male and female, Spaniard and Indian, conqueror and conquered, resulting in a "cosmic race" both national and universal.[20] As U.S. citizens, Chicanos have been a "racialized" minority group since 1848: legally "white," but socially "black."[21] Either choice—1492 or 1942—produces the same mythopoetics, the former transcendent, the latter generational, both articulating a discursive space outside the nation-state, whether in the Mexican indigenous or in the Chicano family.

Political Discourse

The more "political" modality involves a historical narrative with three distinct features: the centrality of great men who initiated different as-

pects of the Chicano civil rights movement: César Chávez and farmworkers, Reies López Tijerina and landowners, José Angel Gutiérrez
and voters, and Rodolfo "Corky" Gonzales and nationalists (many of
them students); the ideological distinction between reformism and radicalism that defined that latter as the appropriate political action and
cultural identity; and the inevitable containment imposed by the state
and manifested through political surveillance and police violence.

By the mid-1960s, as this story is told, diverse and multilocal social
protests in the Southwest and Midwest had coalesced into the Chicano
civil rights movement. In the first years, César Chávez and the United
Farm Workers would in some sense define the political, class, and rhetorical orientations of the Chicano movement. Other local struggles would
acquire national importance in its development. In Tierra Amarilla,
New Mexico, Reies López Tijerina, who founded the Alianza de Pueblos Libres (The Alliance of Free Peoples) in 1963, would seek the return
of the Spanish land grants protected by the Treaty of Guadalupe Hidalgo
(1848). In Crystal City, Texas, a voters' "revolt" in 1963 overthrew the
all-white city government, marking a shift from partisan politics toward a separatist "Chicano politics" that would culminate in the formation in 1969 of a new party, La Raza Unida (headed by José Angel Gutiérrez). In Denver, Colorado, Rodolfo "Corky" Gonzales renounced
his participation in the Democratic Party and founded the Crusade for
Justice, a Chicano community-based organization, in 1966, where he
advocated Chicano nationalism, self-determination, and economic and
political autonomy. Gonzales later mobilized the Chicano student movement when he convened the first Chicano Youth Liberation Conference
in March 1969. The conference platform, "El Plan Espiritual de Aztlán"
(The Spiritual Plan of Aztlán), together with Gonzales's earlier epic
poem, "I Am Joaquin" (1967), articulated an explicitly nationalist identity and ideology. Aztlán, the mythical homeland of the Aztecs, believed
by many Chicanos to have been in the Southwest, located such nationalism in a "mythical geography" that connected both the Aztec empire
and Mexican political history to the Chicano condition in the United
States.[22]

Within the Chicano movement, a generational distinction soon
emerged between Mexican American "reformism" (1930–60) and Chicano "radicalism" (starting in 1963). But these and similar binary oppositions—assimilation and nationalism, reform and revolution, and
egalitarianism and communitarianism—also served to define two con-

flicting notions of social change *during* the 1960s and 1970s. While these terms have been variously defined and debated, they basically point to two strategies: working "within" the system versus working "outside" the system. The former strategy was associated with the established Mexican American organizations oriented toward the political representation system and state bureaucracy. The latter ranged from separatist demands for a Chicano nation to the more prevalent emphasis on community building, from producing cultural expressions to creating local institutions. Despite the apparent binary opposition—and the heated political discourse and struggle between these two strategies—the boundaries between them were much more fluid, since "inside" and "outside" did not so much distinguish between the so-called reformists and radicals as it described the conditions under which both operated. As U.S. citizens of Mexican descent, both groups were *outside* the nation, whether in terms of its social imaginary or its legal rights, while they were *inside* the administrative control and incorporation of the state. It is within this ambivalent context that the state compelled Chicanos and other racial groups to adopt and construct minority identities as the sine qua non of political recognition. Thus, the paradox of incorporation involved exchanging difference for identity.

The Chicano Moratorium

In many ways, the defining moment of the Chicano movement, and of Chicano cinema, occurred on August 29, 1970, when 20,000 Chicanos rallied in East Los Angeles in protest of the Vietnam War. The Chicano Moratorium against the War in Vietnam brought together numerous families as well as groups from across the nation in a peaceful march to Laguna Park, but it ended in an unprovoked police riot that left three dead (including the journalist Ruben Salazar) and hundreds injured. The police action was a purposeful one within a larger agenda. As Carlos Muñoz Jr. notes:

> Political surveillance, infiltration of movement organizations, conspiracy indictments of leaders, and mass arrests of movement activists were forms of ideological repression that played a major role in the decline of the Chicano Movement. Violent repression on the part of police agencies was also a contributing factor.[23]

Indeed, many of the Chicano filmmakers and soon-to-be filmmakers at the moratorium found their own critical observation itself under surveillance. Jesús Salvador Treviño, soon to become the major polemicist of Chicano cinema, was attacked by police as he filmed the aftermath of the riot for public television. In the midst of the riot, students from the UCLA Ethno-Communications Program recorded the event, later producing *Requiem-29* (1971), an example of a direct cinema that stands outside the institutional domains for such objective discourse: television and the state. In fact, the sheriff's department had its own film crew at the moratorium and was able to have its shot-and-edited version of events broadcast on all the local television stations. While *Requiem-29* signals the rise of a Chicano public sphere over and against a national one, it is these students (along with Treviño) who would institutionalize Chicano cinema in independent cinema, public broadcasting, and the philanthropic sector.

Meanwhile, Harry Gamboa Jr., a student organizer of the March 1968 walk-outs in East Los Angeles, was also at the moratorium. While running for cover, he met the longtime community activist Francisca Flores, who recruited him to edit *Regeneración,* and thus began his life as a writer and artist. Gamboa would soon cofound the Chicano avant-garde art group Asco, where he developed a conceptual counterpart to and critique of Chicano cinema: the "No Movie." The No Movies took various forms, although always with Gamboa's camera in mind: performance pieces, published interviews, mail art, and media hoaxes. The No Movies isolated a single 35mm image—as if it were a still from an actual movie—and thereby conjured up the before and after of an implied narrative. Gamboa then applied text to these images in the same way that the sheriff's department had done to secure a narrative to its own visual evidence. In this manner, Gamboa made the processes of mass media (rather than its form or content) the real issue, exploring a postmodern condition in which Chicano identity and history are increasingly mediated and constituted through electronic culture. But if Gamboa questioned the media as inherently objective, he did not so much reject truth claims as identify them as rhetorical strategies within public discourse. Gamboa would turn to video art in the 1980s, first through cable access, then through consumer home video equipment.[24]

Finally, on the outskirts of town, Efraín Gutiérrez sat in a park waiting for a tow truck. His car had broken down on the way to the moratorium and he would miss the event. Similarly at odds with Chicano activists as they oriented themselves toward the professional culture of the industry, Gutiérrez would return to South Texas and over a four-year period produce the first Chicano feature film, *Please, Don't Bury Me Alive!* (1976), about a Chicano whose brother is killed in Vietnam. With no training, little money, and considerable charm, Gutiérrez directed, starred in, and self-distributed three feature films in the late 1970s. Using regional vernacular—"Spanglish"—and a slice-of-life aesthetics rooted in the didacticism of Chicano *teatro,* Gutiérrez built an audience through the Spanish-language theater circuit in South Texas and other parts of the Southwest. Then he and his films disappeared for fifteen years.

When I returned home one day in late 1996 and found Gutiérrez's voice on my phone answering machine, I knew my research was coming to an end. I had already heard the stories about Chicano cinema and No Movies—that is, about the cultural affirmation and critical negation in the face of an exclusionary mass media. Now I would hear the story about the brief creation of a *Chicano* public sphere during the waning days of the Spanish-language theater circuit that had sustained a *Mexican* public sphere in the United States in the 1950s and 1960s.[25] What binds these three stories together is that their myth of origins and political history are narrated through a poetic aesthetic and nationalism, which I will consider in chapter 1.

Telling History

In this book, I will examine the articulation and development of a Chicano cinema as an expression of the Chicano civil rights movement. To some extent, this history has been told a number of times already, first by the filmmakers themselves, and later by scholars.[26] And it is a history that has been told within a metanarrative of cultural resistance that defines *lo chicano* (Chicano-ness) according to its oppositional "experience," "expression," and "identity." Nevertheless, in these accounts, my own included, Chicano cinema inevitably occupies an ambiguous location within the national culture, caught between the conflicting egalitarian and communitarian goals of both its practitioners and its academic critics.[27] In engaging race relations in the United States, Chicanos have produced a metanarrative of cultural resistance that places them both inside and outside the nation. Thus, as a practical matter, the contradictions of this ambiguous location have been addressed at an allegorical level. I want to raise the ambiguous location of Chicano cinema to the level of historiographic operation. My goal is not so much to move "beyond" identity as it is to situate identity within the matrix of both social movements and social institutions. One can find a precursor in Coco Fusco's writings on Black and Latino media in the late 1980s.[28] Working not as an academic but as a media professional actively involved in the object of her study—curator, writer, and program officer—Fusco voiced pragmatic concerns as she sought to define a historical moment of "minority" intellectual and cultural production. More academic accounts necessarily diverted these concerns to an allegorical level, but Fusco openly bristled against her location as the representative for the underrepresented, as the insider for the outsiders, and, consequently, as the outsider who was inside. This ambiguous or dual location, then, became the very methodology by which she read against the grain of oppositional thinking and of "minority" texts. In a similar fashion, I want to raise questions about the function of Chicano cinema within various discourses—nationalist, postnationalist; American, pan-American—in order to distinguish between the idea of Chicano cinema (as an aesthetic, social, or political category) and all those activities and texts that would seem to "belong" to that category *and nowhere else.*

Despite the shift in institutional space for these histories (from filmmaker to scholar), they have usually been told in similarly oppositional terms: first, as a narrative of resistance to dominant cinema, and second, as an internal matter that distinguishes between two paths—one good, the other bad—toward such resistance. Thus, whether told by filmmakers or scholars, whether told then or now, the history of Chicano cinema has been bounded by the essential terms of cultural nationalism. It seeks to define difference—something one can call "Chicano"—against the backdrop of the "non-Chicano," and it does so in the name of an ethnic nation, community, or culture. To do so, however, the mantle of "Chicano" must fall to the filmmakers who follow the good, and not the bad, path, lest the boundaries for "Chicano" become blurred. Since the 1960s, we find this internal distinction expressed a number of ways with respect to Chicano cinema and cultural production in general: nationalism, not assimilation; revolution, not reform; the new mestiza, not the old *veterano;* and, coming full circle, hybridity, not nationalism. Today few Chicano scholars would accept the label of cultural nationalism, but neither would they embrace assimilation. Instead, they would cite works in postmodernism, feminism, cultural studies, and so on that call into question the foundationalist or essentialist positions of either extreme. And yet, at the same time, what is *our* larger goal, if not to reform and reinforce the very borders of ethnic identity that these same social theories would blur, cross, erase, multiply, and otherwise dissipate? In other words, we apply these theories within a discrete social category (Chicano) when, in fact, they speak to the very construction of such categories and of the permeability of the "stable" boundaries between categories. In this manner, Chicano scholarship on *our* hybridity, *our* multiple and shifting subjectivities, argues for a particular type of identity and agency—one that is as monadic as it is exceptional—rather than for a social analysis predicated on the decentered subject. Of course, such a contradiction is not specific to Chicano and other "ethnic" studies, but rather marks an attempt to rearticulate identity and agency within theoretical discourses and social spaces to which they are anathema.

To a large extent, the contradictions of this particular model can be attributed to its articulation within the institutional and disciplinary boundaries of Chicano studies. But this situation is more complicated than it first appears, since Chicano studies claims to speak from (or, at the least, for) another space—the community. And this "speaking for" reflects not so much a naive idealism within the ivory tower as it does the ambiguous location of the minority scholar in the first place. In other words, if such "speaking for" is similar to that of cultural nationalism expressed outside of (or even before) university-based Chicano studies, that is because the inclusion of Chicanos in the university has been structured along the lines of their prior exclusion. This inclusion/exclusion places clear limits on the type of history that can be told, especially insofar as the university and minority scholar want the same thing—a "minority discourse"—though each emphasizes a different word. Of course, all histories can be read as allegories of employment. While histories may speak to an outside community or another time, they are also—as Michel de Certeau notes in *The Writing of History*—"the product of a place."[29] That is, histories speak from a social institution and its constellation of peers, methods, sources, and practices. Thus, to paraphrase David James in *Allegories of Cinema*, a historical text never fails to tell the story of how and why it was produced.[30] Within "body" programs of race, gender, and sexuality, however, that story is qualitatively different from that of traditional appointments insofar as job recruitment and critical analysis are explicitly tied to the same object: a body marked by difference. This situation raises fundamental questions not about affirmative action per se, but about an institution that cannot imagine, let alone enact, an alternative to racial and gender exclusions. For this reason, then, the minority historian often engages in a strategic conflation of critical discourses (rooted in an academic professional culture) with social practices outside the university (mostly local politics and community-based practices).

Chicano anthropologists have raised questions about the institutionalization of "Chicano" in academia and the mass media as well as about the internal construction of "Chicano" as an oppositional term vis-à-vis "Mexican" and "American" that has had a problematic history as a public ethnic identity within the Mexican-descent population of the United States.[31] Indeed, categories are not history, and identity markers are not the same as identities. This insight has methodological implications that undercut the notion of a sui generis object of study. It is not enough, for example, to "read" those films that are easily accessible to the scholar, since that merely leads us to construct a Chicano "tradition" already determined by the market forces we will then claim these films contest. In short, we must seek out the "texts," artifacts, and evidence beyond those cut to the measure of the desires of our political and disciplinary boundaries. We must muddy up the waters, lest we drown, like Narcissus, in the image of our own reflection.

The first two chapters consider the function of poetry within Chicano nationalism as well as the relationship between social movements, the state, and mass media. The remaining chapters represent a social history that attempts to imbricate these two modes of analysis, the aesthetic and the sociological. Placing an emphasis on television, documentary, and media reform, I examine (1) the activism that opened the door to film schools, local television stations, and noncommercial funding sources, (2) the development of independent production companies, media advocacy groups, and international affiliations, (3) continued professional and legal efforts to integrate public and network television, and (4) the aesthetic strategies that related documentary production to the Chicano movement, national audiences, and Third World politics.

As a final word, it is important to note something that the makers often insist upon themselves. All of these films and videos were shot in America. But for some reason they get located somewhere else. . . .

one

"No Revolutions without Poets"
Chicano Poetic Consciousness

One of the distinctive features of the Chicano civil rights movement has been what Tomás Ybarra-Frausto calls its "poetic consciousness," a phenomenon found not just in the ubiquitous poetry of the times, but in the broader function of poetry as a medium for fostering a social movement as well as the development of Chicano studies itself.[1] As Rudolph O. de la Garza and Rowena Rivera explained, "These early writings, most of which are poetry, are closely related to the rise of Chicano militancy. They served to feed the movement and were the medium through which Chicanos became politically aware and active."[2] Poetry—read at political rallies, published in movement newspapers, and circulated hand to hand—exerted a profound influence on the emerging political rhetoric and cultural politics of the late 1960s and early 1970s.[3]

Rodolfo "Corky" Gonzales placed this function of poetry in direct relationship to social change and alongside other social representations that correspond to identity and equity: "There is no inspiration without identifiable images, there is no conscience without the sharp knife of truthful exposure, and, ultimately, there are no revolutions without poets."[4] Gonzales's own "I Am Joaquin" (1967) stands as the most influential poem of the Chicano movement, a first-person narrative that provided many Chicanos with their first exposure to the "big events" and "great men" of Mexican and Chicano history.[5] In presenting this history as an unbroken lineage of indigenous and mestizo resistance to oppression since the conquest, as Bruce-Novoa concludes, "the poem dares to invoke a cosmic, religious, and transcendent principle upon which the Chicano Movement can be founded."[6] The poem was quickly reprinted in numerous community publications and adapted into a film by Luis

1

Valdez and El Teatro Campesino, while Gonzales's Crusade for Justice distributed over 100,000 copies before Bantam Books issued a paperback edition in 1972. Shortly after the poem first appeared, *La Raza* magazine declared,

> "I Am Joaquin" is fast becoming a legend in the Southwest. The version that came to our hands was being passed from hand to hand on a 3rd carbon copy, read aloud and recited in bars and cantinas of the lower Rio Grande Valley. "I Am Joaquin" is also a poem of independence. Independence of the soul of a people and expression of a determination to fight to the end for Freedom and Justice.[7]

Together with Valdez's agitprop skits or *actos,* Gonzales's poem participated in what Ybarra-Frausto calls the "revitalization of Chicano speech" as an aesthetic, didactic, and political expression rooted in the multilingual vernacular speech of everyday life: "Since the people were seen as the true creators of language, Chicano poets began to evolve a poetic diction which saw little essential difference between spoken and literary language."[8] Accordingly, in the late 1960s, Valdez and the poet Alurista named *floricanto* as the concept for Chicano poetry that bridged spoken and literary language by way of the neo-indigenous sacred. The term was taken from the Nahuatl or Aztec-language phrase, *in xochitl in cuicatl,* which translates as "flower and song"—in Spanish, *flor y canto.*[9] More than anything else, however, the concept used the combination of prayer and poetry in Aztec culture to map a transhistorical identity onto the emerging Chicano political culture of the 1960s.

Poetry became the discursive arena within which the movement defined itself and its "appropriate" subjects, providing a language with which to name and narrate the self as a profoundly social act. As such, poetry also provided the discursive arena for challenging a cultural politics predicated on the normative masculine identity of the heterosexual *veterano,* most notably in Chicana feminist and lesbian critiques of Chicano nationalism.[10] For the most part, the function of nationalism in defining a Chicano community remained unchallenged, but the subject position shifts to those "voices" previously considered outside its boundaries: Chicana, *jotería* (queer), mixed marriage, and *coyote* (biracial). Indeed, poetry informs historiographic debates about the Chicano movement itself, from Ybarra-Frausto's effort to situate poetic discourse within its critical purview to Ramón Gutiérrez's use of Chicana poetry to critique the "rhetorical claims of the movement" as a precursor to a more formal history.[11]

I want to examine the way in which a "Chicano poetic conscious-ness" has informed cultural politics since the 1960s. It is my contention that such poetry invents a tradition that not only "incites discourse" but also provides the conceptual parameters and identity-based periods for a Chicano history.[12] Below I will focus on the poetic tradition that operates within the canon of Chicano cinema itself, beginning with the film poem *I Am Joaquin* (1969) and examining the subsequent films that speak back to it as a point of origin. In each instance, these film po-ems serve as a way to recenter and re-form the Chicano community around a new subject: Chicano *veteranos* (*I Am Joaquin*, 1969), post-movement Chicano poets (*Entelequia*, 1978), Chicana workers (*Chi-cana*, 1979), border artists (*Mi Otro Yo*, 1988, and *Border Brujo*, 1990), and Chicano gay men (*Cholo Joto*, 1993, and *St. Francis of Aztlán*, 1997). Rather than conflate poetry with history, however, I want to em-phasize its "rhetorical claims" as one component of a social movement grappling with conflicting notions of history, politics, identity, and representation.

The first generation of Chicano filmmakers emerged from the con-text of the farmworkers' struggle and the student movement, where po-litical activism and poetic discourse developed together as part of a so-cial movement that drew from and addressed the lived experience of Chicanos in the Southwest. In the first years of the Chicano movement, the farmworkers' struggle helped define its political, class, and rhetori-cal orientations, providing the basis for a categorical shift away from the perceived middle-class, accommodationist, and integrationist strategies of the Mexican American Generation.[13] Under the leadership of César Chávez, the United Farm Workers (UFW), founded in 1962, would gain national attention when it joined the grape strike in Delano, California. In a telling concurrence, the predominantly Mexican American mem-bership voted to strike on September 16, 1965, the anniversary of Mexi-can independence from Spain in 1810. Mexican-based historical ref-erences and cultural production played a pivotal role in these social protests (and their political resonance), incorporating more subtle allu-sions to American political history.

Luis Valdez, the writer and director of *Zoot Suit* (1981) and *La Bamba* (1987), was especially important in developing this bicultural political rhetoric in the mid-1960s. In 1965, he founded El Teatro Cam-pesino in order to rally striking farmworkers, developing collaborative agitprop *actos* that were performed on the flatbeds of trucks. Then, in

March 1966, he wrote the influential "Plan of Delano," a manifesto announcing the grape strike as the start of a "social movement"—done in the rhetorical style of the U.S. Declaration of Independence and Black gospel à la Martin Luther King Jr.—which it then related to the Virgin of Guadalupe, Benito Juárez, and the Mexican Revolution of 1910.[14] In this manner, Valdez created a unique expression that coupled together seemingly opposed egalitarian and communitarian goals, so that the call for equal justice within the United States justified an affirmation of a Mexican past and culture that then made such equality its inevitable outcome. As a Chicano rhetorical strategy, Valdez's "Plan of Delano" would have a direct impact on other plans ("El Plan Espiritual de Aztlán" and "El Plan de Santa Barbara"), epic poems ("I Am Joaquin"), films (including Valdez's *I Am Joaquin* [1969] and *Los Vendidos: The Sellouts* [1972]), and—in a more indirect fashion—film manifestos.[15]

By the late 1960s, the emphasis of the Chicano movement had shifted from rural to urban issues and from farmworkers to students, and Los Angeles became a major focal point. In East Los Angeles, some ten thousand high school students undertook a series of "blow-outs" or walk-outs in March 1968 to protest institutional racism and poor education. The blow-outs were initiated by a high school teacher, Sal Castro, who joined the students, and were coordinated by members of United Mexican American Students (UMAS), including UCLA students and the future filmmakers Moctesuma Esparza and Francisco Martinez. In June, Castro and Esparza were among the "L.A. Thirteen" indicted on conspiracy charges for their organizational role in the blow-outs, an act that resulted in increased Chicano activism and radicalism in high schools and colleges across the Southwest within the next year.[16] In March and April 1969, student conferences in Denver and Santa Barbara consolidated the student movement, uniting the four major Mexican American student groups under one banner: MEChA, or Movimiento Estudiantil Chicano de Aztlán (Chicano Student Movement of Aztlán). The rejection of the self-designation Mexican American in favor of Chicano and the fact that *mecha* is vernacular Spanish for "match" underscored the student movement's militant nationalism.

I Am Joaquin

I Am Joaquin (1969), which has been described as the first Chicano film, embodies the above transitions in the Chicano movement and represents the culmination of an intertextual dialogue between the move-ment's rural and urban visionaries: Luis Valdez and Rodolfo "Corky" Gonzales, respectively. Like Valdez, Gonzales had been actively involved in the Democratic Party, becoming disenchanted in the early 1960s. In 1965, he resigned from the party and founded the Crusade for Justice in Denver. The film is Valdez's adaptation of Gonzales's epic poem of the same title. But the poem itself draws upon the rhetorical style of Val-dez's "Plan of Delano," ending with the first person singular expression of phrases that punctuated the earlier manifesto: "I SHALL ENDURE. I WILL ENDURE." [17]

The major shift between plan and poem occurs in terms of the sub-ject of their "poetic consciousness." The "Plan of Delano," although grounded in key figures and moments from Mexican history, addressed a multiethnic membership (mostly Mexican and Filipino) then focused on one class-based social movement rooted in the farmworkers' struggle but ultimately aimed at uniting "all of the races that comprise the op-pressed minorities in the United States," including "poor whites." Fur-thermore, in defining the role of theater and other cultural expressions within that movement, Valdez himself made a clear-cut distinction be-tween its symbolic politics (both theater and demonstrations) and "ac-tual hard-ass, door to door, worker to worker organizing." [18] If commu-nity had to be imagined for a national audience, local politics required an interpersonal expression and organization of that community.

In contrast to Valdez's "Plan of Delano," Gonzales's "I Am Joaquin" envisioned a mestizo historical genealogy for the broad-based Chicano movement, articulating a series of bipolar parameters for Chicano iden-tity that could be subordinated to nationalism: race, religion, class, and, more insidiously, gender. For Gonzales, as echoed in the words of "El Plan Espiritual de Aztlán," "nationalism as the key to organization tran-scends all religious, political, class, and economic factions" within the Chicano community.[19] Nationalism, then, gave a singular political meaning to *mestizaje*. Whereas Valdez used nationalist icons to argue for historical justification as well as internal unity within a working-class struggle, Gonzales turned nationalism itself into the key for unit-ing an admittedly heterogeneous group of Mexican descent.

By 1967, concurrently with the publication of "I Am Joaquin," Valdez had realized the need to develop the aesthetic and political di-mensions of El Teatro Campesino beyond direct involvement with the United Farm Workers.[20] As he explained in 1970,

That was a very hard decision to make—very, very hard. Do you serve the movement by being just kind of half-assed, getting together whenever there's a chance, hitting and missing, or do you really hone your theater down into an effective weapon? Is it possible to make an effective weapon without being bloodclose to the movement?[21]

At stake for Valdez was a question of professionalism and the potential for a national audience for an artistic practice that had begun as a component of grassroots politics. The steps leading up to Valdez's film adaptation of "I Am Joaquin" exemplify his own artistic shift from community-based organizing to addressing a mass audience for which community must be imagined. Prior to the film adaptation, El Teatro Campesino had developed a slide show (in 1967) that combined the photographs of George Ballis, who worked with the United Farm Workers, with a dramatic reading of the poem.[22] Shortly thereafter, Ballis's still photographs were shot and edited together into a film, with Luis Valdez's narration and Daniel Valdez's improvised music recorded in a sound studio in Los Angeles.[23] The film was shown at both farmworkers' rallies and within the urban barrio (as with earlier dramatic readings of the poem and the slide show), but it also reached classrooms, festivals, and a national television audience. Thus the film—like the poem—brought together the diverse aspects of the Chicano movement, while it also expanded the domain for Chicano expressions into the mass media of film and television.[24] In this manner, *I Am Joaquin* signaled both the professional reorientation of El Teatro Campesino (and the Chicano arts, in general), Valdez's own shift from rural-local-grassroots organizing to mass-media communication, and "a new era in Chicano self-determination in film and television."[25]

Still, the film anticipates more than it participates in these shifts, displaying all the hallmarks of a *rasquache* cinema, which is to say, one in which poor means are transformed into a aesthetic style or cultural stance.[26] The camera is unsteady in its pans, tilts, and zooms, nonetheless creating a sense of movement through fast cutting and montage. Perhaps because the content speaks through and transforms these formal shortcomings, *I Am Joaquin* remains one of the most powerful Chicano films ever made, providing a *rasquache* expression of the contradictions of the Chicano experience situated within a 500-year genealogy of indigenous and mestizo resistance. One sign of the film's *rasquachismo* or underdog aesthetics is its irreverence toward the copyright, which gives legal protection to property. *I Am Joaquin* challenges the

Chicano poets Ricardo Sanchez (left) and Alurista, backed up by the music of Con Safos, are featured on an episode of Acción Chicano. The weekly public and cultural affairs series was broadcast on KCET in Los Angeles from 1972 to 1974. Photograph by Oscar R. Castillo.

copyright in assigning it to a collective, El Teatro Campesino, rather than to an individual.[27] But it is the C/S (short for *con safos*) at the film's end that subverts the copyright. When placed at the end of an artistic expression, *con safos* signifies "forbidden to touch, or the same will happen to you," a sort of Chicano copyright. In *I Am Joaquin, con safos* gives the film a discursive framework within and yet in opposition to the legal structure of mass media. Here, in the film's interwoven rhetorical certitude and locational ambivalence, *I Am Joaquin* initiates Chicano cinema.

Entelequia

While rarely discussed, let alone acknowledged, Juan Salazar's *Entelequia* (1978) offers an explicit parody of *I Am Joaquin* that challenges the nationalist and patriarchal context for poetry established by Rodolfo "Corky" Gonzales. The title signals this critique by using a word that also means its opposite: "entelechy" and "pipe dream." In Aristotle's philosophy, *entelekheia* refers to actuality *(energei)* as opposed to potentiality *(dynamis)*. It is, as Dagobert Runes explains, "the mode of being of a thing whose essence is completely realized" as well as "the activity that transforms potentiality into actuality."[28] In this respect, *entelequia* offers a metaphor for Chicano poetry as both a mode of being *(ente)* and a transformative activity based on mediated communication *(tele)*. But in Spanish, *entelequia* also refers to a pipe dream *(fantasía)*, and it is this dissonance in Chicano poetic nationalism—the incongruity and indeterminacy of being, becoming, and believing as mediated through language—that the film explores. That the film uses wordplay to mobilize such a critique makes it self-reflexive about poetic nationalism. Rather than launch realist counterclaims based on authenticity, the film uses puns to expose the discursive construction of identity itself.[29] Thus, the film critiques the autochthonous rhetorical claims of Chicano cultural nationalism while at the same time pointing to state institutions that regulate the body politic: schools, police, and the courts.

The poet Ricardo Sánchez wrote the poem and screenplay for *Entelequia* as an extended critique of Gonzales and Chicano movement poetry. The film begins with an experimental re-creation of the murder of an eleven-year-old Chicano boy by a Dallas police officer, posing the question, "Yes, great poet, where was your stereotypical blade?" The film identifies the social function of Chicano poetry as an increasingly "academic" discourse, identifying the *poeta* as a *puñeta:* literally, a handful or nuisance, but also slang for one who masturbates, suggesting intellectual masturbation. The pun establishes the film's method: that the situational connection between words will be more informing, and more transforming, than the conceptual frameworks that protect the boundaries of a language or culture.

What that situational connection does, however, is conflate poetry and sexuality, placing both at the problematic border between discrete private (female) and public (male) spheres. *Entelequia* depicts Chicanas in two key moments that expand upon this poetic *cum* sexual critique. In the first, the Chicano boy's mother berates the empty rhetoric of various Chicano male types arguing over his death—poet, scholar, pachuco, and *campesino*—calling them all *jotos* or queers. Next, the poet—figured as Gonzales ("Corkus Maximus") but played by Sánchez in a biting poetic masquerade—is shown lying in bed with a naked woman in an open field. The woman implores him to live up to his poetry's promises. When he answers, "I've become the incarnation of Joaquin," she counters, "You've become the joke in 'I Am Joking.'" In using a pun based on the English-language pronunciation of *I Am Joaquin,* the film has an "American" mistake provide the critique of the poem's defiant act of Chicano self-naming. In this way, the film imbricates Chicano nationalism with its dominant doppelgänger, American exceptionalism. But, in having the lover voice such a connection, the film associates her with La Malinche, reproducing the male-female binarism of the conquest with respect to the Chicano "nation": the male poet promises, the female lover betrays. Thus, while the lover critiques the poet's empty rhetoric, she remains nonetheless bound within a love-hate relationship. As she says, "I also want your soul . . . then I want to hate your guts. . . . I want your lies so that I may know myself."

In the end, rather than constitute a feminist critique, the film uses gender, sexuality, and poetic masquerade as part of an overall strategy to "reform" the male identity at the core of Chicano nationalism. The female criticism sexualizes the critique of poetry as an empty promise vis-à-vis the social sphere, setting up *jotería* and machismo as its negative extremes. The poet himself then introduces *puñeta* as the term for a complete isolation from the social sphere located in academia. While sexist, homophobic, and anti-intellectual in its strategy, the film nonetheless fractures the normative male subject of Chicano nationalism into three conflicting parts. First, the film organizes the critique around the verbal sparring among three archetypal Chicanos: Mota Man (drug dealer), a pachuco, and the poet. The film then ends with a debate among three versions of the poet himself. The rapid-fire wordplay among them culminates in a parody of the unifying subject of *I Am Joaquin*. Whereas Joaquin subsumed and resolved all difference, these poets fragment identity claims: "Yo no soy todo" (I am not all), "I am a mockery of myself," and "I am Kennedy, a bit of Nixon, and a dash of Spaniard." But the film goes beyond mere parody, arguing that *I Am Joaquin* offers one aspect of *entelequia* that masks its colloquial other. Here, the philosophical notion of a completely realized essence gives way to the down-and-dirty exposure of a fantasy. In short, the film suggests several times that Gonzales did not write *I Am Joaquin,* identifying Alurista as the ghostwriter. It then goes on to elaborate a critique of the poet as situational identity within a social movement, in contrast to the more prosaic and ongoing practice of writing poetry.

But while critical of the fantasy of the "completely realized" self, the film nonetheless proposes another model for poetic nationalism, one that is self-critical and indeterminant. From this position, the film uses a call and response between the three versions of the poet in order to express community, using gender-neutral language that is implicitly and contextually male. One poet proposes, "Let us laugh at one another," and another concludes, "uncomfortable as it is. . . ." One poet declares, "We can't be mirrors for each other," but another responds, "We'll pretend to be, so it won't hurt as much." The final lines, then, imagine community within an antiessentialist masculine framework that acknowledges itself as incomplete and self-contradictory: "Esclavos liberados, ¿somos qué? ¡Algo, sí! No. Sí." (Liberated slaves, we are what? Something, yes! No. Yes.) Thus, if the film began with a challenge to police violence, it ends not with public policy or social protest, but with the poet fragmented into three parts, speaking to himself in the darkness, claiming to be and not to be. Here then is the self-critical precursor of the border artists and theorists who would later claim to incarnate all things that meet at the border—that is, whose identity would be none other than that of Joaquin. But if the completely realized essence of Chicano poetic nationalism is a fantasy and nothing more, then how can the poet turn that fantasy into political action? Perhaps, the film suggests, the answer is that to be Joaquin one must be joking while also trying to change the world.

Chicana

Sylvia Morales's *Chicana* (1979) presents the first feminist critique of
I Am Joaquin.[30] To a large extent, the two films frame the cultural-
nationalist period and together delineate its historical, political, and
aesthetic vision. As Rosa Linda Fregoso argues, "on the one hand, *I Am
Joaquin* represents an 'instance' of counterhegemony to the racist hege-
monic discourse, and *Chicana,* on the other hand, articulates a critical
discursive tendency within Chicano nationalist ideology."[31] But, in
fact, both films express a "critical discursive tendency" within an emerging counterhegemony based on cultural nationalism: whereas *I Am Joaquin* declares that Chicanos must transcend their internal differences
and identify with a composite male figure, *Chicana* stresses those differences as its narration also depersonalizes the rhetorical mode for nationalist identification. In this respect, it is important to note that both
films actively "imagine" the community for which they then argue an
appropriate identity; in neither case can that identity be assumed.

Both films set forth a worker-based ideology and cultural identity
that are rooted in a pre-Columbian mythopoetics and a 500-year history
of indigenous and mestizo resistance. Camera movements, music, and
the narrators' voices activate the still photographs that constitute the visual texts. But while *Chicana* appears to imitate *I Am Joaquin* in this
ideology and in its skillful use of still photographs, it also presents the
Chicana history that the "seminal" Chicano film overlooks. In a visual
pun on the still photographs that both films use, Morales inserts brief
live-action shots of women at work in the home, bringing movement—
the Movement—into the domestic sphere. In effect, these brief scenes
and the persuasive narration privilege the quotidian and mark it as an
arena for the affirmation and resistance of the other social protests. Finally, whereas *I Am Joaquin* subsumed all difference under the "I" of
the male narrator, *Chicana* ends with interviews of various Chicanas
who add their voices to the film's narrative. In thus documenting the female presence within the nationalist paradigm, *Chicana* is an initial step
in the representation of a Chicano identity that affirms rather than tran-
scends the gender, class, and political divisions within the community.

More significantly, *Chicana* also critiques poetic nationalism itself,
emphasizing the material factors and considerations that are the pre-
requisite for a gendered racial identity. Originally titled *Bread and Roses,*

Chicana references James Oppenheim's poem about women striking against child labor and poor working conditions in the nineteenth century: "Hearts starve as well as bodies. Give us bread, but give us roses." The narration then develops a socioeconomic analysis of the Chicana condition. Thus, while *Chicana* begins with the same poetic impulse as *I Am Joaquin* and *Entelequia,* it locates that impulse not in a neo-indigenous aesthetic *(floricanto)* or the self-critical wordplay of the *puñeta,* but in a gendered labor history that covers much of the same cultural ground as the earlier films.

I Am Joaquin and *Chicana* open and close the first decade of Chicano cinema, a decade in which it functioned as an extension of the Chicano movement. In comparing the two films, it is perhaps most important to note the difference in rhetorical and narrational strategies. In *I Am Joaquin,* Valdez's stentorian voice overpowers the poem's occasional irony and ambiguity. For example, the line that summarizes Mexico's independence from Spain—"Mexico was free?"—is read instead as "Mexico was free!" It is a change of degree, however, and not one of kind, since what Valdez does is to anchor Chicano identity in its own crisis. As he wryly notes in "The Tale of La Raza," "It is not enough to say we suffer an identity crisis, because that crisis has been our way of life for the last five centuries." [32] It is important to note that *Chicana* does not challenge this transcendent identity per se. Instead, the narrator, Carmen Zapata, founder of the Bilingual Foundation, counters Valdez's emotional and confrontational voice of the father with the rational and humorous voice of the mother. The gender dichotomy is further reinforced by Valdez and Zapata's respective roles as founders of rural- and urban-based Chicano *teatro* companies. Within the texts, these differences are registered in the play between the narrative voice and the sequence of images: while *I Am Joaquin* is illustrative, *Chicana* is ironic. If Valdez looked to "flower and song" for the discourse of social change, Morales reversed course and articulated the poetic through the material: bread and roses.

Mi Otro Yo and Border Brujo

Since the 1980s, as Claire Fox notes, "in Chicano arts and letters, the Borderlands has replaced Aztlán as the metaphor of choice in order to designate a communal space." [33] Guillermo Gómez-Peña, a self-styled shaman and performance artist, contributed to this shift within the arts in his role as a founding member of the San Diego–based Border Art

Workshop/Taller de Arte Fronterizo (BAW/TAF) as well as through his widely reprinted polemical and poetic writings on border culture.[34] Gómez-Peña's work follows in the footsteps of the poet-critics Cherríe Moraga and Gloria Anzaldúa in its attempt to explode various "borders" and reconstruct mestizo identities from the fragments of social hierarchies. What distinguishes Gómez-Peña from these writers, however, is his self-identification as a "cross-cultural diplomat" in which the border is neither site specific, reflecting an "art of place," nor tied to Chicano nationalism. Instead, the border becomes a metaphor for a transnational liberal humanism facilitated by artists or "cultural workers" and fueled—ironically enough—by the global movement of capital, mass media, and people.[35]

In two videos produced in collaboration with a fellow BAW/TAF member, Isaac Artenstein, Gómez-Peña develops this poetic globalism, first within the context of Chicano art (*Mi Otro Yo*, 1988), then as a borderless identity (*Border Brujo*, 1990). The first video, *Mi Otro Yo* (*My Other Self*, 1988), documents the Chicano arts in California and includes interviews with Judy Baca, Harry Gamboa Jr., Amalia Mesa-Bains, José Montoya, and Luis Valdez, among others. These interviews are organized around Gómez-Peña's voice-over narration, which is drawn from his poem "Califas" and which centers on the prototypical Chicano male, El Johnny.[36] The poetic narration and the video's title—which refers to the neo-Mayan concept "tú eres mi otro yo" (you are my other self)—situate the documentary within the *floricanto* tradition. But *Mi Otro Yo*, unlike *I Am Joaquin, Entelequia,* and *Chicana,* is an anti-epic whose emphasis is on an avant-garde demystification of the border, rather than on a nationalism that defines the boundaries for Chicano community by transcending, parodying, or foregrounding its internal differences. Instead, Gómez-Peña engages in a simple reversal of the conquest narrative that is designed to have "whites" identify with Chicanos. Gómez-Peña begins his narration with a scenario wherein the Aztecs conquered Europe in 1492. Near the end of the video, Gómez-Peña—now appearing onscreen as a stereotypically drunken Mexican—asks an implied white viewership, "What if *yo* were you *y tu* were us?" In this way, Gómez-Peña proposes expanding "mi otro yo" beyond Chicano nationalism, which defines its "other self" as an internal one of ethnic community and indigenous heritage. Instead, the phrase becomes an idealized model for U.S.-Mexico relations predicated on whites' identification with the nonwhite other. In effect, Gómez-Peña not only critiques Chicano nationalism, but also offers a solution that removes any sense of Chicano agency or participation. What undergirds this maneuver is the very thing Gómez-Peña ostensibly transcends: the nation-state. Indeed, his image of a "borderless future" is populated by the very stereotypes produced by the nation-state: Mixteco pilgrims, Australian surfers, la T.J. (Tijuana) whore, the L.A. junkie, and yuppie tribes.

In *Border Brujo* (1990), which recreates the one-man performance of the same title (1988), Gómez-Peña transforms himself into these various social types who inhabit the border. In this manner, the social drama of *teatro* becomes a stylized *testimonio* or testimonial narrative, making the plural self of the Border Brujo similar to that of Joaquin. But, in many ways, Gómez-Peña's poetic narration—here, performance rather than voice-over—places both Chicano nationalism and Anglo neoconservatism outside his ostensibly all-inclusive social vision. The former is critiqued indirectly: "They say I talk to Gringos; they say I wasn't born in East L.A.; they say I left the committee by choice; they say I promote negative stereotypes of my people." As Fox argues, "[B]y eliminating these two 'extremes'—that is, Anglo and Latino separatists —Gómez-Peña rhetorically constructs a 'middle' of sorts, which consists of those who, in his estimation, would be most receptive to hybrid cultural identities and 'border crossing.'"[37] In a sense, the border becomes the metaphor for a free-floating space of identification for an implied white viewer and a multicultural artistic intelligentsia who share a liberal politics. Ironically, the border becomes the very thing it was used to critique: the universal yet exclusionary realm of the "mainstream."

Cholo Joto

By the late 1980s, Chicano gay and lesbian media artists had begun to work within and subvert the terms of both Chicano nationalism and community-based politics.[38] Experimental videos and dramatic narratives either parodied or rearticulated cultural tropes, from neo-indigenism (*Mujeria: The Olmeca Rap,* 1991) to Mexican traditions (*La Posada,* 1995) to gang culture (*Mi Pollo Loco,* 1995, a drag parody of Allison Anders's girl-gang film *Mi Vida Loca,* 1994). Media artists also worked through community service organizations in order to raise issues of sexual orientation through youth media programs and AIDS educational videos. While not a Chicano queer "film poem" per se, Augie Robles's *Cholo Joto* (1993) incorporates poetry into its *testimonios* by three Chicano gay men.[39] The video's poetry is directed at the normative subjects of the gay and Chicano communities, playfully suggesting the similarity between Chicano machismo and the equally stylized masculinity of the gay community. Ricardo Bracho then reads his poem, "Nothing Personal," which addresses the "gay white male" seeking men of color through the personal ads: "So it's nothing personal, but I wonder why you, 'attractive gay white male,' are searching . . . for some fantasy you find wedged in our dark cracks." The video ends with Valentin Aguirre describing the mural of Che Guevara in San Diego's Chicano Park, which bears his words about how the revolutionary spirit is guided by feelings of love. Aguirre then states: "I'm not just going to fight out of anger. I'm fighting because I love myself, I love my community." In this way, the video—like the writings of Chicana lesbians—signals how homosexuality can serve as the "center" from which to imagine or narrate ethnic community.

For over thirty years, *I Am Joaquin* has set the terms for Chicano cultural politics, validating the need to locate a representative subject and identity within a heterogeneous community.[40] In the end, critiques have amounted to little more than a counterclaim within that same system: Joaquin is a sexist trickster; Joaquin is a border artist; Joaquin is *joto*; the puppetmaster behind Joaquin was his cunning mother, overworked wife, or lesbian sister. In essence, there has been a high degree of consensus about this period and about nationalism itself, such that it need not be examined or questioned beyond a certain point. Instead, one jockeys for the right to occupy the position of Joaquin—that is, to name the "I" and thereby stake a claim to the "we." Such a strategy tends to isolate enunciation and identity, rather than situate them within a broader social horizon. If there is no revolution without poets, neither is there reform without social movements challenging the state; and, as I will show, "Chicano cinema" necessarily pursued both reform and revolution, and other things, too. This book attempts to look beyond the poetic articulation of identity toward the spaces and discourses within which it is made.

two

Setting the Stage
Social Movements, the State, and Mass Media

I Am Joaquin is symptomatic of the struggle for Chicano self-representation within film and television, both as an organizing tool and as a means of representing the Chicano movement to a national audience. But more structural changes came about as a result of the combined efforts of social protests, federal regulation, and foundation initiatives. Widespread Chicano protests against film, television, radio, and print media started in 1968, drawing upon diverse sectors of the Mexican American community in order to address issues of media portrayals, industry employment, and community access to mass communication. These efforts involved older civil rights groups formed before the 1960s, including the League of United Latin American Citizens (LULAC), the American G.I. Forum, and the Mexican American Political Association (MAPA), as well as newer civil rights groups such as the Mexican American Legal Defense and Education Fund (MALDEF) and the National Council of La Raza (NCLR).[1] The last two were formed in the wake of the Civil Rights Act of 1964 as government agencies and foundations intervened in the growing social unrest within minority communities, helping transform unregulated protest into social movements increasingly oriented toward the state and its institutions.[2]

At the same time, media-oriented groups challenged the industry from a number of perspectives: direct action, litigation, and petitions before the Federal Communications Commission (FCC) and other regulatory agencies. These groups included the National Mexican-American Anti-Defamation Committee (NMAADC) in Washington, D.C., Involvement of Mexican-Americans in Gainful Endeavors (IMAGE) in San Antonio, and the Midwest Chicano Mass Media Committee in Chicago, as well as the Los Angeles–based Council to Advance and Restore the Image of the Spanish-Speaking and Mexican Americans (CARISSMA) and Justice for Chicanos in the Motion Picture and Television Industry (Justicia). Unlike MALDEF and the NCLR, these groups never became institutionalized and quickly disbanded, but their more confrontational approach played a significant role in the increased access to the mass media in the early 1970s.

From these various efforts emerged a number of industry trainee programs, film school admissions policies, and local public affairs shows that brought in the first generation of Chicano filmmakers between 1968 and 1974. By the mid-1970s, Chicano media activists and producers were no longer able to pose an effective state-supported challenge to the film and television industry. But because of the nominal integration of the early 1970s, they were able to organize within the professional sphere itself, while establishing and articulating connections with radical cinema in both the United States and Latin America.

Historiography

How are we to understand this history? Two historiographic impulses have delimited my approach to "Chicano cinema." First, if scholars now herald, in the words of the title of one anthology, *The 60s without Apology,* they also continue do so without reference to the Chicano civil rights movement.[3] Indeed, the common assessment of racial politics in this period can best be summed up by the Kerner Commission report in 1968: "Our nation is moving toward two societies, one black, one white—separate and unequal."[4] The report, which also established the centrality of the mass media in race relations, became a major reference point in the emerging media reform movement. But, for a number of racial minorities, the report's black-white dichotomy also added a new inflection to the term "colorblind."

Second, those who study Chicano cinema have done so largely within the realm of aesthetic history. The text has no other context than that of articulating an "oppositional politics" to some dominant realm, from Hollywood to U.S. society at large. But, after years of researching and writing about Chicano cinema, I have slowly come to realize the need to take into account a contradiction that marks this area of study. Despite the claims to examine a "cinematic" practice, most of the relevant texts which we study are products of television, including almost half of the dozen or so Chicano feature films. To take two prominent examples, scholars of Chicano cinema—myself included—have explored the cultural and gender politics expressed in Luis Valdez's *I Am Joaquin* and Sylvia Morales's *Chicana,* but we have failed to consider the material role these "films" played as nationally broadcast or syndicated television programs. These two works, after all, aired at a time in which social protest groups engaged the FCC, the U.S. Court of Appeals, advertisers, and the television industry, and they bookend a decade of professional efforts to create a programming space for Chicano-produced material that could address a dual audience: the Chicano community and the nation. But in the critical literature, an inversion takes place: these film texts become the sole filter through which all other history is read, rather than being seen as participants within a broader field of discourse and practice. As a consequence, text becomes context and vice versa, and we lose any sense of irony or strategy in the spaces between discourse and practice—or, to be more precise, between the films and all the other social practices corresponding to them.

This chapter will attempt to lay out terms for looking at Chicano cinema as the product of the relationships among a social movement, industry practices, and the operations of the state. In other words, rather than place emphasis on an "identity politics" or "cultural expression," I will look at various institutional relations since the mid-1960s and how these have set the terms for representing race, gender, and sexuality in mass media. What I propose to do here is to sketch the broad features of three moments in "minority cinemas," providing examples from each period of Chicano media activism and its relationship to federal activities (legislation, court decisions, and regulation), global technological and economic developments, nonprofit funding policies, and minority textual production.

Two Disciplines

First, I would like to consider some of the disciplinary tendencies that stand in the way of such an approach, since this reveals what is at stake for scholars. Part of the problem is methodological. On the one hand, humanities-based film and television studies tend to shun areas of interest that fall within the domain of mass communication. In fact, the phrase "mass comm" operates as a derogatory shorthand for all empirical, sociological, or policy-oriented analysis, the consequence of which is that film and television studies have isolated themselves from ongoing media debates within the public sphere, regulatory agencies, and legislative bodies. The exceptions are quite recent and are usually limited to the immediate needs of university scholars and teachers—for example, colorization, fair usage, and preservation. On the other hand, telecommunications policy research tends to limit its analytical scope to the technological and economic, for the most part ignoring the state, which is, of course, the domain of policy. While a class analysis might help explain state-market relations (for example, deregulation), it cannot account for the fact that, as Vincent Mosco notes, "organized opposition in the United States and other developed capitalist societies comes from groups whose cohesion is indirectly tied to social class."[5] The main examples here would be gender, race, age, and religion. I want to expand upon these disciplinary differences because they highlight the two "mindsets" that I am trying to bring together: textual analysis as a sign of the historical and largely descriptive policy-oriented reports on funding, employment, and audience. Also, I am trying to locate the grounds from which to generalize beyond the particularities of Chicano cinema to what I call minoritarian media and cultural studies.

The first mindset describes minority scholarship within film and television studies. Insofar as Chicano cinema has been seen as a component of the Chicano civil rights movement, critical discourse has followed the well-trodden path of social movement scholarship more generally, looking at the political, aesthetic, and cultural dimensions of contestation without considering its relationships to the state, the political representation system, industry practices, and the market.[6] Until recently, the exception proved the rule, to the extent that scholars isolated the so-called political accommodation and assimilation of Mexican American organizations from the metanarrative of the Chicano movement *because* these groups worked "within the system" of state institutions.[7] This approach has resulted in a tendency to reduce the Chicano movement period to a monolithic and seemingly autonomous "cultural nationalism" that is then redeemed by contemporary practices or critical discourses.[8]

Here, then, much of the relevant literature deals with the expressive qualities and sociohistorical context for cultural production: defining a vernacular aesthetic and cinema movement and a corresponding community, usually against a backdrop of mainstream exclusion. Despite the theoretical range of these efforts, more than anything else they have contributed to the construction of minority-produced media as distinct genres in critical discourse, funding practices, and public exhibition. In fact, quite often minority cinemas are named and become functional within discourse and institutional practices *before* they exist as a text-producing phenomenon. There is a paradox at work here that speaks to the dynamic of racially marked expression and its circulation in popular and academic discourses. In effect, the articulation of an essential ethnic category created the possibilities for subsequent production and reception. It is not too much of a stretch to argue that, for example, Chicano-produced films did not exist—in either film festivals, foundation initiatives, admission programs, or college courses—until Chicano cinema was named, providing a category that defined prior exclusion and subsequent inclusion in pretty much the same terms. But, as a consequence, Chicano cinema became *the* category, implicit or not, through which Chicano filmmakers and video artists entered the television industry, film festival circuit, grant opportunities, art museums, and college curricula. This is the catch-22 of such a project: it is necessary to posit subnational histories in order to locate texts and thereby incite discourse; but at the same time, any specific text will necessarily exceed the history within which it then circulates and is more or less contained.

If it seems odd that minority cinemas are named before the fact, the reason has more to do with mass communication than with racial identity. Consider the history of over-the-air and under-the-ground media: radio, television, cable, and the information superhighway. At each step along the way, broadcasters have sought concessions from the FCC that deferred fulfilling the "public interest" standard to some new technology: in the 1930s, radio pointed to television, and in the 1960s, television pointed to cable. At that time, and with breathless approval from media reform groups, an argument was made that the public interest now resided *not* in three network channels, but in the fifty cable channels, where, surely, there would be enough space for both public and commercial interests. Similarly, since around 1990, we have been living under the name of an emerging information superhighway and digital revolution that has not quite happened yet, but whose naming sets the stage for "precompetitive" state support, local tax incentives, and diversion of education and library funds—all designed to prepare us for that moment which is, ironically, heralded as the coming triumph of the free market.

With respect to the naming of minority cinemas, what we end up with is a series of body genres for, by, and about women, blacks, Chicanos, queers, and so on that are problematic as genres for the same reason that they are so effective: these social *cum* aesthetic categories

create a space for filmmakers to move into in a very practical and consequential way. After all, films and videos get funded, produced, and
distributed. But that space often ends up being another, more public,
version of the home, ghetto, barrio, and closet from which the filmmakers were trying to escape. For my current purposes, I am concerned
with the historiographic impulse behind the construction of body genres—that is, with a recent critical activity that attempts to write a particular community, subject, or identity into history by way of "film"
genre. What must be repressed in such a move is the fact that one is doing a form of genre analysis that effectively reduces institutional analysis and social history to a textual effect; that is, these social phenomena
exist only as signs circulating within a closed set of texts. But there is
another consequence embedded within the inherent formal and textual
limitations of genre analysis: insofar as one tends to look within and not
across genres, the analysis also looks within and not across racial and
sexual identities.

The second mindset describes mass communication. Here, quantitative studies of minority content and audience reception often end with
a paradoxical shift to moral discourses. Rather than correlate the empirical findings to the messy cultural arena of policy formation, these
studies make a leap of faith from the empirical to a call for enforcement
of the notion of "public interest" embedded in the 1934 Communications Act that established the FCC in the first place. In other words,
these studies do little more than bolster an urgent call to follow a law
that already exists but has rarely been enforced outside corporate parameters. The American Psychological Association has been especially
active on this front.[9] More qualitative work on democratization tends
to be focused on either legal issues or media policies that define state-
industry relations. But it has failed to take into account textual production or the cultural strategies used by "citizen groups" that enter into
or challenge the regulatory process. Indeed, state theorists, policy ana-
lysts, and communications scholars have rarely examined or given much
credence to the role of social movements in contesting existing power
relations.[10] Nor has there been an adequate account of the substantial
role of foundations—most notably, the Ford Foundation—within public television and minority communities (especially given their emphasis on integrating racial minorities into "civil society" and the political
arena). Nevertheless, a "cultural studies" movement within communication studies—which both precedes and is much more discipline iden-

tified than its literary counterpart—has introduced cultural analysis that foregrounds the national, albeit in the problematic terms of a "public sphere" uninflected by the state, let alone global factors. It is here that one can begin to understand foundation activities aimed at the democratization of civil society—a point to which I will return in chapter 5.

What is of note about these two broad fields is the extent to which they implicitly agree that social movements exist *outside* the state, while they also fail to work from the notion that "minority" categories are constructed, provisional, and conflicted. Even when speaking in the language of anti-essentialism, pro-hybridity, imagined communities, or transnationalism, there is a level at which a Latino remains a Latino, a woman remains a woman, and a queer remains a queer, even if these subjects do a lot of dancing around within these categories. In short, these fields fail to account for why previously excluded groups are now included by way of "minority" categories for funding, exhibition, and training. As a preliminary answer, I argue that this particular form of inclusion happened because social institutions, advocates, and scholars were complicit in the wholesale remapping of the terms of institutional analysis with those of minority expression. In this way, we shift from a focus on mainstream exclusion and inclusion to a focus on minority resistance and affirmation. To be fair, this tactical move served the immediate needs of everyone involved—alleviating demands placed upon the state, protecting commercial practices, and ensuring some minority access that, no matter how limited, provided highly charged public symbols of an identity and community marked by otherness. But something else happened, too. Given the absence of other types of institutional practices that involved minorities, inclusion became not the opposite of exclusion, but its mirror image. There was now a space within the institution for the other, but it was the negative space of political exigencies and compromise, an unintegrated space outside aesthetic conventions and professional codes, and, above all else, a transitory space that kept these works outside the institutional imaginary. If we were to describe this space it would be through a series of negatives: not-institution, not-meritorious, and not-always. This space is, in short, the space of affirmative action, prime-time access, and—at the level of an ethos—pluralism, diversity, and multiculturalism, and it suggests the limitations of defending these policies and positions *as such,* except in the continued absence of viable alternatives. In this respect, it is important to remember that affirmative action was a compromise offered by the Right in response to minority demands for equal access and opportunity across the board.

Social Movements

Given this conundrum, how can we move beyond these two disciplinary and methodological extremes and begin to read minority media activism in light of concurrent federal legislation and regulation, global technological and economic developments, nonprofit funding policies, and minority textual production? I propose that we look at a given social formation as the product of the relationships *among* the state, social movements, the market, and other institutional actors. Once we do that, the analytical purity of these categories becomes less important, such that Chicano cinema emerges as a highly contingent practice within the nation-state rather than a purely contestatory one positioned discursively outside and against the nation-state. This contingency explains the contradictory or, rather, complex nature of any contestation, making it difficult to draw clear-cut borders between inside and outside. Thus, although social movements are by definition extra- or noninstitutional efforts to change society, a strict insider-outsider dichotomy misses the point. As Christian Smith notes:

> In fact, the majority of modern social movements possess *moderate* amounts of political and economic resources, enjoy *limited* access to political decision making, employ both disruptive *and* institutionalized means of political influence, mobilize new movement-carrier groups *while simultaneously* collaborating with established political organizations, and vocalize a mix of conciliatory, persuasive, *and* confrontational rhetoric.[11]

Indeed, the numerous Chicano media groups, each with its own internal complexity, formed both alliances and oppositions with each other as well as with other media and civil rights groups, government agencies, industry guilds, and foundations. Whether seen from the perspective of the industry (to contain the movement), the state (to co-opt the movement), or social movements themselves (to capture the state's institutions and reform the industry), contestation necessarily complicates the set of preexisting relationships between the state and mass media that legally define commercial and public broadcast television.[12]

Making matters even more complex, Chicano media activism—as with the broader Chicano movement—worked on three levels at once, challenging the state, regime, and government. Indeed, if the Chicano movement did not speak in one voice, it also did not speak to a mono-lithic power structure. It is for this reason that the broader movement as well as individual groups often articulated seemingly contradictory "radical" and "reformist" goals. In this respect, the traditional politi-cal and ideological spectrum fails to account for the different location and resonance of these goals vis-à-vis the *state* ("the institutionalized claim to a legitimate monopoly over the means of violence within a specified territory"), the *regime* ("the structure of rule and the legiti-mizing myths used to sustain that claim"), and the *government* ("the personnel who actually make authoritative or binding decisions").[13] In fact, what is interesting about the Chicano movement—if not most other social movements in this period—is that movement discourse cir-culated within these three locations, counterbalancing "reformist" po-litical action with "radical" community building. Thus, the Chicano movement reveals the limits of the analytical distinctions that J. Craig Jenkins and other sociologists make between "social movements that challenge the government and its policies, those directed at the regime and its legitimizing myths, and those that adopt the more radical goal of reorganizing the state and its territorial claims."[14] To a large extent, no social movement can pursue one of these goals without also touch-ing upon the others; and, as such, its political and ideological "meaning" will read like a three-level chessboard. Even after the state significantly intervened between protest groups and the mass media, Chicano media activists and filmmakers continued to do all three things at once, sug-gesting a reason for why there have been rather fluid boundaries between reformist demands upon the government, alternative cultural produc-tion aimed at the regime, and radical nation-building efforts vis-à-vis the state. Any one of these activities contradicts the others. But, rather than see this contradiction as a failure on the part of a social movement, I want to argue that a varied approach provided leverage against the state and mass media, precisely by playing with the boundaries that defined "working within the system" for those on the outside.

Periods and Public Spheres

Looked at from this perspective, Chicano cinema—understood here as those activities directed at or located within broadcast television—falls into three overlapping periods, each with a distinctive configuration of demands, discourse, sponsorship, and subject position.

1. Between 1968 and 1977, Chicano media activists made reformist demands upon the news and entertainment media under the sponsorship of the state's civil rights institutions.[15] By and large, these demands were framed within a "discourse of violence" that correlated to ongoing social protests and a general sense of crisis within the imagined community of the nation-state. These demands, and the public and governmental arenas within which they took place, constituted Chicanos as workers and as citizens seeking redress, but not as political actors.

2. Between 1974 and 1984, Chicano filmmakers made radical demands directed at the television industry but were dependent upon noncommercial funding sources for production. This period marks a transition between the social engineering of the Great Society and the rise of neoclassical economics leading to broadcast deregulation by the end of the 1970s. Thus, while filmmakers' sense of their social function became more radical (and associated with New Latin American Cinema and the New Left), their actions operated within a broader "discourse of professionalism" and an increasing reliance upon public funding sources and public broadcasting. The professional arena emphasized the correspondence between Chicano producers and Chicano viewers, leading to the first policy-motivated studies of the "media habits" of Chicano television and radio audiences.

3. Since 1981, the beginning of the so-called Decade of the Hispanic, Chicano media producers and advocates have made increasingly corporatist demands upon both the state and broadcast industry, attempting to gain some control over the "consumer sovereignty" of commercial *and* public broadcasting.[16] As Thomas Streeter notes, "both the practice of funding broadcasting by 'selling audiences to advertisers' and the radical separation of transmission and reception that constitutes broadcasting itself are premised on the production/consumption divide."[17] It is in this period that Chicanos were recognized as consumers. Using a "discourse of citizenship," media producers and advocates did not so much question the legal and political distinction between producers and consumers as stake a moral and economic claim to the Chicano citizen-consumer.

By emphasizing Chicano cinema as a film movement that emerges vis-à-vis television and its regulation by the state, I am proposing a reorientation of the field itself. Rather than take Hollywood as the norm against which the two other media histories—the avant-garde and television—are measured (or ignored), I am arguing that it is television that allows us to organize our objects of study in such a way as to foreground the nation-state itself.[18] Since the 1950s, television has superseded the commercial cinema (or "Hollywood"), in part by becoming the endpoint of almost all feature films, or what Christopher Anderson calls "the informal archive of the American cinema," [19] but more significantly by shifting mass-media viewership from the theater to the home.[20] In the 1990s, the average "white" viewer will go to eight movies per year but will watch nearly fifty hours of television per week. Blacks and Latinos will watch more of both. Television has also become the endpoint of the avant-garde as it has been incorporated stylistically from *Miami Vice* to MTV to the evening news.[21] But there is a larger point to be made. Much of the impetus behind cinema studies stems from the function of Hollywood within the social imaginary, despite the fact that moviegoing has become a relatively minor phenomenon compared to television. This is not to say that Hollywood is not important, since television makes it a central part of its programming and self-referential discourse, but, rather, to shift emphasis from a social imaginary to the public sphere.

When I say public sphere, however, I do not refer to an eighteenth-century political ideal of a "public" located outside the state, market, and family.[22] Nor do I want to counterbalance the exclusions of such an admittedly fictive unity with an emphasis on counterpublics.[23] In other words, I am less interested in analytical distinctions that serve a valuable programmatic function—that is, in conceiving of a public sphere within which democracy *could* actually exist—than in trying to understand the peculiar institution through and against which racial cinemas *did* actually emerge in the 1960s. Therefore, I will engage in what Miriam Hansen identifies as the "disciplinary promiscuity" of the recent critical work on the public sphere. Hansen makes an important distinction between community and counterpublic:

> The ideal of community refers to a model of association patterned on family and kinship relations, on an affective language of love and loyalty, on assumptions of authenticity, homogeneity, and continuity, of inclusion and exclusion, identity and otherness. The notion of a counterpublic, by contrast, refers to a specifically modern phenomenon, contemporaneous with, and responding to, bourgeois and industrial-capitalist publicity. It offers forms of solidarity and reciprocity that are grounded in a collective experience of marginalization and expropriation, but these forms are inevitably experienced as medi-

ated, no longer rooted in face-to-face relations, and subject to discursive conflict and negotiation.

While attentive to this distinction in my analysis, my terminology will be somewhat looser in this book. I will use Chicano "community" in several conflicting senses: as precisely the essentialist political ideal Hansen defines, as a shorthand for the U.S. population of Mexican descent as the object of various discourses, and as a counterpublic.[24]

I propose, then, that we understand the U.S. public sphere in the twentieth century as rooted in a national telecommunications infrastructure that claims to serve the "public interest" but that imbricates private and public via the state. In this respect, television (1) expresses an "imagined community" through a shared national televisual experience broadcast on airwaves owned by the people, and, for that reason, (2) is regulated by the state. At the same time, (3) it operates as a commercial enterprise that presumes property rights; and, when all is said and done, (4) television situates its "public sphere" in the home. But rather than start with television as it is produced by an industry or received in the home, I will emphasize the "in-between" of federal regulation, since it gives rise to a history that these other approaches have not been able to tell: the history of absent texts.

The emphasis on federal regulation also offers a useful vantage point on corporate capitalism, revealing the vested interests of each in the other, while also opening the back door to issues of political representation. Indeed, the rise of the "administrative state" in the early twentieth century raised important questions about the status of emerging federal regulations vis-à-vis the law, including issues of discovery and adjudication. Significantly, concurrent with the rise of television, regulatory bureaucracies became increasingly imbricated in the political representation system, starting with the Administrative Procedures Act in 1946. With respect to television, the U.S. Court of Appeals opened the FCC to direct participation by citizen groups in 1966. What is at stake in my study is the fact that the "public interest" standard for television operated within somewhat contradictory contexts inside the state itself: regulatory, legislative, and judicial. The latter two became the avenues through which the public could express its interests against the private ones of commercial television. It is in looking at television in this way that we can begin to locate Chicano cinema.

three

"The Stereotypes Must Die"
Social Protest and the Frito Bandito

In the fall of 1968, Chicano groups in Los Angeles, Washington, D.C., and San Antonio initiated protests against advertisers, television networks, and the film industry, charging them with disseminating derogatory stereotypes against Mexican Americans, Mexicans, and other Latino groups. In particular, activists objected to media portrayals of Mexicans as "stupid, shiftless, dirty, immoral, and lackey-bandito types."[1] By the spring of 1970, the growing protests would also be directed against the Academy Awards, industry guilds, and television stations, while the Department of Justice—after public hearings by the U.S. Equal Employment Opportunity Commission—negotiated an equal-employment plan signed by seventy-two movie and television production companies. As Armando Rendon and Domingo Nick Reyes concluded in 1970: "Chicanos no longer will stand to be stereotyped— the days of the 'bandito' and the sleepy Mexican caricature are gone. We are making demands of every institution of society and every agency of government."[2]

Before examining the history of these protests, it is important to pose a question about the very terms upon which they took place. Why did these groups initially focus on stereotypes and, furthermore, why did they make them the basis of their demands on social institutions? Did not Chicano demands for social equity have more material things at stake with respect to the mass media, such as employment, access, control, and ownership? A preliminary answer can be found in the Kerner Commission's *Report of the National Advisory Commission on Civil Disorders* (1968), which identified the media as a contributing factor in the race-related riots of the 1960s. The report argued that the media failed to communicate the urgency of "race relations and ghetto problems" to the nation as a whole, and that this failure stemmed from the fact that television "is almost totally white in both appearance and attitude." [3] What the report did, in effect, was to place racial discrimination and growing social unrest squarely within the context of a mediated nation, while linking problematic discourse (stereotypes) not to mass communication per se but to employment within its related industries. This critique acknowledged the central function of mass communication within modern society as well as the need for state intervention, while skirting the regulatory bugaboos of free speech within the free market. Underlying this argument was an understanding of the contradiction inherent in mass media as a basic infrastructure serving the public interest while also operating within a system of private property. As Robert Britt Horwitz explains in *The Irony of Regulatory Reform*:

> Telecommunications constitutes one of the four essential modes or channels that permit trade and discourse among members of a society, the other three being transportation, energy utilities, and the system of currency exchange, or money. . . . [I]nfrastructure industries are always the focus of direct state intervention, whether by way of promotion, subsidy, or regulation. . . . Telecommunications is a peculiar infrastructure because it is a primary medium for the circulation of ideas and information, a realm where, in principle, political life can be discussed openly and in accordance with standards of critical reason. [4]

But insofar as the "public interest" standard originated as what Horwitz identifies as a "commerce-based concept," [5] regulation tended to be between contending corporate interests within the marketplace, rather than serving to counterbalance these private concerns against public ones. Furthermore, access to telecommunications was restricted based on spectrum scarcity and the capital needed in order to broadcast. Only later would the notion of the public interest change to allow the "public" standing within federal regulation, suggesting why initial concerns dealt with stereotypes rather than the specific legal, technical, and aesthetic characteristics of the medium. In effect, regulation safeguarded these concerns from social protest. Thus, the Kerner report made a causal link between social inequities, civil disorder, and mass communication, but limited its critique and solution to "surface" issues within the basic infrastructure: stereotypes and employment.

Beyond the question of the positive or negative images of an ethnic group, then, the critique of stereotypes exposed a set of power relations reinforced by and existing within mass communication. Chicano activists built upon the Kerner report as well as the work of sociologists from Walter Lippmann to Gordon Allport, foregrounding stereotypes within their overall critique of mass media. In *The Nature of Prejudice,* Allport offered a practical definition: "a stereotype is an exaggerated belief associated with a category, and its function is to justify conduct in relation to that category."[6] While this definition assumes the circulation of stereotypes, its emphasis is not on the medium used but rather on the social function served by stereotyping. If going after negative stereotypes provided a strategic approach to the mass media, as argued above with respect to the Kerner report, for Chicano activists this approach also kept attention focused on the "daily life-death reality of the barrio" that motivated their struggle over media representation in the first place.[7] Thus, in refuting the utopianism of Marshall McLuhan's "global village," with its message about the medium being the message, Chicano activists also rejected the underlying formalism that continues to inform media studies. As Thomas M. Martinez noted at the time: "No matter what medium sends the message, the content and context of the message still have important ramifications, which in some cases supersede the importance of difference in media."[8] This position is echoed in all the major media-related documents produced by Chicano scholars and activists during this period, since their larger goal had to do with the "image" of Chicanos within modern society as a whole—from textbooks to commercials to the social sciences—which then spoke to their actual place in the workforce, political arena, education system, and urban environment. But this position also reflects that the message could be questioned much more easily than the medium itself. These documents tend to introduce a sociological understanding of stereotypes as the theoretical fulcrum between their review of the historical injustices against Chicanos and their plan for present-day media activism, whether directed at advertising,[9] broadcast policy,[10] an *institutionalized* social movement,[11] or, more generally, the nation-state.[12]

Thus, stereotypes became a major site of struggle for the Chicano and other social movements, as media representation *of* the community and media use and control *by* the community began to be seen as directly related to other social causes.[13] The focus on stereotypes led in two directions: challenges to the structure of the commercial broadcasting and film industries; and a critique of racism within modern society that identified the media as the determining form of public discourse and hence of social relations. In a prepared statement presented to Senate and

House subcommittees in 1970, Armando Rendon and Domingo Nick Reyes offered the following explanation in a section titled, "The Stereotypes Must Die": "These media do not belong to us, we know that; they are white men's possessions. They have been his strongest and not so subtle instrument of propaganda for spreading the myth of Anglo cultural supremacy." [14] For Rendon and Reyes, television, radio, and print media were "destructive forces" in the Chicano community, especially insofar as they produced "apathy" and "ignorance" that sustained the structure of rule. By the early 1970s, both minority media groups and minority "cinemas" quickly emerged as integral components of broader social movements. Writing in 1974, near the end of this period of activism, Francisco J. Lewels Jr. concluded:

> The power of the media becomes quite clear to the leaders of the social movement seeking relief from discrimination and the hardships of inferior education, poor housing, and low-paying jobs that accompany it. . . . Soon, the issue of identity and stereotype became the major issue of a great deal of political activity within the Chicano movement, which, for the first time, confronted the cultural and racial stereotypes held by the Anglos. [15]

Thus, while institutional reform remained the primary goal, political activity itself turned to the cultural as the underlying determinant, thereby pitting identity against stereotype. This mixture of cultural nationalism and political action created a sense of "newness" that masked the contradictions in these mediated demands for social equity.

For the First Time

Given the sudden and widespread social movement in the late 1960s, together with some initial successes, Chicano activists saw themselves as ushering in the first "organized Chicano protest" against the film and television industry. [16] Thus, although Chicanos had rejected Hollywood stereotypes since the "greaser" films of the 1910s, these earlier responses were now seen as "unorganized criticism" voiced within the home or community. [17] Indeed, the new activists often recalled this earlier "unorganized criticism" by way of family anecdote. In providing historical background for their account of Chicano protest against Hollywood between 1968 and 1971, Thomas M. Martinez and José Peralez explained, "One of our Madres informs us that when she was a young girl, she witnessed Chicano movie viewers who actually shot at the western hero on the screen." [18] In this way, Martinez and Peralez, like other writ-

ers, were able to claim historical and cultural continuity for their protests based on parental respect and shared sentiment, while also marking a crucial distinction between earlier *cultural* resistance and their
own efforts to impact the political and economic mainstream.

Ultimately, the distinction between the past and present had less to
do with being "organized" than it did with a shift in address from community maintenance based on family anecdote (memory) to participation in the national public record (history). Chicano activists no longer
shot at the silver screen; instead, they wanted to address the nation *from*
that screen. But there was a great deal of unstated ambivalence and ambiguity about making this shift, let alone about accepting the critical
distinctions between memory and history, private and public. For one
thing, Martinez and Peralez's article addressed a Chicano movement
readership in *La Raza* magazine, providing historical background, a
brief look at current activism, and a rather militant sense of its importance: "Chicanos are breaking the back of American society." [19] But, as
with Martinez's earlier article on advertising (published in *El Grito* and
reprinted in *La Raza*), this article did not provide a strategy for either
grassroots activism and education or political action and policy formation. So what *did* it do? The last sentence of the article reveals the underlying paradoxes of their position: "If the Chicano way of life is to be preserved and developed, then Chicanos will either have to rely upon limited
access to the mass media, or attempt to change the content and structure of the media while there is still time, for everyone's sake." [20] In effect, the authors admit that the "Chicano way of life" cannot be defined
independently of the mass media, as exemplified by their concern over
the long-term impact of Hollywood stereotypes upon Chicanos, by the
family anecdote that presages "organized" protest, and by the rallying
call to enter into and change the mass media. What, then, is to be preserved and developed? Consider the authors' two options. In the first,
the status quo is preserved: The "Chicano way of life" exists within a
horizon of social relations defined by mass media stereotypes and local-
to-familial resistance. In the second, the "content and structure" of the
mass media are changed to allow for the expression of diverse ways of
life. But how does one group enter into and change a state-regulated,
advertising-supported industry central to the regime's structure of rule
and legitimizing myths? One possible answer is suggested by the emphasis on organized response and in the syntax of the last sentence itself: The
initial goal of preserving the "Chicano way of life" is stated in the pas-

sive voice as part of a conditional statement, allowing the second part of the sentence, the solution (written in the active voice), to redefine the agent's location and motivation. Henceforth, Chicanos will work within the "content and structure" of the mass media in order to effect change "for everyone's sake." It is the universalizing gesture of the final clause, "for everyone's sake," that throws the sentence out of whack, so to speak, since it acknowledges the need to occupy the transcendental space of universal representation—the imagined community of the nation—in order to advocate on behalf of something excluded from that realm to begin with: a "Chicano way of life." [21] Despite their emphasis on "organized" protest, then, Martinez and Peralez could not provide a road map out of this paradox of political representation. In seeking to preserve and develop the "Chicano way of life," Chicano scholars and activists had gone through the looking glass of the nation's self-other dichotomies—consumer-producer, minority-majority, foreigner-citizen, and black-white—finding themselves reflected at neither end. [22] If they were the first, then it was unclear within whose coordinates their firstness unfolded.

Schizo-Cultural Limbo

Writing in 1967, Enrique Hank López addressed the paradox of place that haunted Martinez and Peralez's article and others that attempted to describe the social movement in relationship to the state, mass media, and national culture. López's own political career provided ample experiences from which to theorize this paradox. In 1958, López was a founding member of the Mexican American Political Association (MAPA), which sought the election and appointment of Mexican Americans to public office. He also ran as the Democratic candidate for secretary of state of California, losing by less than one percent of the total vote. In 1960, López served as National Coordinator of the Viva Kennedy Clubs, which played an effective role in Kennedy's election. By most accounts, the failure of the Democratic party to support Chicano candidates such as López in the late 1950s and early 1960s contributed to the rise of a broad social movement at odds with the political representation system itself. This movement included several local protest votes for Republican candidates as well as regional efforts to form a third party, La Raza Unida. [23]

In "Back to Bachimba," López also relied on family anecdote to posit a generational shift. But whereas Martinez and Peralez emphasized a generational shift in terms of political strategy, López articulated a cultural logic that implicitly connected his own reformist efforts at Mexican American political integration in the late 1950s to the current social unrest and more militant political struggle. López starts by contrasting family history with Hollywood representations of the Mexican Revolution:

> I remember how angry my parents were when they saw Wallace Beery in *Viva Villa!* [1934]. "Garbage by stupid Gringos," they called it. They were particularly offended by the sweaty, unshaven sloppiness of Beery's portrayal. "Pancho Villa was clean and orderly, no matter how much he chased after women. This man's a dirty swine." [24]

López's father, "the only private in Villa's army," crossed the border into El Paso in order to escape federal troops and was later joined by his wife and son. In recounting this history and the subsequent "harsh conflicts" within both the barrio and the nation, [25] López uses humor to reveal the complexities of a self-consciously binational, bicultural, and reformed macho identity, locating himself in a "schizo-cultural limbo, with a mere hyphen to provide some slight cohesion between my split selves." [26] Ultimately, López cannot share his parents' anger over *Viva Villa!*, since theirs is a *Mexican* protest against historical representation, while his is that of a hyphenated American jockeying for position within the U.S. cultural and political landscape. But López turns this condition into the basis for action, arguing that it offers a much more pragmatic model for democratization than those of either the melting pot or cultural nationalism. Implicit in López's critique of the melting pot is the fact that the regime operates on an ideology of the assimilated individual, while the political representation system operates on the basis of group dynamics: voting blocs, constituencies, coalitions, and lobbying and special-interest groups. Cultural nationalism, on the other hand, removes one from the political field altogether by discursively rejecting the state, often, as López admits about himself, based on a false sense of being culturally and legally *Mexican* (a belief he was disabused of while in residence at the Centro Mexicano de Escritores). But López forgoes a stable location or "home," instead working between these many spaces, claiming the hyphen as a strategy of citizenship and not as the measure of his identity, which remains open ended. [27]

Thus, starting in 1968, Chicano protests against film and television posited a break with the past in terms of the emergence of "organized" actions against mass media stereotypes. While not entirely accurate, especially with respect to Hollywood, this position had considerable merit within the broadcast media insofar as the federal courts had established "citizen standing" within the regulatory process two years before in 1966. In other words, earlier protests, organized or not, minority or not, meant little until the courts defined the "public interest" in such a way that broadcast policy and commercial broadcasting necessarily incorporated the public itself. This period of citizen participation in the FCC regulation of television stations would be effective until the mid-1970s. Because of the unstable dynamic of the hyphenated American and the nascent standing of citizens (and, hence, political representation) in communication law and policy, Chicano protests exhibited López's "schizo-cultural limbo" during this brief period, maneuvering between reformist and radical strategies and articulating demands from a number of contradictory positions on behalf of consumers, workers, citizens, ethnic communities, social movements, an emergent counternationalism, the American people, state institutions, the Americas, and the world.[28]

While these protests foregrounded negative stereotypes, eventually they would be incorporated into the FCC regulatory process and limited to policy-oriented broadcast reform categories: free speech, access, and the public interest. One of the early protests directed against advertisers, however, reveals the emergence of strategies at odds with this framework that would factor into later "regulated" protests.

There May Be a Frito Bandito in Your House

Caution: He loves cronchy Frito corn chips so much he'll stop at nothing to get yours. What's more, he's cunning, clever—and sneaky!

In 1967, Frito-Lay Corporation launched a national advertising campaign featuring an "unshaven, unfriendly, and leering" Frito Bandito who stole Anglos' corn chips at gunpoint.[29] Initially, Frito Bandito commercials appeared during children's television shows, where they were an "unqualified success," leading Frito-Lay to use the character in all its television and print advertising.[30] Despite growing protests from Mexican American groups, the Frito Bandito, developed by Foote, Cone & Belding Communications, sold a lot of corn chips during its four-year run. In 1971, under increasing pressure as members of the Senate and House, local television stations, columnists, and even the advertising trade journals joined the cause, Frito-Lay reluctantly dropped the Frito Bandito campaign.

Emiliano Zapata, the Mexican Robin Hood and revolutionary, tacked up this notice in a western railroad station: "Any engineer or conductor found not carrying an Elgin watch will be killed for concealing valuables."

It seems that the trainmen were tired of having their expensive Elgins stolen, and were trying to substitute something less valuable. It didn't work then and it certainly won't work now.

At Elgin, we've gained a lot of know-how building 70 million watches in over 100 years. Today's Elgins contain parts accurate to 3/10,000 of an inch. That's just one reason they're better than the Elgins Zapata would kill for.

It's a good thing Emiliano Zapata's gone. He'd be stealing Elgins as fast as we could make them.

ELGIN. MAKING THE MOST OF TIME.

Elgin watch ad, 1970.

But Frito-Lay was not alone in using the "bandito" (an Anglicized version of *bandido*) in order to sell products. Indeed, the bandito appeared to be everywhere within popular discourse, from westerns to advertisements, raising questions about the political and economic concerns embedded within its representation. In the late 1960s and early 1970s, for example, several companies used advertisements featuring

Frito Bandito ad, reproduced in Hispanic *(July 1996).*

Mexican revolutionaries, including Granny Goose (potato chips), Liggett & Myers (cigarettes), the Elgin Company (watches), Bristol-Myers (underarm deodorant), and American Motors (cars).[31] Liggett & Myers introduced "Paco," who never "feenishes" anything, not even the revolution, while Bristol-Myers showed a gang of banditos on horseback whose leader stops to spray on Mum underarm deodorant. The voice-over notes, "If it works for him, it'll work for you." Then, in May 1970, Elgin ran a newspaper ad that portrayed one of the heroes of the Mexican Revolution, Emiliano Zapata, as a common thief willing to kill for Elgin watches.[32]

Before looking at the organized response to the Frito Bandito, it is important to consider something that has escaped notice: why did Mexican revolutionaries make good product spokesmen for largely nonessential consumer items between 1967 and 1971? Critics offered explanations for the negative social impact of these advertisements but failed to explain their primary function: to instill the desire to consume. The answer lies in part in the unique role of the western during this period. As Richard Slotkin argues in *Gunfighter Nation:*

> Through most of the New Frontier/Great Society era, and most markedly between 1965 and 1972, the Western—and particularly the "Mexico Western"—was the only one of the standard Hollywood genres whose practitioners *regularly* used genre symbolism to address the problems of Vietnam and to make the connection between domestic social/racial disorder and the counterinsurgency mission.[33]

Slotkin reads the western as an allegory of national identity and the state, but his analysis nonetheless identifies the narrative terrain within which the issue of "domestic social/racial disorder" emerges: Mexico and a Southwest that was once part of Mexico. The western, then, destabilizes the boundaries between the domestic and foreign, thereby recoding "domestic social/racial disorder" as Mexican. As a national allegory this process goes largely unnoticed, since viewer identification follows those characters whose citizenship remains unquestioned throughout. Perhaps for this reason, scholarship on the western has failed to take into account the genre's function vis-à-vis contemporary Mexican and Mexican American subjects.

In this period, the discourse on Mexico and Mexican Americans shifted as the bracero program (1942–64), which provided Mexican farm labor in the Southwest, was superseded by the emergence of César Chávez and the United Farm Workers Union, signaling, among other things, the Chicano civil rights movement (1965–75). According to Kitty Calavita, the bracero program was "a domestic economic policy hammered out in collaboration with a foreign government" in which the State Department negotiated on behalf of and mediated between the conflicting interests of the Immigration Service and the Labor Department.[34] While she examines this conflict from the perspective of the state, the "bracero solution" also contributed to a broader public discourse—circulating within news and entertainment media and defining social relations—that "deterritorialized" Mexicans and Mexican Americans within the United States even as it also acknowledged the economic necessity of their presence. In other words, "Mexicans" were discursively removed from the body politic in terms of civil rights and citizenship, while their physical presence was understood and accepted on the basis of an economic rationale. The eventual failure of the bracero solution within government policy undercut the economic rationale (though not the system based on cheap labor), shifting regulation from labor issues to immigration control. By the late 1960s, the Chicano movement would challenge the continued deterritorialization of Mexican Americans within the post-bracero economy and political system. Thus, if, as David G. Gutiérrez argues, "the intensifying civil rights movement, urban unrest, and the escalation of the war in Vietnam all served to push the immigration issue out of the political spotlight," [35] the idea of the Chicano population as deterritorialized became the basis for early protests, internal debates, and nationalist conceptions of the Chicano community.

The Frito Bandito, like other Mexican bandits in film, television, and the print media, embodied a cluster of concerns that had to do with both Mexican laborers and Chicano activists as well as with the deepening crisis in the legitimizing myths typified by the western itself. What is interesting about the Frito Bandito, however, is that we are supposed to identify *with* him and even to incorporate him into the normative domestic sphere: "There may be a Frito Bandito in your house." Even in the more offensive ads—such as the ones for Mum deodorant spray or Elgin watches—we are supposed to want what the bandito wants: nonessential consumer items. Our subsequent purchase of these items is recoded as transgressive, on a par with the Mexican revolution, the Chicano movement, and even the Vietnam war. But, rather than connote a radical political sensibility toward racial minorities and the Third World, the Frito Bandito encouraged viewers to co-opt these "outside" threats to the American way of life by adopting their revolutionary and militant style through parodic consumption. In short, these threats were domesticated, rendered humorous, and consumed as a sign of surplus capital within the white middle-class home. Consumption was offered as a form of counterinsurgency.

In 1968, two Chicano groups formed in order to confront racist stereotypes in advertising: Involvement of Mexican-Americans in Gainful Endeavors (IMAGE), in San Antonio, and the National Mexican-American Anti-Defamation Committee (NMAADC), in Washington, D.C. The former group was established in July, the latter in September, although it developed from an ad hoc committee formed in 1967.[36] Both groups wrote letters directly to advertisers and held press conferences stating their case and threatening boycotts, if not more drastic action,[37] while the NMAADC also announced an ambitious ten-step program that signaled its crucial role in a wide array of media-reform activities over the next five years. These proposed steps included buyer boycotts, monitoring the mass media in order to sustain and direct such boycotts, lobbying and letter-writing efforts directed at industry and government, and the development of a "talent bank" in order to facilitate Latino employment within the mass media. In addition, the NMAADC sought government, industry, and foundation support for research on the extent and impact of minority stereotypes while it turned to foundations in order to develop "positive images" of Mexican Americans. Interestingly, the NMAADC also petitioned the government as a media producer, "urging the State Department, Voice of America, and U.S. Information Service to portray favorably the contributions made by the minority and to hire these people."[38]

But the most interesting thing about these two groups had to do with their nominal location within government and the mass media—which further blurred the boundaries between social movement, the state, and industry—and the fact that their initial strategy was based almost entirely on a moral appeal to corporate America to do the right thing. In other words, these groups claimed authority as representatives of the "second largest minority group" (threatening boycotts and pursuing media production), and as employees of an activist state (education programs, legislation, and regulation), but they could not exercise such authority per se. While Mexican Americans constituted a recognized minority group, this status in no way translated into formal inclusion within the political representation system and state bureaucracies,[39] even if IMAGE and NMAADC leaders were also politicians and bureaucrats. In San Antonio, IMAGE was often fronted in the press by Albert Peña Jr., the county commissioner of Bexar County.[40] In Washington, D.C., NMAADC leaders worked within the civil rights bureaucracy itself: Domingo Nick Reyes (executive director) was employed in the Mexican American Study Project of the U.S. Commission on Civil Rights, and Armando M. Rodriguez (chairman) served as chief of the Mexican-American Affairs Unit of the Office of Education in the Department of Health, Education, and Welfare. But, rather than claim an authority that they could not substantiate within existing state-industry relations, IMAGE and the NMAADC reconceptualized power relations to include the state, mass media, corporate interests, *and* the Mexican American community, arguing in moral terms that exchanging "negative" stereotypes for "positive" images would establish stability and unity within this reimagined and inclusive national community. In effect, this morality drew upon and subsumed all other interests within its appeal for positive images: profits for corporations, news and entertainment for the media, quietism for the state, and a positive representational identity for Mexican Americans.

But to see this argument as only a moral one rooted in misguided notions of verisimilitude misses the rhetorical strategy behind "negative" and "positive" stereotypes. These groups knew that stereotypes were reductive representations, whether negative or positive, and that they functioned in mass media to promote ideological, political, and economic ends: The Frito Bandito rearticulated the frontier myth as domestic humor, reinforced Mexican American (and racial) subordination, and sold corn chips. But they also knew that Mexican Americans were largely excluded from active participation in national life, *except as advertising stereotypes circulating within the mass media.* For this reason, the NMAADC addressed the industry directly, using the language of stereotypes to achieve a more fundamental change in the mass media in which Mexican Americans would be seen as members of its constituent elements: consumers and producers. Through the threat of boycotts, the NMAADC redefined Mexican Americans as a consumer group rather than a political constituency, since, after all, consumer rights were apparently universal, while the Voting Rights Act did not yet apply to Mexican Americans. Through the emphasis on a "talent bank," the shift from "negative" to "positive" stereotypes became the entry point for Latino employment and creative control within the mass media. But this strategy required more than a moral appeal, as suggested by the call for monitoring, research, and development funds, and as such it also required mooring in existing power relations—hence the strongly implied equivalence between Mexican American concerns and those of the state.

This strategy can be seen in Rodriguez's letters to advertisers on behalf of the NMAADC, which were written on Office of Education stationery and signed by Rodriguez as Chief of the Mexican-American Affairs Unit. Although the Office of Education informed *Advertising Age* that these letters did not represent an "official pronouncement,"[41] Rodriguez himself appears to have been extremely careful in avoiding such a claim while still positing a connection between his seemingly moral appeal, social and racial unrest, and the interests of the state and other social institutions. But, rather than suggest the political threat of increased regulation, he stresses the economic underpinnings of his social concerns and the business solutions to them:

> I am greatly concerned with the image of the Mexican-American, one which the educational system throughout the U.S. is spending millions to improve.
>
> The U.S. Office of Education, along with many other federal, state, and private institutions, is now making a concerted effort to improve the portrait of the Mexican-American and to provide a symbol which the young Mexican-American can be proud to inherit.
>
> May I suggest to you that advertising of the type you are sponsoring does not help the efforts of educators, nor does it improve the image of the Mexican-American.
>
> Some of the advertisements you are using are misleading because they are based on a stereotype which is the result of ignorance and obliterates the many contributions made by the U.S.'s second largest minority group, the Mexican-American.
>
> Surely a company such as yours can employ its talents to create an advertisement which does not play on or increase the stereotype of human beings who have contributed so much to this country.
>
> If your public relations department insists on using ethnic and racial differences as a basis for advertising, then do it in a selective manner. Have your advertising depict the Mexican-American in a positive manner.
>
> I am approaching you with this letter because I feel that you are one of the leading members of an industry which, during times such as these, should police itself, and begin to build unity in this great country rather than to divide it.[42]

Rodriguez later summarized the NMAADC's basic message to the industry: "Don't stop using us, but use us in a positive way." [43] For him this strategy meant more than just positive images. It meant employment and creative control within the mass media. But the Frito Bandito stood in the way, and, what's more, he was cunning, clever—and sneaky!

As Don McComb notes, "Although Frito Bandito was not the only stereotype targeted by the anti-defamation groups, it was a kind of benchmark in discussions of racial representations in advertising." [44] One reason for this status is that most other corporations dropped the offending advertisements after the initial protests.[45] In the other well-known case, involving AT&T's "Jellow Pages" commercials and print ads, Bill Dana portrayed his comic alter ego, Jose Jimenez, known for his slow-witted antics and mispronunciations. Initially, Dana rejected the criticism, arguing that Jose Jimenez was a "universal character" claimed by all Latin Americans: "Jose is the only one of the commercial images who can possibly be an ambassador." [46] Soon, however, AT&T stopped airing its "Jellow Pages" commercials in areas with large Mexican American populations, while Dana tried to show his support by forming his own advocacy group, Latin-Americans in United Direction (LAUD). [47] Then, in April 1970, after additional pressure, Dana retired his Mexican caricature, announcing at a Los Angeles rally attended by 10,000 Chicanos, "[A]fter tonight, Jose Jimenez is dead." [48] But Frito-Lay stuck to its guns, engaging in a prolonged struggle with the NMAADC and other Chicano groups that would shift protest strategy from direct appeal to the regulatory process.

In response to protests, and in concert with their expansion of the national advertising campaign, Frito-Lay "sanitized" the Frito Bandito. According to Owen J. Burns, who supervised the Frito-Lay account at Foote, Cone & Belding, this meant: "1. Less grimacing. 2. No beard or gold tooth. 3. Change in facial features to guile rather than leer. 4. Friendly face and voice." [49] The NMAADC's Armando Rodriguez also claimed that "Frito-Lay modified its commercials after the assassination of Sen. Robert Kennedy by taking the pistols away from the Frito Bandito." [50] Interestingly, these changes acknowledged the earlier negative stereotype and social impact of the Frito Bandito as grimacing, leering, unfriendly, and pistol shooting, while they nonetheless maintained the basic premise of a Mexican "bandito," although now a domesticated one, who steals corn chips.

But these changes were merely one part of a coordinated response. In addition to the "sanitized" Frito Bandito, Foote, Cone & Belding conducted a survey of Mexican Americans in four cities in California (San Jose and Los Angeles) and Texas (Fort Worth and San Antonio) in July 1969. The results indicated that 85 percent of those polled liked the Frito Bandito, while 8 percent did not, and 7 percent had no opinion. [51] If the NMAADC called for outside funds with which to gather research data on Mexican American stereotypes and consumers as part of an emerging reform strategy, Frito-Lay was already in a position to counter that challenge with empirical evidence of quiescent Mexican Americans who were measured as a demographic group, but not as consumers. For its part, the NMAADC relied upon Thomas M. Martinez's essay on advertising and racism in order to, in the words of *Broadcasting*, "illustrate their feelings" about the impact of negative stereotypes, especially upon the self-esteem of Mexican American children.[52] Bill R. Jones, Frito-Lay's national advertising manager, however, countered these feelings with facts: "Our position is that the facts we have indicate we are not offending a large group. We will continue to survey, and any time we find we're offending a substantial group of Mexican-Americans, we'll be the first to take Frito Bandito off the air."[53] But because Frito-Lay's empiricism did not address racial stereotyping per se, their majoritarian ethos drew attention to the underlying profit motive that was the subject of Martinez's critique in the first place. Even *Newsweek* quipped that Frito-Lay did not object to "offending a small group" if it made money, ending its article with an unflattering quote from Burns: "We don't need the flak if the Bandito wasn't selling Fritos—but he is."[54] Thus, whereas the NMAADC saw the consumer as a social category, Frito-Lay defended it as an economic one; and they did so at precisely that moment when the Supreme Court placed consumer rights above those of broadcaster rights.

Since Frito-Lay would not respond to their complaints, the NMAADC turned to broadcasters. They did so at a time in which consumer groups were demanding free time to respond to commercials that dealt with controversial issues of public importance. This strategy proved to be somewhat effective between 1968 and 1974 as consumers acquired "absolute rights" relative to those of broadcasters. Using the fairness doctrine before the U.S. Court of Appeals in Washington, D.C., law professor John F. Banzhaf III had forced broadcasters to run anti-smoking public service announcements (*Banzhoff v. FCC*, 1968), while an environmentalist group later won an appeal to rebut commercials for automobiles and leaded gasoline (*Friends of the Earth v. FCC*, 1971). In 1969, the Supreme Court issued a landmark decision upholding the fairness doctrine, arguing, "It is the right of the viewers and listeners, not the right of broadcasters, which is paramount" (*Red Lion Broadcasting Co. v. FCC*, 1969). A few years later, in 1973, the Supreme Court also asserted the First Amendment rights of broadcasters over those of would-be political advertisers, arguing that "broadcast licensees are not to be treated as common carriers" such as telephone and telegraph companies (*CBS v. Democratic National Committee*, 1973). In contrast to common carriers, which are predicated on universal access, television viewers did not have the right of access in order to "exercise the guaranteed freedoms of expression"; as a consequence, consumers and producers remained discrete categories.[55] Then, in 1974, the FCC effectively removed most commercials from fairness doctrine consideration except those "which are devoted in an obvious and meaningful way to the discussion of public issues."[56] Interestingly, the report also accepted the Banzhaf case but rejected it as a precedent, a position that made sense given the federal legislation in 1971 that banned cigarette ads from broadcasting. The success of *Banzhaf v. FCC,* then, had less to do with setting a legal precedent with respect to the FCC than it did with opening up a strategy that started within the regulatory process (from petitions to court appeals), then migrated to other political arenas altogether—in this instance, legislation.

In the case of the Frito Bandito, the NMAADC shifted its corporate address from advertisers to broadcasters before entering the FCC regulatory process via the fairness doctrine, then expanding its strategy to that of a public cause. Their first step involved protests directed at local television stations that were also designed to publicize their position. On May 12, 1969, the NMAADC staged an on-the-street protest in front of WTOP-TV, the CBS affiliate in Washington, D.C., since—as one member admitted—it was the easiest to reach during their lunch hour.[57] Waving picket signs that read "Down with the Frito Bandito" and "Stop False Stereotypes," protesters drew attention to derogatory stereotypes and employment discrimination on all the networks and affiliated stations. The NMAADC coordinated similar protests with Chicano media groups in ten other cities, including Los Angeles, San Francisco, Houston, San Antonio, Chicago, and New York.[58]

In early October 1969, after several months of meetings with community leaders, KNBC-TV in Los Angeles stopped selling time for Frito Bandito commercials and began blacking out network broadcasts of the commercials on October 25. The station's general manager, in explaining the decision, cited the "mass feeling" expressed by diverse representatives of the "entire community," which constituted a "major portion" of the station's audience.[59] Thus, KNBC's general manager, while no less attentive to a certain profit-motivated empiricism, both counted Mexican Americans as viewers and incorporated them into the decision-making process. If Frito-Lay saw Mexican Americans as a statistical aggregate to be used by the public relations department rather than as a community or consumer group, KNBC worked within a different regulatory environment where it was predisposed to distinguish between the passive audience of polls and ratings and the active one of community leaders. By early December, two San Francisco stations had joined the ban: KRON-TV and KPIX-TV (the CBS affiliate), setting the stage for the NMAADC to move into the regulatory process itself.

On December 9, 1969, the NMAADC joined with MALDEF and a San Antonio group, Federation for the Advancement of Mexican-Americans (FAMA), in announcing their intention to file a complaint with the FCC under the fairness doctrine.[60] The action was based on the denial of FAMA's request in July for free time from three San Antonio stations in order to respond to the Frito Bandito commercials. The complaint had the potential to affect the more than 600 network affiliates and independent stations that aired the commercials.[61] The turn to the regulatory process, however, was more strategic than sincere. Joseph L. Gibson, legal counsel for the NMAADC, promised to file the complaint in 90 days, thereby leaving the door open in the interim for an "acceptable settlement" with Frito-Lay and broadcasters.[62] This settlement appeared to happen after Senators Cranston and Montoya wrote Frito-Lay, among other advertisers, in early 1970. On February 14, 1970, the company announced that it would replace the Frito Bandito, attributing the change to opposition from "certain leaders of Mexican-American organizations."[63]

A year later, however, the ads were still running, although Frito-Lay had pulled them from California, Oregon, and Washington in July 1970, where it then tested a "Munch-a-Bunch" campaign that "features three western-type cartoon characters not identifiable with any ethnic group."[64] Frito-Lay continued to frame its actions in purely economic terms: "The company has a very sizable investment in the Frito Bandito campaign and from an economic standpoint it cannot be expected to abandon a successful sales effort without having a suitable replacement."[65]

Rather than return to the FCC, the NMAADC announced in January 1971 that it would file a $610 million suit in federal court "for the malicious defamation of the character of the 6.1 million Mexican Americans in the United States."[66] The suit would seek damages of $100 for each Mexican American based on earlier arguments about the psychological damage of negative stereotypes, framing its case in the most extreme rhetoric to date: "Chicanos have thus become the media's new 'nigger.'"[67] By this time, Chicano protests against the Frito Bandito had gained broad support within government, industry, and the press, and had become a rallying point within emerging Chicano publications such as *El Grito, La Raza,* and *Regeneración.* Even *Advertising Age* joined the chorus against Frito-Lay, citing it for its lack of corporate "good faith." [68]

Perhaps the best indication of the change in public attitude can be seen in the difference between two hearings held by the House Subcommittee on Communications and Power to consider resolutions on "films and broadcasts demeaning ethnic, racial, or religious groups." [69] In both hearings, the Frito Bandito served as a common reference point as representatives and select witnesses mostly agreed that stereotypes foment social unrest and undermine democratic institutions but argued over where to draw the line and whether Congress should take action beyond the resolutions' "purely hortatory provisions." But in the first hearing, on September 21, 1970, in which the emphasis was largely on the inclusion of white ethnics, particularly Italian Americans, the Frito Bandito was seen as an "imaginary slur" and Mexican Americans as "hypersensitive." [70] Nine days after the hearings, Reyes petitioned to include the NMAADC position paper "Chicanos and the Mass Media" in the record, where it took up nearly one-third of the published document. By the second hearings, on April 27 and 28, 1971, the NMAADC position paper—as well as a similar, though much briefer, letter from the Japanese American Citizens League—clearly influenced the representatives' own statements. In addition, both the NMAADC and Nosotros testified before the committee. Thus, while the chairman continued to question the Mexican American protest of the Frito Bandito, even the representative who called the ad an "imaginary slur" now sided entirely with the NMAADC position. [71]

Still, while support for the anti–Frito Bandito campaign had grown considerably, skepticism about the resolutions had also grown more vocal, especially over the question of whether the resolution should call for legislative enforcement if the industry failed to respond. [72] In fact, the NMAADC's efforts were applauded as the appropriate type of action since they kept the debate over content issues within the "marketplace of ideas." But Reyes himself was adamant about the need for government intervention given the NMAADC's limited resources. [73] Thus, if these efforts brought an end to the Frito Bandito, they also revealed the limits of government intervention and the need for persistence and a flexible strategy.

Perhaps more than anything else, the $610 million dollar suit signaled a significant reorientation of Chicano media activism. The

NMAADC joined forces with other Chicano media groups that had formed since 1968 — CARISSMA, IMAGE, Justicia, and the Midwest Chicano Mass Media Committee — but its agenda no longer worked for a reformist shift from "negative" to "positive" stereotypes: "The damage done by the Frito Bandito and other similar commercials and programming can be corrected only by providing access to the public media to the currently forgotten and ignored community of 6,000,000 Mexican Americans."[74] Henceforth, access would be the key issue. Or, as Lewels observed at the time, "The fight against the stereotype, although still an important part of the media movement, has taken a back seat in the past year to goals of employment, training, and in-depth coverage of community problems concerning Mexican Americans."[75]

If the larger goals were the same, the movement's approach was entirely different, shifting its address from a mediated society to a regulated industry. In the process, however, the movement became more dependent upon government, which defined the regulatory arena, while media reform groups also acquired roles as producers, making them dependent upon the very industry they challenged. As with other Chicano media groups, the NMAADC and IMAGE became involved in production. According to Martinez and Peralez, "Domingo Nick Reyes was forced to resign from a Washington, D.C., all news radio station because in his capacity as Executive Director of the National Mexican American Anti-Defamation Committee he criticized the media's treatment of Chicanos."[76] By 1971, when the NMAADC described its current activities, media production now figured as a large part of its advocacy plans. These activities included an eight-week television series on WRC-TV, the NBC affiliate in Washington, D.C., which Reyes hosted and Armando Rendon coproduced.[77] Tony Calderon, the executive director of IMAGE, worked as a television producer in San Antonio. In 1972, following a negotiated agreement with several local stations, IMAGE formed a television production company that produced a one-hour special for broadcast.[78]

The irony of the hard-won campaign against the Frito Bandito was not lost on the broadcasting industry. The struggle over content masked a more profound demand for access and control over the means of representation and communication. The irony resided in the fact that Chicano media reform groups sought to replace negative stereotypes with positive images through consumer rights and equal employment, and by becoming producers themselves. On March 23, 1970, shortly after

"What else can he do? They kicked him off television!"

Frito Bandito political cartoon by Sid Hix in Broadcasting *(Mar. 23, 1970).*

Frito-Lay announced it would replace the Frito Bandito, but over one year before it actually did so, *Broadcasting* ran a political cartoon that showed the diminutive Mexican revolutionary robbing two television executives. The Frito Bandito—with his trademark grin and exaggerated handlebar mustache—aimed an oversized pistol at the men's heads while he held out his free hand. In the caption, one television executive explained to the other: "What else can he do? They kicked him off television!"[79] The cartoon does not make sense, of course, unless one accepts the implied equivalence between racial stereotypes ("he") and minority access ("they")—and, hence, between the Frito Bandito and such Chicano groups as the NMAADC and IMAGE. After all, the Frito-Lay Corporation had not been kicked off television. What the text suggests, then, is another rhetorical question: "What else can they do except make demands upon us for access now that they have kicked stereotypes off television?" *Broadcasting* was right in its assessment; but in redeploying the bandito stereotype to depict the very Chicano media groups that fought against it, the trade publication also set the terms for the industry's response to these demands for access.

four

Regulating Chico
The Irony of Approaching
a State-Supported Industry

By the time Frito-Lay finally dropped the Frito Bandito campaign in the summer of 1971, Chicano media groups had proliferated along with the available strategies and government agencies they now used to demand access to the mass media. Demanding access was no simple matter, especially insofar as "access" meant something different to each of the parties involved: equal opportunity for Chicano media groups, regulation for the state, and a concession for corporate interests. The word "concession" carries several conflicting meanings, all of which pertain here: something conceded, something granted by a government for a specific purpose, and the privilege of operating a subsidiary business in a certain place. For television broadcasters, that place resides in the public airwaves—public because they are owned by the "people." But, given the scarcity of bands in the broadcast spectrum and the importance of telecommunications as one of the nation's basic infrastructures, the Communication Act of 1934 established the FCC to regulate broadcasting—that is, determine who gets to broadcast—on behalf of the "public interest, convenience, and necessity." While the FCC grants broadcasters free and exclusive use within the public property of the broadcast spectrum, in actual practice regulation produces first and foremost a marketplace concession with the rights of private ownership. In thus collapsing "public" and "private" interests, the state does not so much regulate the industry as regulate on its behalf.

For this reason, as Thomas Streeter notes, "the discourse of access remains assimilable within a general corporate liberal horizon."[1] In other words, asking for access presupposes the legitimacy of broadcast ownership and control, hence the demand becomes circumscribed within a regulatory environment designed to safeguard that ownership

51

and control. This blurring of state regulation with corporate interests placed outside protest groups in a double bind. In soliciting access and equal opportunity from broadcasters via the state, they also conceded the public airwaves to these corporate interests. Chicano media groups did not see it this way, especially since corporate resistance to their demands had contributed to a more radical and hostile orientation that often circumvented state regulation. Nevertheless, state-industry relations left protest groups with two equally problematic options: either petition the state, thereby endorsing broadcasters' privilege while positioning the protesters' own demands as exceptional and supplementary to the public interest, or pursue confrontational modes of protest, thereby positioning their demands not simply as exceptional but as disruptive or even unlawful, and therefore outside the public interest.

In this chapter, I will be looking at Chicano media groups within the context of state-industry relations. I will necessarily be tracing how their particular needs were articulated and situated vis-à-vis other groups. In this period, media reform addressed a wide range of issues, including civil rights (based on age, gender, race, and sexuality), cultural identity, consumer rights, religious expression, and environmentalism. Many of these efforts, while framed in either national or universal terms, unfolded within local, community-based, and grassroots contexts. But, insofar as the state attempted to "regulate" these protests, all were implicated in each other in at least two ways: through direct interactions based on either coalition or competition and in the discursive social arena that each group conjured up in its public statements before the state and industry. For Chicano groups, the former included extensive networking within the media reform movement, especially after 1970, while the latter created a "space" for Chicano demands by making explicit distinctions from Black groups and implicit ones from women. Gender and race were related in complex ways. Chicano activists often expressed ambivalence toward Blacks, whom they saw as both role models and impediments based on their success in defining the civil rights sector of the state.[2] In response, Chicanos defined their own goals in terms of a masculinity threatened by a white-controlled media and a Black-defined civil rights agenda. Needless to say, these masculine terms influenced relations with all other groups, not to mention gender relations within the Chicano community. Interestingly, they also voiced a male desire that bridged the polar opposites within the Chicano civil rights movement: reform and radicalism, integration and cultural nationalism. In other words, as I will explain later in the chapter, these ideological opposites shared a masculinity shaped by the racial logic of the western itself, and in that respect, both were profoundly "American." Rather than rehearse the failure of panracial coalitions and the ideological impasse between feminism and cultural nationalisms, I will be showing how these inter- and intragroup dynamics all emerged and took place in the shadow of the state.

Beginning with the Civil Rights Act of 1964, the courts and new regulatory agencies challenged and, in some cases, changed or superseded FCC policy, thereby introducing a conflicted state apparatus as mediator between the mass media and disenfranchised groups. But rather than functioning as a "neutral" domain, the state *creates* the market, subordinating political struggles over "public" interests to this overall corporate liberal framework. In policy- and legal-oriented scholarship, this process is seen as one that generates "irony," "illusion," or a "contradictory situation" as citizen and public interest groups are brought within the administrative control of the state.[3] The internal "conflicts" between federal agencies, then, represent an adaptive feature of the state, rather than its Achilles' heel. But this hindsight—"considering television as the product of a set of legal relationships"—often ignores its own advice to look beyond the legitimizing claims of the state itself: "Progressive efforts, therefore, would do well to seek ways to open up this closed door in political discourse, ways to 'defamiliarize' the obvious, taken-for-granted character of the institutional forces that constitute and drive commercial broadcasting."[4] Indeed, the state does not stand outside the social formation, even if it does attempt to bring social conflicts and contradictions under its administrative control. Rather than make the state autonomous—even relatively so—this administrative intervention means that these conflicts and contradictions *constitute* the state and its subjects, at least in part.[5] Thus, if we were to "'defamiliarize' the obvious" about state-regulated commercial broadcasting, the first step would be to bear in mind that minority media groups did not necessarily place much faith in the regulatory process per se. If the "public interest" standard protected private interests, citizen groups responded by approaching the state, industry, and policy arena with an irony of their own. Perhaps the most significant irony about these groups was the fact that they ignored the legal—and, hence, regulatory—distinctions and parameters for their protests, blurring the borders between film and television and between America and the Americas.

In this chapter, I will consider how "minority" groups were constructed, represented, and positioned vis-à-vis the state, the industry, and each other, emphasizing what is usually hidden: the relationship between the state and industry, rights and mediation, as the primary avenue to the social imaginary.

The Americas Boycott

In September 1968, while the NMAADC and IMAGE initiated their protests against advertisers, another group, the Mexican American Political Association (MAPA), confronted the entire film and television industry, pulling together an unusual coalition of a reformist civil rights group (the American G.I. Forum), a labor union representative, an elected official, a Spanish-language radio programmer, two actors, and the Mexican consulate, while also invoking the threat of militant Puerto Ricans and Cubans and a hemisphere-wide boycott of Hollywood.[6] As with the NMAADC's initial campaign against the Frito Bandito, MAPA did not approach the state, but rather invoked it within the language of its demands before the film and television industry. If anything, the threatened harassment and boycott exemplified López's "schizo-cultural limbo" as political strategy, locating its authority in conflicted and contradictory discourses. On the one hand, MAPA's "reformist" demands for equal employment opportunity spoke to inalienable rights as citizens but then set these against the more limited rights of the racialized worker, complaining about losing jobs relative to "Negroes" and "Orientals." On the other hand, MAPA's "radical" threats of pan-American alliances with Mexico, the Caribbean, and South America suggested an incipient, if improbable, Third World transnationalism. This "schizo-cultural limbo" came about as social unrest and militant efforts increased, shifting minority discourse to the left, while also bringing younger Chicano "radicals" into contact with the institutionalized Mexican American groups that had suddenly gained access to the state and business sector. Thus, although the MAPA protest was ineffectual, it reveals much about the media reform strategies emerging within the Mexican American community.

The MAPA action began earlier when two young actors, Ray Martell and Ray Andrade, met during the casting of Twentieth Century Fox's *Che!* (1969) and decided to organize against the motion picture industry after failing to obtain roles.[7] "If we can't get Latin roles," Martell later argued, "where do we go from here?"[8] They went to MAPA.

There they found support and an established organization through which to lodge formal complaints and negotiate with the industry. Martell, who now served as chairman of MAPA's newly created film and television committee, was able to hold a meeting with the Association of Motion Picture and Television Producers (AMPTP) on August 30, 1968. But he came away discouraged: "They were quite indifferent about the situation, quite insensitive about Latins in general. They gave me lip service and rhetoric, but nothing concrete."[9] A second meeting was scheduled for September 25, 1968, to coincide with an AMPTP board meeting that would be attended by representatives of the major studios. There MAPA presented complaints against twelve film and television production companies, demanding implementation of a program to recruit, train, and hire Latinos throughout the industry.[10]

While these complaints and demands used the civil rights discourse of equal opportunity, MAPA did not turn to the three-year-old Equal Employment Opportunity Commission (EEOC) until it held hearings into industry hiring practices in Los Angeles six months later in March 1969. But even then, Martell's testimony challenged the commission's commitment and effectiveness: "I don't really believe the Federal Government will do anything about this, and I have to go back and tell my people that the only way to bring about a change perhaps is to have direct confrontation with these people at their studios, or in their parking lots, or anyplace where we have to deal with these people."[11] The EEOC and, by extension, other Great Society reforms were viewed with considerable suspicion and frustration by the established Mexican American groups oriented toward the political representation system. Several years earlier, in March 1966, the EEOC had convened a southwestern regional conference in Albuquerque in order to discuss problems in Mexican American employment, but the agency quickly offended the fifty participants. Only one commissioner attended the meeting, there were no Mexican Americans present on the EEOC staff, and the EEOC had set a rigid top-down agenda that limited discussion. Within the first five minutes, LULAC and the American G.I. Forum headed a massive walkout, signaling a "growing militancy" among the older civil rights groups.[12] Thus, even though MAPA, LULAC, and the American G.I. Forum continued to try to influence the political representation system, Martell was able to "capture" MAPA in order to stage a more radical and extranational confrontation of the film and television industry.

The day before MAPA presented its demands to the AMPTP board,

Martell threw down the gauntlet, threatening a boycott in Mexico and Latin America if their demands were not met. Since, as Martell claimed, the industry understood only "the language of threats," he went even further and conjured up an image of potential violence: "We have quite a few militants, including Cubans, who are not complacent, and wanted [sic] a direct confrontation over the picture, *Che!*, in which all the meaty roles are going to Anglos."[13] The next day, however, the AMPTP responded with general reassurances of change that nevertheless maintained the propriety of existing industry policy: "We made a commitment on the basis of industry policy and said we will work with them in an effort to eliminate the problem and to eliminate inequities where we find them."[14] For Martell, this statement did not represent a "concrete commitment," and he announced that unless the AMPTP responded to its demands MAPA would go ahead with its boycott and also have Puerto Ricans "harass" the production of *Che!* slated to take place on the island.[15]

Martell walked a rhetorical tightrope, attempting to have MAPA incarnate violence yet also represent a more reformist alternative. To do so, he split violence and the alternative solution between other Latino groups (Cubans, Puerto Ricans, Mexicans, and Latin Americans) and Mexican Americans. Furthermore, he walked without a safety net insofar as MAPA was ill-prepared to carry out a hemisphere-wide boycott, let alone a local one, while its concerns over Mexican American stereotypes and employment were unlikely to inspire Cubans and Puerto Ricans to violent action. The California-based MAPA was a strongly ethnic-identified political group that did not seek coalitions with non-Chicano groups until 1967, when it made tentative overtures to Puerto Ricans, apparently establishing a chapter on the island.[16] What came across, then, was a certain ethnocentrism that defined the group's demand for "equal employment" within the industry against a horizon of other racial groups in the United States and the Americas. Chicano activists were aware of the pitfall of placing themselves in a zero-sum relation to other minority groups, and, in fact, they often identified it as part of the state's divide-and-conquer response to the various social movements. But, in the next breath, they made the argument anyway. For his part, Martell responded in two fairly common ways: first, by qualifying his complaint that Chicanos were "victimized" by efforts to hire Blacks, quickly adding, "[W]e don't begrudge the Negroes anything"; and, second, by broadening MAPA's constituency to include not just all Latins, but Indians as well, arguing, "I am also speaking for the American Indian as we are part Indian."[17]

Beneath this racial discourse one could also see the frustrations of an unemployed Chicano male actor who wanted "dignified roles" that centered him within the national imagination—that allowed *him* to ride off into the sunset of the western. In fact, Martell voiced a recurrent motif among Chicano male critics of the industry at that time: "It's astounding in the history of movies and tv that there has yet to be a Latin actor who has a leading role in a cowboy series, when the very idea of cowboys originated with Spaniards and Mexicans."[18] Instead, Chicanos served as "convenient villains" in the western narrative.[19] In "El Mexicano through the Eyes of the Gavacho," *La Raza* magazine concluded: "This implies that the Anglo is not only smarter than a Chicano but also a better fighter, thus making him a better man altogether."[20] The overall point is well taken, I suppose, but it also reveals—as I noted earlier—the masculine terms that constituted an underlying "resolution" of radicalism and reformism in Chicano media activism: desire for the masculine expressive culture of the Hollywood and television western. Rather than question the masculine ideal that "helped fortify and institutionalize the American tradition of Manifest Destiny," Chicanos complained about being given "dehumanizing roles" that showed them to be "incompetent" men per that very same ideal.[21] For Martinez and Peralez, this incompetence was exemplified by the fact that "the Chicano women, in the movies, often rejects [*sic*] the Chicano man in favor of the super anglo-white hero" and that "one movie showed Emiliano Zapata sitting on a bed with his anglo wife during his honeymoon" . . . *learning to read!*[22] Chicanos wanted to reject the bandito stereotype because it emasculated them and thereby perpetuated their subordination within American society; but at the same time, they wanted to play the leading role in the western *as Chicanos* displaying physical and sexual prowess. But at whose expense? And toward what end? Such questions remained unasked, but their presence can be detected in the failure of MAPA's protest to resonate within the various racial and national groups invoked and in the one group that it did not name: women.

The MAPA protest appears to have ended as soon as it started, while Martell and Andrade pursued other avenues for direct action. The two actors-turned-activists, however, had different advocacy goals: "Martell's aim was to help remedy the injustices existing in the casting practices, whereas Andrade was more concerned with the image."[23]

The distinction between hiring practices and a politics of the image is somewhat misleading—Martell advocated on behalf of himself and other actors who wanted to work within the industry, while Andrade took up a more comprehensive agenda that combined access, employment, and stereotypes. Still, neither was content with MAPA, leaving to form media-oriented groups that addressed their particular concerns: Martell as the executive director of the Council to Advance and Restore the Image of Spanish-Speaking and Mexican Americans (CARISSMA), Andrade as the president of Justice for Chicanos in the Motion Picture and Television Industry (Justicia). Although CARISSMA joined several coalition efforts against the industry, it had an otherwise low public profile. Justicia, on the other hand, engaged in militant protests against the Academy Awards, industry guilds, local television stations, and the broadcast networks. Justicia's activities between 1970 and 1972 proved effective in the short term, as I argue later in the chapter, partly because their strategy was at odds with the increasing state regulation and industry containment of "outside" protests. One of the first signs of that increasing regulation was the EEOC hearings that effectively co-opted MAPA's hiring demands.

Separate but Equal Employment

On March 12–14, 1969, the EEOC held hearings in Los Angeles as part of its national investigation of the "utilization of minority and women workers in certain major industries." [24] These hearings focused on the aerospace industry, "the nation's largest manufacturing employer and the largest single employer in the Los Angeles area," as well as on the motion picture production industry and radio and television networks, which were identified for their "staggering influence on the country's image of itself and . . . the world-wide image of our country." [25] In addressing the culture industry, then, the EEOC drew attention to the combined symbolic and material consequences of its employment discrimination, a sentiment voiced earlier by the Kerner report and such minority protest and reform efforts as those of the NMAADC, IMAGE, and MAPA.

The hearings began on cordial terms, with the EEOC chairman, Clifford L. Alexander Jr., insisting that the hearings were "dialogues" that, while "not an end in themselves," would result in "substantial follow-up activity" over the next year before the commission would even *consider* its next action, possibly more hearings. [26] Company and union

witnesses included the AMPTP, Warner Brothers, Twentieth Century
Fox, Walt Disney, and the International Alliance of Theatrical and Stage
Employees and Motion Picture Machine Operators of the United States
and Canada (IATSE & MPMO). The next day, the television networks'
vice presidents in charge of programs on the West Coast testified.

By the end of the first day of these hearings, however, the EEOC's
general counsel, Daniel Steiner, had cited "clear evidence of a pattern or
practice of discrimination in violation of Title VII of the Civil Rights Act
of 1964" and recommended that the EEOC pursue an immediate lawsuit
against the entire motion picture industry.[27] In particular, Steiner cited
the use of an industry experience roster system established in 1948: "This
system has as its foreseeable effect—and it in fact operates effectively—
to exclude minorities from jobs in the motion picture industry."[28] Under the terms of the collective bargaining agreements between industry
and unions, producers must hire from union rosters ranked according
to seniority; only once the rosters are exhausted can a producer make
"off-roster hires." According to Steiner, this system violated Title VII
and perhaps the National Labor Relations Act. In fact, data compiled by
the EEOC revealed significant underrepresentation of Mexican American and Black employees in white-collar positions in the Hollywood
studios (both 3.5 percent) and television networks (1.2 percent and 2.8
percent, respectively) in the Los Angeles area.[29]

The next day, at the end of the hearings, Chairman Alexander cited
the "callous attitude" of the three networks, calling them "potential
law-breakers" in the areas of equal employment opportunity, antitrust
laws, and FCC regulations, but stopped short of the type of specific actions announced the day before with respect to the motion picture industry. Instead, Alexander called attention to the networks' "greater responsibility" than other industries given their mandate to inform the
American people, while he also warned "that the various American
communities, Anglo as well as minorities, male as well as female,
should worry a good deal about what they heard today."[30] A round-
table discussion with local community groups followed the hearings,
further suggesting the EEOC's role in building upon and coordinating
"publicity" and "pressure" in the public sphere as a counterpart to its
own activism within the state.[31]

Although the EEOC had filed several dozen lawsuits against individual companies, the proposed lawsuit against motion picture production companies and related unions represented its first action against an

entire industry. But because the EEOC did not acquire litigation and enforcement authority until 1972, it had to petition the Department of Justice to pursue the actual litigation process. The Department of Justice then conducted its own investigation, whereupon it agreed that litigation was warranted on the basis of employment discrimination against Blacks and Mexican Americans. (Using catch-22 logic similar to the roster system itself, the Department of Justice did not include women because of their insufficient numbers in the workforce—the very condition motivating their action in the first place.) Rather than face protracted litigation, the AMPTP and IATSE entered into a settlement agreement announced on April 1, 1970. The agreement established a "minority labor pool" from which IATSE local unions would make two referrals for every five referrals from their experience rosters until minority referrals achieved 20 percent of available workdays. Once that occurred, the referral ratio would drop to one to four. The idea was to provide minorities with experience so that after two years the minority labor pool could be fully integrated into the seniority-based roster system. By 1972, however, this integration had not happened, and the agreement was extended for two additional years, then quietly terminated. The EEOC, which now had litigation and enforcement authority, continued to monitor the industry until 1976 but undertook no other action, despite the general failure of the initial agreement.[32]

There are several things that are striking about the EEOC hearings and Department of Justice settlement agreement. First, they substantiated minority underemployment and identified industry practices that resulted in employment discrimination. This information is something that reform groups were not in a position to produce themselves, and it proved very useful in their subsequent protests, petitions, and negotiations.[33] Second, the EEOC intervention was based on the same broad social critique of the mass media that undergirded the reform movement, while the commissioners' aggressive questioning and occasional "hostility" toward the industry were similar to that of protest groups.[34] In this respect, the EEOC was not unlike MAPA in its attempt to confront the entire industry. In fact, Commissioner Vicente T. Ximenes, who pointedly raised issues of Mexican American employment and stereotypes throughout the hearings, represented a strong link between EEOC and such Mexican American groups as MAPA, LULAC, and the American G.I. Forum—groups that had brought about his appointment after the Albuquerque walkout in 1966.

But the EEOC action differed in one key respect: although it too was motivated by social exigencies, it originated and unfolded within the bureaucratic procedures and legal protocols of the corporate liberal state. Thus, as the first of the Great Society regulatory agencies, the EEOC had to "make its own way" in mediating between charges of employment discrimination and the business sector, undertaking this task within a regulatory environment oriented toward competing *business* interests.[35] In fact, in Section 706(a) of Title VII, the Civil Rights Act of 1964 formalizes the EEOC's *informal* mediation on behalf of the corporate liberal state, requiring that it "endeavor to eliminate such unlawful employment practice by informal methods of conference, conciliation, and persuasion."[36] Given the state's orientation toward business, then, the EEOC emphasized what it called the "conciliation process" even after it acquired litigation and enforcement authority—a decision that was more political than it was procedural.[37] This emphasis on "informal methods," more than anything else, explains the slippage between the EEOC's broad social critique, which called for changes in the structure and content of the mass media, and the rather limited agenda it aggressively pursued and turned over to the Department of Justice: equal employment opportunity for off-camera craft and technical personnel. In the end, the EEOC hearings, litigation, and agreement were themselves a form of "conference, conciliation, and persuasion" wherein the limited action was not an end in and of itself, but rather was expected to nudge the industry toward a wider set of reforms.

The settlement agreement negotiated by the Department of Justice, then, had several "unusual aspects," as noted in the daily press. Unlike a court-ordered consent decree, the settlement agreement was voluntary: "Normally, the Justice Department in working out such agreements takes the precaution of getting court-backed enforcement procedures."[38] Furthermore, although the use of a minority labor pool was seen as a short-term plan leading to an integrated roster system, in hindsight it can be seen that the agreement participated in the shift from colorblind policies to an affirmative-action model. This policy shift within the EEOC was, as John David Skrentny argues, a "pragmatic solution" to the overwhelming caseload, a "national race crisis," and the need for cost efficiency and rationalized policies.[39] And, as evidenced by the MAPA protest against the AMPTP, it was congruent with minority demands themselves. But it also perpetuated interracial group conflict over limited "minority" hiring positions. After all, limited minority employment remained inherent in racial quotas, which were usually set well below demographic representation within the workforce. What these quotas did, then, was to subordinate a business practice (discriminatory hiring) to a state "tradition" (affirmative action), thereby changing the tenor, but not the fact, of limited minority employment.[40] In other words, the settlement agreement—as with affirmative action more broadly—kept minorities out of the general labor pool, even as it guaranteed some level of employment; and it articulated this policy as a "conciliation" without enforcement procedures, making any gains temporary and limited ones that satisfied no one. The irony, of course, is not that the agreement failed—since it was clearly neither pragmatic nor a solution in terms of the employment problems it addressed—but that it regulated the protesters much more than it did the production companies.

Outside the Interpretive Community

How, exactly, did protest become regulated, especially insofar as the opposite appeared to be happening? First of all, the EEOC hearings and follow-up activities signaled an increased intervention on the part of the state, leading to more hearings, reports, resolutions, and new policies. Furthermore, these changes and the apparent movement toward change were not limited to the broadcast industry but often superseded or challenged what Thomas Streeter identifies as the state's own "core institutions" for broadcast policy: the FCC, the Federal Trade Commission, the Office of Management and Budget, Congress's Office of Technology Assessment, and the National Telecommunications and Information Administration in the Department of Commerce.[41] Thus, in addition to addressing the industry, the state appeared to be regulating its own regulators, too. In general, this intervention came from two sets of institutions: those that actively engaged in direct oversight of the "core institutions" for broadcast policy (the U.S. Court of Appeals, Congress, and the White House) and those that cut across industry-specific agencies and "regulated the social consequences of business behavior"[42] more generally (the EEOC, the Civil Rights Commission, and related Congressional subcommittees).[43]

In many ways, however, this activity and activism on the part of the state displaced social movements, subordinating them to the "neutral" terrain where political representation meets expert-driven policy formation. It is important to recall that early protests did not turn to the state, even if they sometimes invoked its presence. But once the state intervened, protesters were relegated to two minor roles: serving as witnesses within a process otherwise controlled by the state, as in the EEOC hearings, litigation, and settlement, and acquiring "standing" within the regulatory process itself, which required them to play within the rules of a game established long before such standing existed. In the former, protest groups were co-opted; in the latter, they were simply worn down. Within the state itself there were clear limits to how far the more progressive individuals and agencies could challenge certain major industries, especially one as central to the "structure of rule" as the mass media.

In *Selling the Air,* Thomas Streeter notes that "with one or two possible exceptions, the desirability of the advertising-supported system of broadcasting has never been the subject of policy debate."[44] In short, broadcast policy does not question the legitimacy of its own legal and institutional framework; as a consequence, this discursive boundary provides a mechanism with which to face the "unresolvable ambiguities" and "imponderables" of its corporate liberal principles.[45] Streeter describes the domain for broadcast policy as an "interpretive community" and policy making as a "way of thought" that set the terms for having one's arguments or demands make sense or even to be heard at all: "What makes a ruling appear practical, a legal decision seem sound, or a procedure fair, is the contingent, shared vision of the interpretive community itself, not simply rational policy analysis, legal reason, formal rules of process and procedure, or interest group pressures."[46] But form does count. In order to take part in the policy process one must adhere to an "appropriately neutral and expert policy language" that accepts the legitimacy of the system.[47] Thus, if in the Third World the U.S. military destroyed the village in order to save the village,[48] the state made quite another demand at home: media groups had to accept the system in order to challenge the system.

This paradox was captured in the spatial metaphor used to describe participation in the political and policy process: "inside the beltway."[49] The phrase defines not so much a place, or even the boundaries of the state, as the institutional networks and legitimating protocols that locate power in terms of an inside and outside. For outside groups, then, being inside the beltway was a compelling paradox, to say the least, since there were no other viable alternatives: "The policy arena is after all bounded by the coercive power of law and of the state."[50] This made it difficult for media reform groups to follow Haight and Weinstein's warning that "it is not wise to venture too far into an arena with demands both on resources and on the language defined as acceptable discourse. . . . That route has become a dance of delay, limits, cooptation, and quiescence." [51] Whether one stood on the inside as a supplicant or abdicated that role and stood on the outside, one necessarily acknowledged the state as the locus of coercive power. Such were the politics of dancing, and this impossible two-step was nowhere more evident than in the "expert" testimony of Chicano media advocates.

In general, Chicano testimony fell outside the interpretive framework of the various agencies that were approached or confronted. Chicano media activists understood neither the style nor the substance of the "appropriately neutral and expert policy language" for mass media. After all, they were *not* policy experts, nor were they professionals within the industry; they were outsiders demanding to be let inside. At the same time, however, they were part of a growing social movement that was defining its own boundaries, language, and demands. By the late 1960s, the Chicano movement had begun to theorize its location within power relations, largely by providing a deeply historical and hence transnational dimension to the current socioeconomic and political situation of Chicanos in the United States. In starting with the conquest of the Americas, this historical orientation led to an investment in defining and reproducing a culture of resistance that stood outside the historical forces of the state, whether of Spain (1492–1821), Mexico (1821–48), or the United States (since 1848). To be inside the Chicano movement, then, was to be outside the state, albeit on *cultural* grounds more than anything else. Needless to say, this position colored the demands for access to the mass media, that is, the demands to be let inside, and it helps to explain why the state had to come to Chicano media groups rather than vice versa.

It is these combined factors—ignorance of how to operate inside the beltway and an ethnic identity and politics based on cultural nationalism—that made it impossible for such groups as the NMAADC, IMAGE, and MAPA to calibrate their demands to either the existing policy arena ("core institutions") or the expanded one of Great Society reforms. Chicano media activists wanted to be let inside but did not yet know the rules; at the same time, they wanted to be provided state, foundation, and industry resources in order to develop outside these arenas. In their much-circulated "brown position paper" titled "Chicanos and the Mass Media," Armando Rendon and Domingo Nick Reyes proposed "amalgamating the two extreme concepts" through "intermediary agencies" between Chicano and establishment media: "A balance must be struck between total insulation from outside media contact and influence and the co-opting of Chicano thought and news-reporting by the non-raza communications system." [52] Pushing this argument even further, Rendon and Reyes demanded support for developing a Chicano media through industry "reparations" rather than state-regulated "equal opportunity," and they also announced their intention to enter the regulatory arena in order to bring about reforms in mass media content and hiring practices. [53]

In many ways, "Chicanos and the Mass Media" is an astonishing document. It presents a full-blown theory that builds upon historical and statistical analyses in a more complex way than anything put forth by the state itself. What Rendon and Reyes proposed was nothing less than "amalgamating the two extreme concepts" of inside and outside by allowing both to coexist on equal terms; in short, they offered a real solution to the problem of exclusion rather than the usual "dance of delay, limits, cooptation, and quiescence." But their approach questioned the very legal framework for mass media, suggesting that a noncorporate alternative, "Chicano media," could exist alongside the industry. In this way, their testimony exceeded the interpretive community within which it was presented. It did not make sense. In fact, when read in the context of the numerous published hearings within which it appeared, "Chicanos and the Mass Media" often comes across as an act more of "thinking aloud" within the context of the Chicano movement than of speaking to an addressee within a legally defined set of power relations.

The rhetorical style of Chicano testimony exacerbated this tendency, perhaps even providing a rationale for exile from participation in actual policy making. At their most extreme, Chicano witnesses overplayed their hand, assuming a political power they did not have and calling upon a moral authority that did not exist. During the EEOC hearings in March 1969, for example, Ray Martell served as the minority witness, speaking as a would-be actor rather than on behalf of either MAPA or CARISSMA. No doubt frustrated by the circumspect testimony or "garbage and phraseology" of industry officials, Martell countered by exceeding the boundaries of his location as an aggrieved party before the state: "If we were to conjure world opinion, we would have these people before a world tribunal, and they would sentence them like they sentence war criminals." [54] Martell briefly digressed in order to attack the EEOC for being Black-oriented (whereupon the chairman refuted him) before calculating the "irreparable damage" caused by the film and television industry at "billions and even trillions of dollars," then turning around and asking the government to "bring these dogs to justice." Throughout, Martell claimed to have "mountains and mountains of evidence" against the industry, while he also cited the threat of Mexican American violence—including his own actions. Commissioner Ximenes then stepped in and redirected Martell to procedural questions related to Martell's own demand for a federal investigation. [55]

There are two ways of looking at Martell's testimony. On the one hand, the EEOC hearings *did* lead to an investigation that warranted litigation, and Martell's testimony no doubt helped achieve this end because it legitimated the hearings and subsequent actions as being representative of a broad consensus spanning reformist and radical demands. On the other hand, Martell's testimony clearly placed him outside the policy arena as part of the problem, identifying him with the "crisis" that motivated the hearings in the first place. No matter how much the EEOC and other government agencies sought to address the cause of the crisis, their primary concern had to do with its effects: violence and increased demands on the state. As a consequence, any changes in the mass media were really intended to regulate these effects. Martell, then, was incorporated as a necessary sign of the problem, rather than as a participant in formulating the solution.

But could it have been otherwise? In 1971, in testimony before the House Subcommittee on Communications and Power (which oversaw the FCC), one finds two very different styles of Chicano testimony by the NMAADC and Nosotros, an actors' advocacy group cofounded by Ricardo Montalban in 1969. [56] In the end, however, both are offset by statements from the FCC, which refused to acknowledge Chicano demands, whether framed as "mountains and mountains of evidence" or in "appropriately neutral and expert policy language." In his testimony on behalf of the NMAADC, Reyes begins by paraphrasing his prepared statement, becoming increasingly rushed, ad-libbing about negative stereotypes, and ending his litany with a reference to *Sesame Street* as "the biggest mother sacred cow of them all." At this point, the chairman stopped Reyes and asked him to read the entire statement at his own pace. Their exchange suggests that Reyes was unaware of hearing procedures and of the difference between the hearings as performance and the eventual record into which his statement had been accepted.[57] In sharp contrast, Richard Hernandez, the legal counsel and cofounder of Nosotros, presented a measured statement presenting the problem, Nosotros activities within the industry to address that problem, and specific suggestions for assistance from the House subcommittee, concluding: "Our goals are to be accomplished hopefully within the so-called system."[58] If the NMAADC exceeded or attempted to stand outside the state and industry, Nosotros located itself squarely within the industry itself, asking the state for little more than a level playing field in terms of employment, and doing so within the framework of the interpretive community for broadcast policy. But it did not work. Nosotros members were employees or potential employees of the industry, and as such, if they did not want to be forced to leave it, they could do little more than *suggest* state intervention. For this reason, Nosotros has devoted most of its energies toward more modest and industry-friendly efforts to increase the visibility of Latino actors: acting workshops, awards ceremonies, and face-to-face meetings with industry executives.[59]

When asked about the nature of Mexican American protests against the Frito Bandito (which both Reyes and Hernandez also addressed), the FCC commissioner, Robert E. Lee, answered, "A general objection to the characterization of the Mexican-American being this funny cartoon character, but I have seen no really specific complaints of great substance."[60] Lee did not see these complaints, not because they did not exist, but because nothing compelled the FCC to redefine its parameters in order to take them into account. If the House and other agencies were prepared to solicit Chicano testimony, they likewise refused to see the "mountains and mountains of evidence" no matter how it was packaged. Even in its most accommodationist guise—as with Nosotros—that evidence questioned the legal framework for mass media and therefore exceeded the interpretive community of the policy arena. It did not make sense, even if it made a lot of sense.

The Power to Compel Negotiation

Chicano protest groups, however, were not without power; and, in many respects, their best use of that power came from keeping their actions outside the "legitimate" coercive power of the state. Perhaps the best example of such a group is Justicia, headed by Ray Andrade, who had been a professional boxer, a Green Beret in Vietnam (which led to a role as a technical advisor on *The Green Berets,* 1968), and a movie actor.

Between 1970 and 1972, Justicia engaged in militant protests against the Academy Awards, industry guilds, local television stations, and the broadcast networks. If these activities proved effective, it was in immediate and limited terms calculated in the face of increasing state regulation and industry containment of the civil rights and media reform movements. In many respects, Justicia, more so than other groups, helped bring about Chicano-produced local television shows in the Los Angeles area. While short lived, these shows—which appeared on the local affiliate stations for all three networks and PBS—would then serve as the training ground for the first "generation" of Chicano filmmakers.[61]

Rather than enter into the interpretive community of government regulation, Justicia extended the aggressive techniques used in the earlier MAPA protest against the AMPTP. Likewise, Justicia addressed the entire film and television industry, focusing most of its efforts on prime time programming, whereas other groups engaged increasingly in reforming local television stations.[62] Justicia, fronted by Andrade (president) and Paul Macias (vice president), drew upon a small but committed Chicano membership of professional actors as well as students from California State University, Los Angeles. Sal Castro also took part in the group, both in negotiations and as a member of the board of directors.[63] Castro, a former teacher at Lincoln High School, had been instrumental in the student walkouts in 1968. He now worked as a producer for KNBC-TV. Using a small storefront headquarters on Huntington Drive in East Los Angeles, Justicia set out to publicize its cause before it confronted the industry with specific demands. The first step was a protest of the Academy Awards in April 1970 that received national press coverage.[64] In particular, the protest drew attention to the western, criticizing *Butch Cassidy and the Sundance Kid* (1969), *The Wild Bunch* (1969), and John Wayne, who would win the Oscar for best actor in *True Grit* (1969).[65] By late summer, Justicia had met with the Screen Actors Guild (SAG), which agreed to support the group's demonstrations against films that demeaned Mexican Americans; and, in October, SAG's president, Charlton Heston, chaired a meeting with the other guilds (producers, directors, and writers) that resulted in a similar agreement.[66]

Prior to the agreement with the guilds, Justicia issued an ultimatum to the entire industry that, unless it provided a "better image" of Mexican Americans, there would be "mass walk-ins and demonstrations" at the major studios. Thus, while the negotiating premises and strategy were the same as with MAPA, Justicia made a more credible and immediate threat. Claiming a membership of 738 Chicanos, Andrade concluded, "We are prepared to suffer the consequences of this, but we have to do something in order to let the industry know we mean business."[67] While the protest was undertaken on behalf of a "better image," Justicia's demands for the "Redress of Grievances for Chicanos" addressed four distinct areas: image, equal opportunity, identity, and compensation.[68]

The agreement with the guilds provided symbolic support from within the industry as Justicia articulated its demands, but actual change would have to come from the studios, networks, and production companies. Toward that end, Justicia turned its attention to the television networks in June 1971, situating its demands at the crossroads of its own confrontational strategies and other groups' formal petitions before the state. In particular, Justicia demanded an end to demeaning programs, the right to monitor all scripts with Mexican American characters, and compensation in the form of a $10 million program development fund in order to facilitate significant television roles for Chicanos.[69] These demands were made in concert with other groups as part of a "coordinated attack on the stations in the Los Angeles area,"[70] which were about to come under review by the FCC for license renewal. Justicia had been in communication with such pressure groups as the Congress on Racial Equality (CORE), while Andrade had been instructed in the use of the "petition to deny" before the FCC by the Washington-based Citizens Communications Center. But Justicia did not pursue such state-controlled adjudication. Instead, in a passive coalition, it relied upon the fact that other groups did so, and that the networks were under pressure to avoid the costs of a license challenge, and then it raised the stakes. As one ABC executive recalled, "The challenge was that if we didn't sit up and listen and in fact execute all of the demands of Justicia, they would have Brown Berets up there with guns and force us to meet their demands."[71] And, apparently, the network and local affiliate sat up and listened.

Justicia quickly acquired the right to monitor and comment upon scripts for programming at all three networks, whereupon "standards and practices executives would then negotiate with producers for change."[72] In the end, however, the standards and practices departments represented a containment strategy that brought protest groups in as "technical consultants" and thereby subordinated them to the preexisting relationship between networks and production companies—one in which the producers' "creative freedom" seemingly limited the networks' ability to demand content and personnel changes. That "creative freedom" was based on producers' being outside FCC regulation and on the concurrent failure of the EEOC agreement with the AMPTP. But it was not absolute—that is, "creative freedom" mitigated the social demands routed through networks but not the networks' own demands based on economic rationale. Thus, Justicia's militant threats could not make headway with producers, especially with respect to hiring Chicano creative personnel, something producers considered "really out of the question" or "ridiculous." [73] By 1972, with the license renewal for California stations more or less completed, Justicia had lost whatever leverage it had had in the space between the state and industry and soon disbanded. [74] At the same time, Andrade faced charges for bomb threats against business and government and as one of four Chicanos targeted in a police raid of a picket line at the Million Dollar Theater. [75] If, as state theorists argue, "the state's most important institution is that of the means of violence and coercion," [76] Andrade was an effective interloper during a brief moment of social crisis as it traversed the film and television industry. Then the state arrested him. [77]

Given their investment in communications, the state and industry always get the last word. In fact, the coup de grâce to the broadcast reform movement came two years after Andrade's arrest, when producer James Komack made a situation comedy out of his life. [78] It was called *Chico and the Man* (NBC, 1974–78), and it was, interestingly enough, the first network television series centered on a Chicano character. (It remains the only one to last beyond the first few episodes.) Komack also made Andrade an associate producer on the series in an attempt to defuse Chicano protest and reassure network executives that Justicia would not cause problems. [79] Given the material and the series's symbolic co-optation of Andrade as activist, what it did with his life is all the more revealing.

In short, as the first series centered on a Chicano character, *Chico and the Man* transformed the concurrent Chicano movement into a domestic comedy located in someone else's house-cum-business. [80] The series starred Freddie Prinze as a Chicano ne'er-do-well who lived in a garage owned by a cantankerous bigot (played by Jack Albertson). The predominantly male cast, then, recoded social and racial unrest as a family narrative taking place between a younger Chicano and an older Anglo. Andrade's eventual criticism is telling in this light: "I find the show offensive in some respects. Freddie is too servile to Albertson, he is looking for the white father. There is a certain lack of machismo in Freddie; he doesn't have it on the show. I tried to sell my ideas to the producers, but it was zilch—I got nowhere." [81] The show's bilingual title supports Andrade's point: it translates as "Little Boy and the Man." In this respect, producers and protesters operated on the same register— that of an oedipalized masculinity—and the problem was that each wanted something quite different for Chicanos within episodic television: public machismo versus domestic quiescence. In other words, both sides asked, "Who's the man?" Chicano protests against the series continued, but the demands for machismo and ethnic-specific casting (Prinze was Puerto Rican) failed to resonate within public discourse, while Andrade's effectiveness as an outside agitator came to a decisive end, even after he resigned from the show. [82]

As Kathryn Montgomery concludes,

> Though Justicia's involvement with network television had been brief, its success in gaining access to high-level decision makers had been remarkable. The activist group might have been able to continue working with the networks if it had altered its style. But the explosive, unpredictable behavior of the group's leaders ultimately undermined their effectiveness. As other advocacy groups were learning, dealing successfully with network television required cooperative, as well as confrontational strategies. [83]

This critique, however, assumes that such changes are possible through an institutionalized reform movement; and, in many respects, Montgomery's book represents and exemplifies such advocacy. (Montgomery is currently president of the Center for Media Education in Washington, D.C.) What gets lost in this point of view is the way in which cooperation and confrontation mark boundaries between inside and outside and, in a more specific sense, between social control and social movements. Montgomery is not wrong per se; but her assessment of Justicia fails to take into account the paradox of any social movement. For all the claims to the contrary, the Chicano movement—as with the Mexican revolution it modeled itself after—could not become institutionalized and remain a movement. After all, institutions define an "inside" from which social relations are understood, organized, and controlled; movements are directed from outside and against institutions, in terms of challenging either their particular actions, their legitimacy, or the myths that sustain both. While real life—or history—is more complicated than these categorical distinctions, as I have already shown, they nonetheless "show us whose foot has been on whose neck," as George Lipsitz so aptly argues about historiography.[84] After all, it is from such power relations that social change starts, and it says a lot about how a people underfoot can or do stand up.

Andrade learned this lesson—as political strategy—from none other than the longtime radical community activist Saul Alinsky, who informed him, "You've got to be a little crazy, and you've got to show that you have a sense of humor but a serious side at the same time."[85] Andrade was "a little crazy" in taking on and threatening the entire industry, he had "a sense of humor" in using but not entering the policy arena, and he revealed "a serious side" in making concrete demands and actually achieving some of them. In this respect, as I noted earlier, Andrade used López's notion of "schizo-cultural limbo" as a political strategy, locating his authority in conflicted and contradictory discourses. It is a strategy that Alinsky himself spelled out in *Rules for Radicals. Pace* Alinsky, an organizer must become "a well-integrated schizoid," splitting "himself" into two parts:

> one part in the arena of action where he polarizes the issue to 100 [percent] to nothing, and helps to lead his forces into conflict, while the other part knows that when the time comes for negotiations that it really is only a 10 percent difference—and yet both parts have to live comfortably with each other. Only a well-organized person can split and yet stay together. But this is what an organizer must do.[86]

Herein lie the limits of Alinsky's theory of social change: in effect, he applied revolutionary demands to achieve reformist goals. In *Rules for Radicals,* Alinsky distinguished between the rhetorical radical and the realistic one, noting that the latter cannot be a "true believer" but must take the world on its own terms and work within the system.[87] Tactics, then, were based on producing the illusion of power—*"Power is not only what you have but what the enemy thinks you have"*[88]—in order to turn the system's rules against itself. This strategy required both timing and timeliness lest the illusion wear out before it produced results, since, as Alinsky notes, *"No one can negotiate without the power to compel negotiation."*[89] But if so, the results themselves signaled the end of the power to compel, meaning that any reform would be quite tenuous and difficult to enforce, rather than serve as a prelude to revolution. In the end, Alinsky's strategy could not reconcile the contradictions inherent in his notion of a "realistic radical," leading him to characterize such a person as pathological ("schizoid") and cynical (against "true believers") or as someone forced into exile, like the "first radical . . . who rebelled against the establishment," Lucifer. Demanding access was no simple matter insofar as it *did* require a well-integrated political schizoid.

In this manner, while Justicia was successful in confronting the industry without also being co-opted by the state, it was not able to walk through the very doors it helped crack open. When it did, tragedy turned to farce: Andrade was arrested, then made the subject of a situation comedy. Insofar as *Chico and the Man* was not about women to any degree, the series reiterated the very thing that Chicano groups struggled against in the late 1960s and early 1970s: the representation of the "Mexican" male as an infantilized and emasculated bandito type. Chico, after all, begins the series as an endearing petty thief. Given these terms, Chicano protests could not help but isolate women and other Latino groups. Still, their limited success in this and other struggles had a more profound and determining source: the implicit corporate orientation of the state as it regulated the "public interest." In the end, though, it is important to remember that whatever the structural and tactical limitations of the Justicia leadership once it gained a toehold in the industry, the greatest strength of any protest or reform group resides in its being on the outside. For this reason, Justicia's lasting legacy is in those areas where it put a foot in the door and let others walk through— that is, the actions that led to Chicano public affairs shows.

Interestingly enough, Andrade's lessons were also being learned by those groups that used their standing before the FCC to reform local television stations. If these groups worked "within the system," they did so as a recent supplement imposed upon that system, a supplement whose participation was begrudged, requiring it to work at the margins of regulatory procedures. Media reform groups, then, were able to use the FCC not as an end in its own right, but in order to leverage agreements from the industry itself. Ironically, the Department of Justice showed them how to get around the state. As with my earlier analysis of Chicano protests against advertisers, I want to stress the importance of examining the relationships and tactical maneuvers that locate protest both inside *and* outside. Such an approach does not deny the fact that certain groups have been clearly excluded from equal participation in political representation, economic opportunity, and mass communication, but neither does it fetishize exclusion into an identity out of step with the complexities and paradoxes of the search for social change.

five

Grasping at the Public Airwaves
The FCC and the Discourse of Violence

One of the central paradoxes of broadcast policy has been the "public interest" standard that secures FCC authority in the first place. The FCC regulates on behalf of the "public interest" primarily through licensing, which grants broadcasters free and exclusive use of a specific frequency for a three-year period (now five years), and rulemaking, which directs broadcast station operating procedures. But rather than signal a dynamic between representational and corporatist politics, the "public interest" standard subordinated the legal status of the airwaves as both public property and basic infrastructure to a policy arena defined in terms of commercial interests. In this respect, as Thomas Streeter argues, the "public interest" standard bears a "discursive continuity" with nineteenth-century legal argument based on property and contract:

> The "public interest" here was not being understood as a limit to the market or as a constraint on commercial interests; it was not a limit to the economic system that would eventually be called capitalism. On the contrary, it was typically used to untie perplexing knots in economic systems so that the market as a whole would benefit; it was a necessary element to the nineteenth-century vision of laissez-faire.[1]

One consequence of this "discursive continuity" was that, until the late 1960s, standing before the FCC was effectively limited to broadcasters who could demonstrate a material interest in the proceedings, based on either transmission interference or economic injury.[2] Thus, while the airwaves were the property of the people, the commercial orientation of broadcasting, together with the scarcity of the broadcast spectrum, meant that the "public interest" standard could only be brought to bear on competing and limited *business* interests. As such, there was no basis upon which to challenge discriminatory television programming or hiring practices—among other social issues—before the FCC.

How this situation changed in the late 1960s reveals the extent to which the state and industry have kept the public *qua* public on the other side of the looking glass, claiming to reflect an image *of* the people and *for* the people, but not *by* the people. I am not arguing about the public sphere as an idealized "site" wherein the public debates itself, but rather that the particular "politics" within which television produces a public sphere is not a representational but a corporatist one. In other words, the democratic function of a public sphere emerges as what economists call "externalities" or the unintended consequences of market activities.[3] Thus, if broadcast law and policy placed television outside representational politics, in both senses of the phrase (democracy and mediated public identities), difference necessarily became the bête noire within the public sphere that television produced. After all, difference signaled a body politic, whereas television addressed a mass audience; for this reason, media reform based on civil rights often found itself subordinated to the logic of consumer rights.

In the 1950s and 1960s, racial difference brought this dynamic into high relief insofar as racial minorities did not have the requisite rights of citizenship that television could then rearticulate as consumer rights. Thus positioned "outside" the corporate liberal imaginary for the citizen-consumer, racial minorities encountered the complexities and paradoxes of seeking social change. While the state responded to social unrest by constructing avenues through which racial minorities could seek adjudication, it did so in a way that did not foster structural assimilation. Instead, the state compelled these groups to participate in a "discourse of violence" as well as to base their claims on supplemental racial categories for citizenship. Thus, in their negotiations with the state, racial minorities oscillated between acting the injured party and making unlawful threats, while their status as citizens was itself marked as exceptional in both senses of the word: an exception (in terms of rights) and superior (in terms of identity). These paradoxes pitted a racial identity against an unmarked national imaginary from which it remained excluded. By the mid-1970s, the state would defer issues of social equity to the marketplace, and broadcasters would quickly cast themselves as the victims of the symbolic violence of minority citizenship.

Challenging Television Stations

It would take Black civil rights groups over a decade to bring about changes that allowed public interest groups to have standing within FCC regulation. On March 25, 1966, the U.S. Court of Appeals granted "citizen groups" standing before the FCC in response to a lawsuit brought by the New York–based Office of Communication of the United Church of Christ (UCC) against WLBT-TV in Jackson, Mississippi. But the case had started eleven years earlier when the NAACP responded to requests for assistance from its Jackson chapter. The local television stations, WJTV and WLBT (both established in 1953), were headed by supporters and board members of the all-white Citizen's Council, formed in response to *Brown v. Board of Education* (1954). The NAACP filed a complaint with the FCC charging WLBT with blackouts of network programming that either addressed or embodied racial integration and with failure to implement the fairness doctrine and broadcast the "Negro position" on segregation. The FCC deferred decision on the 1955 complaint and in 1959 rejected the NAACP's 1957 and 1959 complaints, renewing WLBT's license. In this period, the growing civil rights movement in Jackson—desegregation, "freedom riders," and a boycott campaign—received at first little to no local coverage and then extensive but highly inflammatory news reports and editorials peppered with such racial slurs as "negra" and "nigger." Finally, on May 20, 1963, at the height of the boycott and under increasing scrutiny from the FCC, WLBT granted Medgar Evers uncensored airtime to respond to an earlier broadcast statement from the mayor in which he refused to meet with the NAACP. Overnight, the local movement acquired a face and a voice within the local mass media—a mass media that had figured desegregation as something to be spoken against but not represented. Three weeks later, Evers was assassinated outside his home.

Because the civil rights movement sought to bring the state apparatus and national imaginary to bear on local practices, mass media—in both its local and national configurations—played a central role in the process. It is in this context that Dr. Everett Parker of the UCC Office of Communication approached Jackson civil rights leaders with a plan to establish the public as a "party of interest" within FCC regulation. Parker undertook a highly secretive campaign to monitor WJTV and WLBT (using anonymous and mostly white volunteers) and to collect complaints from local African Americans. Using this information, in April 1964 the UCC filed a formal petition to deny license with the FCC. In May 1965, the FCC issued a one-year probationary renewal with no hearings, whereupon the UCC turned to the U.S. Court of Appeals. In March 1966, the court reversed the FCC ruling, established standing for citizen groups, and remanded the case for full hearings before the FCC. When the FCC renewed WLBT's license in June 1968, the UCC again appealed to the court, which in June 1969 again reversed the FCC ruling and denied the relicensing of WLBT. The decision became the first time the courts had revoked a license on the basis of racial discrimination.[4]

It also became the only time the courts so intervened. Thus, while the WLBT case set a number of precedents that facilitated the broadcast reform and consumer reform movements,[5] it remained unique with respect to its raison d'être: racial discrimination. Race was effectively taken out of the equation. Indeed, while the WLBT case was integral to the civil rights movement—a movement that located racial conflict at the crossroads of local politics, mass media, and the state—standing was defined in the formal terms of a television audience concerned with public interest issues. In its rulings, as Steven Douglas Classen demonstrates, the court subordinated the demand for civil rights to an official legal discourse predicated on the individuated American consumer *cum* legal subject, while the FCC itself displaced attention onto the "integrity" of its own standards and procedures.[6] In this manner, standing remained within the formal distinctions of legal liberalism—that the state adjudicates the interests of individual legal subjects. "This symbolic displacement," Classen argues, ". . . allowed the state . . . to address a race-based threat to social and economic stability, via an official legal discourse, without directly appearing to offer such an address."[7]

In assessing this history, media critics have cited the indeterminacy of law or, at a more local level, have pointed to the contradictions in its enforcement. More immediate, however, is the fact that broadcast law and policy have relied upon a circular logic that defines the "public interest" as its sine qua non but then uses that law and policy to close the public sphere to the noncommercial interests of citizen groups. Once the U.S. Court of Appeals established standing in 1966, the FCC displayed what the court itself later described as a "curious neutrality-in-favor-of-the-licensee" and a "pervasive impatience—if not hostility" toward citizen groups, which the FCC treated as "interlopers" or as "an opponent."[8] The FCC consistently sought to contain the court-ordered participation of citizen groups by using circular logic in three areas: evidentiary rules, contract law, and an inclination toward the *informal* regulation of social issues.[9]

First, FCC evidentiary rules placed a citizen group filing a petition to deny license in a catch-22. As Joseph A. Grundfest explains, "[I]t cannot get a license designated for hearing until it makes a sufficient evidentiary showing, but it cannot make a sufficient evidentiary showing until it gains the rights of discovery, which come only after a license has been designated for hearing."[10] Thus, citizen groups that petitioned the FCC—challenging stations on the basis of their employment, ascertainment, and harassment—found their charges dismissed as unsubstantiated. In one of the few such cases to reach the U.S. Court of Appeals, the Bilingual Bicultural Coalition on the Mass Media (BBC) in San Antonio sought admission of statistics as evidence of discrimination in employment. Ironically, this employment data was collected each year by the FCC itself through its Form 395.[11] But if Form 395 provided for FCC enforcement of its EEO rule, it did so on the basis of the *appearance* of such enforcement, since the annual employment reports could not be used as evidence of noncompliance. Thus, on February 13, 1974, nearly three years after the initial petition, the court ruled against the BBC while also noting that "new approaches are clearly necessary," leaving these to the FCC to develop.[12] The court warned, "If minorities are not given *some* means for developing the reasons for statistical disparities, hearings may have to be required based on such disparities alone, in order to provide the tools of discovery."[13]

In effect, the court both acknowledged and reinforced the catch-22 facing citizen groups. Individual complaints or affidavits could not provide evidence of general patterns of discrimination within the industry; and statistical evidence of underrepresentation did not "constitute a prima facie showing of discrimination."[14] Furthermore, while the Court determined that a station's work force should be compared with the population in the station's service area, it also adopted an extremely broad "zone of reasonableness" before such statistical disparity could be used to indicate underrepresentation. In the BBC case, Chicanos made up 12 percent of the workforce at WOAI-TV but 48 percent of the local population, a disparity that fell within the "zone of reasonableness" of the FCC and, later, of the court.

Second, when the FCC modified its hostility and allowed some participation, it did so only "provided that the citizen groups respect broadcasters' ultimate control over their stations." [15] Thus, the "savings clause"—a feature of commercial contracts—became a necessary component of settlement agreements between citizen groups and broadcast stations. Since the FCC did not provide a standard savings clause, however, citizen groups engaged in a hit-or-miss search for an appropriate formula. In 1975, the Television Advisory Committee of Mexican-Americans (TACOMA), in its agreement with KMJ-TV in Fresno, California, hit upon wording that the FCC found acceptable:

> TACOMA understands that communication law and the rules of the Federal Communications Commission require that the final responsibility for all program decisions must remain with station management and nothing contained in the agreement shall be construed to be inconsistent with that requirement. [16]

In the end, the savings clause ensured that broadcasters retained—rather than delegated—authority over programming, and as such, it made settlement agreements less binding and more voluntary. After all, the TACOMA agreement called for a series of citizen group–mandated programs: daily job and consumer information in Spanish and English, a Sunday morning program produced by TACOMA, a monthly program on minority topics, and a half-hour special documentary on minority affairs every ninety days. [17] The savings clause could be used to invalidate these agreements if station management found them "inconsistent" with their authority over programming. Thus, in a simple reversal, citizen groups and not broadcasters were the ones "tightly bound" to the requirements of commercial contracts, which became the formal mechanism for resolving social issues. Unlike a business that has contracted with a broadcast station, citizen groups did not have the economic clout or leverage to offset the "savings clause"—that is, there was nothing inherent in the transaction itself to bind the two parties together. After all, one was doing business, while the other was challenging "business as usual" on moral grounds, with the sole threat of taking up time—and hence money—within the regulatory process. Once a settlement agreement was signed, that threat ended.

Finally, the FCC often engaged in regulation by the "raised eyebrow." [18] As Grundfest notes, "The raised eyebrow technique involves the cooperation of the Commission and the public in convincing broadcasters that certain steps toward self-regulation are in the broadcaster's own interests." [19] The main example is the Family Viewing Hour. Critics and the courts have seen regulation by the raised eyebrow as an informal but powerful tool of state administration—indeed, one that can give the state influence beyond the letter of its own law. But regulation by the raised eyebrow has particular implications with respect to broadcast reform by citizen groups insofar as it essentially delegates FCC authority to the industry, something the savings clause prevents the industry from doing with respect to programming. In this way, social issues raised by citizen groups remained "informal" within the regulatory procedures of the FCC itself, both in its use of the raised eyebrow and in its refusal to specify its own evidentiary and contractual standards.

Legal standing, then, did not offer an end in itself, but rather became a national means by which citizen groups could pursue informal avenues that resulted in local concessions to the public interest. Although the FCC represented at first a closed system and later a circular one, both of which were "hostile" to citizen groups, it was located in a state that did not so much administer social conflicts from an autonomous realm as it embodied them within its bureaucracy. In their internal dealings with the FCC, then, the U.S. Court of Appeals, the U.S. Commission on Civil Rights, and the Department of Justice both raised eyebrows and on occasion slapped hands, though the state was never at odds with itself beyond its corporate liberal principles. Nevertheless, these internal conflicts created a space within which citizen groups acquired leverage to pressure local television stations for public affairs shows, among other demands.

The Community Relations Service (CRS), based in the Department of Justice, played an active role in helping to develop the numerous community-based efforts to challenge the mass media. Established by the 1964 Civil Rights Act, the CRS addressed nationwide problems in "race relations" at the community level. In its efforts to redress the exclusion of racial minorities from mass communications, the CRS Office of Media Relations organized or sponsored regional conferences designed to establish working relations both among the numerous grassroots minority groups and between these groups and the local news media. CRS efforts in the Chicano community began in the summer of 1967 with a preliminary report on news media treatment in Texas and California.[20] The CRS then sponsored three regional Chicano media conferences in San Antonio (January 18, 1969), Denver (May 2, 1970), and Chicago (June 20–21, 1970), the last quickly followed by a national conference in New York (June 29, 1970) that resulted in a short-lived umbrella organization, the National Chicano Media Council. The CRS later played a supportive role in facilitating two workshops for the Bilingual Bicultural Coalition on Mass Media in San Antonio on FCC law (May 22–23, 1971) and negotiating with broadcasters (June 13, 1971).[21]

The goal of these activities was to improve media portrayals and also to increase minority ownership, management, and employment within the industry. The method, however, was based on bringing Chicano community-based groups into "dialogue" with each other, the federal policy arena, and the broadcast industry. CRS travel grants to conferences, together with the published proceedings, allowed Chicano media groups to share information on local tactics as well as to articulate a national strategy. As Francisco J. Lewels concluded at the time, "For years the agency served as the only middleman between minorities and federal agencies, media representatives, and the various public-interest law groups."[22] In short, as middleman, the CRS brought minority groups into alignment with the policy arena in two ways: by helping to constitute a diverse cluster of protest activities as race-specific national groups and by redirecting their protests toward negotiation with the industry against the backdrop of FCC regulation. For the radical sector of the Chicano movement, however, such "negotiation" was little more than a trick, insofar as the state was more interested in containing "valid and explosive protest" than in addressing its cause. As José Angel Gutiérrez argued in *A Gringo Manual on How to Handle Mexicans,* "The trick is to make you think there is a big difference between CRS and local police. There isn't."[23] And, in fact, while the CRS strategy resulted in settlement agreements and headed in the general direction of a national coalition, it also required minority protest groups to accept a policy arena that placed them at the margins of its formal procedures. Then, in early 1973, the CRS budget was cut by the Nixon administration.

What happened in this brief period, then, suggests one of the reasons why the CRS was largely dismantled. Even if the CRS strategy was a "trick," it also produced unintended consequences once citizen groups used formal procedures (the petition) in order to reach informal ends (the settlement). With state support, the margins subverted the center, producing a situation in which the "public interest" was defined by the public itself and was designated outside FCC regulation. Thus, according to Albert H. Kramer, the director of the Citizens Communications Center, settlement agreements created a paradox: "the private enforcement of a public law."[24]

Basically, citizen groups overwhelmed the regulatory system, submitting numerous petitions to the FCC to deny renewal or transfer of a broadcast license. In the early 1970s, the petition quickly became, in the words of two standard textbooks, the "heavy artillery" in the broadcast reform movement.[25] On average, about forty petitions to deny license renewal were filed each year between 1971 and 1976. (The number dropped to under twenty thereafter.[26]) In addition, some twenty petitions to deny transfer or sale of a license were filed each year throughout the 1970s.[27] A single petition could be directed against one or more broadcast stations, while it often involved numerous citizens groups, usually a mixture of local groups, national civil rights organizations, and public-interest law groups. Between 1971 and 1973, the industry trade journal *Broadcasting* provided extensive reports on Black, Chicano, and women groups as they filed petitions to deny license renewal in various states. For Chicanos, the main states included Colorado,[28] Texas,[29] New Mexico,[30] and California,[31] but Domingo Nick Reyes, National Mexican-American Defamation Committee (NMAADC), even challenged stations in Washington, D.C.[32]

Yet, despite the so-called "heavy artillery" at their disposal, and the suggestions in *Broadcasting* that these petitions would leave a "bloody battleground," citizen groups had no better than a 0.0116 percent probability that a petition would lead to a revoked license.[33] Ultimately, what made the petitions a threat was that the FCC was notoriously slow in resolving them. In fact, 53 percent of petitions filed between 1970 and 1974 were still pending at the end of that period.[34] Since the FCC took sixteen months or more to resolve a petition and the U.S. Court of Appeals showed a willingness to overturn FCC rulings, broadcasters had an economic incentive to negotiate settlement agreements in exchange for having a petition withdrawn.[35] Industry estimates for court costs and staff time required to defend a license renewal against a petition ranged from $50,000 to $400,000.[36] Furthermore, the delay could take a station halfway to its next renewal, whereupon the process would start all over again. In the case of a transfer of license (or sale), FCC approval was contingent on the resolution or withdrawal of all pending petitions, providing citizen groups with additional leverage.

Within the brief period during which the petition to deny served as the "heavy artillery" for citizen groups, numerous Chicano media groups operated at the local level.[37] But the petition to deny also functioned as heavy artillery within the Chicano movement as a whole, placing media representation squarely within local politics and grassroots efforts. In addition to Chicano media groups, then, Chicano civil rights organizations, including the American G.I. Forum, MAPA, NCLR, and MALDEF, joined in the petition process, as either claimants or legal counsel. Three of the key figures in the Chicano movement were also involved in petitions against local stations: César Chávez and the United Farm Workers (Bakersfield), Rodolfo "Corky" Gonzales and the Crusade for Justice (Denver), and Reies Lopez Tijerina and the Alianza Federal de Pueblos Libres (Albuquerque). Out of these efforts a number of settlement agreements were reached throughout the Southwest—most of them involving the creation of Chicano programming.[38] The full range of settlement demands reveals a comprehensive agenda to integrate the Chicano community into the local broadcast media, and vice versa: training, advisory councils, employment programs, programming, sensitivity training, minority business aid, scholarships, and public service announcements.

But while these efforts were local, they were also the product of philanthropic, public law, and interracial networks at the national level, which resulted in a certain uniformity in their demands. As *Broadcasting* reported, "They circulate proposed policy statements among themselves, which is why so many statements read alike."[39] What began to emerge, then, were widespread local actions expressive of a regional social movement and increasingly oriented toward the arena of national policy. Chicano local groups formed coalitions in order to file petitions, while Chicano and non-Chicano national organizations provided legal assistance and acted as conduits to broader social and institutional arenas. These informal networks—which the National Association of Broadcasters referred to as a "conspiracy"—were not without conflict insofar as they sustained two social movements that were becoming increasingly institutionalized: civil rights and broadcast reform. Both roles were the subject of concern for Chicano media activists as they attempted to establish a national coalition or umbrella organization for Chicano media.

The NMAADC, building upon its role in the campaign against the Frito Bandito as well as in the petition process, coordinated early efforts to establish such a national strategy. But by 1972, concurrently with the initial settlement agreements, Domingo Nick Reyes had isolated the NMAADC from the more established public interest groups, criticizing the UCC Office of Communication and the Citizens Communications Center (CCC) for intervening in Chicano efforts at self-determination and "ripping off" the community.[40] Reyes's criticism reflects the increasing competition for "clients" among the national public interest groups, but it also indicates the racialized dimension of that competition. Chicano groups were in the process of institutionalizing their social protest, leading some to reject "outside" help in order to keep their efforts "a Chicano thing."[41] The Bilingual Bicultural Coalition on Mass Media in San Antonio, for example, rejected assistance from the UCC, drawing upon Chicano members of the local CRS office instead. As BBC's executive director, Roberto Anguiano, explained, "I've got nothing against the Church of Christ, they've done good things. But no matter how much an Anglo or a black tries to help you, the differences are there, the outlooks are different."[42] But Reyes was less circumspect, making statements that raised the specter of anti-Semitism: "The pattern of institutional racism is perpetuated by one ethnic minority. The Jews have an overconcentration of power."[43] These and other remarks were clearly out of step with the "appropriately neutral and expert policy language" that the reform movement was required to adopt in order to participate in the regulatory process.

Reyes was quickly removed from state-sponsored coordinating efforts as well as from a major petition and settlement. In 1971, Reyes had organized a five-city coalition to petition the transfer of five television stations from Time-Life Broadcasting to McGraw-Hill. In the end, however, the coalition—which included eight Chicano and one Black group—rejected the NMAADC and chose other representation: CCC, UCC, MALDEF, and Black Efforts for Soul in Television (BEST). The subsequent agreement signed in May 1972 became, in Lewels's words, "the most comprehensive contract ever entered into by a broadcaster with a minority group."[44] Then, on June 24, 1972, when the CRS sponsored a second national Chicano media conference to build upon the success of the McGraw-Hill agreement, it excluded Reyes and the NMAADC.[45]

The McGraw-Hill petition and settlement reveal many of the shifts taking place within the Chicano media reform movement, including the decline of the NMAADC and the emergence of MALDEF as national coordinators. But it also reveals the various power relations that traversed the national broadcast reform movement as it worked in and around FCC regulation and the industry. The sale—agreed to in March 1971—was designed to allow McGraw-Hill to enter broadcasting, while Time-Life Broadcasting would shift its emphasis to cable. The FCC banned cross-ownership of television stations and cable systems in the same market, effective August 10, 1973. But FCC policy also prohibited a broadcaster from owning more than two VHF stations in the top-fifty market unless it made a compelling case that doing so served the public interest. Three of the five Time-Life stations were in the top-fifty market. Although the FCC had approved the sale, the coalition had filed petitions to deny renewal of license and had appealed the transfer to the U.S. Court of Appeals. Neither case would be resolved before the contract deadline for the sale (April 12, 1972, later extended to May 1), providing the coalition with the needed leverage to work out an agreement that upheld the top fifty–market policy. In addition to acquiring only four stations, McGraw-Hill also made extensive commitments to establishing minority advisory councils, employment goals, training, and programming. The programs included a *La Raza* series of eighteen documentaries on Chicano culture and history as well as thirty-six prime-time specials on minority issues (twelve on general subjects, twelve on Blacks, and twelve on Chicanos).[46]

In short, the agreement served divergent interests: for public law groups, it enforced the "rule of law" that had become their bailiwick, while for Chicanos, it established a production series and employment programs. The press conference following the agreement revealed a conflict over turf between Albert H. Kramer (CCC) and Domingo Nick Reyes (NMAADC). Both saw the agreement in decisive terms as a "surrender" or "breakthrough," but Kramer emphasized the policy aspects (public law groups versus the industry), while Reyes described the agreement in regional and racial terms (Chicano groups versus an "Eastern establishment" and a Jewish-controlled media). MALDEF's director, Mario Obledo, conciliated between these positions, citing McGraw-Hill for "operating in good faith" and serving as "an example for corporate America" while praising both Kramer and Reyes, then deflecting Reyes's racial rhetoric to a more generalized "white America."[47] Since UCC and CCC specialized in the policy arena, their goals were directed more toward what Kramer called "the private enforcement of a public law," whereas the NMAADC and MALDEF were more concerned with the programming commitment and community-based concessions in a settlement agreement. For Obledo, this concern manifested itself in a less confrontational rhetoric than either "rule of law" policy reform (many of whose specialists entered government in the late 1970s) or Chicano cultural nationalism (which antagonized non-Chicano organizations and support networks).[48]

After the McGraw-Hill agreement, MALDEF pursued other petitions as well as provided legal strategy. In 1972, in the first issue of *Chicano Law Review*, Obledo and a staff attorney, Robert Joselow, provided a blueprint for working the system and making the system work in adjudicating demands of the Chicano community on local television stations.[49] The article followed the pattern of other Chicano "plans" or advocacy texts, beginning with a historical survey of the socioeconomic problems of the Chicano community and the ongoing misrepresentation of Chicanos in the news and entertainment media. The article then outlined the case history that provided citizen groups with legal standing before the FCC, warning citizen groups of the need to "Watch the Watchdog" and take the FCC itself to court, if necessary. In 1973, Vilma Martínez became the president and general counsel of MALDEF. James Perez, who had been a staff member of the CRS office in San Antonio, also joined MALDEF, coordinating media efforts. Until around 1977, MALDEF played an important role in the use of the petition to deny, providing assistance to local Chicano citizen groups, while taking part in an active network of other national civil rights and media reform groups, including the National Association for the Advancement of Colored People (NAACP), the National Organization for Women (NOW), Action for Children's Television (ACT), and Chinese for Affirmative Action (CAA). In this period, MALDEF media activism fit within a broader agenda—immigration, education, voters' rights, and women's rights—that constituted an integrated and holistic social vision that had defined the Chicano civil rights movement.[50]

But if citizen groups were able to use petitions to broker settlement agreements, this leverage came at a price. For the most part, as *Broadcasting* itself noted, the reform movement was necessarily "conservative" (working within the system) and "bourgeois" (predicated on integration), relying on "informal" networks and negotiation strategies to achieve these ends.[51] Thus, while citizen groups were able to appropriate some of the FCC's function, the system of state-supported commercial broadcast remained unchallenged, and stations were able to mount an effective lobby effort for rulemaking changes that returned "control" over the public interest to the FCC. Between October 1975 and January 1976, FCC rulemaking made the regulatory process into make-work rather than something that could work in its own right or as an impetus for working out citizens' agreements.[52] For MALDEF, media soon ceased to be an issue in and of itself. Meanwhile, the role of media within other social movements and national civil rights organizations became an increasingly minor one.

Closing the Public Sphere

The mid-1970s signaled the end of the broadcast reform movement as the FCC moved toward deregulation and local stations canceled the public affairs shows that had been secured through protests or settlement agreements. Cable television was offered as both panacea and Pandora's box, especially for media reform groups working inside the beltway. As Antonio José Guernica declared in *Agenda: A Journal of Hispanic Issues:* "Cable represents the only avenue available for Hispanics to gain substantial control over a communications medium."[53] Guernica's article, together with one in the previous issue,[54] appeared in the publication arm of the Washington-based National Council of La Raza, participating in a shift from petitions to deny license to attempts to secure broadcast and cable ownership. In acknowledging the FCC's failure to consider discriminatory content and hiring practices in license renewals, Guernica identified ownership as the royal road to the public interest. In effect, Guernica internalized the industry's own logic and conceded the public airwaves to corporate interests, at the same time holding out hope that the FCC would act in the "public interest" provided Chicanos approach the FCC by way of the corporate arena. Thus, while Guernica did not equate the marketplace with the public interest, as did proponents of deregulation, his concession meant that the public interest could only emerge out of the marketplace—even if Guernica also hoped that it did not look like the marketplace. In any case, as he conceded, "minority representation . . . is ultimately in the hands of the Federal Communications Commission."[55]

Since the late 1960s, Chicano media activists had sought to form a national coalition or clearinghouse in order to coordinate challenges to the industry and to participate within the policy arena. The National Chicano Media Council, formed after a series of CRS-sponsored conferences, had taken a first step in that direction, electing Ruben Salazar chairman in June 1970. Salazar was a nationally respected *Los Angeles*

Times journalist whose coverage of the Chicano movement provided the sole counterbalance in the mainstream news media. When he was shot and killed by the Los Angeles County Sheriff's Department while covering the Chicano Moratorium Against the Vietnam War on August 29, 1970, the consensus within the Chicano movement was that no one could take his place.[56] Hank López—now a Ford Foundation consultant—continued as executive director until around March 1972, when lack of funds and office space led him to resign.[57] In the end, although Salazar may have been able to provide necessary leadership within the coalition and respectability in the policy arena, chances are he could not have raised the financial support needed to operate the council. "Since we were funded as an organization that was to 'bug' the establishment," as López noted in his resignation letter, "it is highly unlikely that any foundation will risk backing such an organization on pain of losing its tax-exempt status."[58] Thus, while Chicano media advocacy groups continued throughout the 1970s, networking efforts were increasingly sporadic or regional. In 1976, the Los Angeles–based Media Education Group compiled and circulated a "Media Action News Service" consisting of news releases and other documents from media access and community education groups.[59] In February 1977, the Texas Chicano Coalition on Mass Media began publishing *Reporte*, a "monthly" newsletter on print and electronic media activities around the state. The only effective national organization was the National Latino Media Coalition, which was not involved in media reform per se, but rather consisted of television producers lobbying within the industry and among government and nonprofit funding sources.[60]

Given the limited funding sources for social activism designed to "'bug' the establishment," perhaps the biggest setback to both the Chicano and media reform movements came from the withdrawal of their largest nonfederal supporter: the Ford Foundation. Described by some as the sole alternative to federal funds,[61] Ford's "magnitudinous immensity"—with assets then equal to "one-sixth of all 25,000 American foundations"—gave the foundation considerable influence in its more "activist" funding, even though it amounted to less than 10 percent of the total amount the foundation funded in the form of grants.[62] Between 1951 and 1976, the Ford Foundation contributed $300 million to the development and programming of public television in the United States—nearly fifty times more money than the next largest nonfederal funder. Ford played a similarly significant role in the media reform movement, providing an estimated 57 percent of all public-interest funding.[63] In addition to its role in public television and broadcast policy, Ford takes credit for the Community Development Corporation (CDC) as well as other efforts to create a small-scale civil society within Black and Latino communities in this period.[64] Ford's status as the sole or major funder gave it a certain proprietary interest in these projects. In one memo, for example, the foundation identifies the National Council of La Raza (NCLR) as a "wholly-owned subsidiary" between 1968 and 1975,[65] a situation that allowed Ford to micromanage the organization in its start-up years. Beginning in 1974, however, Ford significantly reduced such funding, removing the buffer between these new social institutions and the political and economic forces they sought to change. The loss of these funds sent a "seismic shock through the media reform movement" from which it never recovered.[66] Similarly, civil rights groups that had been "wholly-owned subsidiaries" found themselves quickly reoriented away from a community-based ethos and toward the professional culture of the "American system." NCLR—initially the Southwest Council of La Raza—changed names and relocated to Washington, D.C., in December 1972. By 1977, NCLR was receiving no more than 5 percent of its total funding from Ford.[67]

MALDEF held a similar position vis-à-vis the Ford Foundation, and it is in this light that we must understand both the context, direction, and eventual limit of its media reform activities. Founded in 1967 and funded a year later through a $2.2 million start-up grant from Ford, MALDEF defended the constitutional rights of Mexican Americans. It was modeled after the NAACP Legal Defense and Education Fund, and in fact, Vilma Martínez had been an attorney at the NAACP in the late 1960s, where she helped prepare the Ford grant application for MALDEF as well as provide other assistance. In its first three years, however, MALDEF's regionalism, community-based efforts, and movement rhetoric clashed with Ford's orientation toward securing broad legal rights through the state. Headquartered in San Antonio, Texas, MALDEF operated more as a regional legal aid society rather than as a national legal defense fund concerned with precedent-setting cases; while it also lacked experienced litigators. In addition, MALDEF's close involvement with more "militant and radical" Chicano groups generated considerable political fallout from U.S. Representative Henry B. González, whose district included San Antonio. At issue were "anti-gringo" statements by José Angel Gutiérrez, president of the Mexican

American Youth Organization (MAYO), who called for Chicanos to "resist and eliminate the gringo," including through killing, "if worst comes to worst."[68] González, a Democrat with a mostly liberal voting record, followed the money trail and found that MAYO received funds from the Mexican American Unity Council (MAUC), which was itself funded by the Southwest Council of La Raza, which, of course, was funded by the Ford Foundation. Furthermore, MALDEF employed Gutiérrez as an investigator, which not only provided him with a salary, but also provided him the means to travel around the nation, creating networks and soliciting funds for MAYO and related activities. From the House floor, González led an extended attack on MAYO and the Ford Foundation, charging both with the "emergence of reverse racism in Texas" and claiming that MAYO, MAUC, and other Ford-funded Chicano movement groups "present a real danger to peace and safety" and voice a dogma "as evil as the deadly hatred of the Nazis."[69] While González's claims are questionable, MAYO candidates did pose a significant threat to the Democrat-controlled electoral politics in South Texas, which suggests that González's actions may have been an example of turf war cloaked in the language of virulent patriotism.[70] In any case, Gutiérrez's anti-gringo rhetoric, cultural nationalism, and macho posturing (berating Chicanos for being "psychologically castrated" and "not man enough" to claim their rights), while locally effective, made him open to González's use of a national platform where they did not play so well.

In particular, González's statements resulted in increased governmental scrutiny into Ford's indirect support of political activities, including scheduled hearings by the House Ways and Means Committee. In response, Ford de-funded MAYO and made MALDEF fire Gutiérrez, who returned to Crystal City, Texas, to form La Raza Unida. It also sent an outside evaluation team to examine MALDEF's day-to-day activities in 1970. Using the threat of ending its funding, Ford made a number of "recommendations" that effectively restructured MALDEF. These changes included relocating its headquarters (outside González's district and state),[71] replacing the executive director on two occasions, and implementing working relations with other established civil rights groups. In 1973, when Martínez replaced Obledo, her mandate was to institutionalize MALDEF through an improved litigation record, stronger government relations, and increased fundraising and recruitment.

The Ford directives, together with the changing political and economic climate for social-movement activism and cultural nationalist rhetoric, resulted in MALDEF's necessarily pursuing two contradictory goals: placing Chicano legal rights within a state-defined racial economy while securing the organization's long-term survival within a corporate one. First, as Edward J. Escobar explains,

> [i]n a series of school desegregation cases between 1970 and 1973, MALDEF successfully argued that Mexican Americans should no longer be considered white and should instead be designated an "identifiable minority group" with "unalterable congenital traits, political impotence, and the attachment of a stigma of inferiority." That designation extended to Mexican Americans the same legal protection as blacks and enabled them to take advantage of special programs, notably affirmative action, that sought to redress the effects of racial discrimination.[72]

These efforts culminated in MALDEF's successful campaign to have Congress extend the 1965 Voting Rights Act to Mexican Americans in 1975. At the same time, however, MALDEF would be encouraged to shift its financial base from the Ford Foundation to major support from corporate foundations, private corporations, and government agencies.[73] In contrast to Escobar's assertion that Chicanos developed "their own organizations to protect their rights,"[74] which implies an autochthonous movement, it is perhaps more accurate to argue that these organizations emerged out of complex relationships between a social movement, the state, business and industry, and the philanthropic sector. It is in this context that "rights" were both defined and protected.

If the Ford Foundation remade civil rights groups such as MALDEF and NCLR in its own image of a community-based civil society, it also withdrew this support at a particularly bad time: amid a sharp decline in social protest, government activism, and economic growth. Ford itself was severely affected by the inflation and recession of the mid-1970s. Between September 1973 and September 1974, Ford's assets dropped in value from $3 to $1.7 billion, leading the trustees to change foundation priorities in tandem with implementation of an austerity program designed to cut overall spending by 50 percent over the next four years.[75] But, just as important, Ford had already reached the "extreme limit" of its role as an actor within civil society, as indicated in the incident with González. While the New Left dismissed Ford's funding initiative as a "pacification program" that undermined community-based actions, the more powerful Center and Right carried the day in labeling these efforts an encroachment into their domain: "partisan politics." [76] Thus, as Waldemar A. Nielsen observed in 1972, "despite the small portion of its grants which had trickled into the political process, Ford's Mexican-American program acquired a sensational public reputation." [77] Nielsen's conclusion places Ford's activities in the context of a civil society bounded by the state and its vested interests:

> The net effect of the foundation's program, even though it pursued its goals through acceptable educational, legal, and economic avenues, has been to alter in a subtle way the balance of political forces in those areas where Mexican-Americans are concentrated. A formerly unorganized and inarticulate disadvantaged group has been helped to find its voice and to demand its rights. This development has disturbed various vested interests, created great local sensitivity, and generated most of the criticism of the foundation.
>
> The case illustrates both the internal and external constraints which operate even on the largest and most powerful of the big foundations. It helps define the extreme limit of acceptable foundation action at the present time in the United States in an area of social tension and change—a boundary line well removed from anything that could seriously be termed revolutionary or even radical.[78]

In the end, although Ford's early financial support and managerial intervention made these groups more "professional" on a national stage, it also isolated them to a certain extent from their ostensible communities, reorienting these groups toward and making them dependent upon the very same political and economic arena they sought to challenge. In facing the state, Chicanos were encouraged to change their legal racial identity from white to nonwhite, subject their newly gained rights to an established professional culture that had previously excluded them, and pursue a public sphere operating according to private interests. Such were the complexities and paradoxes of seeking social change.

The Discourse of Violence

Why were the gains of the media reform movement so compromised, problematic, and short term? For Newton Minow and Craig L. Lamay in *Abandoned in the Wasteland,* as for many reform-minded critics, the problem lay in the failure to clearly define the public-interest standard in the 1934 Communication Act: "The broadcast industry's basic structure was essentially untouched, and a thin veneer of public participation served almost no one well—it was simply a source of great expense and growing irritation to broadcasters, who began to lobby Congress for regulatory relief." [79]

While Minow and Lamay are, no doubt, correct in this assessment, especially in terms of the economic underpinnings, their vision of social change is limited to the often contradictory operations of the state toward mass media—regulation, legislation, and court decisions—and the assumption that these contradictions can be sorted out as a policy matter. There is no sense of the role of social movements in the above process. [80] To be fair, Minow and Lamay build a reasonable and rational case, even presenting "A Bill for Children's Telecommunications" at the end of their book, but their own strategy—basically, "let's save the children before it's too late!"—ignores, even as it exemplifies, the social pressures that changed communication policy in the first place. And chief among these pressures was the rise of civil disobedience and outright violence acted out in public space and refracted through the mass media, which prompted the courts to intervene and redefine the "public interest" in order to selectively incorporate and diffuse social movements. As Haight and Weinstein conclude, "Only when a national crisis such as that involving civil rights so transforms the political balance that the state must shift *its* ideology does there appear to be a possibility of some state intervention." [81] This intervention redirected protest groups toward the "rather crude and lengthy" process of petitions *within* and litigation *against* the regulatory system, [82] while it also provided community groups with an immediate outlet on local television through public and community affairs shows during prime-time access.

Throughout, the discourse of violence played a central role within the struggle over mass media and for *other* civil rights. In other words, violence served as both an underlying reality and as something to be invoked as a rhetorical strategy in approaching the mass media, the state, and other institutions within civil society. In this period, for example, Chicano media activism consisted of street protests and rather macho threats of violence. Among Chicano producers there are tales of Chicano Vietnam veterans walking into television stations with flak jackets and live hand grenades and walking out with some of the first Chicano public affairs shows. Television executives recount similar events. [83] True or not, such stories reveal that the discourse of violence worked because it walked hand in hand with an immediate, palpable, and visible social crisis.

If "the state's most important institution is that of the means of violence and coercion," [84] then this period saw a significant challenge to that institution's legitimacy and monopoly—as indicated in the widely accepted phrase, "police riot." Chicano activists saw violence as a necessary tactic within their overall strategy before the state, but it was one that required them to threaten their imminent loss of control over their own community *if* the state did not act on their behalf. In this way, activists attempted to make the state complicit in securing their own community-based power, in essence shifting that power's location and source of violence from a (temporary) social movement to state sponsorship. Needless to say, this tactic was a tricky one in that it drew upon a negative comparison to the Black civil rights movement ("We don't want to have to do what Blacks did, but it seems to be the only thing that gets results"), while it also involved resorting to violent threats in order to change mass media representations of Mexican Americans as people who resort to violent threats. Chicanos, then, found their strategy contained by their own discourse, which reduced the potential for coalitions and defined their power in paradoxical ways. The more often the protests turned violent, the more Chicanos looked like the bandito stereotype, and, consequently, the more that stereotype sustained the power relations being challenged. I am not arguing that there was a better way to proceed, but rather that any resistance starts from *within* contradictory relations to the state. Neither resistance, the state, nor representation can claim to be pure.

In its opening and closing paragraphs, Francisco J. Lewels Jr. frames his *The Uses of the Media by the Chicano Movement* with this discourse of violence even as he marks a shift from grassroots advocacy statements to policy-oriented scholarship. The book begins with an account of a Chicano hijacker in mid-April 1972 as an example of a Chicano will to speak within the nation's mass media in order to redress "nearly two centuries of misunderstanding, conflict, and racism." [85] It ends with a theory of assimilation grounded in such violence and in the redemptive powers of mass communication: "Riots are caused by frustration that evolves from a feeling that no one, not even the government, cares about the problems of the *barrio*. . . . It takes concentrated coverage and in-depth reporting to provide the type of relief that is necessary to prevent this kind of violence." [86] The problem with this theory is that it worked only to the extent that it regulated Chicano protest by making it dependent upon and subject to the state. If Chicano activists and intellectuals willingly followed this path, it should be noted, it was a path paved by the state, and the state's coercive power limited and conditioned the other available routes along the way.

Once the state reasserted its control over the "means of violence and coercion" within its territorial limits, mass media could make an effective counterargument to let the marketplace define the public interest, thereby conflating free speech and free market, with the end result that neither did or could exist. It did so amid political and economic crisis: on the one hand, Watergate seriously undermined public perceptions of elected officials (revealing, among other things, various efforts to manipulate the news media), while Vietnam and OPEC challenged the legitimizing myth of American exceptionalism; on the other hand, by 1973 the economy had entered a severe recession that would last until the early 1980s.[87] Television controlled the means of communication, which were increasingly important in the political representation system and national imagination (what I have referred to as the legitimizing myths of the regime). Thus, the industry was able to co-opt the rhetorical style of the broadcast reform movement itself, effectively removing the public from issues of free speech (fairness doctrine, equal opportunity, access, and control) while gaining federal protection from cable television within the so-called free market.[88]

In so doing, the broadcast industry itself made significant use of the discourse of violence in framing its own response to the court's redefinition of "public interest" and the rapid rise of citizen participation in and around broadcast policy. In fact, the emergence of deregulation can be traced back to discursive changes within the industry in the early 1970s, as its orientation toward citizen groups relied increasingly upon martial metaphors. In the trade journal *Broadcasting,* article titles during the license renewals in 1971 stressed an industry under "attack" and facing "open season," "D-Day," and a "gauntlet" as Chicanos "gang[ed] up" on stations. By conflating full-scale warfare, hunting, and gangs, *Broadcasting* provided a narrative context for subsequent "retaliations" against the ostensible violence of citizen groups' participation within the regulatory process. These references to nonstate violence became more pronounced, moving from the confines of the "executive lunch" to the national press by the mid-1970s.[89] In the *New York Times* (March 19, 1974), a broadcaster was quoted as a sign of the industry's "strike back" against media reform: "Peace in our time may have come for most Americans; it has not come for broadcasters. . . . We must fortify ourselves with sufficient ammunition and extensive legal armament for full-scale warfare." [90] In other words, having lost the living room war in Vietnam, broadcasters should not lose television, too! In this way, civil rights became the object of domestic counterinsurgency.

One year later, *Newsweek* (June 2, 1975), under the provocative heading of "TV: Do Minorities Rule?," quoted a television producer who claimed, "The citizens' groups are getting to be like Frankenstein's monster. . . . By trying to please everybody, the networks will please nobody." [91] What made citizen groups into Frankenstein's monster was that they added up to a reform movement made from motley parts: "blacks, feminists, homosexuals, youngsters, ethnics and religious sects of every stripe." *Newsweek* sides with this point of view at the rhetorical level, describing the industry as under an "unprecedented siege" and the FCC as prepared to revise policy guidelines in order to "give broadcasters some legal ammunition against their attackers." Thus, while *Newsweek* concludes that "being responsive to legitimate minority concerns is an obligation that comes with the franchise," ascertainment of those concerns was meant to follow the same method the industry used in its programming: demographics (age, gender, income), not democracy (political representation).

The reference in *Newsweek* to Frankenstein's monster is a telling one insofar as concurrent changes in horror film production allegorized the process by which "whiteness" itself failed as a universal standard for mass audiences. Indeed, by 1975 Frankenstein was not the monster he used to be: theatrical releases turned to camp and parody—*Andy Warhol's Frankenstein* (1974), Mel Brooks's *Young Frankenstein* (1974), and *The Rocky Horror Picture Show* (1975)—or had to be viewed as such, if at all, as did the final two films from the Hammer cycle (1957–74). But if the cinema recast the horror genre in an attempt to reach or exploit various subcultures, the made-for-television version went in the other direction and appealed to the "thinking man" by making the monster into a dashing rogue who undergoes physical and psychological degeneration. *Frankenstein: The True Story* (1973) provides a 200-minute spectacle about a monster whose seamless "wholeness" is an illusion. As such, the television movie itself becomes allegorical of the breakdown of the ideology that sustained a normative "white male" viewer as the industry standard. Made from motley parts—and motley means both heterogeneous and multicolored—*this* monster cannot hold together under the façade of an unmarked subjectivity. This monster is the mass audience of a diverse and conflicted nation, which makes the television industry none other than Frankenstein—the one who produces the monster, that confused sum greater than its parts, whose revolt and death often leads "us" to confuse the poor creature with its maker, Dr. Frankenstein. Once this reversal takes place, once effect obscures cause, the discourse of violence points in one direction alone: the status quo.

By the time the U.S. Commission on Civil Rights issued its two-part report, *Window Dressing on the Set* (1977 and 1979), violence no longer functioned as an impetus for social change.[92] Thus, even though *Window Dressing on the Set* provides an invaluable insight into the nature and extent of racial and gender discrimination in television and lays out policy recommendations that are substantive, practical, and legally sound, the report falls flat in its reliance on the discourse of violence first articulated in the Kerner report (1968) and embedded in the EEOC hearings (1969). In other words, the report had little to no impact insofar as the state sanctioned the marketplace as the arena within which to resolve these problems. Two decades after their publication, the reports' findings and recommendations continue to apply, but are not applied.[93]

In examining the discourse of violence, however, there is more at stake than meets the eye. Industry and government documents constitute a vast portion of the existing primary sources for telling this history. In the 1970s, *Broadcasting* was an important source of information on the industry, FCC policy, and the reform movement, but its $35 per year subscription rate meant that most media reform groups could not afford to obtain copies.[94] In any case, historical sources—whether generated by the state, industry, or Chicano activists—now reside in the archive of the state and industry, in both a metaphorical and a literal sense. In fact, the only place I could find the NMAADC pamphlet *Chicanos and the Mass Media* was in the Federal Trade Commission library.[95] Such a situation says a lot about who knew this history, when, and to what ends. It is ironic, to say the least, that the early history of "Chicano cinema" resides in the archive of those institutions that placed it on their margins: the state and industry.

In the late 1960s and early 1970s, the struggle over access to and control of the mass media brought together conflicting notions of ethnic community and national identity, communication and capital, stereotypes and employment, while violence provided a rationale for linking these social spheres, basic infrastructures, and symbolic and material representations into an agenda for social equity. When Chicanos protested the broadcast media, the state intervened and redirected their protest to the policy arena, offering them a quid pro quo: the state would participate in constituting minorities as distinct groups with an identity and place within the body politic; and, in exchange, that place would be an informal one that did not challenge the structure of rule. Nevertheless, in the gaps between quid and quo, citizen groups were able to assert the public interest, creating employment opportunities and programming that corresponded to their local communities. But by the mid-1970s, social and economic conditions had changed, causing media activists to shift from a representational to a corporatist arena. The next chapter examines the early trainee programs and public affairs shows that were concurrent with this first period of media activism. It is here that the history of Chicano cinema usually begins.

six

Training the Activists to Shoot Straight
A Political Generation in U.S. Cinema

Between 1968 and 1973, media trainee programs and film school admissions policies brought Chicano student activists into the "industry" within the context of the ongoing Chicano civil rights movement. These programs were notable for being multiracial, bringing together mostly working class students who often had limited interaction with other racial groups and limited experience with higher education. These students did not know the "class" codes—that is, the confluence of social class and the classroom—that made professional training as much an issue of social networking as of acquiring technical expertise. Furthermore, because their access to higher education was secured by and tied to a social movement predicated on cultural nationalisms, minority film students challenged an educational system based on class rise (or maintenance), "addressing issues of culture, identity, and social protest."[1] But class rise took place, too, and that goes some way toward explaining the conflicts and contradictions inherent in this period. Thus, when we write about Chicano cinema, it is important to remember that its pioneers were not just militant activists, but also first-generation college students caught up in the "shock of the new," who were, above all, quite young and inexperienced. In other words, these agents of social change —these *veteranos* of the movement—were also, as Mauricio Mazón notes about the pachuco zoot-suiters of the 1940s, "youth facing problems of maturation, rebellion, and identity confusion."[2] It is this combination that generated social change.

In addition to direct confrontations with faculty members and administration, minority film students challenged their programs' object of desire: Hollywood. As Luis Garza explains, "we were going to revolutionize the whole film industry and present opposite points of view and document what had never been documented before."[3] Thus, Chicano film students whose personal motivations were to make Hollywood feature films nevertheless devoted themselves to documenting ongoing social protests, among other organizing activities. In this respect, Sylvia Morales's account of her own career is typical: "I am an artist, and my goal has always been to make feature films, [but] I got sidetracked into documentaries."[4] She explains: "The non-color students were involved with films concerning personal relationships, personal films. But for us there was a sense of urgency, so we set aside our desire to make personal films in order to make ones which reflected our communities."[5] The decision was a political one—made in contradistinction to the personal, affiliated with the communal, and laden with professional consequences.

As an experiential cohort entering the film and television industry through its professional schools, these nonwhite students were both thrown together with each other and segregated from whites in minority programs. The situation was somewhat similar to the minority hiring pools established by the EEOC in its settlement agreement with the industry in 1970. For the most part, the classroom became secondary to ongoing social protests and the students' own social parties, both of which brought together different racial groups as well as male and female students. These encounters expanded affinities and affiliations but also revealed conflicts based on "insensitivities" and "personalities" that were often presented as ideological differences.[6] Whites were not the only ones who had to learn to deal with racial and sexual difference, but the minority students had political, curricular, and professional reasons for undertaking the effort.

The Education of a Political Generation

Two Los Angeles–based programs provided the main entry points for Chicano filmmakers: New Communicators (1968) and the UCLA Ethno-Communications Program (1969–73).[7] These programs, especially the latter, are often credited with giving rise to independent film movements based on racial identity groups: Chicano, African American, Asian American, and Native American.[8] While these "cinemas" are often relegated to separate histories and read as distinct genres, the students' shared experiences of social crisis and change during their formative years provide the basis for a sociology of a multiracial "political generation" in the U.S. cinema. As the historian Mario T. García explains, "[A] political generation consciously and politically reacts to its historical era. . . . Moreover, a political generation emerges not just in reaction to history but in order to make history—that is, to produce and consolidate significant social changes in an environment conducive to such changes."[9] Between 1968 and 1973, film schools provided a space within which a political generation emerged for whom race organized a loose set of socioaesthetic influences that are consistent for being largely auteur driven. These influences included the "golden age" of television documentary, the Mexico western of the Vietnam era, a "new wave" within the industry (including Francis Ford Coppola, at that time a recent graduate of UCLA and "the first major American director to have graduated from a university film program"[10]), the rise of U.S. independent cinema, and exposure to Third World films (especially as theorized by the filmmakers of the New Latin American Cinema). The students in the UCLA Ethno-Communications Program were largely conscious of being a "generation" within this milieu. In fact, the Chicano filmmakers often refer to each entering class between 1969 and 1973 as a distinct "generation," indicating the volatility of social change in the period, but also establishing internal distinctions among an experiential cohort who are now working in the industry.

The New Communicators

In the summer of 1968, the U.S. Office of Economic Opportunity funded a program called New Communicators that was designed to train minorities for employment in the film industry. With a board of directors composed of various progressives within Hollywood, the program "recruited about twenty students, largely Blacks and Chicanos, with a few Indians and one or two token hippie-type white guys."[11] Through intensive hands-on training with film graduate students from the University of Southern California, the students were to advance from Super-8 to 16mm over the course of one year. The program fell apart within eight months due to internal conflicts, including demands for minority teachers as well as more aggressive and extremist dissent by a student representative who was possibly an agent provocateur. Nevertheless, the program provided several Chicanos with their first exposure to the film industry: Jesús Salvador Treviño, Esperanza Vásquez, Francisco Martinez, and Martín Quiroz. It also provided access to film equipment that allowed the Chicano and Black "communicators" to film events in their communities.

Treviño, who had just received a bachelor's degree in philosophy from Occidental College, used a Super-8 and later a 16mm camera from the New Communicators to document the events surrounding the high school walkouts in East Los Angeles. Treviño was already involved in the Educational Issues Coordinating Committee (EICC) formed in the Chicano community after the March 1968 blow-outs.[12] With his camera, he documented the board of education hearings into the firing of a high school teacher, Sal Castro, for his role in the walkouts, and the EICC sit-in and arrests after the board refused the appeal to reinstate him. Treviño himself was later arrested after he drove off in an effort to save the film, although the police never checked his trunk, where the undeveloped film was hidden.[13] Using ten to twelve hours of raw footage, Treviño edited together several films in early 1969 as part of his training at New Communicators. These include La Raza Nueva (The New People), on Super-8 with sound and narration on a separate tape cassette, and Ya Basta! (Enough Already!), on 16mm. La Raza Nueva documents the March 1968 blow-outs, the conspiracy trial of the L.A. Thirteen, and the Castro hearings and sit-in. In Ya Basta! Treviño experiments with jump cuts, dramatic re-creations, and multiple story lines, which re-emerge in Treviño's later television documentaries La Raza Unida and Yo Soy Chicano (both 1972). The free-form docudrama intercuts blown-up footage from La Raza Nueva with a dramatic sequence about a teenage boy with troubles at home and school. By the end of the film, the boy's death seems almost a direct outcome of the Board of Education's refusal to reinstate Castro.

While these films appear primitive and incoherent according to mass media conventions, their effective use within the EICC and Chicano community at that time suggests another way of understanding early artistic expressions within the movement. As Treviño himself argues, the free-form style of Ya Basta! relied upon the fact that "so much of this was self-evident to the audience."[14] Thus, the film—as with the emerging Chicano visual arts, performance, and literature—served the needs of an audience whose main concern was the organization of a "community" and not the craft of an autonomous, objective, or artistic statement. To that extent, watching a Chicano film about an event experienced firsthand by many of the audience members played a role in community building, becoming more important than the actual form and content of the film, even, for the moment, more important than its ability to function within the mass media. Soon after, however, Treviño would enter public television.

The Ethno-Communications Program

While the New Communicators provided Treviño and others with an abbreviated introduction to the industry, UCLA served as the main entry point in the early 1970s for those filmmakers whose work would also define Chicano cinema: Moctesuma Esparza, David García Jr., Luis Garza, Sylvia Morales, Alex Nogales, Jeff Penichet, Susan Racho, Tony Rodriquez, and José Luis Ruiz, as well as former New Communicators Esperanza Vásquez and Francisco Martinez. As was the case with Treviño and Luis Valdez (before he joined the farmworkers' movement), the student movement served as the context for the UCLA group. As Esparza explains:

> We were all students at the time, deeply involved in the walk outs, completely engaged, living that as our daily life. And we were at that time film students. And we applied what we were learning to what we were living in the social protest movement. . . . We were all making documentaries at that time and the film was being defined by the social protest movement.[15]

But although Chicanos such as Racho, Morales, García, and Esparza had entered UCLA between 1966 and 1968, it was not until the creation of the Ethno-Communications Program, in 1969, that the film school enrolled "the first group of Third World film students."[16] The program was initiated by Eliseo Taylor, a Black professor in film production who brought in Esparza as a "hired gun" to recruit students, design the curriculum, and raise funds.[17] Although he was a history major, not a film student, Esparza drew upon his considerable skills as an organizer within the Chicano student movement. (In fact, at the time, Esparza was one of the L.A. Thirteen fighting conspiracy charges for the 1968 blow-outs.) Esparza and twelve other minority students, including Martinez and Garza, formed a multiracial group called the Media Urban Crisis Committee, with "Mother Muccers" as its acronym.[18] The group staged sit-ins and other protests that resulted in the establishment of a pilot program for ethnocommunications, with the Mother Muccers as its first class.[19] Ethnocommunications operated as an affirmative action program that opened the doors to minority undergraduates in other departments. But it existed outside the film department proper, hiring its own instructors (graduate film students David García Jr. and Charles Burnett) and implementing its own curriculum (modeled after the departmental one). The Mother Muccers continued to agitate, however, bringing about a new policy that 25 percent of all undergraduate and graduate admissions to the film department should be from racial minority groups.[20] The students also reached outside the department for material support, receiving university-wide tuition waivers and financial aid as well as work-study and research assistantships from the newly created ethnic studies centers. The program continued as a student-driven recruiting mechanism until about 1973, enrolling a number of students who remain active filmmakers today: Black students Larry Clark, Haile Gerima, and Ben Caldwell; Asian American students Eddie Wong, Betty Chin, Duane Kubo, Steven Taksukawa, and Robert Nakamura; and Native American student Sandy Osawa.[21]

Needless to say, students entered the program with a strong sense of mission. Garza—who was already a photographer for *La Raza* magazine—describes the program's students as alternative journalists: "We went about covering campus demonstrations, street demonstrations. We were the journalists of the time, but from a totally different perspective that wasn't done before."[22] In addition to documenting local events, the students hit the road in order to learn about location shooting, traveling through the Central Valley and into the Bay Area, gathering footage on the Black Panthers, Asian American farmworkers in the Central California Loc region, Chicano studies at Berkeley, and the Bay Area Native American Center. As Steven Taksukawa explains, "[T]hese visits stimulated films. The Loc footage became a Visual Communications film on Asian American farmworkers in the Delta entitled *Pieces of a Dream*."[23]

But perhaps the most significant example of how these students acted as the "journalists of the time" is *Requiem-29* (1971). As Renee Tajima writes, "The essentially political orientation of the Ethno program was evident in the film *Requiem 29*, a major production of the pilot group (along with the teaching assistant, David García)."[24] The students documented the Chicano Moratorium against the Vietnam War on August 29, 1970, a peaceful march involving over 20,000 people, including many families, that ended at Laguna Park, where a cultural program was staged. Musical groups played corridos while children performed Mexican folk dances. Shortly after a musical performance of "La Punitiva" (about Pancho Villa), while the audience applauded, police entered Laguna Park in military formation, apparently in response to a minor incident one block from the park. Soon numbering 1,200 officers, they fired tear gas canisters, clubbed fleeing or prone marchers, made numerous arrests, and repeatedly maced marchers whom they had already handcuffed and detained in buses. Three people were killed, two of them by tear gas projectiles. During the riot, a sheriff's deputy shot a ten-inch tear gas canister into the Silver Dollar Cafe, not up into the ceiling, but down into the journalist Ruben Salazar's head, killing him instantly. Despite pleas from two of Salazar's colleagues, police left his body in the bar for two hours before entering.[25]

The moratorium was the culmination of a series of earlier demonstrations organized by the National Chicano Moratorium Committee, which was formed by the Brown Berets in order to protest the high casualty rate among Chicanos fighting in Vietnam (roughly twice their demographic representation). Salazar, a columnist for the *Los Angeles Times* and the news director for KMEX-TV, "provided a voice for the millions of Chicanos who had been denied a public forum for years by institutions such as the *Times.*"[26] Thus, although Salazar rejected the label of "Chicano newsman," seeing himself as a professional journalist, his reportage on the increasing police-community tensions went against the grain of a news media whose status as a fourth estate brought it no closer to minority communities. In fact, Salazar was already under investigation by the FBI and LAPD for his coverage of police abuse in the Chicano community, including the recent killing of two Mexican nationals. The police chief, Ed Davis, had tried to have Salazar fired from the *Los Angeles Times,* and shortly before the moratorium a sheriff threatened Salazar in person, warning him, "You had better stop stirring up the Mexicans."[27]

Following Salazar's death, a coroner's inquest held hearings that were broadcast in their entirety on the local television stations. For an inquest, a hearing officer without judicial standing provides impartial oversight over the proceedings. Seven jurors then vote on the probable cause of death. In this instance, however, the hearing officer red-baited Chicano photographers offering visual evidence of police abuse in an attempt to discredit their testimony. Meanwhile, he also allowed the sheriff's department to introduce immaterial facts unrelated to Salazar's death. The sheriff's department opened the televised proceedings with an edited movie of the riots produced by its own film crew and later introduced selected photographs of looting around the Silver Dollar Cafe, as well as other testimony that suggested that the Chicano community was by its nature inclined to riot. In the end, despite a four-to-three vote finding "death at the hands of another," the district attorney decided not to prosecute, leading to other demonstrations over the next five months that also ended in riots incited by police officers or agents provocateurs. In each case, the news media looked no further than police information, which presented the demonstrators' retaliation as an unprovoked attack and also red-baited movement leaders.[28] Many Chicanos believed that the televised inquest and other media accounts represented blatant propaganda that used photographs and film in order to reverse causality.

Requiem-29 took up the difficult challenge of a counterstatement: how to represent the "truth" when the means of representation are controlled by a mass media working with the justice system. After all, these two institutions effectively redirected attention from the issue at hand to the "immaterial" facts that reinforce the status quo. In response, *Requiem-29* necessarily refuses to adhere to one of the major documentary modes—expository, observational, interactive, and reflexive[29]—that would then offer a stable orientation toward the truth: that it can be either told, observed, solicited, or exposed as a construct. Instead, *Requiem-29* modifies the observational mode—a "direct cinema" in which the filmmaker records in the midst of breaking events—making the film not so much a "document" of the truth as a "requiem" for the truth as embodied in Ruben Salazar's death. The film then extends its requiem to include the futile testimony of Raul Ruiz as well as the filmmakers' own efforts. It is important to remember that the film spoke against media representations influenced by the police's own production of visual narrative, whether in edited film (broadcast on television) or selected photographs (printed in newspapers).

The film makes an explicit contrast between the inquest (as mass media event) and its own project (as alternative cinema) in opening with a juxtaposition of two "truths" about Salazar's death: the legal (the inquest hearings) and the spiritual (the requiem). If the former was intended to determine the probable cause of Salazar's death, it did so as a public, hence, political event, while the latter represented a private, hence, familial ceremony—a mass for the repose of Salazar's soul. *Requiem-29* uses this distinction in order to step outside the objectivity associated with the mass media and justice system without also giving up a notion of the truth. The film opens with a shot of the start of the inquest, cuts to the requiem, returns to the inquest as it introduces the first exhibit (the projectile that killed Salazar), then returns to the requiem as mourners pass by the casket. It is the requiem that motivates a flashback to the moratorium as a sound dissolve removes mourners' sobbing and introduces chants of "Chicano power." The film then cuts from a shot of Salazar in an open casket to a shot of the back of a marcher whose shirt bears an image of the Mexican flag and the words "Viva la Raza" (long live the Mexican people; literally, long live the race). The shot sequence establishes a causality: the affirmation of the Mexican race will end in Salazar's death by the American system. But, in reversing chronology, the film moves from death to life, also suggesting a rebirth rooted in the cause. In this way, the film identifies its documentary project with the requiem in contradistinction to the inquest, identifying the latter as part of a broader institutional realism bounded by the state (which also includes television). Like a requiem, the film seeks life in death, and, as such, its concerns over causality are not about chronology per se, but about the rupture in institutional realism—whether understood as a leap of faith, an epistemological break, or consciousness raising—that will result in social change.

Following the opening sequence, the film documents the march through the streets of East Los Angeles followed by a musical performance at Laguna Park, alternating between ground-level and overhead shots. In the midst of recording the marchers applauding, the film does a swish pan away from the stage (from ground level), then cuts to an overhead shot (from the stage) of the police entering the park in military formation and full riot gear. In the ensuing police riot, the cameras document the melee as police fire tear gas and club marchers, while some Chicanos retaliate and throw rocks and tear gas canisters back at the police. The scene ends with an on-the-spot interview of a young Chicana who cannot believe police attacked the peaceful event and who recounts taking refuge in a restroom with a mother and her children, whereupon the police tear-gassed them.

If the scenes from the march and police riot posed the question "Why did the police attack the moratorium?," the next scene upsets viewer expectations of an immediate answer, revealing instead how the inquest itself displaced that question onto one about Chicanos' criminality. The film cuts to the inquest, where the hearing officer is questioning Raul Ruiz, the photographer and editor of La Raza magazine, about whether he has evidence of Chicanos breaking police car windows. Instead, Ruiz presents a photograph of a Chicano who is being lifted off the ground by an officer holding a club around the man's neck while nine other officers beat him, including one who is laughing. The hearing officer, however, questions Ruiz's ability to determine that the officers are using force. A frustrated Ruiz then challenges the hearing officer's line of questioning, since it has nothing to do with the inquest proper, but also since he did not question the sheriff's photographers as well. What is at stake is a struggle over the evidentiary status of Ruiz's photographs: for the hearing officer, photographs of looting are self-evident, while photographs of police violence require an authoritative interpretation. In effect, the film reveals that the Salazar inquest is not even about Salazar's death—and hence police violence against Chicanos—but about Chicanos as violent criminals who can only provide visual evidence against themselves.

In this context, Ruiz becomes the voice of reason, first in challenging the hearing officer, then through on-the-spot interviews filmed outside the courtroom. For example, Ruiz is the one who explains the legal role of the hearing officer as someone who is supposed to be impartial, rather than represent the sheriff's department and allow immaterial evidence to be entered. That this "rule of law" statement occurs outside the courtroom shifts authority to Ruiz and, by extension, the filmmakers. *Requiem-29* then alternates between the inquest and the Ruiz interview throughout the rest of the film, using Ruiz's outside commentary to motivate subsequent cuts to the inquest. Describing the hearing officer's red-baiting, Ruiz says, "but he said," and the film cuts to the hearing officer's question about Ernesto "Che" Guevara (whom he refers to as "Mr. Castro's man"). In the next scene, Ruiz explains how the hearing officer has clouded Chicano testimony and distracted the hearings from the question at hand: "Who killed Ruben Salazar?" The film then cuts to a close-up of the deputy who fired the tear gas canister into the Silver Dollar Cafe, now testifying before the inquest. In this manner, Ruiz's recollections supersede the present tense of the inquest established in the film's opening shot, reinforcing the nonchronological time established in the transition from the requiem to the moratorium. Occurring in medias res, the Ruiz interview occupies an ambivalent present tense insofar as it marks the inquest as both a foregone conclusion (past) and something still ongoing (future). The film then uses this ambivalent time frame to argue Salazar's death and inquest as the cause of the moratorium itself. In fact, the film works against chronology not just in the editing but in the cinematography, creating a sense of anticipation about the immediate past. During Ruiz's commentary on the hearing officer's red-baiting, for example, the camera tilts up and zooms in on a poster of "La Raza Peace Moratorium," pans lefts to a poster of Che Guevara, and then pulls back as Ruiz describes the hearing officer's question about a marcher's "¡Viva Che!" sign in one of Ruiz's photographs.

After the deputy's description of the shooting, the film returns to Ruiz a final time. Here he concludes, "In reality the rights which people thought that they had are no longer really there." Ruiz ends by arguing that Chicanos "must look to themselves . . . for justice . . . because there's nobody else who's going to help them, absolutely nobody." As he speaks, the film dissolves to the start of the moratorium with a shot of a Brown Beret banner passing the camera, followed by uniformed Brown Berets marching in tight formation. A trumpet call and marching drums underscore the militant sense of the shot and Ruiz's words. The film then cuts to a shot of the Mexican flag passing the camera, followed by numerous Chicanos in street clothes who amble along the march route. It is at this point—in the final shots of the film—that the marching drums break into a full orchestral rendition of "La Adelita," a Mexican love song that is the unofficial anthem of the Mexican revolution. Mexican revolutionary nationalism—invoked by the flag and "La Adelita"—brokers the leap from the militantly separatist position of Ruiz and the Brown Berets to the shots of "everyday" Chicanos participating in the moratorium. These people are, in fact, the addressees of Ruiz's final call to action; it is in this sense that the moratorium becomes the afterlife of Salazar's death.

If, as Mario T. García notes, Salazar's death and inquest "silenced an expression of hope that American society would keep its promises,"[30] *Requiem-29* found itself in a peculiar relationship to documentary production. On the one hand, as Bill Nichols argues in *Representing Reality,* documentary filmmakers can "talk about anything in the historical world," and, to that extent, they are not regulated.[31] On the other hand, for Chicanos, the "fluid nature of an institution, apparatus, or discourse" for documentary proved to be more viscid when it came to matters of broadcast and distribution.[32] Not everything flowed into the social imaginary. In this respect, the ethnocommunications filmmakers understood documentary not as an abstract form but as a specific mode of discourse circulating on television and upholding the violence of the state in the service of "whiteness." It is this self-consciousness about their exclusion from the mass media that figures into the film's unique relationship to documentary realism. While not self-reflexive in formal terms, the fact that *Requiem-29* exposes the construction of "truth" within its subject matter cannot help but be read back into the film itself, even as it attempts to return the Chicano viewer to the material world.[33] In this sense, *Requiem-29* fulfills the function Nichols ascribes to the reflexive mode: "As a political concept, reflexivity grounds itself in the materiality of representation but turns, or returns, the viewer beyond the text, to those material practices that inform the body politic."[34] But the materiality to which the film returns its viewer is, in fact, a situation in which neither the state nor the mass media acts as a guarantor of rights—that is, neither rule of law nor objectivity can be called upon to make the system work. And so the film makes another argument. Salazar had represented the possibility of an "objective" and professional journalism incorporating Chicanos into the body politic. Given his brutal death, however, the "journalists of the time" necessarily stepped outside the body politic, and it is from this position that Ruiz— as the film's implied narrator—calls for Chicanos to go it alone in the search for justice. As such the film is an example of a direct cinema about the impossibility of objectivity—direct or otherwise—for Chicanos as U.S. citizens. But its critique is institutional, not epistemological.

If the film riffs off a traditional realist mode in order to question the "truth" of its subject matter, it does so without quite becoming reflexive. Instead, the film offers a requiem that mourns the democratic possibility of *the* public sphere, turning instead to a Chicano public sphere where the truth could be asserted, just not broadcast. Then the exception proved the rule: its student producers—beaten up by police, fighting conspiracy charges, and under political surveillance—went on to become media professionals, making documentaries for a "public" that can only be reached through a state-regulated, commercially driven industry. In this respect, Chicano cinema begins with its own requiem.

By most accounts, ethnocommunications never had strong support within the department, especially given its challenge to the department's own mission of training filmmakers for the entertainment industry. As Duane Kubo recalls: "David García and other advisors to Ethno were constantly under fire from the rest of the faculty to produce competent filmmakers, as opposed to political activists." [35] Ironically, the program itself experienced an internal conflict along pretty much the same lines. The earlier militant students who had opened up the film school felt that later students did not appreciate their efforts, arguing that these new students presented themselves as "individuals" wanting to make it in Hollywood.[36] This perceived split between radical and reformist goals would become the focus of intellectual debate over the function of Chicano cinema into the early 1980s. To a large extent, however, the distinction had less to do with whether to "go" Hollywood than with how to approach the industry.

For the students at that time, however, the split between "activists" and "individuals" marked rather pure boundaries between being inside and outside the movement. But it also masked a question about gender insofar as the masculine orientation of these debates precluded the role of women within the movement.[37] Indeed, minority women encountered sexism among their cohort in the program as well as racism and sexism in facing the department and, later, the industry.[38] For such militant activists as Esparza, being involved in "feminist issues" was distinct from being involved in "the movement." In this manner, Sylvia Morales and Susan Racho were "there at the beginning," but also not there as equal participants in the development of the idea of a Chicano cinema predicated on social change.[39] Women's issues were effectively outside its definition, an exclusion that extended to most other identity groups, wherein feminism became coded as "white."[40] This catch-22 placed Chicanas—and other women of color—both inside and outside the movement. As Patricia Zavella writes: "Framed by larger historical forces and political struggles, identifying myself as a Chicana feminist meant contesting and simultaneously drawing from Chicano nationalist ideology and white feminism—being an insider and outsider within both movements and ideologies."[41]

But for Morales, the problem had less to do with placing "feminism"—since she didn't identify with the term—on the margins than with her growing disillusionment over the inconsistencies in her male colleagues' radical rhetoric.

> I recall in one film class led by David García, he sat there . . . and he looked at me and he said, "Well, the film is the thing." "That's the thing to be involved in," he says. "Boy," he says, "once you get going you have money, you can have women following you all over the

place." I was really idealistic. I thought we were going to change the world. So . . . after he said that I was kind of stunned, and [then] he said, "Okay, I want to know from all of you what kinds of movies you want to make." And he started down the line and most everyone, until it came to me, put out . . . essentially this time the man who was going to ride in on the white horse was going to be a Chicano. He was going to clean up the town, and he was going to get that white woman at the end. I was stunned and very hurt. And when he came to me I said, "I'm not going to tell you the kind of movies I want to make because I'm shocked at everything you're saying here. I thought we were here to change the world and what you're talking about is just replacing what is with yourselves." I think this was the beginning of my disillusionment. . . . And when I said that David said, "Well, Sylvia's right, you know. We've got to be serious." I mean this is my recollection, and recollections of course can take on mythic proportions, and I don't remember any more about that class, but I do remember that as being my first like, what I thought was like a slap in the face.[42]

Morales's equanimity reflects her present-day understanding of the past as a site where Chicano and Chicana youth mediated between the political and the personal. I do not mean to excuse sexism as a function of youth, but rather, *pace* Morales, to acknowledge the particular coordinates within which the ethnocommunications students engaged these and other conflicts based on difference. In a sense, the "mythic proportions" belong less to the present than they do to the past, when first-generation students negotiated between a national social crisis, militant demands for change, institutional racism, and their own ambivalent class rise. The myth, of course, is that these students had the answer to these problems, when, in fact, their lives became increasingly marked by the peculiar contradictions and limitations of social change in the United States. In short, by subscribing to a divide between the political and the personal—what has been called the public and private spheres—Chicano students found their public demand upon the "representational system" undercut by their own private desires to reproduce its social imaginary. Morales and most other Chicano students turned to documentaries cut to the needs of a social movement, but they really wanted to make Chicano feature films in Hollywood. For the men, this private desire produced an even more startling contradiction with their political ideals. Like their counterparts—the actor-turned-activist Ray Martell, the critics Thomas M. Martinez and José Peralez, and the editors of *La Raza*—Chicano filmmakers railed against Manifest Destiny while they also sought to reshoot its masculine metanarrative as a Chicano western. In contrast to these highly personal desires, which then found symbolic political expression in Chicano cultural nationalism, Chicana filmmakers produced documentaries wherein the personal either embodied a pastoral "Mexican" tradition set against "American" capitalism (Esperanza Vásquez's *Agueda Martinez: Our People, Our Country* [1977]) or gave way to a political critique of gender strongly based on class analysis (Susan Racho's *Garment Workers* [1975] and Sylvia Morales's *Chicana* [1979]). Contrary to stereotype, both Chicanos and Chicanas developed cultural identities strongly vested in gender and sexuality; but whereas the men foregrounded an implicitly masculine and heterosexual norm, the women subordinated race, gender and sexuality to a largely socioeconomic nationalism. In either case, however, for the filmmakers the personal remained outside the political, the one obscuring the other.

As a "political generation," the ethnocommunications students lived through these contradictions with each other, and it is in this sense that the political became quite personal, and vice versa. This generation learned to work together despite their differences—out of necessity and shared purpose—crewing for each other on their UCLA projects and later on their public affairs series, documentaries, and dramatic films.[43] This generation also founded and organized the key institutions for the new minority cinemas. These included two public broadcasting consortia—the Latino Consortium (headed first by Ruiz and later by Morales) and the National Asian American Telecommunications Association—as well as numerous movement-oriented production entities, most notably Visual Communications.[44] The immediate goal, however, was to shoot straight.

Prime-Time Access

Given the ongoing social crisis and an impatience to gain access to equipment and make relevant films, a number of the students in the Ethno-Communications Program dropped out after a year or two in order to produce newly created public affairs shows.[45] José Luis Ruiz and Luis Garza dropped out of UCLA and produced television series for the local ABC affiliate, hiring their fellow students Sylvia Morales, Jessie Corona, and Betty Chin (Ruiz, *Unidos,* 1970–71); and Susan Racho, David García Jr., and Tony Rodriguez (Garza, *Reflecciones,* 1972–73). After *Unidos,* Ruiz went to NBC, where he produced the series *Impacto*

(1973) as well as the Emmy Award–winning documentary specials *Los Vendidos* (1972), *Cinco Vidas* (1973), and *The Unwanted* (1975). Other Chicano public affairs series in Los Angeles included *¡Ahora!* (1969–70) and *Acción Chicano* (1972–74), both KCET-TV, and *The Siesta Is Over* (1972–973) and *Bienvenidos* (1973), both KNXT-TV (now KCBS-TV). These local television shows and specials provided initial, albeit contested outlets for Chicano-produced film related to the issues, protests, and goals of the Chicano movement. These and other minority programs aired during prime time as part of the Prime Time Access Rule (PTAR) established in 1970.[46] In an effort to increase local programming, the PTAR limited network programming to three hours during prime time: 7–11 P.M. eastern and Pacific time (6–10 P.M. central and mountain time). The first hour of prime time became the "access" hour, situated between the evening news and network programming. In the early 1970s, concomitant with the media reform movement, the PTAR facilitated the emergence of community-based programs during prime time, providing the training ground for a "political generation" of minority producers.

Chicano documentaries—produced as specials or as segments within public affairs series—reflected the aesthetic priorities of the Chicano movement, the stylistic influence of the network documentary of the early 1960s, and a willingness to experiment that came, by and large, from ignorance of television conventions. Chicano students thrust into new roles as television producers set out to "revolutionize the industry," although many of them did not know what a producer did in the first place. When Luis Garza applied to the ABC affiliate for a position as a cameraman, he was offered the opportunity to produce a television series instead. "And I debated whether to pursue the job as an assistant cameraman or take the job as a producer . . . because I didn't know what a producer was!"[47] Thus, as they attempted to address social issues within the television industry, these novice producers quickly learned about and confronted its aesthetic, economic, and ideological constraints. In fact, Garza was hired to produce a replacement series for *Unidos,* which often ran afoul of the station for its coverage of the Chicano community, including sympathetic interviews with welfare mothers and *pintos* (Chicano prisoners). *Unidos* also included episodes on Native Americans and Asian Americans, groups that did not have public affairs programs, while the production crew worked together closely to create a community-based program and style that stemmed, in part, "out of ignorance of the rules."[48] Eventually, KABC fired the producer, José Luis Ruiz, his staff resigned in protest, and the station—still under pressure to respond to community needs—hired the inexperienced Garza. "It was designed to fail," as Garza explains, especially since the station budgeted less than $3,000 per show, including salaries and production costs for a two-week period. "It was really sink or swim. I had never done a television show before in my life. I had no idea."[49]

Against the odds, *Reflecciones* became one of the more innovative Chicano series, subverting the "objective" discourse of reportage in order to pioneer a new form of television, the political documentary series. *Reflecciones* protested the Vietnam War, advocated a farmworkers' union, and exposed the racism of the criminal legal system, while it also reported on Wounded Knee and the civil rights struggles of Puerto Ricans in New York. Because of the overt and radical positions the program took, the station "tried to prevent us from airing some of the shows we did."[50] But because Garza conformed to the legal parameters of journalism—the presentation of both sides of the story and the documentation and verification of sources and information—the station was unable to censor or withhold controversial shows.[51]

Reflecciones was as unique in style as in its radical objectivity. The show used no on-air host; instead, each episode began in medias res and developed its critique through shot composition, fast cutting, and perspective shots, all reinforced or counterpointed through the use of diverse musical styles. Even the conventional "voice of God" narration proved different on two accounts. First, Alfonso Tafoya's otherwise unmarked, implicitly "white" voice-over would drop into Spanish-language pronunciation for such Spanish-origin place-names as "California" and "Sacramento." Second, the narration, written by Tony Rodriguez, relied heavily upon direct quotations, either juxtaposing outrageous statements with the narrator's pointed commentary, providing the semblance of balance, or using a historical figure to assert a point of view (for example, quoting Jack London on strikebreakers). Thus, *Reflecciones,* unlike *Unidos* and other Chicano talk shows, was able to synthesize the various techniques and styles previously used to interrupt the talk show format, creating instead a consistent, hybrid documentary format:

> The thematic variety of the shows dealt with Chicanismo, Mexicanismo. Chicanismo in the sense that we were exploring who we were here within the context of the United States. Mexicanismo in terms of

the tradition and the legacy of our history. So, we took the documentary approach, but not just in terms of documentaries, in that we attempted to weave in story lines, in that we attempted to create images that were beyond just a documentary format. It was exploratory for us, there were no rules.[52]

Like earlier Chicano series, *Reflecciones* mixed an eclectic coverage of current issues with cultural investigations, incorporating dramatizations and low-budget special effects into its documentaries. In the opening sequence of an episode on Wounded Knee, for example, Garza worked out a shot of a slowly rotating Indian-head nickel, simulating a coin toss, while the narrator read a list of broken treaties, massacres, and so on. Between coin tosses, Garza interspersed rapid-fire montage of images related to the conquest of Native Americans. *Reflecciones* also developed an extensive network of progressive sources that often resulted in material previously not shown on commercial television. For an episode on a Chicano pilot shot down over Vietnam, for example, *Reflecciones* acquired Vietnamese footage of captured American pilots. But *Reflecciones* was perhaps most effective in its subversion of objective journalism, presenting both sides of a story while using visual techniques to contextualize statements, much in the same way that the narration provided historical context for contemporary events. In the episode on the Chicano pilot, *Reflecciones* juxtaposed interviews with the pilot's anti-Communist father and antiwar sister but placed a rear-projection screen beside the sister, running slides of bombing devastation and napalm casualties to underscore her point about the war. Later in the episode, aerial footage from a training film of bombing missions and dogfights was offset with a song by a Vietnamese woman, producing an eerie dissonance. In the end, the series's multiethnic and international perspective (and sources) reflected Garza's own involvement with the socialist Left, which included travel to Russia as part of a twenty-five-member American peace delegation in 1971. Garza was able to articulate that perspective within the framework of Chicano public affairs programming on prime-time commercial television for two years.

As these shows came to an end by 1974, producers set up independent production companies and turned toward professional advocacy and networking largely directed at public television. By the time the PTAR was rewritten in 1975,[53] local television stations had started running syndicated game shows (*Wheel of Fortune* and *Jeopardy*) and entertainment magazines (*P.M. Magazine, Entertainment Tonight, Hard*

Copy, and *A Current Affair*), while grouping together minority public affairs programming under multiracial series: *Pacesetters, Community Feedback,* and *Let's Rap.* In fact, although the PTAR voiced "local" concerns, the rule actually originated with broadcast corporations competing with the three networks. Indeed, the major force behind the PTAR had been Group W (Westinghouse): it owned five affiliated stations and produced syndicated programs, including *P.M. Magazine,* which began as a local "access" program called *Evening Magazine* in 1976. What made the PTAR briefly effective in facilitating community-based programming, then, had less to do with the corporate forces and motives behind the rule than with the legal and public pressures brought by the media reform movement before 1974. With the decline in effectiveness of these pressures, the PTAR mostly served the interests of the nonnetwork broadcast corporations. As Thomas Streeter notes, "The prime-time access rule in particular provides a clear illustration of mechanisms by which public complaints are subsumed under the question of competition, and by which the social aspects of the 'public interest' are supplanted by the interests of the various members of the broadcast industry." [54]

Given the reduction of federal regulation and foundation support on behalf of social issues, Chicano producers quickly lost their "access" to a regular prime-time audience through which they were able to address the public interest and participate in the public sphere. In effect, they became "independent" producers in the face of an exclusionary industry. What bridged the widening gap between this political generation and the social imaginary, then, was the "mere hyphen" of their own professionalism. It was a space Enrique Hank López had called "schizo-cultural limbo," and it would characterize Chicano television production in the quarter century since these shows ended. Before turning to the rise of Chicano professionalism, however, I want to examine two works by Luis Valdez and El Teatro Campesino that register this shift between the early and late 1970s.

Location and Narration

Luis Valdez occupies a number of central points in the Chicano movement, both as multitalented *veterano* and as object of critique—for his neo-indigenous spiritualism, for his desire to inhabit the mainstream, and for his paradoxical position as great-male founder and auteur of a collective ensemble. In addition, his career provides a template for Chicano activists who rejected reformism, turned to a cultural politics rooted in Mexican history and Third World radicalism, became professional artists and intellectuals, then returned—with a difference—to a reformist and integrationist "American" position. In 1964, before the Chicano movement, Valdez traveled to Cuba as a member of the Progressive Labor Party delegation. Like many Chicano student activists, he had been involved in reformist efforts directed at the Democratic Party, such as the Mexican American Political Association (MAPA), and had been active in the Viva Kennedy! clubs of 1960. Upon his return from Cuba, however, Valdez coauthored one of the first radical student manifestos, "Venceremos! Mexican American Statement on Travel to Cuba," which anchored its rejection of reformist politics in a pan-American solidarity and concluded, "Having no leaders of our own, we accept Fidel Castro."[55] In the late 1960s, Valdez cofounded El Teatro Campesino (ETC) under the aegis of the United Farm Workers (UFW), wrote the influential "Plan of Delano," worked on the film adaptation of "I Am Joaquin," then broke with the UFW, developing ETC as a professional theater group and articulating an aesthetic agenda based on neo-indigenous spirituality.[56] In this way, the earlier agitprop *actos* (skits), which addressed specific and pressing political issues, were now framed with *mitos* (myths) that explored spirituality and culture at large. The fact that Valdez placed social protests within a mythical and religious context caused Chicano critics to accuse him of mystification. In response, Valdez combined the *acto* and *mito* through the structural frame of musical performance—first using the corrido or ballad, then the stage musical—thereby emphasizing the artifice and reflexivity of the earlier didactic forms.[57]

By the 1970s, Valdez and ETC had become involved in television productions, most notably *Los Vendidos: The Sellouts* (1972) and *El Corrido* (1976). The revival of *teatro* in the mid-1960s, together with Valdez's movement toward film, provided Chicano cinema with a ready-made narrative form. Indeed, the use of *teatro* solved budget and schedule limitations, since a piece could be performed before several cameras in a television studio, then cut together as a video.[58] Between 1974 and 1975, ETC briefly attempted to establish a film production department at its headquarters in San Juan Bautista, recruiting José Luis Ruiz and Jesús Salvador Treviño to produce documentaries it had contracted with the McGraw-Hill *La Raza* series. Within a year, however, McGraw-Hill canceled the contract and shelved the first film, then in post-production.[59] In the 1980s, ETC ceased operation as an ensemble group, and Valdez turned to more mainstream projects, writing and directing two feature films for major studios (*Zoot Suit*, 1981, and *La Bamba*, 1987) and one made-for-cable movie (*The Cisco Kid*, 1994), among other projects.[60]

Yolanda Broyles-González has raised significant questions about the usual "great-man/text-centered/chronological-linear approach" to El Teatro Campesino, an approach that inscribes Valdez's biography as the ensemble's history.[61] What I am interested in here, however, has to do less with questions of authorship than with the specific institutional arenas within which Valdez emerged as a Chicano auteur. After the break with the UFW, Valdez's audience expanded beyond the Chicano movement, moving toward national, international, and mass audiences defined largely in terms of "whiteness." But as Valdez's address broadened, minority access to television narrowed, resulting in a shift from network to public television productions: *Los Vendidos* appeared on NBC, while *El Corrido* appeared on PBS, as did *Corridos* (1987) and *La Pastorela: A Shepherds' Tale* (1991). In adapting his work to television, then, Valdez encountered a cruel irony, moving from the local to the national, while also moving from prime-time commercial broadcast to the noncommercial, decentralized, and elite-oriented alternative of public television. It is in this context that Valdez became an auteur. While all his productions credit ETC, by the mid-1970s the group ceased to be associated with the title, becoming instead an adjunct to Valdez's authorship. *Los Vendidos* begins with the title sequence "El Teatro Campesino presents / Los Vendidos / The Sellouts," later adding the credit, "created and written by Luis Valdez." In contrast, *El Corrido* begins with the title sequence "El Corrido / by Luis Valdez / and El Teatro Campesino." In *La Pastorela,* the opening credits identify the producer (Richard D. Soto) and the writer-director (Luis Valdez). But ETC is only "credited" within the diegesis itself. After Valdez's credit appears, the camera pans to the right to reveal a tree with a poster for the performance later that night: "El Teatro Campesino / presents / La Pastorela." It is also in this context that Valdez shifted from defining the multivalent location within which a Chicano text becomes both particular and universal *(Los Vendidos)* to defining the culture-specific narrative structure through which it articulates a minority identity *(El Corrido, Corridos,* and *La Pastorela).* In short, becoming a Chicano auteur meant accepting a marginal location in the mass media, one that was allegorized in Valdez's narratives through the expression of an identity politics. Thus, if *teatro* provided a narrative form, the relationship of that form to local and national audiences, as well as to minority and mainstream discourses, posed more difficulties.

Location: *Los Vendidos*

The sense of emplacement, or that social space from which the text "speaks," is one that finds expression within early Chicano films, often through a direct reference to Aztlán, the Aztec homeland, which is thought to have been in the Southwest.[62] In the mythohistorical introduction to *Los Vendidos*, Valdez, dressed as an Aztec calendar, uses Aztlán as the fulcrum between the particularities of the Chicano movement and the universal, proclaiming, "We are El Teatro Campesino— the Farmworkers' Theater of Delano, of the grape strike, of the Chicano movement, of the *raza;* the Farmworkers' Theater of Aztlán, of the Southwest, of America, of the Earth; the Farmworkers' Theater of the Universe." Valdez's statement reveals a complex sense of the competing geographies within which the Chicano artists and intellectuals operated, interestingly positioning Aztlán as the summation of the particularities of *raza* politics, then locating "America" as a midpoint between these particularities and the universal. Here, the nation-state implicitly "mediates," producing a democratic public sphere in which, according to Ernesto Laclau, "different groups compete to give their particular aims a temporary function of universal representation."[63] In Valdez's statement, then, one finds a core metaphor for the project of Chicano *teatro cum* television to impact the Chicano community as well as broader audiences. One does not, after all, stand in Aztlán without also occupying the other spaces.

But, despite its mythohistorical introduction, *Los Vendidos* does not establish an equivalence between these spaces and their corresponding modes of social organization. Thus, while the *mito* that frames the video makes universal claims about the role of Chicano theater and indigenous culture,[64] the *acto* that makes up the core of *Los Vendidos* distinguishes between a "Chicano" audience able to identify with the characters and a "white" national one that is constituted as outsiders. The *acto,* "Honest Sancho's Used Mexican Shop," depicts Miss Jimenez (pronounced JIM-en-ez, instead of he-MEN-ez), a secretary from the governor's office who enters the shop "looking for a Mexican-type model for our Administration." The premise allows the shopkeeper to

Close-up of Luis Valdez in an Aztec calendar. Production still from Los Vendidos *(1972).*

present and comment upon a range of Mexican stereotypes *cum* robots, including a Frito Bandito–style revolutionary, the 1944 East L.A. zoot-suiter ("an American classic"), a farmworker couple, a campus militant, and, finally, Eric, the 1972 Mexican American model. In the end, Miss Jimenez leaves with Eric to add a "brown face in the crowd" to the governor's luncheon. After she leaves, however, Sancho is revealed as the true robot. The Mexican models drop their stereotypes, grab the money from Sancho, and gather around the *campesino* (Luis Valdez), who announces, "According to the map, we've got Chicanos infiltrated into every major urban center in the U.S." When the pachuco model looks out the window and into the camera, he cries out, "Están watchando" (They are watching us), whereupon the crowd peers into the lens and Valdez announces, "I'm sorry, Honest Sancho's is closed," pulls down the shade, and concludes menacingly, "Buenas noches" (Good night).

The *acto* conflates stereotypes with economic and political subordination—hence, the pun on "used" Mexicans—then introduces a conspiracy narrative beneath this surface: Chicanos themselves will infiltrate the political arena and mass communications by mimicking the very stereotypes that secure their exclusion, but that nonetheless introduce "Mexicans" into discourse. In this sense, *Los Vendidos* is the Chicano response to the political cartoon in *Broadcasting*, which conflated the Frito Bandito with the Chicano groups challenging the stereotype and seeking access to television and asked, "What else can they do? They kicked him off television!"[65] In this case, however, *Los Vendidos* rearticulated the Frito Bandito's illicit consumption into a political narrative that placed Chicanos inside the television screen looking out at the "white" mainstream.

While the televised *acto* retains the us-versus-them dichotomy of the original, its ending is radically different. In fact, the difference between the staged *acto* (performed first in 1967) and the televised version (broadcast in 1972) reveals what is at stake in expanding the audience context on a number of levels: from an immediate, specific, and local setting to a television broadcast; from public to private spaces; and from participatory to imagined communities. In the stage performance, the *acto* ends with Miss Jimenez run off by the Mexican American and the other stereotypes when they unmask their Chicano identities.[66] The Chicanos remove the money from Sancho's hand, divide most of the proceeds among themselves ("we're going to be rich"), invest the remainder "back into the business," and head to a party. Here the politics are subsumed by a profit motive and a pleasure principle that are as localized as the performance itself, requiring an audience that understands robbery as a politically symbolic act. In the televised version, however, the audience must be assumed to be mostly "white," so robbery and the profit motive are replaced by conspiracy and political infiltration. In this way, both versions of the *acto* are able to convey

Production still from Los Vendidos *(1972).*

Production still from Los Vendidos *(1972).*

the same point to different audiences—one within the barrio, the other within the mainstream—namely, that exploitation and counterexploitation are the only avenues of exchange between the barrio and a "white" body politic. And both versions express this politics through the figure of La Malinche, the woman who betrays her culture by "sleeping with the enemy": in other words, Miss Jimenez.

Narration: *El Corrido*

In its stage performances, *La Gran Carpa de los Rasquachis* (1973) likewise presented an *acto* on the farmworkers' struggle framed by two *mitos*. The title can be taken as either reflexive or metaphoric—on the one hand, referring to the narrative itself as a bigger-than-life tent-show performance about the Rasquachi family, and on the other, describing the truck used to drive farmworkers to the fields (literally, the big tent of the underdogs). In the feature-length television adaptation, now titled *El Corrido,* the *acto* and *mito* are combined to create a mythical narrative about the life and death of an archetypal Mexican male immigrant: Jesús Pelado Rasquachi, the irreverently named Jesus Poor Tramp. The *acto-mito* functions as a performance within the performance: in the back of a truck carrying strikebreakers to the fields, an older Mexican man (Luis Valdez) sings a corrido for his younger Chicano namesake (Daniel Valdez), inspiring him to join the United Farm Workers in strike when they finally arrive. While the older Mexican sings, the corrido narrative is performed as an *acto-mito* on a stage decorated like the truck itself and framed by a curtain made from farmworkers' burlap sacks. The singing of the corrido mediates between the realist scenes in the truck and the *acto-mito* performance featuring Diablo (Devil) and Calavera (Skeleton) as various U.S. characters. But it also links the *carpa* tradition of tent theater and circus in the Southwest from the 1850s to the 1940s with its agitprop revival in the 1960s, now performed on the flatbeds of trucks.[67] In this way, *El Corrido* equates Mexican and Chicano vernacular forms—the corrido, the *carpa,* and the *acto-mito*—setting them against the realist depiction of the narrative frame that is formally aligned with television itself.

The performance-within-a-performance critiques racial *cum* class hierarchies, even lampooning the church for serving the interests of the "boss" and revealing gender differences within the family as the point beyond which the macho will not be subordinated. But *El Corrido* remains profoundly ambivalent about these hierarchies within the private

realm of love, desire, and belief, signaled most explicitly in the conflation of Pelado's mother (Mamá), his wife (María), and La Virgen María.
That Pelado's first name is Jesús places him in a preoedipal relationship
to all three mother figures and, by extension, to the "violated" Mexican culture they symbolize and reproduce; but it also constitutes U.S.
capitalism—the *patrón* (owner) and *patroncito* (managerial class)—as
the new father figures of the conquest.[68] Pelado's oedipalization—
wherein he submits to the "Law of the Father"—occurs as a racialized
form of class and national subordination, but it is lived within the family as the very terms of his love, desire, and belief. When Pelado crosses
the border, symbolized by a rope, the Diablo/Patrón ties one end
around Pelado's neck. The turning point occurs when Pelado internal-
izes the border, tying the loose end around his waist. Similarly, when
Pelado marries a Mexican American, he places a clothesline around her
neck, which she shruggingly accepts, draping the loose end over her
shoulders. In this manner, *El Corrido* equates undocumented labor (for
men) and marriage (for women) as forms of subordination, the former
producing the terms of the latter. Both roles require the subjects to internalize their subordination. But if, in the biblical and conquest narratives, the "father" literally produces the son (Jesus Christ or Mexico's
"hijos de la chingada"), here it is done indirectly as a usurping of
Pelado's *patrimonio* (cultural patrimony) by the Diablo/Patrón. U.S.
capitalism provides the context within which Jesús finds María—he expresses his love by placing his produce into her box—while U.S. culture
provides the context within which his children are raised as *not* Mexican. Thus, while Pelado remains a Mexican, his wife is Mexican American, and his children are Chicanos, and it is his death that marks the
tragic border between becoming and being an "American."

In *El Corrido,* as in most of his work, Valdez explores the inter-
relation between myth and history as, in Mircea Eliade's phrase, "the
paradigms for all significant human acts." [69] Eliade further argues "that
in one way or another one 'lives' the myth, in the sense that one is seized
by the sacred, exalted power of the events recollected or re-enacted." [70]
It is in this way that the *mito* and the *acto* share a direct relationship to
social agency. The representation of oppression—whether done as allegorical realism *(acto)* or mythical divagation *(mito)*—is intended to
incite action, thereby bridging the gap between art and life. But Valdez
works between Brechtian critical distance and a realist transparency,
subverting those who would seek "the thing itself and not the myth" as

if representation were not also part of social relations, while also confounding those who believe the two are exactly the same thing.[71] The sense that one "lives" the myth is expressed in the song that opens and closes the video, "Yo Soy el Corrido" (I Am the Corrido), together with the singer's claim that the lives of "mucha gente" or many people wrote the song in the first place. Hence, at the end of the video, the corrido and strike become interwoven: the young Chicano paraphrases the corrido's class analysis in persuading the other scabs to join him in the strike; and the corrido characters themselves emerge at the picket line to help him learn the song. This equivalence between the realist and allegorical narratives—mirrored in the formal equivalence between the corrido, *carpa,* and *acto-mito*—resolves social differences within the realist narrative itself between Mexican and Chicano, urban and rural, striker and strikebreaker.

But the television special can never do more than *represent* the equivalence between the allegorical world and the "real" one and the leap from theory to practice. Social agency is created, but only within the text itself. The fact of a mass audience remains. In *El Corrido,* however, viewer identification with the *acto-mito* is restricted by way of language. The corrido lyrics are *not* subtitled, removing their articulation and structuring of an identity politics within the narrative from the lingua franca of the American mainstream. In this way, *El Corrido* creates an insider's discourse that could not be broadcast in English. When Pelado takes a train to the Mexico–United States border, for example, the Diablo and Calavera act as engine and caboose, chanting a telling onomatopoeia for the sound of the train: "chíngate, chíngate, chíngate" (fuck you, fuck you, fuck you). More significantly, *El Corrido* takes the *acto* format—which had originally been used to convince farmworkers to join the strike—and transforms it into a metaphor for identifying oneself as different from the mainstream. Unlike *Los Vendidos,* which situates its politics and mythopoetics within a universal context, *El Corrido* uses Spanish-language dialogue and music rooted in Mexican-Chicano vernacular culture in order to limit direct identification to a specific bilingual audience.[72] In this instance, the act of identifying with the Spanish-language discourse becomes the desired response for viewers outside the text, one that finds its counterpart in the act of identifying with the corrido by joining the strike within the television narrative itself. In terms of viewer response, then, taking action by occupying a social space gave way to assuming a cultural identity.

The concern with "space" has been a complex one in Chicano thought since 1848, with the "lost lands" of the Mexican-American War often the catalyst for political action and the maintenance of a communal identity.[73] During the Chicano movement, however, the major spatial metaphor—Aztlán—became increasingly tied to an identity rather than a space, a process that is notable in the shift between *Los Vendidos,* where a collective identity is located within concentric geographical spaces until it becomes, quite literally, universal, and *El Corrido,* where a performative space provides the occasion for narrating an identity in which the individual becomes the expressive form of social agency: a "real" Chicano can sing the corrido, which claims, "Yo soy el corrido" (I am the corrido) and "Yo soy el alma de mi pueblo" (I am the soul of my people). This shift—marked by a shift from English to Spanish—is part of a larger process of naming oneself as a mythical space *outside* the mainstream. The Chicano movement's "Plan Espiritual de Aztlán" (1969), which laid out a seven-point "plan of liberation" for "a nation autonomous and free," nonetheless concluded in terms of social identity: "We are Aztlán."[74] As the poet Alurista notes, the first Chicano articulation of the myth of Aztlán established it as "more than a geographical location . . . [but rather as] . . . a mission and a state of mind, a way of facing contemporary reality and social conditions."[75] In Rudolfo Anaya's novel *Heart of Aztlán* (1976), set amid a railroad strike in the 1940s, the wayward protagonist searches for Aztlán in the mountains outside Albuquerque, only to realize at a crucial moment, "I AM Aztlán!"[76] Thus, Aztlán, like earlier conceptions of a "lost land," proffered an alternative, if not utopian, geography from which Chicanos could negotiate and perform ethnic identity within the United States. The irony of Valdez's *El Corrido* is that the articulation of such a nationalist identity becomes an insider's discourse situated within an "American" myth (the immigrant narrative) and state-regulated communication (television).

Valdez embraced that irony, contradictions and all, upsetting others' desire for a more clear-cut political representation. To that extent, he was prescient, not of a new and improved mode of representation, but of the complex and variegated arena within which Chicanos represented themselves. The concept of Aztlán emerges concurrently as the Chicano arts start to become distinct, professional components of the Chicano civil rights movement. Thus, for example, early Chicano filmmakers may have looked to Aztlán and a separatist "raza cinema" but entered into professional programs or institutions: New Communicators, Ethno-Communications, and Chicano public affairs series on PBS and network affiliates. In this manner, the call to nationalism put out by "El Plan Espiritual de Aztlán" provided an accurate description of the multiple geographies or spaces that the movement had entered: "Nationalism as the key to organization transcends all religious, political, class, and economic factions or boundaries."[77] Rather than transcend these boundaries, however, this political generation—of Chicano students, professionals, community activists, artists, and scholars— would henceforth negotiate within and between them.

It is perhaps no accident, then, that the shift from an emphasis on social space to one on cultural identity occurs simultaneously with the shift from student activists to media professionals. But it also occurs amid a shift from state-regulated, prime-time minority series on the public airwaves to an occasional state-sponsored special on public television. The narration of an exceptional cultural identity, then, became the quid pro quo for the absence of a secured location on the public airwaves. The problem was twofold insofar as minorities' access to the "public" had shifted to a public television that had already conceded the popular to the commercial networks and stations. The "public" of public broadcasting could not at the same time be popular. PBS became an elite location even as it also became the one broadcasting outlet within which the state secured some level of minority participation. This peculiar reconfiguration of racial minorities' demands for social equity—wherein these demands were rearticulated as cultural nationalist identities in an elite public culture rooted in noncommercial television and federal bureaucracy—was bound to clash with the political representation system. Indeed, Chicanos and other racial minorities had been deracinated in a very public way.

seven

"Our Own Institutions"
The Geopolitics of Chicano Professionalism

The question of violence or nonviolence in the struggle is a misleading one, for while many Chicanos theorize about the question and never have to confront the answer, they also avoid facing questions of how to best utilize the possibilities that are open to them.

—Jesús Salvador Treviño, 1974

Social change, real and lasting change, has never been obtained through the "appropriate" channels.

—David Morales, 1976

In his report on the Civil Rights Media Hearings in October 1976, Felix Gutiérrez concluded, "The tactics of the late '60s and early '70s have run their course."[1] This assessment was echoed by David Morales in his review of Chicano media reform activities, who noted that "since 1973, not only has there been a change in the attitude of government towards community access, but there was also a change in the attitude of the Chicano community towards institutional change."[2] Morales, writing for the Committee for the Development of Mass Communications in El Paso (established in 1970), described the dilemma facing Chicano media groups in the late 1970s: how to use the media to address the "life and death" issues in the barrio in the face of "a more unified and powerful business community," "police harrassment and false arrest," and the "'limited' access" brokered by the welfare state.[3] Morales considered the three alternatives: continue attempting to make the media industry responsive to the community, "develop our own media resources," or engage in the "one-to-one communications system" of grassroots community organizing. For Morales, all three alternatives had inherent limitations, making his account of the committee and other Chicano media reform groups one of the more evenhanded and self-critical. In the end, Morales identified three areas in which Chicano media groups had failed. First and foremost, these groups had lost community support, the sine qua non of any viable reform strategy. Second, they had failed to bring about relevant programming after obtaining settlement agreements, mostly due to lack of experience, office support, and time within their volunteer memberships.[4] Because there were few Chicano "production specialists" or "media professionals" outside California (given its film schools and Hollywood), the Chicano employees hired by local stations rarely created new programming, leaving the media groups to take on the task themselves. Third, Chicano media groups were mired in local issues—from employment to production—that made it difficult to organize at the national level, where most programming originated. In any case, the conflict between the overwhelming struggle to address local needs and an ill-defined and panethnic "national question" made local groups suspicious of the national efforts in which they nevertheless participated. Morales himself, for example, headed the West Texas regional office of the Texas Coalition on Mass Media and served as Southwest chairman of the National Latino Media Coalition.

The articles by Gutiérrez and Morales, as well as similar statements, were reproduced through carbon copies or mimeographs and circulated through the informal and sporadic networks of the Chicano media reform movement. In the end, these statements amounted to a last rallying call during a period of media activism that situtated itself within a community-based movement dealing with "life and death" issues, from police repression, to inadequate education, health care, and housing, to lack of political representation. For the most part, activists recounted tactics that no longer worked for an audience of other Chicano media activists, looking ahead with little hope for change, especially with respect to the media professionals who were expected to change the system from within, but, according to Morales, "simply take up space and pay checks." As Morales himself admits, however, "the media advocacy groups cast a 'naive' lamb into the lion's den and expected 'miracles,' which eventually never came." The groups' own efforts to enter the lion's den were no less sanguine: "As we break down more doors, others are found; we are no where close to dealing the racist media industry a death blow than we are close to electing a Chicano president, but we are wiser. And that perhaps makes a greater danger to this system than ever before."[5] Thus, although still confronting the media, Chicano activists were left with little more than a hard-and-fast resolve based on an acute insight into the structural underpinnings of their own failure.

In the same period, Chicano media professionals began publishing accounts of their own activities within public television. Unlike the *rasquache* or make-do circulation of activist statements, these articles appeared in the publication arms of two Washington-based groups: the National Association of Educational Broadcasters' *PTR: Public Telecommunications Review* and the National Council of La Raza's *Agenda: A Journal of Hispanic Issues*. Here, media professionals narrated their advocacy efforts for an audience involved with broadcast practices, not-for-profit funding, and public policy. Still, these articles—as with earlier movement literature—placed advocacy efforts in the historical context of race relations in the United States, while detailing Chicano and Latino struggles within public television. But these authors took a more passive position with respect to social change: "The Latino culture is a living workshop spread throughout the nation. It would be a tragic and irrevocable loss if in the third century of this country, a culture which has remained intact, despite all odds, disappears because of human ignorance and biases."[6] Since these articles were designed to influence public broadcasting from inside the beltway, their tone was more informational and persuasive, rather than confrontational and demanding, deferring to the state for the final decision. The overall strategy consisted in persuading the state to live up to its own ideals by noting the historical and legal precedents for bilingual programming, calling for equal representation within public television, and appealing for funding to support Latino programs and advocacy efforts that would enrich the nation as a whole.[7]

Together these two sets of texts represented the first histories of Chicano media reform, although their audiences and functions were quite different, revealing a change in reform activities from an outside activism predicated on a "discourse of violence" to an inside advocacy predicated on a "discourse of professionalism." In both instances, however, the publications signaled an increasing concern over keeping clear-cut boundaries between activists and professionals, between outside and inside. One group, the National Latino Media Coalition (NLMC), did so within its own ranks, requiring an equal mix of activists and professionals in order to bring both outside and inside pressures to bear upon television and related government agencies. Even so, by the start of the Carter administration, federal deregulation and the decline of left-of-center social movements shifted the predominant site for media reform efforts from activism to professionalism. This shift manifested itself on a number of levels, redirecting attention from local to national politics, from cultural nationalism to minority citizenship, and from the corporate mass media to public television.

Nevertheless, as the NLMC example indicates, effective efforts were marked by both sets of tactics, and, in this respect, Saul Alinsky's "realistic radical" did not so much end as a viable type within media reform as reemerge within the ranks of the Chicano media professionals. More than any other filmmaker, Jesús Salvador Treviño embodied the "schizo-cultural limbo" of such earlier activists as Ray Andrade, albeit as someone now operating as a "well-integrated political schizoid" *within* the film and television industry. As a polemicist, advocate, and filmmaker, Treviño laid out the practical and theoretical dimensions of Chicano cinema along the lines of Alinsky's "realistic radical," who takes the world as is and works within the system for social change. According to Treviño, "My approach has been to go for the opportunities that exist within the system and try to make the best of them, at times changing them, subverting them. I've been successful at doing this in certain areas." [8] In thus situating himself both within and against the establishment, Treviño calibrated the demands of a minority social movement to the corporate professional arena within which the mass media operated and within which it also produced a national public sphere.

Treviño's strategy is notable for the way it insinuates Chicano social protest into prevailing media theory and public policy—a theory and practice whose universalist terms excluded racial minorities. As a first measure, he turned from the social realm per se and addressed the medium in aesthetic terms, making a distinction between ethnic-specific content (a set of issues) and a universal form (film artistry). By identifying media conventions as a "film artistry" distinct from its content, Treviño was able to argue that Chicano content could also express universal humanism and thereby appeal to all audiences. In practical terms, Treviño then argued for the need to address Chicano issues within both ethnic-specific *and* general programming in order to reach both Mexican American and Anglo-American audiences. Needless to say, Treviño's humanist rhetoric elided, even as it relied upon, an implicit equivalence between media production and mass reception. In other words, Treviño subscribed to the "hypodermic needle" theory of media impact, but only insofar as it allowed him to argue for diversified content and, by extension, the hiring of minority producers whose experiences reflected that content.

In effect, Treviño engaged in a humanist rhetoric that redirected critical attention from the medium to the message itself. He did so as an effort to rearticulate Marshall McLuhan's "The Medium Is the Message" from its systemic analysis to a local strategy.[9] Indeed, despite the historical reach of McLuhan's argument, it remained somewhat vague about the industrial and regulatory context for present-day mass media. Treviño's resultant tactics, then, were both practical and self-reflexive, laying the foundation for an argument to change programming and hiring practices while also pointing out the inherent limitations of telecommunications itself: "By its nature . . . television will distort, edit, and stereotype. It is the media that is the mistake."[10] Thus, for Treviño, the medium was effective precisely because its message was a "mistake" that had become "the basis of most of our impressions and access to information."[11] But rather than look back to an idealized print culture or ahead to the promise of technological solutions for social problems, Treviño called for "more accurate representation" within the context of a medium that could be neither objective nor ignored:

> Perhaps we must begin "exposing" television to the public, denouncing its shortcomings, perhaps we can provide people with the tools to discern between the "true" facts and the "truer" facts, between the stereotype and the real person in front of them. But the question is how to communicate this information . . . through television?[12]

Like Thomas M. Martinez's "Advertising and Racism: The Case of the Mexican-American," Treviño's writings engaged McLuhan's systemic analysis of the mass media while also struggling to develop a viable reform strategy that necessarily started with the message and its societal context. It is here that an argument could be made to hire minorities able to produce the former in order to redeem the latter.

What is especially interesting, however, is that Treviño developed this position through a series of publications and presentations aimed at diverse constituencies that effectively expanded the domain of discourse for Chicano cinema beyond the professional arena proper: local television stations,[13] PBS and CPB,[14] and broadcast policy seminars,[15] but also community newspapers,[16] the Catholic Church,[17] the U.S. Conference for an Alternative Cinema,[18] and El Comité de Cineastas de América Latina (at meetings in Mexico City and Havana, Cuba, designed to further the cause of New Latin American Cinema).[19] In this way, Treviño located Chicano cinema within divergent local, national, and transnational contexts, thereby blurring the boundaries between a state-regulated professional arena and transnational institutions and movements. Treviño's writings, together with his television productions and organizational activities, developed a strategy based on the juxtaposition of conflicting goals: on the one hand, working within the system in order to challenge the film and television industry and related social institutions, while, on the other hand, creating an alternative cinema by aligning Chicano cinema with liberation theology and radical film movements in Latin America and the United States. In this context, Treviño's writings articulated a rhetoric that served to more or less reconcile the dilemmas facing Chicano media professionals whose raison d'être emerged out of community-based politics, but whose paychecks came from the margins of an intransigent industry.[20] Until the early 1980s, this rhetoric proved effective in bolstering Chicano efforts to secure limited production funds and programming outlets through the state, thereby maintaining a toehold within the industry.

Unlike the media activists of the late 1960s and early 1970s, Chicano media professionals were able to institutionalize their efforts, although not through their own advocacy groups, which were likewise underfunded and staffed with volunteers, but through production companies and a public broadcasting consortium. Echoing "El Plan Espiritual de Aztlán," Treviño identified these various efforts as an attempt to create "our own institutions."[21] These were, however, institutions that attempted to speak on behalf of both the Chicano community and Chicano media professionals from within the mass media, rather than institutions whose domain was that of the community itself. Furthermore, given the federal transition from social engineering to deregulation by the end of the 1970s, situating "our own institutions" within the mass media resulted not in structural but in weakly "affirmative" access. As a consequence, advocacy required leverage from outside the industry and the state, something Treviño's radical rhetoric and international networking provided. Ironically, it did so by defining Chicano cinema as that point where Hollywood meets its antithesis—that is, where the American film and television industry overlaps with a Latin American film *cum* social movement—when, in fact, Chicano cinema did not exist in either location.

What did exist were a handful of documentaries produced for public affairs series. Interestingly, while the direct political action that created these series followed a masculine code derived in large part from the Mexican and Cuban revolutions and the Black Power movement, the resultant shows and their social function—as with Chicano cultural production in general—were self-consciously modeled on the family. This gendered distinction between masculine activism and family-oriented cultural production is also found in Treviño's own writings, albeit in slightly different terms. Here the object of activism is described as a universal "man" who stands to be either influenced by media stereotypes or informed by film artistry. At the same time, however, Treviño defines the role of Chicano filmmakers—he begins using "he or she" by the mid-1970s—as a didactic one rooted in the Chicano family: "When you talk about independence, about standing up for justice, you're talking about your mother, your sisters and brothers, your family, your people. It's not something you mess with, it's something you respect as you would yourself." [22] The father is placed outside Treviño's description of the family, as is the "you" associated with the filmmaker, suggesting an equivalence between the two as they "stand up" for the Chicano family *cum* community. But if so, the father position was more implied than presented in Chicano public affairs programs. In one of the first Chicano public affairs series, *¡Ahora!* (KCET, 1969–1970), the avuncular host was quickly replaced by Treviño and Rita Sáenz, whose youth and heterosexual pairing symbolized the new generation within the Chicano community. In the early 1970s, other shows were similar to *¡Ahora!* in their primary address to the Chicano community and in their use of the family as a model through which to educate, entertain, and engage that community.

Between 1974 and 1984, Chicano filmmakers—like their activist counterparts—combined radical and reformist demands directed at the film and television industry. But even as filmmakers' sense of their social function became increasingly radical, their actions operated within a broader "discourse of professionalism" that placed an emphasis on funding sources, production schedules, aesthetic conventions, market analysis and ascertainment, broadcast and syndication, the policy arena, and, above all, an ongoing participation in the social networks or "interpretive community" within which these things meant something. For those Chicanos attempting to work within the mass media, being a film-maker meant an increasing reliance upon noncommercial funding sources and public broadcasting. Indeed, while later series worked at the crossroads of a pan-Latino national audience, they did so mostly in family-oriented educational and children's public programming. Thus, one of the ironies of the discourse of professionalism—as with the discourse of violence—was that while it challenged the corporate mass media in terms of access to the public sphere, social change itself required not the machinations of a civil society, but a dynamic among those things outside civil society: the family, the state, and transnational social movements. It is in this sense that the two epigraphs at the start of this chapter, while marking a conflict between activist and professional tactics, express a larger strategy that found expression first in Andrade's grassroots activism, then in Treviño's professional advocacy: one must work within the system *and* outside "appropriate" channels. It was a lesson learned first at school and then on the job, and it would be modified over the next three decades in response to changes in the industry and regulatory arena. In the 1970s and 1980s, Chicano producers mobilized a discourse of professionalism that relied upon state support and public television, situating this reformism vis-à-vis U.S. and Latin American alternative cinemas. Since the late 1980s, as the next chapter outlines, with deregulation and the rise of new technologies and a global mass media, Chicano producers have turned increasingly to a "discourse of citizenship" wherein the public sphere is defined in market terms and its subjects as citizen-consumers.

Entering Public Television

If public television has been the major outlet for Chicano cinema, the two have also been coterminous, intimately bound up in each other's history from the very beginning. As I argued at the end of chapter 4, this relationship had a profound effect on racial minorities, who acquired "voice" by way of an elite media culture susceptible to political pressures precisely *because* it lacked both public support and commercial viability. In some respects, however, public television was created for just such a purpose, rerouting more substantive demands away from commercial television without becoming an autonomous alternative in and of itself.

In January 1967, the Carnegie Commission on Educational Television proposed a national public television system that would supplement the commercial networks, producing programs about "all that is of human interest and importance which is not at the moment appropriate or available for support by advertising."[23] While the commission called for a decentralized system outside government control (rather than an elite "fourth network"), it also reinforced the centrality of the marketplace, particularly in maintaining the distinction between programming and reception. In this way, public television also constituted viewers as passive consumers, rather than as active participants in a public sphere, even though its mandate ostensibly placed public television outside market forces.[24] In November 1967, the Public Broadcast Service Act became one of the last Great Society programs, and the only one concerned with communications. But in establishing the Corporation for Public Broadcasting (CPB), the act defined "public" negatively and in market terms—as "noncommercial" rather than as a way of understanding how a society constitutes itself through communication—while it subordinated the CPB to political pressures and corporate underwriting. Indeed, as an administrative structure, CPB had a board that reflected political appointees rather than community participation, and the corporation's effectiveness was limited by its ill-defined interconnection with the Public Broadcasting Service (PBS) and local stations.[25]

Though established in 1967, CPB did not deal with race at the national level until the mid-1970s, when a combination of political and public pressures led it to sponsor surveys of the Mexican American audience (1973–74),[26] adopt an affirmative-action plan (1975),[27] fund a national Latino public affairs series (Realidades, 1975–77),[28] and, in 1979, provide first-time funds to the Latino Consortium (established five years earlier), the first minority public broadcasting consortium.[29] In the interim, efforts to incorporate Chicanos and other racial minorities within public television came either from grassroots efforts aimed at local stations or from national initiatives outside CPB and PBS. In particular, two funding sources provided the impetus behind the development of national programming aimed at Latinos: the U.S. Office of Education and the Ford Foundation. By 1976, the former had granted nearly $15 million for Latino bilingual children's television series as part of its mandate under the Bilingual Education Act of 1968.[30] And in the late 1960s, the latter had funded various pilot programs in an effort to develop a model for national Latino public affairs programming.[31] In many cases, these Latino-themed series became the start-up productions of local stations within the newly minted Public Broad-

casting Service, allowing one in particular—KCET-TV in Los Angeles—
to emerge as one of five national production centers in the system.[32] By
the end of the 1970s, that history, like the funding itself, would be
erased from the institutional memory of public television.

Bilingual Children's Programming

Beginning in the late 1960s, the U.S. Office of Education became a major funding source of educational children's programming, supporting
the creation of *Sesame Street* in 1969.[33] That same year, the office also
provided initial support for the creation of bilingual programming in
response to the Bilingual Education Act. While these and other minority programs funded through the Emergency School Aid Act (ESAA)
were made available to commercial and noncommercial stations, for all
intents and purposes educational children's programming became the
stepchild of public television. After all, on commercial television, children's programs consisted mostly of Saturday morning cartoons, for
which stations could run nearly twice as many commercials as they
could during prime-time programs (sixteen minutes per hour).[34] In contrast, bilingual education programming became circumscribed by the
"compensatory" orientation of the War on Poverty, so that participants
were seen as "disadvantaged" children. "Instead of promoting multicultural and multilingual environments," notes the producer-turned-
scholar Aida Barrera, "the legislation was often used to keep children
in isolated, poverty-linked programs."[35] Unlike classroom programs,
bilingual education on television entered the public sphere. But, stig-
matized as a program for nonwhite, low-income, and undereducated
children, it had neither commercial appeal for network television nor
the elite cultural status associated with public television, both of which
catered to the underlying ideal of a white, monolingual, middle-class
audience.

Nevertheless, given its multimillion-dollar governmental funding
and emphasis on cultural and linguistic diversity (following desegregation), educational children's programming became one of the major
"training grounds" for Chicano filmmakers in the 1970s.[36] Moctesuma
Esparza and Jesús Salvador Treviño worked briefly as executive producers on, respectively, *Villa Alegre* (1973–74) and *Infinity Factory*
(1975–76), creating opportunities for other Chicano filmmakers, many
of whom also produced segments for other "modularized" children's
television series.[37] In 1973, for example, Sylvia Morales directed seg-

ments of *Sesame Street* for a Cinco de Mayo program. But in addition to providing a training ground for filmmakers otherwise excluded from the industry, *Carrascolendas* (1970–78) and *Villa Alegre* (1974–79) represented the first *national* programs that addressed the Latino population. These series, which started with a regional emphasis on Chicano culture, soon incorporated Puerto Rican and Cuban American cultures, themes, and performers, thereby constituting a panethnic public on the basis of language and shared problems in integrating "white" social institutions.

In 1969, Aida Barrera, who produced nearly 500 Spanish-language programs at KLRN-TV in Austin, Texas, during the 1960s, convinced the U.S. Office of Education to extend its bilingual education funding into television. Her concept, *Carrascolendas,* became the first such program, funded as a regional series for two years, then airing nationally on PBS from 1972 to 1978, eventually reaching over 200 stations.[38] Unlike "modularized" or segmented series such as *Villa Alegre* and *Sesame Street, Carrascolendas* used a single story line for each episode, while its use of the musical comedy genre provided an alternative to the usual "realist" framing devices of other series. Set in the mythical town of Carrascolendas, each episode included a half dozen original fully scored and choreographed musical numbers, together with at least one slapstick sequence. In this manner, the series emphasized affective concerns related to cultural difference rather than instruction and the "politics" of interpersonal relations. This emphasis is captured best in the title itself, which represents an oral transmutation of the town name Carnestolendas (which means "carnival"). In drawing upon stories from her own childhood, Barrera validated not only Latino cultural heritage, but also its informal transmission, mutability over time, and linguistic playfulness. That one should break the rules in saying the word "carnival" and thereby produce a word that sounds like "expensive schooling" *(cara + escolaridad)* expresses many of the contradictions facing both Barrera and her target audience (Latino children between three and nine years old). Indeed, standardized approaches to English, bilingualism, education, and desegregation—let alone the reactive purity of cultural nationalism—prevented an affective engagement of cultural difference and an effective resolution of cultural conflicts. Perhaps for this reason, *Carrascolendas* appealed to both children and adults and Latinos and non-Latinos, as well as audiences in Canada and Latin America.[39] In effect, it created a profoundly ludic mixture of high and low cultures, "expensive schooling" and "carnival," wherein cross-cultural pedagogy starts with the mispronounced name at the heart of any culture. Barrera pursued a notion of heritage in which its origin bespoke two disparities: its own incongruity and the inequality that occasioned a genealogy in the first place. As Michel Foucault writes, "What is found at the historical beginning of things is not the inviolable identity of their origin; it is the dissension of other things. It is disparity. History also teaches how to laugh at the solemnities of the origin." [40]

But such laughter can be painful, too. Barrera's programming ran counter to the institutional operations and cultural orientation of public television itself. As Barrera concludes:

> The ESAA programs were not segregated per se, but a number of factors placed these productions in isolated scheduling ghettos, both within the public broadcasting community and the educational establishment, virtually guaranteeing their demise. . . . PBS stations, especially smaller stations whose . . . principle [sic] focus was broadcast and not production, did not necessarily see their role as assisting minority production. Since funding was generally unavailable from PBS-CPB, productions came to an end at the conclusion of government funding. [41]

When *Carrascolendas* ended, KLRN-TV dismissed most of Barrera's multiethnic staff, which had reached fifty-five full-time and forty regular part-time people, on the grounds that they were too inexperienced, despite six years' work on an award-winning national series that had also bankrolled the station. In a move that would be repeated at other PBS stations throughout the mid-1970s, Barrera would be the only minority person offered a continuing position. She refused the favor.

Televisual Fordism

While the U.S. Office of Education was funding bilingual education programming, the Ford Foundation launched a funding initiative in response to the Kerner Commission findings on the role of the media in race relations. [42] In addition to minority training programs and advocacy efforts in broadcast law, Ford funded the development of minority programming at public television stations across the United States. These included Black public affairs series such as *Soul!* and *Black Journal* as well as pilot programs for five Chicano series.

In Los Angeles, between 1968 and 1970, Ford funded three Chicano programs at KCET-TV, starting with *Canción de la Raza* (Song of the People), a bilingual *telenovela* or soap opera set in East Los Angeles and dealing with social issues facing the barrio. The seventy-episode series aired weekdays at 3:00 P.M. and 7:30 P.M. for fourteen weeks and was subsequently rerun during the evening time period. *Línea Abierta* (Open Line), a community call-in service that aired between 3:00 P.M. and 9:00 P.M., provided the basis for a Monday evening discussion panel that aired before the *telenovela*. By 1969, the local success of the *telenovela* led to its being rebroadcast by about fifteen other stations in cities with significant Latino populations.[43] The attempt to elevate the local series to a national one, however, failed on several counts. Audience surveys found that the East L.A. drama did not resonate with Puerto Ricans in New York and New Jersey. Meanwhile, Chicanos in other parts of the Southwest often objected to what they perceived as racial stereotypes and improper dialect.[44] On the basis of these surveys, Ford then funded three community-based public affairs shows—*¡Ahora!* (KCET-TV) in Los Angeles, *Periódico* (KLRN-TV) in Austin, and *Fiesta* (KUAT-TV) in Tucson[45]—with the expectation that the local stations would continue to produce them after the grant period had run out. But in almost all cases, when Ford funding ended, stations dropped the Black and Chicano programs, often despite their popularity.

Assessing the failure of its initiative in 1974, Ford cited the lack of minorities in decision-making positions at television stations, while it also backed away from the Kerner Commission findings about the centrality of the mass media, arguing instead that overcoming racism "depends upon the condition of the larger society, which the media shape only in part."[46] If Ford discovered that its training programs, advocacy efforts, and production grants did not change the structure of the mass media, it blamed the larger society, then withdrew. Ford-funded surveys, however, pointed to another consideration: "In the minds of the Mexican Americans the need is *not* for a single series, but rather for a total programming strategy."[47] What they got, however, were single series. Even though these series succeeded in addressing the needs of Chicano viewers, they could not carry the burden of changing an industry by example alone.

In the end, ironically enough, Ford found itself undone by Fordism.[48] After all, television stations concerned themselves with mass audiences. If Henry Ford offered the Model-T in any color as long as it was black, station managers did something quite similar for programming aimed at an implicitly "white" broadcast audience. Under Fordism, mass production meant mass consumption, the only problem being that women, racial minorities, and the Third World were excluded from the benefits at either end. As David Harvey writes in *The Condition of Postmodernity,*

> The resultant inequalities produced serious social tensions and strong social movements on the part of the excluded—movements that were compounded by the way in which race, gender, and ethnicity often determined who had access to privileged employment and who did not. . . . All these threads of opposition began to fuse into a strong cultural-political movement at the very moment when Fordism as an economic system appeared to be at its apogee.[49]

In response, the Ford Foundation placed its emphasis on creating prototypes of a new "product" that served the needs of minority audiences alone, informing them about educational opportunities, social services, civil rights, community action programs, and even "proper diet." Like other race-based initiatives in this period, these programs were a prelude to integration and not the thing itself, isolating nonwhite racial groups on the problematic assumption of their deficiency relative to the (white) national culture.[50] In short, these series functioned as part of Ford's overall efforts to bring impoverished minority groups into what they perceived as the mainstream of American society. Rather than understanding racial groups as a resource for expanding and enriching the so-called mainstream, Ford identified Chicanos in narrowly socioeconomic terms as a "targeted audience" consisting of Spanish-speaking families with low incomes, blue-collar employment, and below-average education.[51]

Looked at from another perspective, Ford took a decidedly non-Fordist approach to an industry well suited to Fordist principles, especially given the limited competition and ineffectual "public interest" regulation. Either way, racial minorities remained unincorporated by design. The resultant series were understood in *social* terms as a stopgap effort to shore up impoverished and disenfranchised communities; in consequence, they were understood in *industry* terms as a sidebar to the proper functioning of public television and, more generally, the public sphere. When the Fordist regime came apart amid the recession of 1973, the Ford Foundation lost half its assets, which ended much of its activist funding; meanwhile, network television continued to operate on Fordist principles for the next two decades, even as deregulation signaled both the decline of their monopoly over the televisual public sphere and the rise of narrowcasting and niche marketing.

Ford *did* open the door to public television for the Chicano producers who were hired for its pilots. If the programs were canceled, it proved more difficult to remove the producers. But in the absence of a well-funded "total programming strategy" for integrating Chicanos into public television, these producers straddled a racialized divide between production line and picket line, cultural capital and community needs, broadcast and narrowcast. Chicano producers negotiated between these conflicting demands, both as professionals and in the programs that they produced. They also laid the groundwork for a national programming rooted in local differences, setting the stage for the professionalism and institution building of the mid-1970s. The local was not sufficient, after all, but neither were the national models offered by the Ford Foundation and the U.S. Department of Education. Nevertheless, these efforts and the entrance of a "political generation" into public television provided the basis for the development of pan-Latino advocacy and organization at the national level.

The Discourse of Professionalism

By the mid-1970s, minority cinemas had shifted to a professionalism that was correlated not to social protests or state and foundation intervention—both of which were then in decline—but to the idea of a community within the nation and of pan- or transnational cultural formations. Treviño himself would develop and articulate this position through a series of publications over the next decade, wherein he argued that "the films that have resulted are at once an expression of the life, concerns and issues of the Chicano people, and at the same time, the northernmost expression of a political and socially conscious international cinema movement known as New Latin American Cinema."[52] Such claims were more than just rhetorical, insofar as Treviño and others participated en masse in organizational efforts to develop a radical cinema at the national and international levels. These included the U.S. Conference for an Alternative Cinema at Bard College in June 1979, which represented the first such gathering since the 1930s but which also signaled the end of a class-based leftist politics, amid protests from the racial and sexual minorities in attendance.[53] In the mid-1970s, Treviño also participated in the meetings leading up to the first International Festival of New Latin American Cinema in Havana, Cuba, in December 1979, which he and sixteen other Chicano filmmakers attended. Treviño's cultural argument and organizational efforts imbricated minority discourses of cultural identity and civil rights with Third World debates over national identity vis-à-vis neo- and postcolonialism. Film scholars have followed suit with this cultural argument, so that U.S. minorities now factor into most discussions of Third Cinema, but they conveniently ignored the professional discourse that held it all together at a practical level for the filmmakers themselves. Indeed, when looked at from the filmmakers' perspective, one sees that professionalism subordinated the ongoing radical rhetoric challenging the state's legitimizing myths and territorial claims to an overall agenda designed to challenge the government and its policies to intervene on their behalf within the television industry.

Beginning in 1974, Chicano filmmakers formed various organizations as part of a general movement from waning social protests to an emergent professionalism. These included public television syndication (Latino Consortium) and professional groups (National Latino Media Coalition, Chicano Cinema Coalition). But the full range of activities suggests something much more than mere professionalism—or, rather, it suggests the extent to which Chicano filmmakers had to create the discursive and performative contexts within which they could then emerge as professionals. Thus, in addition to writing for trade and policy-oriented publications, filmmakers introduced the notion of Chicano cinema into debates over alternative and independent cinema. Equally important, they also participated in the emerging community-based publications and cultural activities that developed out of the Chicano movement. Treviño and others published both in movement-oriented magazines (*Caracol* and *Chismearte*) and in new, advertising-based "Latino" general-interest magazines (*Nuestro* and *Caminos*).[54] In 1980, the Spanish-language newspaper *La Opinión* published a Sunday cultural supplement on "cine chicano" that brought together and translated many of the formative essays by Chicano filmmakers.[55]

Meanwhile, Chicano and Latino film festivals provided community members with an opportunity to see these films and the filmmakers with some measure of celebrity and publicity, not to mention moral support, with which to bolster their careers. The main festivals include the Chicano Film Festival in San Antonio, Texas (established in 1975, renamed the International Hispanic Film Festival in the late 1970s and known as CineFestival since 1981), the National Latino Film Festival in New York (established in 1981), and the Chicago Latino Film Festival (established in 1985).[56] These and numerous other community- and university-based exhibitions created an important alternative circuit for Chicano independent films. But they also signaled the need for a panethnic, if not hemispheric, framework for public exhibition in order to reach non-Chicano audiences as well as to imbue the public consumption of ethnicity with national and international resonances. In this manner, festivals constructed a viable counterpublic in opposition to the mainstream, exchanging the universal appeal of the latter's homogeneous subject for the self-selected appeal of a heterogeneous one. In San Francisco, for example, Cine Acción (established in 1980) eschewed a strictly nationalist orientation in favor of an approach that was panethnic, hemispheric, and gender balanced. The group's exhibition efforts have included a regular "cineteca" screening program, the groundbreaking Women of the Americas Film and Video Festival (1988), and the annual ¡Cine Latino! festival (since 1993).[57] By the early 1980s, most public festivals followed the Cine Acción paradigm, even in cities with Chicano-majority populations. In this manner, festival programmers situated the ethnic specificity of individual films within the panethnic and hemispheric viewing context of public exhibition, providing an alternative to the particular-as-universal formula of the mainstream.[58] Here, the particular became public against the backdrop of the universal; or, put another way, Chicano films entered America under the aegis of América.

In this same period, Chicano filmmakers began to leave television stations in order to form independent production companies. The move was at once a response to the limited opportunities within television stations and an attempt to acquire greater control over the development, production, and distribution of Chicano-themed films. The first production companies stemmed from the various settlement agreements and bilingual education funding sources and were often extensions of advocacy groups such as NMAADC and IMAGE. McGraw-Hill's *La Raza* series helped establish Moctesuma Esparza Productions (1974; now Esparza/Katz Productions). Other production companies included Ruiz Productions, later InterAmerican Pictures (José Luis Ruiz, 1975–80); Learning Garden Productions (Severo Pérez, 1976–82); New Vista Productions (Jesús Salvador Treviño, 1977–78); Chispa Productions (Daniel, Juan, and Susan Salazar, 1978–81); and, starting with independent works in 1979 and continuing into the present, two Chicana producers who would eventually form their own companies, Sylvan Productions (Sylvia Morales) and Xochitl Films (Lourdes Portillo).

These production companies were located in a "schizo-cultural limbo" where their independent status was measured against an increasing deregulation that would turn them toward the public sector while their rhetoric became simultaneously corporate *and* radical. Chispa Productions in Denver, Colorado, made explicit this dual framework of cultural identity and integrationism.[59] To some extent, this impulse had always been present, but its terms began to change in the late 1970s. In a twist on more nationalist rhetoric, for example, Chispa's Juan Salazar situated *mestizaje* within a reformist vision of American culture:

> We are the last ingredient to make the American Dream real. . . . I believe that the Mestizo . . . is the real existential, modern, paradoxical man. He is bilingual, bicultural, divided. We must find a way to reconcile the divisions, to explore our lives, to understand ourselves and to give the other culture a way of understanding us.[60]

In effect, *mestizaje* meets the melting pot. Below I examine the way in which Chicano filmmakers negotiated the terms of minority professionalism in the decade after the Chicano movement, focusing on three instances: national broadcast and syndication efforts within public television (*Realidades* and the Latino Consortium), national advocacy (National Latino Media Coalition), and the Chicano Cinema Coalition's efforts to work among antithetical locations: Hollywood, U.S. alternative cinema, and New Latin American Cinema.

Protest Locally, Broadcast Nationally

While the creation of "our own institutions" did not occur until the mid-1970s, their foundations were laid as Chicano producers struggled to remain on the air amid the decline of media reform activities and extra-industry production initiatives. After the Ford-funded *¡Ahora!* was canceled, for example, Eduardo Moreno and Jesús Salvador Treviño would be the only Chicanos who remained as full-time staff at KCET.[61] Treviño quickly produced several award-winning documentaries, including *América Tropical* (1971),[62] *Soledad* (with Sue Booker, 1971),[63] *Yo Soy Chicano* (1972),[64] and *América de los Indios* (1972).[65] He also documented the first national convention of La Raza Unida for the series *L.A. Collective* in the fall of 1972. In addition to producing documentaries related to the ongoing Chicano movement, Treviño became active in public television at the national level, joining with other Chicano producers in approaching the Public Broadcasting Service (PBS), the Corporation for Public Broadcasting (CPB), and the National Association of Educational Broadcasters (NAEB). In May 1972, for example, he wrote and submitted a report to the NAEB president on the lack of "Spanish-surnamed" employment and programming.[66] The report resulted from a conference with four other Chicano producers from Colorado, New Jersey, Michigan, and California, as well as Mario Obledo (MALDEF), Domingo Nick Reyes (NMAADC), Congressman Edward Roybal, and Lionel Monagas (NAEB Office of Minority Affairs). Over one month later, after follow-up letters from Treviño and Reyes, NAEB's president sent a pro forma response assuring them of his concern while claiming that "no funds exist" to hire Chicanos.

Treviño continued his efforts, writing CPB about the need to fund Chicano-related programming, for which he included a list of Chicano journalists as potential consultants. But by September 1972, when Treviño addressed the general assembly of the PBS Public Affairs Conference in Atlanta, Georgia, he had become less circumspect. One of only two Chicanos at the conference, Treviño opened by inveighing the assembly in Spanish, calling them "un montón de tapados" (a group of idiots), before presenting his critique of the "narrow parochialism" of public broadcasting for ignoring the Latino population as part of the nation. Treviño then ended by translating his opening quotation of the Mexican president Benito Juárez (1858–72), "Respect for the rights of others is an assurance of peace."[67] Although Treviño remained within the bounds of professional discourse (at least in English), his use of selectively translated Spanish signaled not only his growing frustration with CPB and PBS, but also his development of a rhetorical strategy to conjure the specter of support from outside that exclusionary arena. For Treviño, that support included U.S. Latino groups (as a panethnic constituency) and Latin American political history (as an implied threat). Within two years, however, he would enter into actual dialogue with Latin American filmmakers, setting a geopolitical stage for creating "our own institutions."[68]

For the moment, Treviño's advocacy introduced him to the national professional arena, but it did not result in changes in either local or national programming. In order to secure another series that addressed the concerns of the Chicano community, Treviño had to apply activist strategies within KCET. He organized the fifteen to twenty "Spanish-surnamed" employees of the station—mostly janitors, secretaries, and various technicians—"to sign a petition that said, unless the Chicano community had a weekly television show, we were all going to resign en masse. . . . and that was the birth of *Acción Chicano [sic]*." [69] By the time *Acción Chicano* first aired in December 1972, Treviño had decided to reproduce the "high production values" of the station's other shows, even though his budget of about $1,500 per weekly episode limited him to a talk show format: "I would tape two or three shows and make them all talk shows so that I could take that budget and invest it in film stock." [70] In this manner, Treviño was able to film such short documentaries as *Carnalitos* (1973) and *Somos Uno* (1973), airing them as segments on his series. Treviño also used these films as a way to train other Chicano filmmakers, such as Bobby Páramo, who coproduced *Carnalitos*. [71] Because he was diverting his budget to producing short documentaries, Treviño had airtime to fill on his own series and filmed segments to distribute to other stations. In its first year, then, *Acción Chicano* pooled resources with a new Puerto Rican series in New York City called *Realidades,* and the two shows traded five episodes each for local rebroadcast. The arrangement signaled the emergence of national "Latino" programming based on multilocal and multiethnic production as well as the first instance of a bicoastal Chicano and Puerto Rican coalition.

Realidades

Like *Acción Chicano, Realidades* was created through protest, though in a much more confrontational form. In 1972, members of the Puerto Rican Education and Action Media Council took over the WNET studio during the station's pledge drive. In the months before, José García Torres and others had attempted to negotiate with the station management for a public affairs series. When the station refused, the activists, who had planted volunteers as telephone operators on the pledge drive, read a statement on the air and shut down the studio. Under a banner reading "20% Hispanic population, 0% programming," some 250 people demonstrated outside the station, including sympathetic WNET staff. As García Torres wryly notes, "Power concedes nothing without demand.

As a result of that community action [the station] stated to the press the next day that they had found discretionary funds within their budget to guarantee this new series called *Realidades* for the first year."[72]

In its first two years, the series was similar to *Acción Chicano*, mixing filmed segments with the talk show format. Then, in 1974, CPB awarded *Realidades* $60,000 to produce a one-hour pilot for national broadcast. The next year, *Realidades* became the first national Latino public affairs series, hiring a Chicano producer to join the three other staff producers in New York City: Humberto Cintrón, Raquel Ortiz, and Mercedes Sandoval. Antonio Parra, an associate producer on *Acción Chicano*, took the position, producing segments on employment and politics. According to Parra, "[I]t was the first time Chicanos, Puerto Ricans, and Central Americans came together to work in one project on a national scale. . . . and there were a lot of frictions and a lot of misunderstandings."[73] The experience allowed the different groups to learn about each other, while the series itself provided the opportunity to commission numerous Chicano films, including Severo Pérez's *Cristal* (1975), Susan Racho's *Garment Workers* (1975), Jay Ojeda's *De Colores* (1975), José Luis Ruiz's *Guadalupe* (1976), Bobby Páramo's *Salud and the Latino* (1976), Ricardo Soto's *Cosecha* (1976), *Migra* (1976), and *Al Otro Paso* (1976), and Adolfo Vargas's *Una Nación Bilingüe* (1977).[74] Several of these segments dealt with national Latino issues, with footage shot on both coasts and the Midwest: *Garment Workers*, *De Colores*, and *Salud and the Latino*.

In its two years as a national series, *Realidades* received $553,687 from CPB and produced twenty-three half-hour programs. After two years of CPB funding, the PBS series had to be picked up for subsequent funding by the national station cooperative. "But," as Raquel Ortiz noted at the time, "WNET didn't support the series when it went to the Station Program Cooperative (SPC)."[75] WNET management objected to the outspoken executive producer, Humberto Cintrón, and they considered the coverage of Puerto Rican Solidarity Day, among other topics, to be too controversial, even though, as Ortiz explained, "All we did was cover an event."[76] Without support from WNET as well as other stations, the SPC turned down the series for a third season. In the end, funds from CPB proved to be limited and short term. Even during the national run of the series, CPB's Latino funding represented less than 3 percent of CPB's total production budget, and in the three years following the series, that level would drop to 1 percent.[77] For both *Acción Chicano* and *Realidades,* the initial commitment of funds was the consequence of bringing street protest into the station on behalf of local ethnic groups, while the programming itelf strove to represent Latino groups around the nation. Thus, if protest and production remained locally and ethnically specific, programming and professional advocacy necessarily became national and panethnic under the banner of Latino media.

Latino Consortium

Ironically, the first "Latino" organization began not as a coalition, but as a consortium among stations seeking to cut the cost of their Chicano public affairs programming. During the two-year run of *Acción Chicano,* KCET looked for ways to meet the local demand for Chicano programming without at the same time expanding its production. By 1973, KCET management had developed the idea of a programming cooperative among PBS stations with large Chicano audiences, which they then proposed at the PBS national meeting in Washington, D.C., the following year. Nine other stations participated in the first season of the Latino Consortium: KLRN (San Antonio), KERA (Dallas), KRMA (Denver), WKAR (East Lansing), KVIE (Sacramento), KQED (San Francisco), KAET (Tempe), KUAT (Tucson), and KPBS (San Diego). KCET coordinated the "bicycling" or shipment of tapes within the consortium, which proved to be a "scheduling nightmare," since many stations did not allocate money for dubbing and would wait until after the scheduled broadcast before sending the tape to the next station. In the first year, consortium programming consisted of episodes of *Acción Chicano.* Although other stations soon began to contribute their own programs, they were often of such low quality that KCET would not rebroadcast them. As Parra noted in his brief history of the consortium, "The participating stations wanted Latino programming at the cheapest price possible." [78]

Despite its insistence on broadcast quality, KCET also sought to reduce its Chicano production costs, dropping *Acción Chicano* and limiting its programming commitment to the Latino Consortium, which only required members to produce between one and four programs per season and broadcast at least 50 percent of the syndicated programming.[79] In 1975, KCET hired José Luis Ruiz as executive director in order to make the operations more effective and develop a more national presence.[80] With a $30,000 grant from CPB, Ruiz convened a national conference with representatives from twenty-nine stations across the

United States. The conference resulted in over twenty additional member stations, but it failed to involve stations with Puerto Rican and Cuban American producers and/or audiences in order to make the consortium more Latino oriented, as intended. For the next four years, then, the consortium continued as a Chicano programming exchange financed by an assortment of local stations, often as a cost-cutting replacement for their previous community-oriented production. "In the original meeting of 1976," Ruiz notes, "the biggest fear that Latinos had was that stations would stop producing locally and depend on the consortium to supplement its Hispanic programming, and so we tried to draw guidelines."[81] But it happened anyway. Nevertheless, the conference brought together many of the Latino producers in public television, facilitating interethnic working relationships and quid pro quo agreements that would develop over the next two decades. Thus, while WNET (New York) and WGBH (Boston) did not join the consortium at that time, *Realidades* producers and the Latino Consortium agreed to support each other within CPB/PBS.[82]

When Ruiz left the Latino Consortium in 1976, the organization migrated to Detroit, under Cecilia Garcia at WTVS, before returning to KCET in the late 1970s. But the consortium did not develop into a truly national programming syndicator until it secured funds from CPB, providing the consortium with some autonomy from the more limited purposes it served for KCET and member stations. Starting in 1979, CPB provided annual support for the Latino Consortium, initially $92,000 a year but reaching around $200,000 a year by the end of the 1980s. In the early 1980s, the consortium also switched to satellite feed by buying time through the Central Educational Network in Chicago, which allowed the entire system to access its programming. Over the next decade, three executive directors—Rick Tejada-Flores (1979–81), Sylvia Morales (1981–85), and Mark J. Carreño (1985–89)—expanded the consortium's membership to fifty-three stations, packaging drama, documentary, and entertainment programs under an omnibus series (*¡Presente!* for seven seasons, followed by *Vistas*—hosted by Rita Moreno—starting in the fall of 1986).[83] But these were make-do alternatives to an actual series, cobbled together from diverse and uneven local programming and reaching only a small portion of the PBS system. For its part, CPB never pursued the goal of a "strand" or nationally broadcast series on Latino issues as expressed in its own 1979 report, *A Formula for Change,* submitted by the Task Force on Minorities in Public Broadcasting. As Tejada-Flores noted at the time, "CPB is not putting in any production monies; it's just packaging programs which are locally produced."[84] The CPB funds for the Latino Consortium were earmarked solely for promotion.

By the end of the 1980s, public television programming had changed in several significant ways as deregulation both increased corporate funding and decreased the commitment to local community-oriented production. In essence, the local disappeared and was replaced by public affairs programming funded by transnational corporations (mostly in finance or electronics), made outside PBS and its major production centers, and offered direct to local stations at little to no cost. Whereas local public affairs programs had served as a vital forum for debate within racially and economically diverse urban populations, these programs reflected elite concerns, consisting of either corporate showcases (*Adam Smith's Money World, Wall Street Week,* and *Nightly Business Report*) or conservative talk shows (*Firing Line, The McLaughlin Group,* and *One on One*). As William Hoynes concludes, "[T]hese programs exist in such abundance because of a convergence of two factors: local public television stations' need to obtain inexpensive programs, and the desire of corporate funders to have such perspectives aired on a regular basis."[85] If the local had been replaced by corporate production of "public affairs" programs, CPB/PBS likewise came under an increasingly corporatist framework, calculating risk in production decisions not in terms of some notion of the public interest or even of ratings, but according to the concerns of corporate underwriters, local station managers, and conservative legislators.[86]

It was during this period that Latino producers left local stations and became independent producers, often shifting from public affairs to cultural affairs programs, since the latter allowed racial minorities to cross over into a national audience, in large part by dropping the politics and entering into the realm of the aesthetic, wherein, *pace* Horace, one both instructs and delights at some remove from the social formation. The public sphere—as exemplified by the local public affairs programming of the early 1970s—had become privatized around corporate-funded business news and corresponding ideological commentary. What Latino and other minority producers faced, then, was an instance in which the cultural not only challenged the corporate, but did so while standing outside a public sphere within which to participate in political debate and decision making. If pundits and politicians bemoaned the rise of cultural and identity politics, pointing fingers at PBS and the national endowments, they conveniently ignored the fact that such "politics" were the only available strategy for minority groups seeking access to the mass media. They also ignored the fact that PBS and the national endowments already served their own interests to a much greater extent than those of the minority groups that they blamed.

Meanwhile, local stations dropped the minority public affairs series format and began cherry picking from the consortium package, slotting individual programs around the PBS national schedule and corporate-funded syndicated series.[87] The Latino Consortium went from being a syndicator of locally produced programs packaged into regular series to becoming a "weak access point" for independent producers "where we couldn't even tell the filmmakers when they were going to be broadcast."[88] In any event, regular CPB funding did secure institutional status for the Latino Consortium, ensuring its long term survival, while providing an access point, however weak, for the Latino independent producers who had left local stations since the mid-1970s. When Ruiz returned to the Latino Consortium in 1989, he would remake it into an independent entity within public television, one that attempted to participate in the system's entrepreneurial zeitgeist. In the interim, Chicano producers would continue efforts to build a coalition with other Latino groups in order to acquire a critical mass with which to address the nation-state. Since Chicanos, like Puerto Ricans and Cuban Americans, were understood in regional and not national terms, they turned to "Hispanic" or "Latino" as a necessary fiction for engaging the national. These terms offered neither identity markers nor de facto political categories; instead, they represented the bumpy road of coalition building among diverse groups unable to achieve a national representation in their own name or in their own image.

Addressing the Nation-State

By the time *Realidades* went off the air in 1977, its executive producer, Humberto Cintrón, realized the need for a pan-Latino organization in order to secure ongoing funding for Latino programming at the national level. The series itself provided the foundation for such advocacy, since it both established a national network of local producers and provided an arena for working out a panethnic coalition based on identifying differences and shared concerns. In the period between *Realidades* and CPB funding of the Latino Consortium, Cintrón and other Latino producers used the National Latino Media Coalition (NLMC) as a platform for challenging CPB and PBS policy. The NLMC represents a hybrid advocacy group, starting in the early 1970s as an outgrowth of the media reform movement but becoming more producer oriented by the time the group incorporated in April 1977.[89] In this respect, NLMC embodies the shift from activism to professionalism, revealing not just the conflicts between the corresponding tactics, locations, and personnel, but also a rather self-conscious attempt to use both outside and inside as part of a larger reform strategy.

By 1973, earlier Chicano-specific efforts to create a national umbrella organization had failed, including the National Mexican American Anti-Defamation Committee and the National Chicano Media Council. In contrast, NLMC emerged through happenstance at a time when Chicanos and Puerto Ricans had come to realize the need to collaborate on areas of mutual concern. In May 1973, during the first meeting between the FCC and minority media reform groups, Latino advocates withdrew as an ad hoc group when they felt that their particular concerns—for example, bilingual programming—were not being addressed. The group demanded and received a separate meeting with the FCC for the next day. The experience convinced the participants of the need to decouple Latino interests from the catchall category of "minority," while it also required creating a viable coalition between different Latino groups in order to be effective at the national level.

In creating an organizational infrastructure, the NLMC struck a balance along two axes: Puerto Rican and Chicano; and activist and producer. The chair position alternated between the two major ethnic groups, while the board consisted of representatives from six regions. Furthermore, as the bylaws specified, "No more than three of the six regional representatives are to be employed within the media industry and to earn more than twenty percent of their income from that industry."[90] In many respects, however, the bylaws signified the increasing presence and influence of media producers within the coalition. In April 1975, the coalition held its first national conference in San Antonio, Texas, followed by others in Los Angeles (April 1976) and New York (April 1977). The first conference, as Treviño notes,

> would turn out to be this free for all because everybody was polarized.
> It was Chicanos against Puerto Ricans, and Texas Chicanos against
> California Chicanos. I mean, it was just a madhouse. . . . But, you

know, actually what happened at that time is that a lot of friendships were formed, like with Raquel. Since then we've worked very closely together over the years.[91]

Thus, by the second conference, Cintrón and other producers identified the NLMC as a way to lobby public television, government agencies, and Congress. Thus, rather than pursue litigation as in the media reform of the early 1970s, the NLMC engaged in a strategy to integrate professionals into the administrative structure and funding protocols for public television. In this way, the NLMC played an instrumental role in several concessions on the part of CPB: the appointment of Louis P. Terrazas to the board of directors, the hiring of José Luis Ruiz as a consultant for the development of another national Latino series, and NLMC participation in the CPB's Advisory Council of National Organizations (ACNO). These efforts, and the NLMC's resignation from ACNO in September 1976, coincided with congressional budgetary pressures on CPB over its EEO record, providing the group with some leverage.[92]

In the end, when Ruiz recommended another public affairs series using the magazine format, CPB decided upon a dramatic series, awarding research and development grants to four projects during 1977: *Oye Willie* (Lou De Lemos), *Bless Me Ultima* (José Luis Ruiz), *La Historia* (Jesús Salvador Treviño), and *Centuries of Solitude* (KERA-TV).[93] CPB delayed decisions on the subsequent production of pilot programs, leading Treviño and Ruiz to present a written statement to the CPB board in October 1979, which was followed by protests from a national contingent of Latino producers that November.[94] For Latino producers, as Treviño and Ruiz noted, CPB had exchanged its agreement to develop and fund another series for the endless deferral of "research and development as a way of life," while it also turned to the Latino Consortium as a "panacea for national Hispanic programming."[95] These pressures resulted in short-term funding for pending dramatic projects by Puerto Rican and Chicano producers. In 1980, CPB funded *Oye Willie* for one season and provided partial support for two dramatic features that had already received funds from the National Endowment for the Humanities (NEH): *Sequin* (1981), the pilot program from Treviño's *La Historia* series; and *The Ballad of Gregorio Cortez* (1983). But by December 1980, when Ruiz organized a Hispanic Southwest Regional Conference aimed at facilitating additional Chicano projects funded by the NEH,[96] Latino producers had hit a brick wall in terms of public television policy, and the NLMC came to a quiet end. Producers had also identified another funding source in the NEH, one that offered an opportunity to develop and direct feature-length films based on historical events or literary works.[97] In effect, Latino producers looked outside CPB and PBS, making alliances with other governmental agencies, often in order to return with programs for broadcast and syndication within the PBS system. In short, Chicanos joined with Puerto Ricans in order to stake a claim to the nation-state, learning their way around the political and bureaucratic landscape within which public television operated. But these same producers also looked outside the nation-state itself, defining Chicano cinema and their own professional activities within an international context.

Going International

One of the interesting paradoxes of the Chicano movement is that its political discourse continued to look to Mexico, Cuba, and, more generally, the "Bronze Continent" as the necessary backdrop for its efforts to imagine a Chicano community within the political, socioeconomic, and legal structures of the United States. For Chicano filmmakers, this "imagined" location in the Americas became the context for local political action as well as professional reform within the U.S. film and television industries. More than any other media group in this period, the Los Angeles–based Chicano Cinema Coalition (1978–80) exemplified the mixture of professional, radical, and community-based tactics used to establish the idea of a Chicano cinema as well as to create "our own institutions" for production, distribution and exhibition.[98] In its brief existence, the coalition served as a resource for over forty producers, writers, directors, and film students and as a platform for protests against exploitation films and industry hiring practices. Members included Jason Johansen, Sylvia Morales, José Luis Ruiz, Luis Torres, Jesús Salvador Treviño, and Adolfo Vargas. The coalition held workshops, hosted visiting Latino and Latin American filmmakers, and even screened classic Hollywood films in order to learn about the industry and its cinematic style. Organized protests included detailed press statements upon the release of the gang film *Boulevard Nights* and the made-for-television movies *Act of Violence* and *Streets of L.A.* in 1979.[99] The coalition also pressured educational and funding institutions, often successfully incorporating Chicanos into existing programs. On December 15, 1978, for example, coalition members met

with the American Film Institute (AFI) to discuss the underrepresentation of Chicanos within the organization. In a follow-up letter to the directors on January 10, 1979, the coalition noted that "(1) there are no
Hispanics on the AFI Board of Directors, (2) that only one Chicana has
participated in the women's director program, and (3) that only two or
three Hispanics have ever participated in the ten-year history of the AFI
independent film grant program." Consequently, in late February, three
coalition members were awarded AFI grants: Aldolfo Vargas, David
Sandoval, and Francisco Martinez.[100]

In addition to professional advocacy and membership support, the
coalition called for "a Chicano alternative cinema ideology and philosophy which stress the use of film and videotape for the decolonization,
independence, advancement, *concientización* and national liberation of
the Mexican and Chicano people in the United States."[101] The development of such an aesthetic was seen as "intrinsically linked" to the alternative cinema movements of other ethnic groups in the United States
as well as in Latin America and the Third World.[102] The coalition was
not alone in making this argument: Cine-Aztlán (Santa Barbara) and
Francisco Camplis (San Francisco) had earlier placed the emergent film
practice within the context of Third World politics.[103] Interestingly,
both were heavily influenced by Jesús Treviño—the former incorporating his research for *¡Ahora!* into its publication, the latter drawing upon
an extensive interview with Treviño.

In any case, the connection between ethnic and Third World politics found resonance in the concurrent scholarship by Mario Barrera,
Carlos Muñoz Jr., Rodolfo Acuña, and others who described the barrio
as an "internal colony."[104] The difference between "internal" and "external" colonialism was not so much geographical as legal. Chicanos
had the same "formal legal status" as all other United States citizens;
but, as Barrera and the others argued, the conditions of colonialism remained the same: "Internal colonialism means that Chicanos as a cul-
tural/racial group exist in an exploited condition which is maintained
by a number of mechanisms . . . [and] . . . a lack of control over those
institutions which affect their lives."[105] In "Notes on Chicano Cinema,"
Johansen articulated the cinematic counterpart to an internal colony
model implicit in all the manifestos: "Hollywood cinema is one of intellectual colonization." For this reason, all three manifestos opposed
Hollywood while looking to revolution in Latin America as the appropriate international catalyst and context for Chicano cinema: "our films

should strive to connect our struggle internationally. . . . Our films should prepare Raza for that eventuality" (Camplis); "La Raza film-makers have an international responsibility . . . to unify Raza interpretations with the total human circumstance in a class structured society" (Cine-Aztlán); and, "[g]iven the ability of the medium to reach a wide audience, Chicano film must remain linked to and be an integral part of the revolutionary process" (Johansen).

But if the manifestos rejected Hollywood, they nonetheless relied upon the terms of its liberal humanist discourse in order to effect or prepare audiences for international revolution: "Yet, our struggles, hopes and dreams are universal because we are human beings" (Camplis). Rejection of the "liberal" filmmakers who sought change or reform from within the established modes of production and distribution existed simultaneously with the call for a "radical" practice that sought revolution based upon an assumption of Hollywood-type distribution. This contradiction also manifested itself in the practical efforts of the Chicano Cinema Coalition to seek access to the U.S. film and television industry while developing relations within Latin America on the basis of an antithetical position toward Hollywood.

The manifestos, then, reveal the way in which Chicano political thought built upon a Third World politics of national liberation while at the same time focusing its efforts on the politics of incorporation vis-à-vis existing U.S. social institutions. In fact, in the case of Camplis and Cine-Aztlán, their understanding of New Latin American Cinema was almost entirely limited to its manifestos, which were translated and reprinted in *Cinéaste* in 1970.[106] Thus, if their rhetoric was international and revolutionary, their political orientation was actually grounded in the more immediate experience of the Chicano movement circa 1974. It was not until Jason Johansen published his "Notes" in 1979 that Chicano filmmakers, under the direction of the Chicano Cinema Coalition, started to develop a concrete relationship or "active solidarity" with the films and practitioners of New Latin American Cinema.[107] But the imagined solidarity served a purpose, too. In the expression of an oppositional political and aesthetic stance, the Chicano film manifestos, like those of the Chicano movement itself, provided an alternative geography or conceptual space within which to approach U.S. institutions.[108]

In this respect, José Limón's application of Harold Bloom's concept of the "anxiety of influence" to the Chicano movement offers some insight.[109] But whereas Limón identifies the Mexican Revolution of 1910 as the object of the movement's anxiety of influence, it is perhaps more historically accurate to argue that anxiety over the more prevalent "gringo" influences motivated Chicanos to research and identify models in the Mexican and Cuban revolutions. Likewise, Chicano filmmakers' appeal to New Latin American Cinema masked a considerable anxiety over the pervasive influence of Hollywood, an anxiety also expressed in the manifestos of New Latin American Cinema. For Chicano filmmakers, especially those who lived and worked in Los Angeles, Hollywood constituted *the* U.S. film and television industry, one from which they remained excluded, except as stereotypes. The Chicano Cinema Coalition and other community-based groups reiterated that point in organized protests against *Walk Proud* (1979), a gang film starring Robby Benson in brownface. Shot on location in Venice, California, the film production increased tensions between the police and the local Chicano community.[110] It is within this context that Chicano filmmakers theorized, sought out, and developed other influences.

Postrevolutionary Cuba provided both rhetoric and experience for the development of the Chicano movement's radical politics as well as its reformist achievements, starting with Luis Valdez's trip to Cuba in 1964 as part of a student delegation. For filmmakers, however, the most lasting impact has been the result of Treviño's involvement with New Latin American Cinema. In 1974, Treviño was recruited into the Cuban-sponsored Comité de Cineastas de América Latina (Latin American Filmmakers Committee), an international committee of a dozen or more filmmakers committed to the advancement of New Latin American Cinema. The committee met six times between 1974 and 1978 and worked toward the organization of the Annual Festival of New Latin American Cinema, which premiered in December 1979 in Havana, Cuba. At its sixth meeting—held in Havana, July 12–17, 1978—the committee issued a declaration about the festival that in the second paragraph spelled out the relationship of the Chicano filmmakers to New Latin American Cinema:

> Igualmente nos declaramos solidarios con la lucha llevada a cabo por el cine del pueblo chicano, manifestación cultural de una comunidad que combate por afirmar su identidad de raíz latinoamericana en medio de la opresión y discriminación a que es sometida en el territorio de los Estados Unidos de Norteamérica. Esta realidad casi o total-

mente desconocida por una gran parte de nuestros pueblos, o que ha llegado a ellos a través de las tergiversaciones de la información imperialista, tiene hoy sus cineastas, cuenta ya con un conjunto de obras y demanda de nostros el compromiso de fortalecer los lazos histórico-culturales que nos unen a ella, contribuyendo a la difusión de sus filmes, de sus experiencias y de sus luchas.

[We also declare our solidarity with the struggle of Chicano cinema, the cultural manifestation of a community that combats the oppression and discrimination within the United States in order to affirm its Latin American roots. This reality remains almost or entirely unknown by most of our people, or reaches them through the distortions of the imperialist news media. Yet today (the Chicano community) has its own filmmakers and films and demands of us the commitment to strengthen the cultural-historical ties that join us together, contributing to the dissemination of their films, their experiences, and their struggles.][111]

The Chicano Cinema Coalition led a delegation of seventeen Chicano filmmakers and media advocates to the first festival.[112] The Puerto Rican producer Raquel Ortiz also attended. As Treviño explains, "[I]t was a real eye opener experience for a lot of Chicanos that went, because for the first time they were seeing a lot of Latin American—not just Cuban—cinema."[113] One of those who attended was Eduardo Díaz, soon to be the director of the San Antonio CineFestival, who adds:

> The organizers of the event had certainly opened up their perspective—Chicanos were regarded as a nation of Latin American derivation living within the confines of the United States. The Festival even programmed a special series of Chicano films and honored it with a special poster (a wonderful graphic depicting the thorns of a bright green cactus tearing away at an American flag).[114]

The Chicano films screened received an award as a group, and Treviño's *Raíces de Sangre* (Mexico, 1977) won the award for best feature script. In subsequent years, Chicano cinema functioned as a national category within this and other Spanish-language festivals. Chicanos thus continued to participate in the festival—for example, as jurors—as well as in a new Cuban film production program established in January 1987 for students from Third World countries. Graciela I. Sánchez from San Antonio participated in the first eighteen months of the program, producing the first documentary in Cuba to deal with homosexuality: "*. . . no Porque lo Diga Fidel Castro*" (1988).[115]

While the experience in Cuba seemed to confirm the predictions of the earlier film manifestos, the social context for racial and radical

Premiere of Raíces de Sangre in East Los Angeles with director Jesús Salvador Treviño (left). Photograph copyright Harry Gamboa Jr., 1978.

politics in the United States had changed quite a bit since the heyday of the Chicano movement and of New Latin American Cinema.[116] Contacts with Latin America did foster an increased international political perspective in the 1980s, although it is difficult to separate this perspective from the filmmakers' increased awareness of and attention to the international film market and festival circuit. In this respect, the Festival of New Latin American Cinema served an important symbolic role in doubling the "location" of Chicano cinema, making it into a movement that was at once reformist and revolutionary. But rather than constitute a contradiction, this dual location provided Chicano filmmakers with an effective political strategy within the United States. Chicano cinema both juxtaposed and straddled two locations, America and América, not so much as a matter of an either/or choice (even though it was presented and debated as such), but rather as an attempt to define tightly coupled oppositional terms—nationalism and assimilation, revolution and reform—so that the one would inevitably produce the other. Early successful reforms came about in this manner as a result of shifting the center leftward during public protests and press statements, providing filmmakers with a vantage point from which to negotiate for more moderate goals within the film and television industry and related social institutions. Without a doubt, such a strategy put Chicano cinema on the map in both a literal and a figurative sense, constructing an alternative to Hollywood. But it was an alternative in both senses of the word, something different from Hollywood, yet something that also aspired to take its place.

eight

This Is Not a Border
From Social Movement to Digital Revolution

While the Chicano media strategy developed by the mid-1970s continues to the present, numerous changes have made it an increasingly rhetorical one that fails to account for either individual careers or institutional operations. The rhetorical appeal to a "revolutionary" Latin America no longer works as part of a strategy to secure U.S. public funding, in large part because of the rise of aggressive neoliberalism or market-driven policies throughout the hemisphere. Furthermore, during the 1980s, the so-called Decade of the Hispanic, public funding sources, which had been the mainstay of Chicano-produced film and video, were cut back under the Reagan and Bush administrations. With deregulation as the official policy within the Federal Communications Commission (FCC), the "public" dimension of broadcast television became increasingly privatized, first on the commercial networks, then on public television itself.[1] If Chicano filmmakers had developed a rhetoric and practice based on moving inside and outside a professional arena bound by the nation-state, the new terrain—best described as the disappearance of the public into the private—required another approach: courting the citizen-consumer. But how?

With the Telecommunications Act of 1996, the deregulated "consumer sovereignty" of the corporate mass media went global and brought broadcast networks into direct "competition" with six other transnational industries: film, cable, telephone, computer, publishing, and consumer electronics. But competition is somewhat of a misnomer, insofar as these industries are increasing grouped under U.S.-based vertically integrated media conglomerates, the largest being News Corporation, Time Warner, Disney, Viacom, and TCI. (European-based Bertelsmann is ranked third, after Time Warner, among these global media groups.) Computer corporations stand alongside these conglomerates, with Microsoft, Intel, and Compaq having a higher net worth than all the Hollywood studios combined. And, last but not least, joint ventures and cross-ownership are the norm among these corporations. Thus if the activity taking place is competition, it is not the type idealized by capitalism itself—the type that leads to better product at lower prices. Quite the contrary, especially insofar as it is *consumption* and not the *consumer* that has become sovereign. The reason has to do with regulatory law itself. Since the 1930s, the public interest had been defined as a national ideal regulated at the local level, hence the regulation of over-the-air broadcast stations but not networks. The purpose of regulation had to do with a particular cause (commercial broadcasting) rather than a general effect (a public sphere based on reception alone), and that made it easier for telecommunications to loosen its regulatory moorings in the local market once "broadcast" became just one of a number of delivery mechanisms. Going global, then, meant that there were no borders, because there were no publics to be served, only markets. Fittingly, as Robert W. McChesney points out, the Telecommunications Act of 1996 was largely reported as a business or technology story, rather than as a public policy issue with profound societal and global implications.[2]

From the wired nation to the global village, communications technologies have been at the center of utopian visions of community. And for good reason: print as a commodity ushered in the modern era, creating "monoglot mass reading publics" that were secular, nonhierarchical, and simultaneous.[3] In this manner, a nation could begin to imagine itself in terms of a "deep, horizontal comradeship" among individuals.[4] With respect to U.S. telecommunications, the free market and new technologies promised a consumerist path to social equity and democracy. Today, as Edward S. Herman and Robert W. McChesney describe this ideology, "Any social problems not addressed by the 'magic of the market' will be resolved by the near-mystical powers of digital technology."[5] Under deregulation, the prevailing assumption has been that diversity of channels will lead to diversity of content and ownership, when, in fact, it has intensified merger activity, leading not just to concentration and downsizing, but to a global integrated oligopoly. Meanwhile, new technologies are promoted for their presumed ability to blur the boundaries between producers and consumers. Cable, interactive television, video on demand, and similar proposed services through an "information superhighway" are framed in such a way as to imply that a proliferation of consumer choice creates something akin to producing the product itself. In a recent media conference, for example, Dean Valentine, then the president of Walt Disney Television and now heading the United Paramount Network, claimed that such choice allowed viewers to act as their own network stations, apparently by using the remote to cobble together programming that reflects their individual interests.[6] In effect, freedom of choice becomes freedom of expression, and consumption is thereby confused with production and public speech.

But once one moves beyond such utopianism, a simple fact remains: broadcasting continues to be based on two premises—"the radical separation of transmission and reception" and, in consequence, "selling audiences to advertisers."[7] Broadcasting itself factored into the global privatization of the very communication networks that served as basic infrastructures undergirding the nation-state:

> Communication was and is becoming central to the global market economy; business wanted and needed high-speed communication networks to manage global operations. In this context, the move toward privatized communication was the key to admission to the global economy, and there was simply no other alternative within the existing set of social relations. . . . In many respects this need to have privatized communication to participate in global capitalism accounts for the lack of democratic participation in communications debates, and the narrow range of the debates that have ensued. The only issue to be debated was the speed of the liberalization program, not the merits of it.[8]

As a consequence, while both capital and the mass media have gone global, consumers have become increasingly local—that is, consumers no longer belong to an imagined national community, but rather to a highly individuated one that provides an illusory sense of control and autonomy over industry product. Surfing the Web or flipping through eighty-odd channels gives us the sense of global reach and, hence, power, but we are rarely more than consumers. The quantitative expansion of choice obscures its qualitative sameness, contributing to a moment in which the business contract secures the social contract and the private transaction makes the public sphere, thereby conflating the consumer with the citizen. Citizens are assumed to be passive—that is, their choices and expressions are geared toward personal consumption and not toward re-producing community. The commonweal, national community, civic duty, and other productive social acts become little more than "externalities" of a business transaction between global mass media, global capital, and the state, on the one hand, and individual consumers, on the other hand.

While drawn in extremely broad strokes, the above account signals the democratic consequences and global dimensions of the decline of Latino television programming in the 1970s and 1980s. In short, as minority public affairs series migrated from network to public television, only to be replaced by corporate-sponsored public affairs series, the "public" became a private matter while "minority" became a cultural one. The hope was that "minority" culture could now serve as the parameters for both a (global) commodity and a (niche) market.[9] Consequently, the press discourse on Latinos and the media increased exponentially in the 1990s. But it did so in restricted terms, creating a handful of "Latino" celebrities (sometimes without a body of work) while defining the Latino population almost entirely in terms of an elusive yet desirable market to be penetrated. Even the increased press on the absence of Latinos in the media framed the discussion in terms of emerging celebrities and an exploding market.[10]

This approach appears to have started in the Latino press as an alternative to the earlier "discourse of violence," with its emphasis on rights and expression. Civil rights? Social equity? Cultural diversity? These ideals require a public sphere within which they can be articulated, whereas the marketplace uses another language. Thus, for example, while *Hispanic Business* (1982–) devotes its July issue to the entertainment industry, Latino producers tend to be discussed in the context of "consumers." It is the highest-paid performers whose "careers" and social agency are spotlighted. Other significant publications include *Hispanic* (1988–), *Más* (1989–93), and *Hispanic Link* (1983–). For actors and even some producers, press-generated celebrity became an avenue into the industry, rather than vice versa, most notably for Edward James Olmos. Along these lines, Bel Hernandez publishes *Latin Heat* (1993–), a bimonthly Latino entertainment industry trade publication that also hosts an annual Latino Entertainment Conference (since 1995). Despite intentions to the contrary, this approach necessarily pits Latinos against each other insofar as it works from a traditional assimilation model: Latino actors and producers must adapt themselves to the industry, competing with each other for that right, while also serving as the front line against calls for more structural industry reforms. In the mid-1990s, the Cuban American producer Nely Galán became the ubiquitous poster child for the claim that Hollywood had at last opened its doors to Latinos, offering upbeat quotes in pointed contrast to the statements by media reform and identity-oriented advocates.[11] The cruel irony is that Galán's development deals—like all other such deals since the late 1980s—yielded no Latino productions in the English-language media. If only assimilation worked—but its first premise is that the problem resides entirely in those who have been kept out.

At the same time, U.S.-based Spanish-language television as well as the Latin American market became regular news items in the business press, the former as a "new" market phenomenon seeking its share of advertising revenues, the latter as an object of global media activities. In the United States, Spanish-language television mostly recycled Latin American programming, thereby sidestepping "public interest" pressures for community-based productions. Thus, I have not dealt with Spanish-language television until now since it has generally not been part of a history of local ethnic-produced programming serving the public interest.[12] In the early 1990s, however, Spanish-language television became the object of various concerns. The A.C. Nielsen Company developed a "Hispanic Television Index" to measure viewing habits and ratings on Spanish-language television (paid for by Univisión and Telemundo),[13] while the mainstream press ran several features as a prelude to more-regular business coverage throughout the decade. Although their activities were much less reported, U.S. Latino groups began pressuring these networks for both local and independent production relevant to a U.S.-based population.[14]

By the late 1990s, bilingual programming re-emerged, not as a public-interest or education issue as in the political arena, but as a marketing strategy for Spanish-language networks associated with an older immigrant and working-class audience base. Despite their high ratings, these networks lagged behind their English-language counterparts in advertising revenues.[15] Bilingual programming promised to encompass the entire ethnic market, appealing to the equally large but more assimilated and middle-class population of second- and third-generation Latinos.[16] It is in this context that Nely Galán re-emerged in late 1998 as part of the new management team at Telemundo after its purchase by Sony Pictures Entertainment. Having failed in developing Latino-themed English-language programming, Galán had played a central role in producing Spanish-language promos for U.S. English-language programs being sold to and broadcast on the Latin American networks. Now, as Telemundo's new entertainment president and its only Latino or Spanish-speaking executive, Galán quickly announced that Telemundo would shift to "a more bilingual format," following the lead of Galavisión.[17]

What Telemundo did, however, was to mine the Sony Pictures library, using the format and scripts from 1970s police series as the basis for "new" Spanish-language programming reflecting the Latino experience: *Reyes y Rey* (adapted from *Starsky and Hutch*) and *Angeles* (a remake of *Charlie's Angels*).[18] Telemundo also added English-language subtitles. The recycled format and scripts, as well as the Tijuana location shooting, reduced production costs to a small fraction of those of their English-language equivalents. These series created opportunities for Latino actors and directors who had been excluded from episodic television in the United States, but they did so without creative or financial rewards—other than that of being able to use their experience to move into English-language television. Not surprisingly, these series failed to attract an audience, ranking well below the standard *telenovela* fare from Mexico. The corporate strategy itself overrode the goal of reaching a wider U.S. Latino audience. After all, what better way to attract assimilated Latino viewers than to recycle 1970s police series and resituate them in Mexico? The strategy strained credibility, but it also cost less than doing anything else. In the end, as commodity and market, Latinos facilitated the incorporation of Spanish-language television within global media, but they remained a structured absence within the media itself.

Meanwhile, Chicano cinema, like the public sphere that it sought, disappeared within most accounts of the rise of global media and the information superhighway—as did independents generally. Nevertheless, U.S. independent producers and media groups joined together and organized around pending telecommunication legislation, starting with their successful lobbying for a separate funding source for independent productions—the Independent Television Service (ITVS)—in 1988, then in response to the clarion call to develop a National Information Infrastructure (NII) or "information superhighway" in the 1990s.[19] In 1992, Jeffrey Chester and Kathryn Montgomery, the codirectors of the Center for Media Education, astutely identified "a narrow 'window of necessity'" of no more than five years within which independents had an "opportunity . . . to assert the public interest, reframe the debate in terms of democratic and social consequences, and involve legislators and the public in deciding the key questions of public policy." [20] Independent producers and advocates did engage these very issues in quite sophisticated and strategic ways—but they did so almost entirely outside media-controlled public discourse. [21]

If the independents fought for access, public policy concerned itself with the fantasy of the citizen-consumer. For example, in the *Aspen Institute Quarterly,* subtitled *Issues and Arguments for Leaders,* Francis D. Fisher described the social impact of telecommunications in the year 2002 by using the example of a hypothetical Latina welfare mother who has trouble speaking English and lives in a public housing project. [22] "Rosa Gonzales" has two teenage children: Maria, herself the mother of a two-year-old girl and pregnant with a second child, and John, an illiterate ex-con working as a grocery bag boy. Fisher baldly asserts that it is such families for whom the NII will make "the greatest contribution," helping them with education, health care, and government—but never explaining why these are no longer available or reliable offline in the public sector. What makes this essay significant, rather than merely laughable, is that Fisher operates within the policy arena itself, moving between university research centers, policy institutes, and the public sector, including stints at the U.S. Department of Education and the Office of Technology Assessment. In the end, he offers a fantasy about "choice"—the choice to do without social services while purchasing new computer equipment and accessories instead. Where does the money come from? Fisher's fantasy consists in having the poor pay for their own social control *and* subvent new technologies: "If the Gonzaleses had a camera for transmitting video, John could confirm his whereabouts to his parole officer." [23] Poor John.

And so, as Chester and Montgomery predicted, the "window of necessity" closed in less than five years with the Telecommunications Act of 1996. Subsequently, the fact that access to the public sphere had to be purchased raised no eyebrows, even when the Mexican American Legal Defense and Education Fund (MALDEF) began running "the first-ever image ad for an ethnic group" in February 1998. [24] The television ad—which ran in Southern California prior to the vote on Proposition 227 (eliminating bilingual education)—stressed image rather than policy, appealing to the 54 percent of whites who held negative views of Latinos as a group unconcerned with the quality of *American* life. Even more telling, the image ad ran during the evening news. But its function as a supplement put the image ad in a double bind in that it attempted to counteract the biases of the evening news while also associating itself with journalistic notions of objectivity. Ironically, the press covered the image ad as an "advertising and marketing" story, which, in many ways, was all too true. In buying the ether, as the public airwaves were once called, MALDEF also bought into its ethos that everything had a price.[25] Likewise, other civil rights groups found corporations and corporate foundations quite willing to fund either studies about the social disadvantages of being an untapped market or awards ceremonies celebrating the emerging celebrities of a phantom culture and exploding market.

In the remainder of this chapter, I will examine three instances of Chicano advocacy, distribution, and production in the 1990s, offering not so much a comprehensive history as a glimpse of contemporary events as they are unfolding. The three instances are the deregulated protest of the National Hispanic Media Coalition (established in 1987), the privatization of public television and transformation of the Latino Consortium into the National Latino Communications Center in 1990, and the re-emergence of Chicano internationalism around issues of gender and media production in the Americas.[26] Here I am necessarily more speculative than in the previous chapters; but this moment is also one in which I am complicit—as critic, curator, archivist, advocate, and even producer.

If I began this book claiming that "I was not there" and that I was an observer after the fact, the same has not been true during the period in which I have researched and written about Chicano cinema, which is also the period covered in this chapter. Indeed, these events have formed me as much as I have also formed an account of them. In starting this book with the 1960s, however, I claimed otherwise. As Michel de Certeau notes, "[I]t is an odd procedure that posits death, a breakage everywhere reiterated in discourse, and that yet denies loss by appropriating to the present the privilege of recapitulating the past as a form of knowledge."[27] But this past is not yet past. It shares the stage of the present with the historian. The death was metaphorical, or, at most, generational; it is located in the writing of history and not in the course of events still unfolding.

Deregulated Protest

While the mass media went global, Chicanos remained mired in the "numbers game" of federal regulation. Before considering how media activists responded to this situation, I want to make two points about numbers.[28] First, numbers are relative. While the figures for Latino portrayal and employment have stayed roughly the same over the past three decades (something Treviño has called "the 2 percent factor"),[29] the percentage of racial minorities continues to increase relative to the total U.S. population. The Latino population in particular has more than doubled since 1970. But neither the industry nor media advocates have revealed how the exponential increase in the Latino population changes the significance of the near-constant industry figures. This change occurs because the Latino population has doubled both in real numbers—from 9.1 million (1970) to 20.1 million (1990)—and as a percentage within the total U.S. population—from 4.5 percent (1970) to 8.2 percent (1990).[30] Thus, beneath the apparent statistical stasis within the industry lurks a situation in which actual employment opportunity and equitable representation have decreased by about 50 percent for the Latino population.

Second, numbers are selective. From a market-based perspective, minority underrepresentation is explained as a result of the need for a "universal appeal" that will satisfy the perceived taste and expectations of the primetime audience.[31] Minority themes and characters represent too much of a risk factor—or so we are told. But around 75 percent of new television series are canceled in their first year. In fact, of the thirty-four television series that premiered in 1992, only eight continued to 1993, a success rate of 23.5 percent.[32] In other words, following formats and actors with proven track records fails to achieve a "universal appeal" three out of four times. By its very nature, prime-time programming is a high-risk enterprise, so it is not a question of whether the industry takes risks, but of whom it allows to do so. In any case, FCC regulation and cross-ownership minimize their impact, protecting the system as a whole.

These contradictions reveal an unspoken problem with the numbers game: Those who opt to play must assume or attribute some notion of merit, rationality, and authority on the part of the system or institution whose rules define the game. But the game often becomes an end in itself, the impossible first step toward obtaining the rights and protections already written into the law and the supposed opportunities or "level playing field" of the free-market system. Surveying the past thirty years, one quickly notes that progress has been the product of protests more often than of direct government intervention. As a consequence, it has also been sporadic and piecemeal. There is, after all, a problematic assumption behind the numbers game: namely, that the statistical substantiation of discrimination will reform the film and television industries once that information is brought to light. In another context, Henri Lefebvre refers to this assumption as the "illusion of transparency" in which communication alone acts to transform social space.[33] The result is a belief in "freedom of expression" that pays no attention to the physical and institutional structures that limit access to social space. What Lefebvre suggests, then, is that the numbers game is more a strategy of power than a search for knowledge. What these numbers ultimately "mean" depends on the power relations within which they are asserted.

In the 1970s, regulated protest limited the scope of reform, but it also facilitated the ability of social movements and professional groups to pressure the industry for minority public affairs series and employment. Since the 1980s, deregulated protest has had neither a secure footing in the state nor the benefit of having the other foot either on the streets or in the international arena. Thus, not only did public affairs shows go off the air, but Latino broadcast journalists started to lose their jobs in the mid-1980s. In response, the National Hispanic Media Coalition developed a new twist on old strategies to pressure the television industry in an era of FCC deregulation and media mergers. The coalition came together during 1986 as the end result of "a brilliant thought that all these different people had at the same time."[34] Armando Durón was finishing his term as president of the Mexican American Bar Association and looking for something more consequential than "press conference" advocacy; Esther Renteria—an associate producer of such early public affairs series as *¡Ahora!, Bienvenidos,* and *The Siesta Is Over*—operated a public relations firm and had just founded the Hispanic Public Relations Association in 1984; and Alex Nogales, then a producer at KCBS, served as president of the Hispanic Academy of Media Arts and Sciences (HAMAS), which was then in the midst of a contentious struggle between traditional advocates and an influx of actors concerned with their profile within the industry.[35] These three principal members would alternate four-year terms as chair, Durón from 1987 to 1991, Renteria from 1991 to 1994, and Nogales from 1995 to 1998.

The "brilliant thought" that brought these and other Chicano professionals together was based on a historical understanding of Chicano media activism, recounted for them in part by the veteran activist Bert Corona, who had helped secure initial funding for Justicia in the 1970s. The coalition studied media reform history, its successes and failures, developing not just a viable strategy but a general theory about the nature of power—namely, that power had as much to do with perception as it did with coercion. By having no professional involvement with the media and by accepting no cash settlements, the coalition could avoid the blacklisting and cooptation that brought an end to earlier advocacy efforts. As Renteria explains, "We designed the coalition to be a group that could speak for those in the industry without having to go back the next day and say, 'We need a job.' We could be the battering ram!"[36] Thus, the coalition involved mostly nonmedia Latino groups, and Renteria and Nogales quit their media-related jobs in order to pursue media activism.[37] Durón specialized in family law. This autonomy produced the appearance of "incredible strength" in the way theorized by Saul D. Alinksy: *"Power is not only what you have but what the enemy thinks you have."*[38]

In addition to its autonomy, the coalition understood the peculiar way in which the "petition to deny"—the so-called heavy artillery of the broadcast reform movement in the 1970s[39]—became increasingly viable in the midst of deregulation. While petitions to deny are almost never upheld, a transfer of license cannot be approved until all pending petitions have been resolved. Since the FCC is understaffed (and has been subject to repeated cutbacks), "the wheels grind very, very slowly," producing an economic incentive to enter into a settlement agreement to remove the petition.[40] One of the defining features of deregulation—and the move toward global media—has been the intensified rate of mergers and acquisitions. In other words, deregulation not only increased the opportunities for media reform groups to intervene, it produced the very time-based pressures that made settlement preferable to waiting for the FCC to reject a petition.

The coalition focused on employment figures derived from Form 395, following FCC guidelines established in 1978 according to which stations should employ women and minorities at no less than half parity with the civilian labor force for their market area. With one exception, network stations in Los Angeles and New York were not in compliance (and public television and radio were the worst offenders). Starting in 1986, the Los Angeles–based coalition met with general managers of the local stations, working out an agreement with KCBS. When the new general manager refused to honor the agreement, he made the mistake of writing to the coalition on corporate letterhead informing them that "CBS Inc. and the station do not subscribe" to the concept of "goals and timetables for Hispanic employment at KCBS-TV"—even though affirmative action and equal opportunity policies were FCC license requirements at the time.[41] Renteria faxed the letter to a friend in Washington, D.C., who specialized in FCC law. Bob Thompson, who would thereafter serve as the coalition's pro bono lawyer, informed her that the general manager, as an officer of the corporation, had placed the entire CBS network in jeopardy. In a carefully orchestrated move that played off the time difference between the two coasts, Thompson faxed the letter to CBS in New York at 8:00 A.M. so that when the coalition arrived to set up a picket line in front of KCBS in Los Angeles at 9:00 A.M., they were promptly informed that the manager had been fired four hours earlier and that the network was prepared to meet with them. The coalition would play similar roles in removing several other biased station managers and news directors in Los Angeles.[42] In addition, the coalition teamed up with local groups in other cities across the nation, filing over fifty petitions by 1995.[43] Many petitions resulted in "reporting conditions" that shortened the license renewal period, requiring the station to report on its EEO efforts on a quarterly basis. The coalition also negotiated affirmative action agreements with the ABC and CBS stations in Los Angeles (1988) and New York (1989). By 1995, after nearly a decade of coalition efforts, only two television stations were not in compliance in Los Angeles and New York: KCAL (owned by Disney) and WWOR.

Between 1989 and 1992, the coalition became involved in Spanish-language television, negotiating agreements with Telemundo (1990) and Univisión (1992). Telemundo agreed to increase Latino representation within its seven owned and operated stations as well as on the network's board, create local news and public affairs programming, and solicit community participation (in everything from advisory boards to procurements from Hispanic-owned vendors and suppliers). Univisión, in the process of being sold by Hallmark Card to two major media magnates in Latin America, agreed to develop children's educational programming in exchange for the coalition's dropping its appeal of the FCC decision to deny its petition. Both agreements included benchmark dates that required contributions to scholarship funds if the networks did not meet certain deadlines—$100,000 for each missed deadline in the case of Univisión.[44]

The occasion for these negotiations grew out of internal conflicts at two Los Angeles stations: KMEX (Univisión) and KVEA (Telemundo).[45] In May 1989, 80 of the 150 employees at KMEX signed a vaguely worded petition than nonetheless implied that Mexican Americans were losing senior management positions at the station and within the network. The next month, KVEA fired its news director, Bob Navarro, who was the sole Mexican American in the station's senior management. Navarro, a veteran reporter who had covered the Patty Hearst case and Robert Kennedy's assassination for CBS, had joined KVEA ten months earlier with the goal of improving local news coverage on Spanish-language television. At the time, both networks were owned by U.S. holding companies and often filled management positions with non-Latinos who did not even speak Spanish. For the Spanish-language newspaper *La Opinión,* however, the primary concern had to do with what it called the "cubanización" of the networks.[46] Univisión had announced that it would consolidate its production operations in Miami, even though Los Angeles accounted for half its revenues.[47] At KVEA, Navarro was replaced by a Cuban American, while two other management positions held by Chicanos—the general manager and the executive producer— were filled by a non-Latino and a Spaniard. For Frank del Olmo, writing in *La Opinión* and the *Los Angeles Times,* the "Chicano-Cuban rivalry" revealed the myth of "Hispanic" unity.[48] But the rivalry itself was a myth, a reenactment through identity politics of a more structural conflict, one between corporate networks importing Latin American product for national broadcast and U.S. Latino urban populations that had just developed a political and economic presence at the local level. Latino demands upon these networks were no different than those upon the English-language media, although in this case Latinos were not a minority audience, they were *the* audience, and still they found themselves excluded.

In 1993, the coalition entered into its most recent phase, focusing its efforts on one network: ABC. The strategy reflected the coalition's limited resources, but it also dovetailed with increased media hearings and reports in advance of the planned overhaul of the Communications

Act of 1934. Renteria herself testified before the U.S. Civil Rights Commission (June 17, 1993) and the National Telecommunications and Information Administration (February 16, 1994). The first hearing coincided with dismal minority employment reports from the guilds, generating considerable press.[49] In September 1994, the National Council of La Raza sponsored a study that showed Latino portrayals on prime-time programming had declined from 3 percent in 1955 to 1 percent in the 1990s.[50] Unlike local stations, television networks are not licensed by the FCC and are therefore outside direct regulation, limiting reform efforts to an economic approach that correlated audience size and spending power to improvements in employment and portrayals. But writing to production companies and holding meetings with network presidents and division heads resulted in empty promises: CBS Entertainment Division agreed to hire a Latino writer for each of its shows (which fell apart when Jeff Sagansky left the network), and the president of Capital Cities/ABC, Robert Iger, promised a Latino-themed program for fall 1994 as well as increased walk-on and supporting roles for Latino actors (which never happened). In response, the coalition convened a National Latino Summit on the Media in January 1995, bringing together delegates from thirty organizations in order to define a national strategy. They settled upon a boycott of ABC. The boycott—which started with protests outside the network's owned and operated stations but also included contacting advertisers for support—functioned primarily as a public relations offensive, providing the coalition with a platform for presenting its case to the public and generating "bad press" for the network.[51] For its part, ABC denied it had made a promise to the coalition, but shortly initiated a Latino Freelance Writers Project.[52] When the Walt Disney Company announced its plans to purchase Capital Cities/ABC that July, Nogales met with Michael Eisner, but he came away with no guarantees, whereupon the coalition filed a petition to deny transfer.[53] The following fall, ABC launched a short-lived Latino sitcom, which Nogales claimed as a partial victory.[54] But in the absence of lasting and structural changes, the coalition extended its boycott to include both Disney and ABC in April 1997, gaining support from Los Angeles County Supervisor Gloria Molina and, indirectly, from the newly formed U.S. Congressional Hispanic Task Force on Arts and Entertainment, which subsequently met with Disney executives in Washington, D.C.[55] The coalition also filed petitions to deny license renewal of Disney's three radio stations in the Los Angeles area. But one consequence of such sustained pressure from a group that can be neither bought nor sold is that it increases the attractiveness of more moderate groups. Thus, in December 1997, ABC entered into an agreement with the National Council of La Raza to air its two-hour awards ceremony during prime time the following summer, while Disney gave money to the League of United Latin American Citizens (LULAC).[56] *Plus ça change.* To its credit, the coalition did not change.

If the coalition has helped to redefine post–civil rights Latino advocacy, it has done so because its cultural politics are fundamentally different from the radical and reformist models of the 1960s and 1970s. Whereas earlier groups worked within an environment nominally open to social change and thus developed a strategy predicated on being outside the system and defined by circulating knowledge about and against that system, the coalition worked within an environment defined by long-term deregulation and global technological and economic transformations. As such, their strategy depended not upon confronting the remnants of the state's regulatory system per se, but upon creating an appearance of power by tapping into the inherent instabilities within a deregulated and globalizing market. To some extent, the coalition succeeded by inserting itself into the loop of an increasingly corporatist system wherein social claims find expression through economic representation. But rather than sell an "untapped market" on the promise of residual benefits, the coalition demanded equitable employment at all levels, trading its demand against the cost of slowing down mergers and acquisitions. In an undefined global media environment, speed became the basis upon which conglomerates "competed" for stability and advantage; and so for the coalition time became power. The Telecommunications Act of 1996 seriously undermined such media activism and was followed two years later by a U.S. Court of Appeals ruling that rescinded the FCC affirmative action program.[57] The requirement that the electronic media reflect their public *cum* market no longer served a compelling public interest. For media reform groups, only economic pressure and "bad press" remained viable strategies. But another fact remains, although mostly forgotten until the serious global economic crisis in 1998. The state necessarily intervenes in both infrastructure industries and the system of currency exchange; or, as one pundit noted, "Free markets cannot exist without a supporting set of political institutions."[58] Ironically, the U.S. Court of Appeals ruling is a case in point insofar as it represents the still-prevailing political response to economic crises: deregulate. In other words, court decisions can be rather transparent responses to social unrest or economic crisis, while deregulation must be seen as a regulatory policy, not the absence of regulation. But therein also lies the potential for the coalition and other reform groups. It is not that government will save the day, but rather that community groups can always attach the "and" of political contingency to their encounters with the corporate media. Political paradigms shift when they can no longer bear the weight of the supplement. For Nogales, then, the strategy is a simple one: "How do we get in their way? We're doing it through economics *and* politics *and* existing law." [59]

Needless to say, the above is neither a progress narrative nor a fall from grace. Instead, it maps out the shifting terrain upon which the relationship between social movements and the state create the specific opportunities for textual production. With respect to the coalition, its strategy is based on the usual confrontation between the industry and an oppositional identity, but the resulting reforms produce a hybrid entity. This strategy is perhaps most apparent in the coalition's Hispanic Film Project, sponsored by Universal Television, which has produced two half-hour dramas each year since 1989. Though outside the formal activities of the coalition and functioning as an independent project, it reveals much about the relationship the coalition establishes with the industry. In its first four years, the Hispanic Film Project resulted in two films about families in which the father takes a political or cultural stand in the public sphere,[60] one film about an activist priest,[61] and five films about either adult women or biracial youth and their relationships with their parents and peers.[62] It is the latter group, which makes up nearly two-thirds of the films produced, that runs counter to the general nature of Chicano narrative films, which tend to privilege strong male characters in hostile environments. These new narratives represent the mutual interest and common cause between the National Hispanic Media Coalition and Universal Television (which have an equal number of votes in the selection process)—and to that extent the arrangement must be seen as a constructive force, rather than as a compromise, especially insofar as it produces two new types of narrative: Chicana dramas and biracial dramas. At the risk of being reductive and deterministic, I want to suggest that these two types of narrative represent a space in which each "side" finds a point of identification in what is, in fact, a unified subject. The Chicana dramas represent a commonality on the basis of gender identification, while the biracial dramas allow each side to find its racial identification expressed in the protagonist. But in neither case does the protagonist fit the norm for each group, especially insofar as racial conflict usually produces a cultural nationalism on each side that requires a male subject: women-as-mothers are the potential betrayers of racial purity, and biracial youth are the living proof of said betrayal.

So what does this all mean? If I were to conclude with a moral, it would be necessarily and passionately ambiguous. And it would be as follows: In the reconfiguration of the state, mass media, and social movements over the past three decades from a representational to a corporatist structure, minority politics lost sight of the fact that *entrance is not acceptance*. This phrase is taken from the title of an installation by Richard Lou and Robert Sanchez that depicts door frames along the U.S.-Mexico border.[63] But I would go even further than these artists and add that acceptance itself is a problematic concept insofar as it requires an authority—that is, someone or something that can confer acceptance upon the supplicant. For better or worse, the National Hispanic Media Coalition learned these lessons, and troubled the categories that defined entrance and delimited acceptance, even as they also walked through the door. In this respect, the female and biracial dramas provide an allegory of the coalition's strategy as it seeks the ephemeral power of deregulated bodies. And, in both this strategy and the ones discussed in earlier chapters, the text tells only one part of the story, albeit a telling one.

Privatized Public

In 1989, José Luis Ruiz returned to the Latino Consortium and initiated a three-year process to make the organization independent of KCET. Within a year, the Latino Consortium reorganized as the National Latino Communications Center (NLCC), incorporating as a nonprofit media arts and production center with its own board of directors.[64] By 1992, the NLCC had severed its ties with KCET and relocated to separate headquarters in Los Angeles.[65] The reorganization contributed to a shift within the minority public broadcasting consortia from station-based operations to independent production centers. The first consortium to do so had been the National Asian American Telecommunications Association in San Francisco.

Undergirding these changes was the Public Telecommunications Act of 1988, which increased minority funding and created the Independent Television Service (ITVS), both as a result of an aggressive lobbying effort by independent producers for greater access and more diverse programming. Congress affirmed that "minority programming is an essential foundation of public broadcasting," directing the CPB to distribute "a substantial amount" of its production grants "to producers of programming addressing the needs and interests of minorities." [66] In particular, Congress earmarked $3 million per year out of the CPB Television Program Fund for the production of national minority programming; it also required that the CPB file an annual report on its provisions of service to minority and diverse audiences. Starting in 1991, then, one-third of these production funds went to the minority consortia ($200,000 each), which had previously received only administrative support from the CPB, and the remaining $2 million went to a Multicultural Program Fund. Overnight, the consortia went from program syndicators dealing with individual stations and regional groups to program producers working with PBS and other national organizations. But the production funds for each consortium amounted to less than the budget for a one-hour documentary; the consortia mission was systemic but the resources meager. Congress also established ITVS—against the wishes of the CPB and PBS—with a $6 million annual budget for independent productions for public television. But, as Patricia Aufderheide notes, "[I]t also replicated traditional organizational problems by putting CPB in charge of ITVS, by making ITVS an ancillary service to what was already an ancillary service, and by perpetuating public television's financial agony." [67] These limited concessions, then, signaled a "crisis of mission" in public television that would only get worse. [68]

With its share of annual minority production monies, the NLCC established a program development fund that included a re-grant program with the New York–based Latino Collaborative as well as a Latina screenwriters grant. The NLCC also commissioned a survey of multicultural content on PBS's major strands, including *Frontline* and *The MacNeil/Lehrer Newshour,* as well as a feasibility study for a National Latino Film and Video Archive. [69] But by the mid-1990s, with the increasing loss of federal funding, the NLCC looked for "self sustaining streams of revenue," staking a claim as an "investor" in its funding and distribution activities. [70] NLCC Educational Media created a video distribution service that not only became self-sustaining, but even expanded rapidly at a time when other distributors were downsizing or folding. [71] The NLCC Video Collection targeted both the educational and home markets, bringing together Latino-themed documentaries, short narratives, independent features, and forgotten "classics" from the Hollywood studio era. NLCC Educational Media also became involved in merchandising, most notably around the four-part NLCC documentary series *Chicano! The History of the Mexican American Civil Rights Movement* (1996), selling a CD-ROM, an educator's kit, a companion book, T-shirts, baseball caps, and a poster.[72]

Started in 1992 and modeled on the *Eyes on the Prize* series chronicling the Black civil rights movement, *Chicano!* became the first major Chicano documentary series on PBS.[73] In many respects, the series revisited the conventional markers for Chicano movement historiography, presenting episodes on the land grant movement, the farmworkers' struggle, the East Los Angeles high school walkouts, and La Raza Unida. The producers included many veterans of Chicano documentary, including José Luis Ruiz (executive producer), Jesús Salvador Treviño (co–executive producer), Hector Galán (series producer), Sylvia Morales (episode producer), and Susan Racho (episode producer). Because of the series's entrepreneurial function, however, it differed subtly from the history related by these same filmmakers in *I Am Joaquin* (1969), *Yo Soy Chicano* (1972), *Chicana* (1979), and *Yo Soy* (1985). First, the producers did not include a separate episode on women, as originally planned, but attempted to integrate gender issues and female interviewees into the entire series. Second, the documentary absolutely refuses to connect the past to present-day issues, with the explicit intent of not "dating" the series for classroom sales and rentals in subsequent years. (The series was purposely aired in advance of elections, however.)[74] Third, and perhaps most significant, *Chicano!* became the first Chicano civil rights documentary to break free from a poetic nationalism in its voice-over narration. Instead, Henry Cisneros, then the Secretary of Housing and Urban Development and now the chairman of Univisión, narrates in the mellifluous tones of a professional discourse, while the objects of earlier protest—politicians, educators, and landowners—are interviewed in a straightforward and evenhanded manner.

It is within this context that the documentary locates its poetic nationalism in the Chicano interview subjects, and not in the narration or the text as a whole. Indeed, with one exception, the Chicanos interviewed in the series constitute a self-identified generational cohort that actively participated in the events described. Thus, the nationalist "I" first proclaimed in *I Am Joaquin* becomes a generational "we" associated with the producers and their peers in front of the camera. Nearly thirty years after the period covered, the documentary constructs a dialogic history within which Chicanos are able to speak alongside the very forces that had silenced them. The paradox is almost sublime: these veteran activists produce their autobiography, a commodified "history" with no expiration date, a corporatist product with no corporate backers; these former students return to the scene of their youth as media professionals and confront the teachers and police who tried to silence their protests for social equity, and they do so with more fairness than they ever received; and these middle-aged men and women tell their story for perhaps the last time that it will be told by them, a story that still remains outside the national imagination they first challenged three decades earlier. Cameras do not make films, people do.

The pressure to privatize reflected a conflict within the CPB toward the minority consortia: on the one hand, the CPB wanted to minimize if not eliminate the impact of the consortia on its budget; on the other hand, it wanted to maintain control over them rather than have them become autonomous or semiautonomous entities as in the case of ITVS. Most CPB monies go directly to PBS and the stations; the remaining monies (6 percent of the total budget) cover the program fund and consortia. In other words, the consortia allocations represent a significant percentage of the funds the CPB itself controls. In 1994, the minority consortia negotiated with the then executive vice president, Robert Coonrod, for a $5 million allocation that would increase production monies and allow the consortia to build "capacity" or infrastructure.[75] In the process, the Multicultural Program Fund was shut down in protest after failing in its mission to fund minority-themed programs. Starting in 1995, its $2 million allocation was turned over to the consortia, tripling their production monies ($650,000) and nearly doubling their administrative support ($350,000). But the consortia never received the monies to develop capacity.

For its part, the NLCC's production of a major documentary series during its rapid expansion resulted in both merchandising opportunities and managerial challenges. In the end, the NLCC alienated its constituency—in part due to a lack of follow-up and services, in part due to personality conflicts—while the day-to-day operations became rife with financial mismanagement. Between August and October 1997, the CPB Office of the Inspector General conducted an on-site audit that resulted in the grand jury indictment of Roy L. Casares, the NLCC's former business manager, who then pleaded guilty to six counts of fraud during the period between January and November 1995.[76] The audit documented various inappropriate expenditures as well as conflicts of interest with respect to the board, then presented twenty procedural recommendations. But the CPB's response appeared more predatory than procedural. In March 1998, the NLCC shut down, since the CPB had withheld funding for nearly a year.[77] The board then negotiated with the CPB, which made reinstatement of funds contingent on the firing of José Luis Ruiz. Even after Ruiz was removed as executive director, however, CPB continued to withhold funds, placing Latino production funds in limbo throughout 1998.

In the interim, a Latino producers' coalition approached the CPB seeking the release of the production funds that had been frozen for nearly two years.[78] Another group addressed the need to reform the NLCC (as "our own institution") and to reclaim the $1.2 million infrastructure support that the CPB had committed to for the NLCC but never delivered.[79] The CPB responded to neither group (which included nearly one hundred members combined); nor did it seek input from other Latino organizations. In November 1998, the CPB selected Edward James Olmos as head of an interim organization.[80] Olmos, a celebrity actor with good intentions, commercial ambitions, and limited understanding of public television, represented a third option between independent producers and "our own institutions." The CPB's option: a publicity coup that denied Latino producers equitable participation in public television. Since that time, the two Latino producers groups have joined in protest of CPB's failure to engage and support Latino producers, establishing political alliances and calling a national conference wherein Latinos would be able to define the institution serving their needs and goals.[81]

If I end here with a glimmer of hope, it is that producers have an opportunity to enter the larger political and policy arena within which public and commercial media operate. Oddly enough, that arena has become somewhat more representative than the media itself, and the two are very much imbricated in each other. There are more Latino political actors than dramatic ones! In any case, I end here unable to separate history from my own untimely actions in these events. I began the "real" research for this book in 1991 when José Luis Ruiz approached me after I had made a presentation on Chicano cinema and rather bluntly told me I did not know what I was talking about. He was right. And he was also generous. Now the future, and not the past, beckons; and it is of necessity that I say no more within these pages.

Gendered Transnation

If I started the previous chapter with Treviño and his rearticulation of McLuhan with Third World and minority politics, I am compelled to end this chapter and the book with Lourdes Portillo and her role within independent film and video. Rather than developing a cultural politics with which to confront the industry and related institutions, Portillo engages in an expression of the transidentification that remains outside an industrial framework. I want to suggest not that Portillo offers a panacea to Treviño's professional activism in the 1970s and 1980s, but rather that she stakes out another approach rooted in the ability of the aesthetic itelf to cross the borders between contending notions of ethnicity, gender, sexuality, and nationality. The medium is not the only message.

Portillo, a cofounder of Cine Acción in 1980, contributed to organizational efforts aimed at the role of women in Latino and Latin American film production in the late 1980s and early 1990s. Part of the problem that Latina filmmakers faced had to do with the conceptual parameters that failed to take them into account, first on the basis of gender, and second for their "transnational networks."[82] Living in San Francisco, for example, Portillo came into contact with people from "all over Latin America" and participated in an independent scene far removed from Hollywood.[83] But, as Rosa Linda Fregoso pointedly argues, Chicano scholars have had difficulty making sense of Portillo's transnational and cross-cultural concerns:

> Of course, all these seemingly different ways of re-presenting reality are only confusing and perplexing to thôse who assume that there is only one way of being a Chicana, that there is only one voice that can speak for all Chicanas, or that there is only one concern that interests Chicanas, in sum, to those who assume that there is an "essential" Chicana subject.[84]

Several events laid the critical and organizational groundwork for a pan-American film practice by women. The first, "Cocina de Imágenes: Primera Muestra del Cine y Video Realizado por Mujeres Latinas y Caribeñas" (Kitchen of Images: First Festival of Film and Video By Latin and Caribbean Women), took place in Mexico City on October 1–8, 1987. Inspired by that event, Luz Castillo and Liz Kotz organized the

"Women of the Americas Film and Video Festival/Festival de Cine y Video: Mujeres de las Americas" in San Francisco and Berkeley on October 19–23, 1988. The festival title itself—"Women of the Americas"—was an attempt at an "imperfect" reconceptualization of gender, culture and the media:

> This project—Cine Acción's major undertaking for 1988—is an effort to counter the common misperception that all major Latin American directors are men, that all successful women filmmakers are white. The other issue, harder to formulate, revolved around a shared sense of dissatisfaction with the existing labels—"Latino," "Chicano," the hopelessly artificial "Hispanic," the even worse "Spanish-surnamed." How to talk about this group of people, not all of whom were born in Latin America, not all of whom speak Spanish?[85]

Then, in November 1990, Portillo and Nancy de los Santos, together with Rosa Martha Fernández (director of TV-UNAM) and Norma Iglesias (Colegio de la Frontera Norte) in Mexico, organized the first conference of Chicana and Mexican women filmmakers, media professionals, and film scholars. The event—"Cruzando Fronteras: Encuentro de Mujeres Cineastas y Videoastas Latinas/Across the Border: Conference of Latin Women Film and Video Makers"—was hosted by the Colegio de la Frontera Norte in Tijuana and represented an attempt to counter the sexism within media advocacy, most notably in the all-male roster for "Chicanos 90," an event hosting Chicano filmmakers in Mexico City.[86]

Although Chicanas such as Susan Racho, Sylvia Morales, Esperanza Vásquez, María Muñoz, Grace Castro Negata, Esther Renteria, and Lourdes Portillo were instrumental in the first decade of Chicano cinema, their work has not received the same critical attention as male-produced films. The neglect is amplified since Chicanas have not produced feature films, which tend to be the focus of most film scholarship. Many Chicanas choose to work in shorter formats, since these provide a greater measure of artistic freedom.[87] In fact, for Chicanas, video offers the same access and immediacy that television did for an earlier, mostly-male generation; and, as Portillo argues, video may lead to an increase in the number of Chicana media artists, if not the development of a distinct video aesthetic.[88]

Portillo's work is itself pivotal in the development of an alternative Chicana/Latina film practice, challenging assumptions about an essential subject, style, and genre for the female, ethnic, and bicultural filmmaker. Her films are often codirected; and even when they are overtly political, there is a subtle attention to the objects that define social space and the mise-en-scène in national and cultural terms. Portillo also playfully invokes popular Latino genres and in some respect can be said to have pioneered the use of the *telenovela* style in short narratives in order to discuss such taboo social issues as domestic violence, female sexuality, homosexuality, and AIDS within the Latino community. Ironically, for Portillo, the use of the *telenovela* was unintentional at first:

> I think I was more influenced by the neo-realists. . . . I wanted to do this other thing and it came out like a *telenovela*. So I got a slap, you know. You have the intention to make a film and then you look at your footage and you realize that your limitations are infinite, not your possibilities. So you have to work with that—even though I had the romantic notion that I would make something that would deal with something more realistic.[89]

But infinite limitations resulted in a culturally specific possibility. In the late 1960s, *Canción de la Raza* used the *telenovela* format to address the social concerns of the Chicano community. In the absence of subsequent funding for television series, Chicano filmmakers adapted the *telenovela* to short dramas and docudramas, starting with Portillo's *Después del Terremoto* (After the Earthquake, 1979).

Unlike soap operas, "*telenovelas* always have clear-cut stories with definite endings that permit narrative closure; they are shown during prime-time viewing hours; and they are designed to attract a wide viewing audience of men, women, and children."[90] Although it is a popular industrial form that expresses dominant ideologies, the *telenovela* also carries the potential "to serve a demystifying cultural function" as it addresses social issues.[91] Ana M. López describes that paradox in the relationship between the *telenovela* and New Latin American Cinema:

> It is ironic that at the moment when the New Latin American Cinema rejected the melodrama as the embodiment of cultural dependency, television used the melodrama in order to establish a solid audience base and as a result, created a nationalistic (or, at least, pan–Latin American) form with which to begin to challenge that very same cultural and economic dependence.[92]

Since the late 1980s, the *telenovela* has been the genre par excellence for Latino films about AIDS and domestic violence in the barrio, including *Ojos Que No Ven* (1987), *Dolores* (1988), *Face to Face with AIDS* (1988), *Vida* (1989), *Mi Hermano* (1989), and *Between Friends* (1990). These films are sponsored by health organizations and are in-

Production still from Después del Terremoto/After the Earthquake, *a film by Lourdes Portillo.*

tended for educational use within the community rather than for broad distribution.[93] As single-episode narratives intended for narrowcast, these *telenovelas* construct a public sphere derived from yet outside both Latin American and U.S. English-language networks.

In *Después del Terremoto,* codirected with Nina Serrano, Portillo broadens the discourse on immigration and the barrio to include Central Americans as well as the gender politics of barrio assimilation.[94] As Rosa Linda Fregoso notes, "The theme of gender conflict is represented in terms of the tension between male and female discourses, that is to say, between formal politics (the idea of oppression as framed by the discourse of anti-imperialism) and an informal politics (the actual ex-

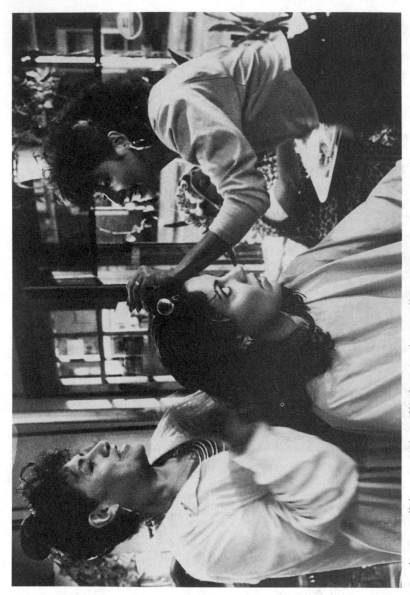

Production still from La Vida, a film by Lourdes Portillo.

perience of oppression in the daily life of a woman)."[95] But Portillo uses the *telenovela* to imbricate these discourses and politics. As in the conventional *telenovela*, mise-en-scène becomes synonymous with the traditional Latino home, setting up a conflict between a young immigrant woman's desire to buy a television and her fiancé's desire to foment revolution in Nicaragua. Portillo frames this narrative with bilingual title cards and an accordion score that together evoke silent cinema. Within the diegesis itself, the fiancé's slide show on the conditions in prerevolutionary Nicaragua makes explicit the difficult process of constructing progressive narratives that can bridge the gendered gap between private and public. When nostalgia for the homeland gives way to explicit political critique, an aunt jumps up and stops the slide show, albeit with the troubling consequence that the political images are now projected onto her body. These self-reflexive elements undercut the family melodrama, then redirect its exposed fictional status toward a feminist political parable with an open ending. The status of the relationship remains undecided, although the woman's self-proclaimed autonomy means that the proposed conversation that ends the film will be between equals. The final intertitle reads, "y empezó así . . . /and so it began. . . ."[96] Ironically, the film itself represents the obverse of the slide show: Portillo and Serrano made *Después del Terremoto* in support of the Sandinistas, although the Sandinistas did not quite appreciate the effort.[97] Portillo later produced an AIDS *telenovela*-style narrative addressed to Latinas: *Vida* (1989). In both cases, what proves transgressive is that the narratives represent female sexuality within a bicultural framework rather than a strictly familial or nationalist one.

Portillo's documentaries confront political issues from the personal perspective of Latina resistance. *Las Madres: The Mothers of Plaza de Mayo* (1986), codirected with Susana Muñoz, for example, documents the mothers of the disappeared in Argentina and their struggle against the military regime. Two recent documentaries—*La Ofrenda: The Days of the Dead* (1989), codirected with Susana Muñoz, and *El Diablo Nunca Duerme/The Devil Never Sleeps* (1994)—mark a significant development in her work as a documentary filmmaker. Here, Portillo explores the cultural ritual and sociopolitical transformation of modern Mexico while foregrounding the filter of her childhood experiences in Mexico as remembered from adulthood in the United States. In *La Ofrenda,* the alternation between male and female narrators, Mexican

Production still from Las Madres, *a film by Lourdes Portillo.*

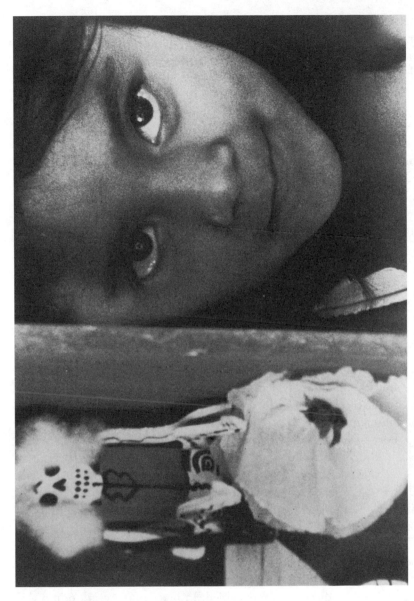

Production still from La Ofrenda: The Days of the Dead, *a film by Lourdes Portillo.*

and U.S. locations, contrapuntal montage and long tracking shots, among other techniques, establishes a poetic cultural narrative within the documentary form.[98] While not explicitly autobiographical, the film nevertheless introduces a first-person voice through the female narrator, whose memories contrast with the historical facts and figures presented by the male narrator.

In *El Diablo,* Portillo places herself in the documentary as she explores the sudden death and possible murder of her uncle in Mexico.[99] But while evocative of other self-reflexive documentaries—notably *Roger & Me* (1989) and *Sherman's March* (1986)—*El Diablo* refuses to establish a boundary between filmmaker and subject matter. Instead, Portillo uses irony and autobiography as a way to explore the changing relationship or boundaries among the middle-class family, mass culture, and the state in contemporary Mexico. In the end, Portillo offers a uniquely open-ended vision of cultural and social relations in the United States and Mexico at a time when those relations are undergoing intense conflict and change, from anti-immigration legislation in the U.S. to the recent dual citizenship legislation in Mexico. As with *Chicano! History of the Mexican American Civil Rights Movement,* Portillo's "I" is situated alongside the "you" that would otherwise silence her identity: in *La Ofrenda,* masculine rational discourse; in *El Diablo,* the imbrication of family, nation, and state. She thereby produces not a counterdiscourse but a dialogic history, precisely that which global media must suppress.

Portillo's *El Diablo* appeared in a feature-length format at film festivals, while an hour-long version aired on PBS. If Chicanos were the proverbial "sleeping giant," Portillo's film allegorized an exclusion wherein the devil never sleeps, recalling Luis Valdez's *diablo* in the morality tale of *El Corrido* (1976). In the 1990s, Chicano efforts to institutionalize advocacy, production, and distribution became increasingly marginal with the consolidation of global media. The geopolitical outlook of Chicano professionalism was quickly superseded by the global reconfiguration of the media industries. In short, the medium changed, but its message did not: access denied. In place of integration into the industry or even minority public affairs series, independent filmmakers struggle to produce and distribute their works at irregular intervals spanning several years. Meanwhile, the press focuses on the "ethnic" celebrity and market, as if consumption were its own reward.

Epilogue

If, as Lourdes Portillo argues, "your limitations are infinite, not your possibilities," she does not mean that there are no possibilities. Chicano filmmakers and media activists exemplify the complex and even paradoxical search for possibilities in the face of infinite limitations.

In this book, I have focused on Chicano cinema as it relates to television, media reform, and state regulation, considered in the contexts of social movements and professionalism. But there are more histories to be told, histories that account for other texts and practices. These include feature films drawing upon a range of financial sources: Mexico's state-controlled industry in the 1970s (Jesús Salvador Treviño's *Raíces de Sangre*, 1977), Hollywood (Luis Valdez's *Zoot Suit*, 1981, and *La Bamba*, 1987; Richard "Cheech" Marin's *Born in East L.A.*, 1987; and Gregory Nava's *Selena*, 1997), U.S. state agencies such as the NEH and CPB (Robert Young's *The Ballad of Gregorio Cortez*, 1983; Isaac Artenstein's *Break of Dawn*, 1988; and Severo Pérez's *. . . and the Earth Did Not Swallow Him*, 1994), and private or personal sources (Efraín Gutiérrez's three feature films; Alejandro Grattan's *Only Once in a Lifetime*, 1978; Robert Diaz LeRoy's *River Bottom*, 1994; and Luis Meza's *Staccato Purr of the Exhaust*, 1996). But it also includes short narratives often circumscribed to the film festival and classroom (Sylvia Morales's *Esperanza*, 1985; Carlos Avila's *Distant Water*, 1990; Gary Soto's *The Bike*, 1991, and *The Pool Party*, 1992; Mario Barrera's *The Party Line*, 1996; and Jim Mendiola's *Pretty Vacant*, 1996).

Perhaps the largest body of work falls into the avant-garde or experimental category. Several Chicano filmmakers have worked in the context of underground and personal cinema and thereby represent links between the "visionary film" associated with such figures as Maya

Production still from Desi del Valle's Cruel. *Photograph by Amy Davis.*

Deren, Stan Brakhage, and Andy Warhol and the identity- and rights-oriented discourses of Chicano cinema. These filmmakers include Severo Pérez and Ernie Palomino in the 1960s, and Guillermo "Willie" Varela since the 1970s. Chicano avant-garde art groups—notably Asco, the Border Art Workshop/Taller de Arte Fronterizo (BAW/TAF), and the Chicano Secret Service—have been involved with video documentation, appropriation, installation, and conceptual- or performance-based narratives. Chicana video artists have transformed the *testimonio* into a format for a social autobiography located in the embodied Chicana subject: Frances Salomé España, Sandra P. Hahn, Laura Aguilar, Rita González, and Sandra "Pocha" Peña.[1] Since the late 1980s, Chicano and Latino gay and lesbian media have reclaimed and redefined the community-oriented concerns of Chicano cinema: AIDS *telenovelas* (José Gutiérrez-Gómez and José Vergelín's *Ojos Que No Ven*, 1987; Lourdes Portillo's *Vida*, 1988; and Edgar Bravo's *Mi Hermano*, 1989), short dramas (Desi del Valle's *Cruel*, 1994; and Andrew Durham, Rico Martinez, and Victor Vargas's *Mi Pollo Loco*, 1994), experimental identities (Osa Hildalgo de la Riva's *Mujeria: The Olmeca Rap*, 1991; Danny G. Acosta's *A History of Violence*, 1991; and Eugene Rodriguez's *Straight, No Chaser*, 1995), and queer youth media programs addressing the

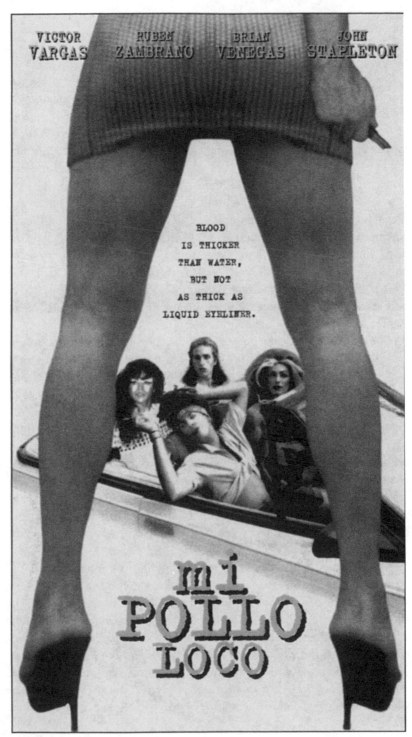

Advertisement for Mi Pollo Loco, *a drag parody of Allison Anders's*
Mi Vida Loca.

needs of Latino students (Divas-in-Training, Los Angeles, and Drama Divas, San Francisco).[2]

While these films signal an area outside the immediate subject of this book—basically, public exhibition across the movie theater, the festival, the community center, the classroom, and the museum—they also require consideration in terms of the relationship between a social movement, the state, and corporate capitalism. Harry Gamboa Jr. and the No Movie—mentioned in the preface—provide the basis for a useful avant-garde commentary on the history told in this book. The No Movie offered both a Chicano commentary on the role of language and the mass media in race relations and a satirical critique of Chicano cinema, especially the filmmakers associated with KCET-TV, the Chicano Cinema Coalition, and the Latino Consortium. The image on page 199 is from one such No Movie. Performed and photographed in 1976, "Chicano Cinema" appeared in print for the first time in 1983 as part of a conference and exhibition on the U.S.-Mexico border at the Center for Third World Economic and Social Studies in Mexico City. In this No Movie, Gamboa portrayed a fallen gunshot victim (visually coded as a Latin revolutionary) whose last gesture had been to scrawl "Chicano cinema" on the nearby wall. While the gesture links Chicano cinema with street expressions (murals and graffiti), it adds an insightful ephemeral dimension: "Chicano cinema" is written on a paper roll taped to the wall, with small portions of the first and last letters spilling over onto the wall itself. Thus the No Movie comments on the film medium as a tool for social protest. The paper roll, like the silver screen, lacks the material "fact" of graffiti, but it is nevertheless portable and reproducible, leaving behind some traces of its impact. Still, for the noncommercial and ethnic-identified filmmaker the "message" worth dying for amounts to no more than the naming of a new genre: Chicano cinema.

This early performance, done for the still photograph that appeared in the conference proceedings and elsewhere, entered the public sphere at the high point in the development of a Chicano cinema. By 1983, its practitioners had gained a toehold in noncommercial circuits (public television, national endowments, and foundations), had directed studio-released feature films (*Zoot Suit*, 1981; *The Ballad of Gregorio Cortez*, 1983; and *El Norte*, 1983), and had become regular participants and manifesto writers in a modified New Latin American Cinema. The Chicano Cinema Coalition was a major force in these efforts to situate

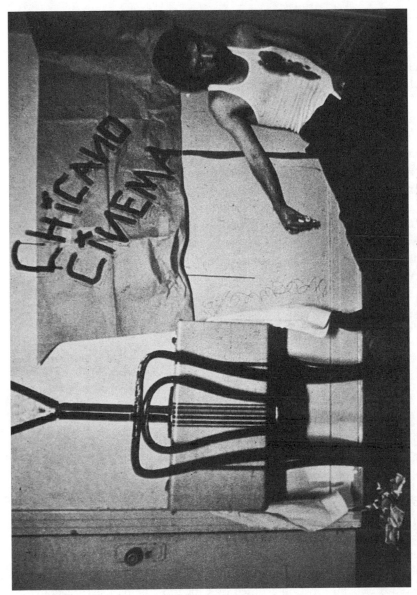

"Chicano Cinema" No Movie. Photograph copyright Harry Gamboa Jr., 1976

Chicano cinema within the divergent institutional contexts of New Latin American Cinema, New American Cinema, and Hollywood. The coalition also fought against itself over whether the apparent access to Hollywood represented an extension of a radical agenda or middle-class reformism. By 1984, this would be a moot point: access to Hollywood ended abruptly and radical politics became more moderate in the face of a hemispheric neoliberalism.

For his part, Gamboa parodies the debate over a liberal versus a radical ideological function for Chicano cinema, pointing out that both camps sought the same goal: access to and success in the American film and television industry. And he makes this argument through one of the first public critiques of the masculinist sexual politics that undergird Chicano cinema: Gamboa's bloodied revolutionary leans against the wall, one hand holding a gas fixture by the nozzle, the other hand shoved down his pants feeling his genitals. In neither case does the revolutionary achieve what he wants as the product of his defiantly public act of self-naming and self-stimulation: a feature film and sexual intercourse. Writing a decade and a half later, Rosa Linda Fregoso made this critique manifest within academic discourses:

> In a society where feature-length films signify mastery over cinematic practice and in which 35-mm symbolizes power, the accumulation of "cultural capital" becomes a self-generating process. In other words, making a Chicano 35-mm feature film translates into a certain prestige that virtually guarantees greater critical and scholarly attention as well as film reviews in the mainstream media. In a phallocentric society, power is measured by *big-ness* (as in feature-length films) and *penetration* (as into the Hollywood industry). These are the crucial markers or signs of success, of "making it," of *coming . . .* into fruition, that is.[3]

Gamboa's explicit and equally humorous commentary on the congruence between discourse and intercourse in Chicano cinema nevertheless exemplified its very ideals. The No Movie did not negate Chicano cinema, but rather pointed to a double standard that conflated public ethnic demands with private masculine desires. The No Movie then enacted the social function claimed by Chicano cinema itself: reaching a Third World international audience and disrupting the status quo. Even more, the No Movie served as a pointed reminder that Chicano cinema had perhaps foregrounded the politics of access and revolution at the expense of the make-do aesthetics and local orientation of the Chicano movement.[4]

The No Movies suggest the paradoxical nature of Chicano resistance to Hollywood and the mass media. There are no easy "messages" here that take for granted the existence of a value-free medium. And yet, as Gamboa's work testifies, there remains an urgent need to communicate both within and across communities. Gamboa shifts the analysis of minority representation away from its usual focus on textual content and toward the structure of exclusion itself. But as an auteur, as a social actor, Gamboa must also speak beyond the peculiar conditions of his expression, lest he fall into self-referential abstraction and aestheticism. In reversing David James's argument in *Allegories of Cinema,* Gamboa's No Movies begin as an allegory of exclusion from cinema in order to address other social relations within a mediated national community.

What unites the history told in this book with Gamboa's No Movies and other Chicano film and media-arts practices resides in neither a cultural essence nor a cinematic style, but rather in a political imperative: "The fox knows many things, but the hedgehog knows one big thing." [5] And the hedgehog must find many ways to voice the one big thing that it knows, since the fox controls the communications networks and refuses to listen to anything else. Such has been the life's work of a political generation born of the 1960s and of the filmmakers who followed upon their precedent but who have found the fox no less exclusionary. This group was and has been, as E. P. Thompson notes of the English working class, "present at its own making." [6] And, with camera in hand, they have shot right back so that others could see as well.

And you, dear reader, how do you participate in this world of knowledge and power as something other than a viewer?

Notes

Introduction

1. Américo Paredes, *"With His Pistol in His Hand": A Border Ballad and Its Hero* (Austin: University of Texas, 1958), and Gloria Anzaldúa, *Borderlands/La Frontera: The New Mestiza* (San Francisco: Spinsters/Aunt Lute, 1987).

2. Paredes's study was later made the basis for the feature film *The Ballad of Gregorio Cortez* (1983), produced by Moctesuma Esparza for theatrical release as well as broadcast on the PBS series *American Playhouse*.

3. See José E. Limón, *Mexican Ballads, Chicano Poems: History and Influence in Mexican-American Social Poetry* (Berkeley: University of California Press, 1992), and Ramón Saldívar, *Chicano Narrative: The Dialectics of Difference* (Madison: University of Wisconsin Press, 1990).

4. Saldívar, *Chicano Narrative*, 39, 41.

5. Anzaldúa, *Borderlands/La Frontera*, 61.

6. Whereas these writers articulate a political function for Spanish as a private and public language, Richard Rodriguez identifies Spanish as a "private" language against the "public" language of English. See *Hunger of Memory: The Education of Richard Rodriguez* (New York: Bantam Books, 1982).

7. Anzaldúa, *Borderlands/La Frontera*, 78.

8. For an insightful critique of this tendency in Anzaldúa and other "border" theorists, see Scott Michaelsen and David E. Johnson, eds., "Border Secrets: An Introduction," in *Border Theory: The Limits of Cultural Politics* (Minneapolis: University of Minnesota Press, 1997), 1–39, esp. 10–15.

9. Paredes, *"With His Pistol in His Hand,"* 247. On Paredes's use of irony and understatement within an overall "idealization of a primordial patriarchy," see Renato Rosaldo, "Changing Chicano Narratives," in *Culture and Truth: The Remaking of Social Analysis* (Boston: Beacon, 1989), 150–55.

10. For a useful discussion of canon formation in Chicano literary studies—especially useful given the author's ironic self-awareness—see Bruce-Novoa, "Canonical and Non-Canonical Texts," *Americas Review* 14, no. 3–4 (Fall–Winter 1986): 119–35; reprinted in Bruce-Novoa, *Retrospace: Collected Essays on Chicano Literature* (Houston: Arte Público, 1990), 132–45.

11. Cherríe Moraga, "Queer Aztlán: The Re-Formation of Chicano Tribe," in *The Last Generation: Prose and Poetry* (Boston: South End Press, 1993), 145–74.

12. Michel Foucault, *The History of Sexuality*, vol. 1, *An Introduction*, trans. Robert Hurley (New York: Vintage Books, 1978), 8–11. In drawing upon Foucault's "repressive hypothesis," however, I do not so much reject the "transcendent impulse" as make it one object of an overall discursive and institutional analysis.

13. Paredes, *"With His Pistol in His Hand,"* 34: "Men should sing with their heads thrown back, with their mouths wide open and their eyes shut. Fill your lungs, so they can hear you at the pasture's farther end."

14. Anzaldúa, *Borderlands/La Frontera*, 79.

15. Esperanza: "Whose neck shall I stand on, to make me feel superior? And what will I get out of it? I don't want anything lower than I am. I'm low enough already. I want to rise. And push everything up with me as I go. . . . [After her husband Ramón raises his hand to slap her] That would be the old way. Never try it on me again—never." Michael Wilson, *Salt of the Earth*, ed. Deborah Silverton Rosenfelt (New York: Feminist Press, 1978), 82. Esperanza means "hope" in Spanish.

16. Benedict Anderson, *Imagined Communities: Reflections on the Origin and Spread of Nationalism*, 2d ed. (New York: Verso, 1991), 5.

17. See, e.g., Rodolfo Acuña, *Occupied America: A History of Chicanos*, 3d ed. (New York: HarperCollins, 1988); Matt S. Meier and Feliciano Ribera, *Mexican Americans/American Mexicans: From Conquistadors to Chicanos*, rev. ed. (New York: Hill and Wang, 1993); and John R. Chávez, *The Lost Land: The Chicano Image in the Southwest* (Albuquerque: University of New Mexico Press, 1984).

18. I borrow this line from El Pachuco in Luis Valdez's *Zoot Suit* (1981).

19. See René Girard, *Violence and the Sacred*, trans. Patrick Gregory (Baltimore: Johns Hopkins University Press, 1977), 306.

20. The idea of Mexicans as a "cosmic race" comes from José Vasconcelos, *La Raza Cósmica* (Barcelona: Agencia Mundial de Librerías, 1925). For English-language sources, see José Vasconcelos, *The Cosmic Race: A Bilingual Edition*, trans. Didier T. Jaén (Baltimore: Johns Hopkins University Press, 1997), and also Octavio Paz, "The Sons of La Malinche," in *The Labyrinth of Solitude*, trans. Lysander Kemp (New York: Grove Weidenfeld, 1985), 65–88.

21. On "racialization," see Tomás Almaguer, *Racial Fault Lines: The Historical Origins of White Supremacy in California* (Berkeley: University of California Press, 1994), 3–7. For a consideration of race in Chicano historiography, see Almaguer, "Ideological Distortions in Recent Chicano Historiography: The Internal Colonial Model and Chicano Historical Intepretation," *Aztlán: A Journal of Chicano Studies* 18, no. 1 (Spring 1987): 7–28; and Alex Saragoza, "Recent Chicano Historiography: An Interpretive Essay," *Aztlán: A Journal of Chicano Studies* 19, no. 1 (Spring 1988–90): 1–78. An earlier version of Saragoza's essay appears in *Ethnic Affairs* 1, no. 1 (Fall 1987): 24–62.

22. Luis Leal, "In Search of Aztlán," trans. Gladys Leal, in *Aztlán: Essays on the Chicano Homeland*, ed. Rudolfo A. Anaya and Francisco A. Lomelí (Albuquerque: Academia/El Norte Publications, 1989), 8.

23. Muñoz, *Youth, Identity, Power*, 173. In fact, in Oct. 1970, Eustacio (Frank) Martinez, an undercover agent for the Alcohol, Tobacco, and Firearms Division of the U.S. Treasury Department, infiltrated the National Chicano Moratorium Committee. By Nov. he had ousted and replaced Rosalio Muñoz as chairperson. Working with four Chicano officers in the Criminal Conspiracy Section of the Los Angeles Police Department, Martinez then advocated more militant and violent tactics in subsequent protests on Jan. 9 and 31, 1971, both of which devolved into riots, leading to numerous arrests, injuries, and one death. See ibid. and Acuña, *Occupied America*, 351.

24. See Harry Gamboa Jr., *Urban Exile: The Collected Writings of Harry Gamboa Jr.*, ed. Chon A. Noriega (Minneapolis: University of Minnesota Press, 1998).

25. Prints for all three films have been recovered: *Please, Don't Bury Me Alive!* (1976), *Amor Chicano Es Para Siempre* (Chicano Love Is Forever, 1978), and *Run, Tecato, Run* (1979). Working with Gutiérrez, I have undertaken restoration of these films through the UCLA Film and Television Archive.

26. I discuss this genealogy in my introductions to two edited works, *Chicanos and Film: Representation and Resistance* (Minneapolis: University of Minnesota Press, 1992): xi–xxvi, and "El Hilo Latino: Representation, Identity, and National Culture," *Jump Cut* 38 (June 1993): 45–50. Of the filmmakers, Jesús Salvador Treviño has been the most prolific and influential, publishing in Europe and the Americas and in some ways setting the terms for subsequent scholarship. See, e.g., his "Jesús S. Treviño Habla para Cine Cubano: Entrevista," *Cine Cubano* 83 (1977–78): 11–16; "Cinéma Chicano aux États-Unis," in *Les Cinémas de l'Amérique Latine*, ed. Guy Hennebelle and Alfonso Gumucio-Dagron (Paris: Nouvelles Editions Pierre Lherminier, 1981), 493–99; "Chicano Cinema," *New Scholar* 8 (1982): 167–80; "Latinos and Public Broadcasting: The 2% Factor," *Jump Cut* 28 (1983): 65; "Presencia del Cine Chicano," in *A Traves de la Frontera* (Mexico, D.F.: Centro de Estudios Económicos y Sociales del Tercer Mundo, A.C., and Instituto de Investigaciones Estéticas de la U.N.A.M., 1983), 194–201; "Chicano Cinema Overview," *Areíto* 37 (1984): 40–43; "Latino Portrayals in Film and Television," *Jump Cut* 30 (Mar. 1985): 14–16; and "El Desarrollo del Cine Chicano," in *Hojas de Cine: Testimonios y Documentos del Nuevo Cine Latinoamericano* (Mexico: Fundación del Nuevo Cine Latinoamericano, 1986), unpaginated. In their extensive introduction on Chicano art, Shifra M. Goldman and Tomás Ybarra-Frausto situate Chicano cinema within the context of Chicano cultural production and social history. See Goldman and Ybarra-Frausto, *Arte Chicano: A Comprehensive Annotated Bibliography of Chicano Art, 1965–1981* (Berkeley: University of California, Chicano Studies Library Publications Unit, 1985). Books on Chicano cinema include Gary D. Keller, ed., *Chicano Cinema: Research, Reviews, and Resources* (Binghamton, N.Y.: Bilingual Review/Press, 1985); Noriega, *Chicanos and Film*; Rosa Linda Fregoso, *The Bronze Screen: Chicana and Chicano Film* (Minneapolis: University of Minnesota Press, 1993); Gary D. Keller, *Hispanics and United States Film: An Overview and Handbook* (Tempe: Bilingual Press, 1994); David R. Maciel, *El Bandolero, el Pocho, y la Raza: Imágenes Cinematográficos del Chicano*, Cuadernos de Cuadernos, no. 5 (México, D.F.: Universidad Nacional Autónoma de México, 1994); Frank Javier Garcia Berumen, *The Chicano/Hispanic Image in American Film* (New York: Vantage, 1995); and Christine List, *Chicano Images: Refiguring Ethnicity in Mainstream Film* (New York: Garland, 1996).

27. I draw upon Mario Barrera's insightful analysis of the historical role of egalitarian (integrationist) and communitarian (cultural nationalist) goals in the Mexican-origin community. See *Beyond Aztlán: Ethnic Autonomy in Comparative Perspective* (Notre Dame: University of Notre Dame Press, 1988), chaps. 1–6.

28. Coco Fusco, "Fantasies of Oppositionality: Reflections on Recent Conferences in Boston and New York," *Screen* 29 (Autumn 1988): 80–93, and "Ethnicity, Politics and Poetics: Latinos and Media Art," in *Illuminating Video: An Essential Guide to Video Art*, ed. Doug Hall and Sally Jo Fifer (New York: Aperture/BAVC, 1990), 304–16.

29. Michel de Certeau, *The Writing of History*, trans. Tom Conley (New York: Columbia University Press, 1988), 64.

30. David E. James, *Allegories of Cinema: American Film in the Sixties* (Princeton: Princeton University Press, 1989), 5.

31. See José E. Limón, "The Folk Performance of 'Chicano' and the Cultural Limits of Political Ideology," in *And Other Neighborly Names: Social Process and Cultural Image in Texas Folklore,* ed. Richard Bauman and Roger D. Abrahams (Austin: University of Texas Press, 1981), 197–225; Rosaldo, *Culture and Truth;* and Patricia Zavella, "Feminist Insider Dilemmas: Constructing Ethnic Identity with 'Chicana' Informants," *Frontiers* 13, no. 3 (1993): 53–76.

1. "No Revolutions without Poets"

1. Tomás Ybarra-Frausto, "The Chicano Movement and the Emergence of a Chicano Poetic Consciousness," *New Scholar* 6 (1977): 81–109.

2. Rudolph O. de la Garza and Rowena Rivera, "The Socio-Political World of the Chicano: A Comparative Analysis of Social Scientific and Literary Perspectives," in *Minority Language and Literature: Retrospective and Perspective,* ed. Dexter Fisher (New York: Modern Language Association, 1977), 50–51.

3. On a Chicano rhetoric, see John C. Hammerback, Richard J. Jensen, and José Angel Gutiérrez, *A War of Words: Chicano Protest in the 1960s and 1970s* (Westport, Conn.: Greenwood, 1985); Michael Victor Sedano, "Chicanismo: A Rhetorical Analysis of Themes and Images of Selected Poetry from the Chicano Movement," *Western Journal of Speech Communication* 44 (Summer 1980): 177–90; and Lloyd D. Powers, "Chicano Rhetoric: Some Basic Concepts," *Southern Speech Communication Journal* 38 (Summer 1973): 340–46.

4. Rodolfo "Corky" Gonzales, introduction to *I Am Joaquin* (New York: Bantam Books, 1972), 1.

5. As Rodolfo Acuña argues, "[I]ts impact was immeasurable." Acuña, *Occupied America,* 341. See the literary critiques of the poem in Juan Bruce-Novoa, *Chicano Poetry: A Response to Chaos* (Austin: University of Texas Press, 1982), chap. 3, and José E. Limón, *Mexican Ballads, Chicano Poems: History and Influence in Mexican-American Social Poetry* (Berkeley: University of California Press, 1992), chap. 6.

6. Bruce-Novoa, *Chicano Poetry,* 68. He also writes: "The poem's power derives, first, from its simplistic ideology and form; second, ironically, from its pretentiousness." Similarly, Limón writes: "Adolescent in its rebellious attitude toward the father, *I Am Joaquin* remains a primer for poetic and political adolescents, which we all were in 1969." Limón, *Mexican Ballads, Chicano Poems,* 129.

7. "I Am Joaquin," *La Raza,* Sept. 16, 1967, 4.

8. Ybarra-Frausto, "Chicano Poetic Consciousness," 88–89.

9. According to Cordelia Candelaria, the term expressed both opposition and communion, and "embodies the holistic, synthetic power of poetry to transform mundane experience into mystical insight." Candelaria, *Chicano Poetry: A Critical Introduction* (Westport, Conn.: Greenwood, 1986), 34–35.

10. For an overview, see Mary Louise Pratt, "'Yo Soy La Malinche': Chicana Writers and the Poetics of Ethnonationalism," *Callaloo* 16, no. 4 (1993): 859–73. See also the influential works by Cherríe Moraga and Gloria Anzaldúa: Moraga and Anzaldúa, eds., *This Bridge Called My Back: Writings by Radical Women of Color* (Watertown, Mass.: Persephone, 1981; 2d ed., New York: Kitchen Table, 1983); Moraga, *Loving in the War Years: Lo Que Nunca Pasó por Sus Labios* (Boston: South End, 1983); Anzaldúa, *Borderlands/La Frontera;* and Moraga, *The Last Generation: Prose and Poetry* (Boston: South End, 1993).

11. Ybarra-Frausto, "Chicano Poetic Consciousness," and Ramón Gutiérrez,

"Community, Patriarchy and Individualism: The Politics of Chicano History and the Dream of Equality," *American Quarterly* 45, no. 1 (Mar. 1993): 44–72.

12. See E. J. Hobsbawm and Terence Ranger, eds., *The Invention of Tradition* (Cambridge: Cambridge University Press, 1983).

13. See Carlos Muñoz Jr., *Youth, Identity, Power: The Chicano Movement* (London: Verso, 1989).

14. The "Plan of Delano" is reprinted in Armando B. Rendon, *Chicano Manifesto* (New York: Macmillan, 1971), 327–30. In fact, Rendon reprints the "Plan of Delano" with three other manifestos under the appendix title "Four Declarations of Independence."

15. As I will discuss below, this influence can be seen in the use of specific phrases as well rhetorical strategies. The "Plan Espiritual de Aztlán" is reprinted in Rudolfo A. Anaya and Francisco Lomelí, eds., *Aztlán: Essays on the Chicano Homeland* (Albuquerque: Academia/El Norte Publications, 1989), 1–6. The "Plan de Santa Barbara" is reprinted in Muñoz, *Youth, Identity, Power*, 191–202. Three film manifestos from the 1970s are reprinted in Noriega, *Chicanos and Film*, 275–307.

16. The charges against the "L.A. Thirteen" were dismissed as unconstitutional after two years of appeals. Acuña, *Occupied America*, 338.

17. "I/WE SHALL ENDURE" appears in capital letters in both texts.

18. Luis Valdez, "Notes on Chicano Theater" (1970), in *Luis Valdez, Early Works* (Houston: Arte Público, 1990), 8.

19. "El Plan Espiritual de Aztlán," in Anaya and Lomelí, *Aztlán*, 2. See also Rodolfo "Corky" Gonzales, "Chicano Nationalism: The Key to Unity for la Raza," *Militant*, Mar. 30, 1970.

20. As Rolando Hinojosa observes in "*I Am Joaquin*: Relationships between the Text and the Film," "By 1970, like many of us, El Teatro Campesino, while not abandoning the farmworkers' movement, moved on to other topical issues, such as barrio problems, Vietnam, and racial discrimination." In Keller, *Chicano Cinema*, 143.

21. Quoted in Ybarra-Frausto, "Chicano Poetic Consciousness," 87.

22. The slide show presentation remains a powerful tool for the dissemination of Chicano histories and the source of key films: Sylvia Morales's *Chicana* (1979), often seen as a feminist response to *I Am Joaquin*, also developed out of a slide show by the Chicana scholar Ana Nieto-Gómez. Yolanda Lopez's *When You Think of Mexico* (1986) is based on her slide show *Mexicana*. Since the late 1970s, Harry Gamboa Jr. has created "fotonovelas" (slide shows with prerecorded soundtracks and live performance) that on one level spoof the Chicano cinema project, while also commenting on local events and struggles.

23. The production dates cited for the film range from 1967 to 1970. Treviño, on the basis of interviews with the Valdez brothers, states that the film was shot and recorded "[o]n a hot summer evening in 1967," the same year the poem was written. The film itself has a 1969 copyright, which may indicate that the film was shown before it was copyrighted, or that it took over a year to edit the film. Treviño, "Chicano Cinema Overview," 40.

24. See Rolando Hinojosa's comments on the changes made in the film in order to make it more commercial. Hinojosa, "I Am Joaquin: Relationships between the Text and the Film," in Keller, *Chicano Cinema*, 142–45. For another comparison of poem and film, see Eliud Martinez, "*I Am Joaquin* as Poem and Film: Two Modes of Chicano Expression," *Journal of Popular Culture* 13, no. 3 (Spring 1980): 505–15. The United Farm Workers Service Center continued to document events on film, and produced at least two Spanish-language documentaries for internal use: *Nosotros Venceremos* (1971, We Will

Overcome), which uses photographic stills to relate UFW struggles and goals; and *Sí, Se Puede* (1973, Yes, We Can), on César Chávez's hunger strike in Arizona.

25. Treviño, "Chicano Cinema Overview," 40.

26. See Tomás Ybarra-Frausto, "Rasquachismo: A Chicano Sensibility," in *Chicano Art: Resistance and Affirmation, 1965–1985*, ed. Richard Griswold del Castillo, Teresa McKenna, and Yvonne Yarbro Bejarano (Los Angeles: Wight Art Gallery/UCLA, 1991): 155–62.

27. For a history of El Teatro Campesino that also explores the issue of authorship in terms of gender relations, see Yolanda Broyles-González, *El Teatro Campesino: Theater in the Chicano Movement* (Austin: University of Texas Press, 1994).

28. Dagobert D. Runes, *The Dictionary of Philosophy*, 16th ed. (New York: Philosophical Library, 1960), 91–92.

29. For an insightful discussion of puns, including macaronic or bilingual ones, see Gregory Ulmer, "The Puncept in Grammatology," in *On Puns*, ed. Jonathan Culler (Oxford: Blackwell, 1988), 164–89.

30. For an account of the film's production, see Sylvia Morales, "Filming a Chicana Documentary," *Somos* 2, no. 5 (June 1979): 42–45; reprinted in Noriega, *Chicanos and Film*, 308–11.

31. Fregoso, *The Bronze Screen*, 3. See Fregoso's extended reading of *Chicana* and *I Am Joaquin* in chap. 1 and in "Chicana Film Practices: 'Confronting the Many-Headed Demon of Oppression,'" in Noriega, *Chicanos and Film*.

32. Luis Valdez, "The Tale of La Raza," reprinted in *The Chicanos: Mexican American Voices*, ed. Ed Ludwig and James Santibañez (Baltimore: Penguin Books, 1971), 95.

33. Claire F. Fox, "Mass Media, Site Specificity, and the U.S.-Mexico Border: Guillermo Gómez-Peña's *Border Brujo* (1988, 1990)," in *The Ethnic Eye: Latino Media Arts*, ed. Chon A. Noriega and Ana M. López (Minneapolis: University of Minnesota Press, 1996), 228.

34. See Guillermo Gómez-Peña, *Warrior for Gringostroika: Essays, Performance Texts, and Poetry* (Saint Paul: Graywolf, 1993); and idem, *The New World Border: Prophecies, Poems, and Loqueras for the End of the Century* (San Francisco: City Lights, 1996).

35. See Fox, "Mass Media, Site Specificity, and the U.S.-Mexico Border."

36. The entire poem is reprinted in Guillermo Gómez-Peña, *Warrior for Gringostroika*, 67–74.

37. Fox, "Mass Media, Site Specificity, and the U.S.-Mexico Border," 235.

38. The notion of a queer Chicano nationalism is articulated most forcefully in Cherríe Moraga's polemical essay "Queer Aztlán: The Re-formation of Chicano Tribe," in *The Last Generation*.

39. Ramón García and Rita González's video *St. Francis of Aztlán* (1997) illustrates García's poem, an AIDS allegory that situates an Echo Park "cha cha" boy at the crossroads of Catholicism and Chicano nationalism.

40. Interestingly, Ray Santisteban is attempting to produce a new version of *I Am Joaquin* that will narrate the entire poem, drawing upon a diverse and intergenerational group of Mexican and Chicano readers.

2. Setting the Stage

1. For an early account of these groups based on the distinction between a reformist period (the 1920s through the 1950s) and a militant one (since the 1960s), see Kaye Briegel, "The Development of Mexican-American Organizations," *The Mexican-Americans:*

An Awakening Minority, ed. Manuel P. Servín (Beverly Hills: Glencoe, 1970), 160–78. In a similar vein, Armando Gutiérrez and Herbert Hirsch correlated self-identification as Chicano (rather than Mexican American) to increased political consciousness. See "The Militant Challenge to the American Ethos: 'Chicanos' and 'Mexican Americans,'" *Social Science Quarterly* 53, no. 4 (Mar. 1973): 830–45. Political activism within the Mexican-descent community was much more complex than these binarisms allowed, especially insofar as militant activism played a crucial role in the emergence of Chicanos within national politics, including federal legislators, national political appointees, and Washington-based organizations. But, as Rudolph O. de la Garza notes, the results were marginal: "Prior to 1967 . . . Chicanos *qua* Chicanos had no presence in Washington, D.C., and in national politics. . . . As of 1980, these actors have enjoyed some specific and real successes, but overall they have not had a major or continuous impact on public policy." See "'And Then There Were Some . . .': Chicanos as National Political Actors, 1967–1980," *Aztlan: A Journal of Chicano Studies* 15, no. 1 (Spring 1984): 18.

2. At the same time, however, police intelligence units initiated surveillance of Chicano groups and used infiltrators as agents provocateurs. In at least one instance, the Los Angeles Police Department (LAPD) collaborated with a state agency (the Treasury Department's Bureau of Alcohol, Tobacco, and Firearms) in an effort to discredit the Brown Berets and the National Chicano Moratorium Committee. The LAPD intelligence unit also testified before the U.S. Senate on subversive activities among minority high school and college students. See Edward J. Escobar, "The Dialetics of Repression: The Los Angeles Police Department and the Chicano Movement, 1968–1971," *Journal of American History* 79, no. 4 (Mar. 1993): 1483–1514. For a more general account of CIA domestic surveillance and use of agents provocateurs against student groups, see Angus Mackenzie, *Secrets: The CIA's War at Home* (Berkeley: University of California Press, 1997).

3. Sohnya Sayres et al., eds., *The 60s without Apology* (Minneapolis: University of Minnesota Press, 1984).

4. *Report of the National Advisory Commission on Civil Disorders,* Otto Kerner, chairman (New York: Bantam Books, 1968). See John David Skrentny's discussion of the report in *The Ironies of Affirmative Action: Politics, Culture, and Justice in America* (Chicago: University of Chicago Press, 1996), 91–103.

5. Vincent Mosco, "Toward a Theory of the State and Telecommunications Policy," *Journal of Communication* 38, no. 1 (Winter 1988): 121.

6. For an early consideration of the state in terms of "internal colonial" theory, see Mario Barrera, *Race and Class in the Southwest: A Theory of Racial Inequality* (Notre Dame: University of Notre Dame Press, 1979), esp. chap. 6. Barrera's "internal colonial" model, together with his critical review of state theory, rejects the notion of "state neutrality" in a pluralist society, instead explaining conflict as a result of "the fact that the state looks after both the particular *and* the general interests of capitalists, and that the two sometimes get in the way of each other" (158, 172). In order to sustain his argument, however, Barrera must posit the Chicano population as being outside both the state and capitalist interests.

7. See, e.g., Muñoz, *Youth, Identity, Power;* Acuña, *Occupied America;* and Juan Gómez-Quiñones, *Chicano Politics: Reality and Promises, 1940–1990* (Albuquerque: University of New Mexico, 1990).

8. See, e.g., my introduction and essay in Noriega, *Chicanos and Film;* Fregoso, *The Bronze Screen;* and Gutiérrez, "Community, Patriarchy, and Individualism."

9. See, e.g., the report of the APA task force on television and society: Aletha C. Huston et al., *Big World, Small Screen: The Role of Television in American Society* (Lincoln: University of Nebraska Press, 1992).

10. Jo Freeman makes this point with respect to the relationship between social movements and public policy in *The Politics of Women's Liberation: A Case Study of an Emerging Social Movement and Its Relation to the Policy Process* (New York: David McKay, 1975), 4. Two decades later, J. Craig Jenkins echoes Freeman's assessment with respect to the relationship between social movements and the state in his essay "Social Movements, Political Representation, and the State: An Agenda and Comparative Framework," in *The Politics of Social Protest: Comparative Perspectives on States and Social Movements*, ed. J. Craig Jenkins and Bert Klandermans (Minneapolis: University of Minnesota Press, 1995), 15.

In the past two decades, U.S. sociological literature on social movements has fallen into three areas: rational choice, resource mobilization, and political process. While the latter two place social movements within political contexts, they share the instrumental framework of rationalists, wherein external resources and opportunities explain actions. See, e.g., Sidney Tarrow, *Power in Movement: Social Movements, Collective Action, and Politics* (Cambridge: Cambridge University Press, 1994). More recently, U.S. sociologists, often influenced by European scholarship on social movements, have begun to consider the impact of culture. See Hank Johnston and Bert Klandermans, eds., *Social Movements and Culture* (Minneapolis: University of Minnesota Press, 1995), and James M. Jasper, *The Art of Moral Protest: Culture, Biography, and Creativity in Social Movements* (Chicago: University of Chicago Press, 1997).

11. Christian Smith, *Resisting Reagan: The U.S. Central American Peace Movement* (Chicago: University of Chicago Press, 1996), 130–31; quoted in Jasper, *The Art of Moral Protest,* 35.

12. As Freeman argues, "[I]t is shortsighted to view the whole political system as limited to established institutions and governmental channels. . . . One can say that change happens only outside the political system, only if one limits one's conception of that political system." *The Politics of Women's Liberation,* 2.

13. Jenkins, "Social Movements, Political Representation, and the State," 15. Jenkins draws upon Max Weber's classic definition of the state. As John A. Hall and G. John Ikenberry point out, "there is a great deal of agreement amongst social scientists as to how the state should be defined." Hall and Ikenberry, *The State* (Minneapolis: University of Minnesota Press, 1989), 1.

14. Jenkins, "Social Movements, Political Representation, and the State," 15.

15. Robert Britt Horwitz identifies the Great Society period between 1965 and 1977 as an era for the creation of agencies that "regulated the social consequences of business behavior" on behalf of consumers and public interest groups—from the creation of the Equal Employment Opportunity Commission (1965) to the failure to secure passage of the proposed Consumer Protection Agency (1977). In contrast, regulatory agencies formed during the Progressive Era and New Deal—such as the FCC—were oriented toward producers. Horwitz, *The Irony of Regulatory Reform: The Deregulation of American Telecommunications* (New York: Oxford University Press, 1989), 76. In terms of minority media, the Great Society period can be framed by industry hearings held by the Equal Employment Opportunity Commission in 1969 and a media report issued by the Commission on Civil Rights in 1977.

16. Thomas Streeter, *Selling the Air: A Critique of the Policy of Commercial Broadcasting in the United States* (Chicago: University of Chicago Press, 1996), 302–8.

17. Ibid., 287.

18. For revisionist scholarship that examines the "symbiotic relationship" between the film and broadcasting industries, see Michele Hilmes, *Hollywood and Broadcasting: From Radio to Cable* (Champaign: University of Illinois Press, 1990); William Boddy,

Fifties Television: The Industry and Its Critics (Champaign: University of Illinois Press, 1990); Tino Balio, ed., *Hollywood in the Age of Television* (Boston: Unwin Hyman, 1990); and Christopher Anderson, *Hollywood TV: The Studio System in the Fifties* (Austin: University of Texas Press, 1994). For an examination of the "generic similarity" of film and television family melodramas that also takes the differing industrial contexts into account, see Nina C. Liebman, *Living Room Lectures: The Fifties Family in Film and Television* (Austin: University of Texas Press, 1995).

19. Anderson, *Hollywood TV*, 291.

20. See Lynn Spigel, *Make Room for TV: Television and the Family Ideal in Postwar America* (Chicago: University of Chicago Press, 1992).

21. For an excellent analysis of the "performance of style" that has refigured American television since the 1980s, see John Thornton Caldwell, *Televisuality: Style, Crisis, and Authority in American Television* (New Brunswick: Rutgers University Press, 1995).

22. The key text here is Jürgen Habermas, *The Structural Transformation of the Public Sphere: An Inquiry into a Category of Bourgeois Society,* trans. Thomas Burger (Cambridge: MIT Press, 1989). Hannah Arendt makes a similar distinction based on the Greek polis in "The Public and the Private Realm," in *The Human Condition* (Chicago: University of Chicago Press, 1958), 22–78. For a feminist critique of the universal public sphere that nonetheless maintains the public as being distinct from the market, state, and family, see Nancy Fraser, "Rethinking the Public Sphere: A Contribution to the Critique of Actually Existing Democracy," in *The Phantom Public Sphere,* ed. Bruce Robbins (Minneapolis: University of Minnesota Press, 1993), 1–32.

23. See Fraser, "Rethinking the Public Sphere," and Oskar Negt and Alexander Kluge, *Public Sphere and Experience: Toward an Analysis of the Bourgeois and Proletarian Public Sphere,* trans. Peter Labanyi, Jamie Owen Daniel, and Assenka Oksiloff (Minneapolis: University of Minnesota Press, 1993).

24. See Hansen's foreword in Negt and Kluge, *Public Sphere and Experience,* xi, xxxvi.

3. "The Stereotypes Must Die"

1. Dave Kaufman, "Mexamericans Prep Boycott despite AMPTP," *Daily Variety,* Sept. 27, 1968, 1, 6.

2. Armando Rendon and Domingo Nick Reyes, *Chicanos and the Mass Media,* prepared statement with exhibits, in U.S. Congress, Senate Select Committee on Equal Educational Opportunity, *Hearings on Equal Educational Opportunity,* part 2—Equality of Educational Opportunity: An Introduction—Continued, hearings on July 30, 1970: "Effect of Television on Equal Educational Opportunity" (Washington, D.C.: U.S. Government Printing Office, 1970), 928AH–928AR, 928AO; also submitted for the record in U.S. Congress, House Subcommittee on Communications and Power, *Films and Broadcasts Demeaning Ethnic, Racial, or Religious Groups,* hearings held Sept. 21, 1970 (Washington, D.C.: U.S. Government Printing Office, 1970), 67–97; reprinted as *Chicanos and the Mass Media* (Washington, D.C.: National Mexican-American Anti-Defamation Committee, 1971).

3. *Report of the National Advisory Commission on Civil Disorders,* 382–83.

4. Horwitz, *The Irony of Regulatory Reform,* 11–14.

5. Ibid., 12.

6. Gordon Allport, *The Nature of Prejudice* (Cambridge: Addison-Wesley, 1954), 191; quoted in Francisco J. Lewels Jr., *The Uses of the Media by the Chicano Movement: A Study in Minority Access* (New York: Praeger Publishers, 1974), 51.

7. Rendon and Reyes, *Chicanos and the Mass Media*, 928AO.

8. Thomas M. Martinez, "Advertising and Racism: The Case of the Mexican-American," *El Grito: A Journal of Contemporary Mexican-American Thought* 2, no. 4 (Summer 1969): 5; reprinted as "How Advertisers Promote Racism," *Civil Rights Digest* 2, no. 4 (Fall 1969): 5–11; and "The Profit of Advertising: Racism," *La Raza* 1, no. 4 (June 1971): 27–31. A fascimile of "How Advertisers Promote Racism" appears as an exhibit with Rendon and Reyes's prepared statement, *Chicanos and the Mass Media*, in *Hearings on Equal Educational Opportunity*, 928AY–928BE, and *Films and Broadcasts Demeaning Ethnic, Racial, or Religious Groups* (1970), 83–89. The article was also adopted as the position paper of the National Mexican-American Anti-Defamation Committee.

9. Martinez, "Advertising and Racism." See also Domingo Nick Reyes, "Testimony on Modern Advertising Practices," presented to the Federal Trade Commission (FTC), dated Nov. 18, 1971. The eight-page manuscript is located in the FTC Library.

10. Mario Obledo and Robert B. Joselow, "Broadcasting: Mexican-Americans and the Media," *Chicano Law Review* 1, no. 1 (Summer 1972): 85–98; revised and reprinted as Mario G. Obledo, "Mexican Americans and the Media," in *La Causa Chicana: The Movement for Justice*, ed. Margaret M. Mangold (New York: Family Service Association of America, 1972), 6–16.

11. Lewels, *The Uses of the Media by the Chicano Movement*.

12. Rendon and Reyes, *Chicanos and the Mass Media*.

13. As Timothy R. Haight and Laurie R. Weinstein note, "Fundamentally, the media reform movement was originally a 'second issue,' involving groups wanting to influence the media in the name of other goals." Haight and Weinstein, "Changing Ideology on Television by Changing Telecommunications Policy: Notes on a Contradictory Situation," in *Communication and Social Structure: Critical Studies in Mass Media Research*, ed. Emile G. McAnany, Jorge Schnitman, and Noreene Janus (New York: Praeger Publishers, 1981), 135.

14. Rendon and Reyes, *Chicanos and the Mass Media*, 928AO.

15. Lewels, *The Uses of the Media by the Chicano Movement*, 53.

16. Thomas M. Martinez and José Peralez, "Chicanos and the Motion Picture Industry," *La Raza* 1, no. 5 (1971): 60–64, esp. 63.

17. Ibid., 63.

18. Ibid.

19. Ibid., 64.

20. Ibid.

21. Here I am drawing upon Ernesto Laclau, "Universalism, Particularism, and the Question of Identity," *October* 61 (Summer 1992): 83–90, and Anderson, *Imagined Communities*.

22. Though not male-female! I make reference to Teresa de Lauretis, "Through the Looking Glass," *Alice Doesn't: Feminism, Semiotic, Cinema* (Bloomington: Indiana University Press, 1984), 12–36. For de Lauretis, "[t]o perform the terms of the production of woman as text, as image, is to resist identification with that image. It is to have stepped through the looking-glass" (36). Interestingly, de Lauretis draws upon the similar use of the phrase in an early feminist text concurrent with this period of Chicano media activism: Sheila Rowbotham, *Woman's Consciousness, Man's World* (Harmondsworth: Penguin Books, 1973), 25, 27–28.

23. See, e.g., Marvin Alinsky, "The Mexican-Americans Make Themselves Heard," *The Reporter*, Feb. 9, 1967, 45–48. López would later serve as executive director of the National Chicano Media Council (1970–72), an attempt to coordinate Chicano groups and activities directed at the media.

24. Enrique Hank López, "Back to Bachimba," in *The Chicanos: Mexican American Voices,* ed. Ed Ludwig and James Santibañez (Baltimore: Penguin Books, 1971), 263; reprinted from *Horizon* (Winter 1967).

25. López voices two recurrent concerns about conflicts within the barrio: those between Mexican Americans and recent Mexican immigrants, and those between Mexican Americans and African Americans.

26. López, "Back to Bachimba," 269.

27. López's rejection of home contrasts with nationalist efforts to claim a homeland—Aztlán—as the basis for cultural identity and direct action. There are some similarities between this performative text, where many of the arguments remain implicit, and Juan Bruce-Novoa's theoretical discussion a few years later about the space of Chicano identity. While Bruce-Novoa rejects the terminology of the "hyphen," his description of that "space" actually conjures up the hyphen-as-identity to a greater extent than does López: Chicano art creates a space outside Mexican and U.S. influences, "while at the same time creating interlocking tensions that hold the two in relationship." In a way, the difference between the two can be attributed to the fact that Bruce-Novoa places a higher importance on Chicano art as a category, while also making a universalist claim to Art, whereas for López these categories are political constructs and are meant to be used rather than occupied. Juan Bruce-Novoa, "The Space of Chicano Literature Update: 1978," in *Retrospace: Collected Essays on Chicano Literature* (Houston: Arte Público, 1990), 93–113, esp. 98; the original article, "The Space of Chicano Literature," appeared in *The Chicano Literary World: 1974,* ed. Philip Ortego (Las Vegas: New Mexico Highlands University, 1975), 22–51, and was reprinted in *De Colores* 1, no. 4 (1975): 22–42.

28. It was not until 1973, as this period of activism came to an end, that scholars first drew attention to the historical dimension of Chicano resistance, revealing organized protest against film and print stereotypes since at least 1910. José E. Limón, "Stereotyping and Chicano Resistance: An Historical Dimension," *Aztlán: International Journal of Chicano Studies* 4, no. 2 (1973): 257–70; reprinted in Noriega, *Chicanos and Film,* 3–17. See also Mario T. García's account of the "antidefamation cultural strategy" of the Asociación Nacional México-Americana in the 1950s, in *Mexican Americans: Leadership, Ideology, and Identity, 1930–1960* (New Haven: Yale University Press, 1989), 215–16. While these appear to have been isolated incidents, they bear consideration given their simultaneous local and national orientations.

29. "Ban the Bandito?," *Newsweek,* Dec. 22, 1969, 82, 86.

30. Ibid. I recall watching these ads on Saturday morning cartoons and being quite taken with them—much to the dismay of my father (who was then involved in the "Boycott Grapes" campaign) especially when my sister and I compared his mustache to that of the Frito Bandito.

31. Martinez, "Advertising and Racism," listed eight advertisers who were subsequently targeted by NMAADC, IMAGE, and CARISSMA, as well as by Senators Alan Cranston (California) and Joseph Montoya (New Mexico). *Advertising Age* later reported that three of these companies had been misidentified. For example, Arrid deodorant was cited for an ad run for Bristol-Myers's Mum spray deodorant. See Martinez, "Advertising and Racism," 13, and "Mexicans' Defenders Err," editorial, *Advertising Age,* Mar. 16, 1970, 24. The mistaken charge against Arrid is repeated in a recent sidebar to an article on Hispanics in advertising: Octavio E. Nuiry and Alex Avila, "Hall of Shame," *Hispanic* (July 1996): 30–31.

32. Lewels, *The Uses of the Media by the Chicano Movement,* 58. The ad ran in Sunday supplements on May 24, 1970—e.g., *Chicago Tribune Magazine,* 24—and was reprinted as an exhibit in Rendon and Reyes, *Chicanos and the Mass Media,* in U.S. Con-

gress, House Subcommittee on Communications and Power, *Films and Broadcasts Demeaning Ethnic, Racial, or Religious Groups* (1970), 91. See also Mike Royko, "Mexicans Fix Admen's Clock," *Chicago Daily News,* June 9, 1970.

33. Richard Slotkin, *Gunfighter Nation: The Myth of the Frontier in Twentieth-Century America* (New York: HarperPerennial, 1992), 536.

34. See Kitty Calavita, *Inside the State: The Bracero Program, Immigration, and the I.N.S.* (New York: Routledge, 1992), 179–83.

35. David G. Gutiérrez, *Walls and Mirrors: Mexican Americans, Mexican Immigrants, and the Politics of Ethnicity* (Berkeley: University of California Press, 1995), 182.

36. "San Antonio Bell Unit Criticized for 'Jellow Pages' Ads," *Advertising Age,* Aug. 5, 1968, 4; "Anti-Defamation Group Fights Ads Using Spanish Name Stereotypes," *Advertising Age,* Sept. 30, 1968, 94; "Bill Dana Defends 'Jellow Pages' Spots," *Advertising Age,* Sept. 30, 1968, 94; and the prepared statement by Domingo Nick Reyes in U.S. Congress, House Subcommittee on Communications and Power, *Films and Broadcasts Demeaning Ethnic, Racial, or Religious Groups: 1971,* hearings held Apr. 27–28, 1971 (Washington, D.C.: U.S. Government Printing Office, 1971), 49–55, esp. 52–53. The ad hoc committee is referred to as a loose confederation of groups called La Raza Unida in "Anti-Defamation Group Fights Ads." Reyes identifies the original members as Albert Peña Jr., Armando Rodriguez, and himself.

37. Albert Peña Jr. suggested a letter-writing campaign against Bell Telephone for their "Jellow Pages" commercials by the comic character Jose Jimenez (comedian Bill Dana), but added: "If they do nothing, rip out the 'Jellow Pages' from your phone books. At a designated time and place, we will start us a huge 'Jellow Pages' bonfire." Bell later claimed to have received just two complaints. Peña quoted in "San Antonio Bell Unit Criticized for 'Jellow Pages' Ads"; on complaints to Bell, see "Bill Dana Defends 'Jellow Pages' Spots."

38. "Anti-Defamation Group Fights Ads Using Spanish Name Stereotypes."

39. Concurrent efforts addressed this exclusion: protest votes against the Democratic party, the formation of a locally successful third party, petitions to expand the Voting Rights Act (1965) to include Mexican Americans, and court-mandated redistricting.

40. Peña also cofounded NMAADC and, after 1963, headed the Political Association of Spanish-Speaking Organizations (PASSO).

41. "Anti-Defamation Group Fights Ads Using Spanish Name Stereotypes."

42. Armando M. Rodriguez, letter to Liggett & Myers, quoted in "Anti-Defamation Group Fights Ads Using Spanish Name Stereotypes."

43. "Spanish Americans Hit 'Derogatory' Stereotypes in Ads," *Advertising Age,* May 19, 1969, 112.

44. Don McComb, introduction, special issue, *Minority Images in Advertising, Journal of Communication Inquiry* 14, no. 1 (Winter 1990): 4.

45. Companies that quickly dropped their bandito ads included American Motors, Granny Goose, Rainbow Bread, and Liggett & Myers. See "Spanish Americans Hit 'Derogatory' Stereotypes in Ads."

46. "Bill Dana Defends 'Jellow Pages' Spots."

47. "Spanish Americans Hit 'Derogatory' Stereotypes in Ads"; and "As We See It," *TV Guide,* Oct. 5, 1968, 5.

48. Richard Vasquez, "Jose Jimenez 'Dies'—and Pride Lives," *Los Angeles Times,* Apr. 5, 1970. Dana was one of a number of actors and entertainers showing support for the Chicano community in Los Angeles at an event organized by the Congress of Mexican-American Unity. Latino performers included Anthony Quinn, Ricardo Montalban,

and Vicky Carr. See also Oscar Zeta Acosta's fictionalized account in *The Revolt of the Cockroach People* (New York: Vintage Books, 1989), 168–75, esp. 170.

49. "Ban the Bandito?"

50. "Spanish Americans Hit 'Derogatory' Stereotypes in Ads." In its announcement, Frito-Lay made a more general claim that Frito Bandito would no longer fire a gun "because of the recent concern regarding violence in America." See "Frito Bandito Is Still Around," editorial, *Advertising Age,* Jan. 11, 1971, 10; reprinted in *Regeneración* 1, no. 9 (1970): 20.

51. "Time to Answer Frito Bandito? Mexican-American Groups to Seek Fairness Ruling on Frito-Lay Commercials," *Broadcasting,* Dec. 15, 1969, 37, 40.

52. Ibid.

53. Ibid., 40.

54. "Ban the Bandito?"

55. The quotations from *CBS v. DNC* are taken from an extended passage reprinted in Haight and Weinstein, "Changing Ideology on Television," 121–22.

56. *The Handling of Public Issues under the Fairness Doctrine and the Public Interest Standards of the Communications Act* (1974), quoted in Erwin G. Krasnow, Lawrence D. Longley, and Herbert A. Terry, *The Politics of Broadcast Regulation,* 3d ed. (New York: St. Martin's, 1982), 81. The FCC's report was upheld in the U.S. Court of Appeals for the District of Columbia Circuit.

57. "Spanish Americans Hit 'Derogatory' Stereotypes in Ads."

58. Ibid.

59. "Time to Answer Frito Bandito?," 40. Reyes claims that NBC dropped the ad, too, after NMAADC met with their Bureau of Practices and Standards, headed by a Spanish-surnamed executive, Hermino Traviesas. I have not been able to find confirmation of this action by NBC. In any case, on this basis, NMAADC did not include NBC in its $610,000,000 lawsuit. The networks, which are not regulated by the FCC, appear to have had a different position from that of the local stations, as represented in a letter to the House Subcommittee on Communications and Power from Richard W. Jencks, the president of the CBS Broadcast Group: "Of course, broadcasting, by its very nature, insures the application of reasonable standards. As a mass medium, viewed in the home, and supported by advertisers whose desire is clearly not to offend, it is inconceivable that, in programs intended to entertain, we would seek to offend or fail to be sensitive to members of our audience." In order for this statement to be true, the networks would have had to consider Chicanos as consumers and viewers—something Frito-Lay's position as well as industry hiring patterns called into question. *Films and Broadcasts Demeaning Ethnic, Racial, or Religious Groups: 1971, 56, 65.*

60. "Mexican-Americans Assail Commercials," *New York Times,* Dec. 10, 1969, and "Time to Answer Frito Bandito?," 37.

61. There were about 700 commercial stations in the United States at this time. "Time to Answer Frito Bandito?," 37.

62. Ibid.

63. "Frito Bandito Is Still Around."

64. Letter from John R. McCarthy, Vice President of Public Relations, Frito-Lay, to Dr. Hector García (founder of the American G.I. Forum), n.d.; reprinted in "El Mexicano through the Eyes of the Gavacho," *La Raza* 1, no. 4 (June 1971): 23.

65. Ibid.

66. The suit was directed at Frito-Lay, Foote, Cone & Belding, CBS, and ABC. "$610,000,000 Suit: The National Mexican American Anti-Defamation Committee," *La*

Raza 1, no. 4 (June 1971): 26; and "Frito Bandito Is Still Around." Nevertheless, NMAADC also continued to approach state institutions regarding advertisers. In Nov. 1971, Reyes testified before the Federal Trade Commission, presenting ten policy recommendations aimed at regulating advertisers on behalf of minority groups. See Reyes, "Testimony on Modern Advertising Practices."

67. "$610,000,000 Suit."

68. "Frito Bandito Is Still Around." The columnist William Raspberry viewed the case in the context of *racial* discrimination rather than *ethnic* stereotypes in "How About Frito Amigo?" See also Raspberry's follow-up column responding to a letter about his "left-wing liberals . . . 'nitpicking'": "Who's the Real Bandito?," *Washington Post,* June 7, 1971.

69. *Films and Broadcasts Demeaning Ethnic, Racial, or Religious Groups* (1970), and *Films and Broadcasts Demeaning Ethnic, Racial, or Religious Groups: 1971.*

70. These comments were elicited and expressed by the committee chairman, Torbert H. Macdonald. *Films and Broadcasts Demeaning Ethnic, Racial, or Religious Groups* (1970), 41–42, 45.

71. See Frank J. Brasco's remarks in both hearings. *Films and Broadcasts Demeaning Ethnic, Racial, or Religious Groups: 1971,* 14, 16, 24, 32, 56–58. For Macdonald's comments, see 18, 36, 58.

72. Chief among dissenting voices was Rep. Lionel Van Deerlin (California), who in the late 1970s—as chair of the subcommittee—would propose a "rewrite" of the Communication Act to eliminate or reduce equal employment opportunity, the equal time rule, the fairness doctrine, and ascertainment of community needs. While his proposal was rebuffed by media reform groups, it signaled the start of the deregulation of the industry in the 1980s.

73. *Films and Broadcasts Demeaning Ethnic, Racial, or Religious Groups: 1971,* 59.

74. Ibid. The actors' group Nosotros still clung to the reformist strategy in its complaint before the House Subcommittee on Communications and Power. Richard Hernandez, legal counsel for Nosotros, suggested "a Frito Amigo who gives away corn chips instead of stealing them." William Raspberry, "How About Frito Amigo?," *Washington Post,* June 2, 1971.

75. Lewels, *The Uses of the Media by the Chicano Movement,* 60.

76. "Chicanos and the Motion Picture Industry," 64.

77. *Films and Broadcasts Demeaning Ethnic, Racial, or Religion Groups: 1971,* 53–55.

78. Lewels, *The Uses of the Media by the Chicano Movement,* 78.

79. Sid Hix, cartoon with Frito Bandito character, *Broadcasting,* Mar. 23, 1970, 80.

4. Regulating Chico

1. Thomas Streeter, *Selling the Air: A Critique of the Policy of Commercial Broadcasting in the United States* (Chicago: University of Chicago Press, 1996), 195; see also Haight and Weinstein, "Changing Ideology on Television by Changing Telecommunications Policy, 124. Streeter defines corporate liberalism: "Corporate liberal social organization does not simply mean control by private corporations. It involves a complex, dynamic pattern of interactions among corporations, small businesses, the state, and an electoral polity. In general, the pattern involves a hierarchal distribution of power, with a core dominated by an alliance of corporate and government elites, orbited by less powerful—but not powerless—peripheries: an economic periphery of smaller enterprises and a political periphery of electoral politics. . . . Corporate liberalism, in other words, is a

dynamic response to complex social contradictions and conditions, conditions that include various forms of resistance to corporate control" (39–40).

2. For an example of an early piece that addressed this issue, see Ruben Salazar, "Chicanos Would Find Identity before Coalition with Blacks," *Los Angeles Times,* Feb. 20, 1970; reprinted in Ruben Salazar, *Border Correspondent: Selected Writings, 1955–1970,* ed. Mario T. García (Berkeley: University of California Press, 1995), 239–41.

3. Streeter, *Selling the Air;* Horwitz, *The Irony of Regulatory Reform;* William D. Rowland, Jr., "The Illusion of Fulfillment: The Broadcast Reform Movement," *Journalism Monographs* 79 (Dec. 1982): 1–41; and Haight and Weinstein, "Changing Ideology on Television."

4. Streeter, *Selling the Air,* 21, 197.

5. For a critique of the relative autonomy of the state, see Bob Jessop, *State Theory: Putting Capitalist States in Their Place* (University Park: Pennsylvania State University Press, 1990), 85–103.

6. Dave Kaufman, "2-Mil. Mexicans Can't Be Conned, Says Martell; Also-Angry Negro Actors Copping Latin Roles," *Variety,* Sept. 25, 1968, 17; and Kaufman, "Mexamericans Prep Boycott despite AMPTP," *Daily Variety,* Sept. 27, 1968, 1, 6.

7. I am extrapolating from a number of sources: Martinez and Peralez, "Chicanos and the Motion Picture Industry," 63; Kaufman, "2-Mil. Mexicans Can't Be Conned"; Kaufman, "Mexamericans Prep Boycott despite AMPTP," 6; and Kathryn C. Montgomery, *Target: Prime Time, Advocacy Groups and the Struggle over Entertainment Television* (New York: Oxford University Press, 1989), 56. Martinez and Peralez place Martell and Andrade on the set of *Che!,* but the film had not gone into production when Martell first announced the boycott, complaining about the casting for the film. In the end, Martell had a small part in *Che!,* playing Camilio Cienfuegos.

8. Kaufman, "Mexamericans Prep Boycott despite AMPTP," 6.

9. Kaufman, "2-Mil. Mexicans Can't Be Conned."

10. Kaufman, "Mexamericans Prep Boycott despite AMPTP," 6.

11. Ray Martell, in U.S. Congress, House Subcommittee on Communications and Power, *Films and Broadcasts Demeaning Ethnic, Racial, or Religious Groups: 1971,* 145. See also Roy Reed, "Movies Face U.S. Suits on Hiring Bias," *New York Times,* Mar. 14, 1969.

12. Mario T. García, *Memories of Chicano History: The Life and Narrative of Bert Corona* (Berkeley: University of California Press, 1994), 222–25. See also Marvin Alinsky, "The Mexican Americans Make Themselves Heard," *Reporter,* Feb. 9, 1967, 45. Corona, the president of MAPA, also attended the EEOC meeting, although he arrived late as the walkout was in progress. After the walkout, Vicente T. Ximenes was appointed to the EEOC (June 1967), and then named head of the newly created Inter-Agency Committee on Mexican American Affairs. The EEOC does not mention the walkout in its summary of "technical assistance" for the year. U.S. Equal Employment Opportunity Commission, *First Annual Report,* submitted to the House of Representatives (Washington, D.C.: U.S. Government Printing Office, 1967), 23.

13. Kaufman, "2-Mil. Mexicans Can't Be Conned."

14. Kaufman, "Mexamericans Prep Boycott despite AMPTP," 6.

15. Ibid., 1.

16. See the comparison between MAPA and PASSO in Leo Grebler, Joan W. Moore, and Ralph C. Guzman, *The Mexican-American People: The Nation's Second Largest Minority* (New York: Free Press, 1970), 544.

17. Kaufman, "2-Mil. Mexicans Can't Be Conned"; and Martell, in U.S. Equal Employment Opportunity Commission, *Hearings on Utilization of Minority and Women*

Workers in Certain Major Industries, Mar. 12–14, 1969, Los Angeles, Calif. (Washington, D.C.: U.S. Government Printing Office, 1969), 142.

18. Kaufman, "2-Mil. Mexicans Can't Be Conned." Martell's statement, of course, ignores a notable exception: *The Cisco Kid* (1950–56), starring Duncan Renaldo and Leo Carrillo. The show was the first popular syndicated program and one of the first *filmed* programs on television (filmed in color, but broadcast in black and white).

19. Blaine P. Lamb, "The Convenient Villain: The Early Cinema Views the Mexican-American," *Journal of the West* 14, no. 4 (Oct. 1975): 75–81.

20. "El Mexicano through the Eyes of the Gavacho," *La Raza* 1, no. 4 (June 1971): 24.

21. Martinez and Peralez, "Chicanos and the Motion Picture Industry," 61.

22. Ibid.

23. Ibid., 63.

24. U.S. Equal Employment Opportunity Commission, *Hearings on Utilization of Minority and Women Workers.* For press accounts of the hearings, see Jack Jones, "U.S. Board to Ask Suit Charging Film Job Bias," *Los Angeles Times,* Mar. 14, 1969; Ruben Salazar, "Gilbert Roland Raps Films Portraying Mexicans as Foolish," *Los Angeles Times,* Mar. 14, 1969; "Film Studios Flunk Hiring Quiz; Send Untutored, Don't Know 'Voices,'" *Variety,* Mar. 19, 1969, 17; Dave Kaufman, "U.S. Equal Opportunity Commission Puts Network TV Coast Execs on Hot Seat Re Jobs for Minorities," *Variety,* Mar. 19, 1969, 78; and Dave Kaufman, "EEOC Brushed Off One IA Union: Costumers Local 20% Minorities," *Daily Variety,* Mar. 20, 1969, 1, 8.

25. U.S. Equal Employment Opportunity Commission, *Hearings on Utilization of Minority and Women Workers,* 2.

26. Ibid., 3.

27. Ibid., 227–28.

28. Ibid.

29. Ibid., 353, 357.

30. Ibid., 346.

31. See, e.g., Kaufman, "U.S. Equal Opportunity Commission Puts Network TV Coast Execs on Hot Seat."

32. I rely upon the following report for details about the EEOC hearings, Department of Justice agreement, and subsequent results and follow-up efforts: California Advisory Committee to the U.S. Commission on Civil Rights, *Behind the Scenes: Equal Opportunity on the Motion Picture Industry* (Washington, D.C.: U.S. Government Printing Office, 1978), esp. 11–14, 36–40. For press accounts of the agreement, see Paul Delaney, "Major Moviemakers Agree to a Fair-Hiring Plan," *New York Times,* Apr. 1, 1970; and Vincent J. Burke, "Film and TV Minority Job Plan in Effect," *Los Angeles Times,* Apr. 1, 1970; reprinted as "New Movie, TV Plan Bans Job Bias," *Washington Post,* Apr. 1, 1970, A6.

33. See, e.g., Jesús Salvador Treviño's comments to this effect in his "Chicano Cinema," 170–71, and "Chicano Cinema Overview," 41.

34. Kaufman describes the commissioners as displaying "disbelief and, at times, hostility" in "U.S. Equal Opportunity Commission Puts Network TV Coast Execs on Hot Seat." Most press reports cite the forceful nature of the hearings, something that is readily apparent throughout the published transcript.

35. The quoted phrase is taken from U.S. Equal Employment Opportunity Commission, *First Annual Report,* 17.

36. U.S. Equal Employment Opportunity Commission, *Second Annual Report,*

submitted to the House of Representatives (Washington, D.C.: U.S. Government Printing Office, 1968), 8–9; for a discussion of the conciliation process, see 8–15.

37. Of course, the critique of the EEOC made within government itself ignores these "contextual" factors, focusing instead on such procedural failings as "management problems" in defining and executing "administrative operations," and citing just one factor "outside EEOC's control": "the frequent turnover in top management positions of chairman and executive director." See U.S. General Accounting Office, *The Equal Employment Opportunity Commission Has Made Limited Progress in Eliminating Employment Discrimination,* report to the Congress (Washington, D.C.: U.S. Government Printing Office, 1976), esp. 62–66.

38. Burke, "New Movie, TV Plan."

39. Skrentny, *The Ironies of Affirmative Action,* esp. 141–44.

40. See Skrentny's argument about how affirmative action became seen as a "tradition" in ibid., chap. 6.

41. This list is taken from Streeter, *Selling the Air,* 118.

42. Horwitz, *The Irony of Regulatory Reform,* 76.

43. Enforcement agencies for the latter include the Department of Justice and the Department of Labor. The Department of Labor enforces Presidential Executive Order 11246 (1965), amended by 11375 (1967), which prohibits discrimination on the basis of race, religion, sex, or national origin by federal contractors and subcontractors. The department delegates federal contract compliance in the entertainment industry to the General Services Administration. See *Behind the Scenes,* 38–39.

44. Streeter, *Selling the Air,* 114. The main exception here would be the creation of PBS in the 1960s.

45. Ibid., 114, 116.

46. Ibid., 114. Streeter cites Stanley Fish, *Is There a Text in This Class? The Authority of Interpretive Communities* (Cambridge: Harvard University Press, 1980), but also points to earlier work in anthropology and sociology.

47. Ibid., 135.

48. See Slotkin, *Gunfighter Nation,* chaps. 14–17, for an extended analysis of this trope during the Vietnam era.

49. See "Inside the Beltway as an Interpretive Community," in Streeter, *Selling the Air,* 117–20.

50. Ibid., 143.

51. Haight and Weinstein, "Changing Ideology on Television," 141.

52. Rendon and Reyes, *Chicanos and the Mass Media,* 75.

53. Ibid., 75–77. For a similar statement by NMAADC before the National Association of Broadcasters, see Reyes, "Anti-Defamation Committee Says Media Do Not Depict Mexican Americans Fairly," *TV Code News* 3, no. 12 (Feb. 1971): 2.

54. *Utilization of Minority and Women Workers,* 142.

55. Ibid., 140–49.

56. *Films and Broadcasts Demeaning Ethnic, Racial, or Religious Groups: 1971,* 29–36, 45–60.

57. Ibid., 45–46.

58. Ibid., 32.

59. See Kathryn Montgomery's discussion of Nosotros in *Target: Prime Time,* 64–65.

60. *Films and Broadcasts Demeaning Ethnic, Racial, or Religious Groups: 1971,* 21.

61. These included *Impacto* (1970–74, KNBC-TV); *Unidos* (1970–71) and *Reflec-*

ciones (1972–73), both KABC-TV; *¡Ahora!* (1969–70) and *Acción Chicano* (1972–74), both KCET-TV; *The Siesta Is Over* (1972–73) and *Bienvenidos* (1973), both KNXT-TV (now KCBS-TV). Ibid. and Harry Gamboa Jr., "Silver Screening the Barrio," *Equal Opportunity Forum* 6, no. 1 (Nov. 1978): 6–7.

62. Montgomery, *Target: Prime Time*, 55–56. Montgomery provides a useful case study of Justicia in her chapter, "Managing Advocacy Groups," which examines the role of standards and practices departments in containing protests. See esp. 51–65.

63. The board also included Bert Corona, who had been president of MAPA during the AMPTP protest.

64. While Andrade acted as the spokesperson, the protest was associated in the press with the National Mexican-American Anti-Defamation Committee. Ted Thackery Jr., "John Wayne and Maggie Smith; 'Midnight Cowboy' Top Picture," *Los Angeles Times,* Apr. 8, 1970; "'Midnight Cowboy' Gets Oscar; Wayne and Maggie Smith Win," *New York Times,* Apr. 8, 1970; and Bill Edwards, "Chicanos Picket Academy Awards," *Daily Variety,* Apr. 8, 1970, 1, 8. For an account of smaller protests the year before, see "Crowd Outside Awards Was Scant but Very Enthusiastic," *Daily Variety,* Apr. 15, 1969, 17.

65. Later, in a move similar to the MAPA position on Black gains in the industry, Justicia would add the Jim Brown westerns *100 Rifles* (1969) and *El Condor* (1970) to their list.

66. Ricardo Montalban, the president of Nosotros, and Walter Pidgeon joined Justicia in its meeting with SAG. Richard Vasquez, "Chicano Protest on Movie Image Backed by Guild," *Los Angeles Times,* Aug. 27, 1970; "Film Guilds Vow Aid for Chicano Image," *New York Times,* Aug. 28, 1970; and "Film Guilds Air Needs of Chicanos," *Los Angeles Times,* Oct. 16, 1970.

67. "Chicanos List 'Grievances,' Issue Ultimatum to Px, TV," *Daily Variety,* Oct. 9, 1970, 1,6. See also "Mexican-Americans Seek New Film, TV Image," *Los Angeles Herald-Examiner,* Oct. 10, 1970.

68. "Chicanos List 'Grievances.'"

69. "Chicanos' Question: What About Us?," *Broadcasting,* June 28, 1971, 23; "Justicia Now Moves against NBC-TV," *Broadcasting,* Aug. 2, 1971, 38; and "NBC Answers Chicano Beefs on Portrayals," *Variety,* Aug. 4, 1971, 2.

70. Montgomery, *Target: Prime Time*, 58.

71. Quoted in ibid., 59.

72. Ibid., 60.

73. Ibid., 61–62.

74. Late in 1971, Justicia called for a boycott of the Dean Martin western *Something Big* (1971), then clashed with Nosotros, which also served as a script consultant for the industry, but whose position within the industry made it more moderate. "Rated X: Racist Films," *La Raza* 1, no. 7 (Jan. 1972): 57; and "Justicia o Muerte," *La Raza* 1, no. 8 (Apr. 1972): 14. See also "Justicia, Nosotros Iron Out Differences for Bowl Bash," *Daily Variety,* Aug. 6, 1971, 19.

75. "Million Dollar Four Acquitted: Courts Admit to Bias against Chicanos in Jury Selection," *La Raza* 1, no. 11 (July 1973): 32–33; "Andrade Jailed on Bomb Charge," *Los Angeles Herald-Examiner,* July 11, 1972; "Andrade Hearing Is Set," *Los Angeles Herald-Examiner,* July 13, 1972; and William Farr, "Militant Chicano Faces Three Felony Charges in Bomb Cases," *Los Angeles Times,* July 12, 1972.

76. Hall and Ikenberry, *The State,* 1–2.

77. Of course, Andrade faced local police and the municipal court. My point, however, is that the Chicano movement existed in the interface between the local and the national, and that Andrade posed a direct challenge to the "means of violence and coercion"

that define state power and legitimacy. For an account of the collusion between local police and state agencies against the Chicano movement, see Edward J. Escobar, "The Dialectics of Repression: The Los Angeles Police Department and the Chicano Movement, 1968–1971," *Journal of American History* 79, no. 4 (Mar. 1993): 1483–1514.

78. Cecil Smith, "Chico and the Man: A Hit in Spite of the Controversy," *Los Angeles Times,* Nov. 10, 1974, "TV Times," 2. See also the response by John H. Brinsley, "Chico and the Man," letter to the editor, *Los Angeles Times,* Nov. 18, 1974. In a radio interview in 1975, Komack claimed both Andrade and Cheech Marin as early models for Chico. See Victor Vazquez, "Who's behind Chico and the Man?," KPFK, 1975, 61 minutes, Pacifica Radio Archive.

79. See Montgomery, *Target: Prime Time,* 62–64; Vincente Aceves Madrid, "The Controversy Surrounding NBC's 'Chico and the Man,'" *Latin Quarter* 1, no. 2 (Oct. 1974): 5–7; Victor Vasquez, "More on 'Chico and the Man,'" *Latin Quarter* (Jan.–Feb. 1975): 13–15; and Harry F. Waters, "Hot Hungarican," *Newsweek,* Nov. 11, 1974, 74–75.

80. Likewise, in such feature films as *Walk Proud* and *Boulevard Nights* (both 1979), Chicano movement discourse was resituated within gang narratives.

81. Quoted in Dave Kaufman, "'Chico' Associate Producer Andrade Unhappy over Show's Chicano Image," *Daily Variety,* Sept. 19, 1974, 7.

82. See the protest statement by the faculty of the Los Angeles Hispanic Urban Center, "Under Fire: Chico and the Man," *Los Angeles Times,* Sept. 30, 1974. For a contemporary assessment of *Chico and the Man,* including interviews with Andrade, Prinze, and Komack, see the radio program by Victor Vazquez, "Who's behind Chico and the Man?" Andrade later worked as military technical advisor on both Haskell Wexler's *Latino* (1985) and Frank De Palma's *Private War* (1990).

83. Montgomery, *Target: Prime Time,* 62.

84. George Lipsitz, *Time Passages: Collective Memory and American Popular Culture* (Minneapolis: University of Minnesota Press, 1990), 214.

85. Quoted in Montgomery, *Target: Prime Time,* 58. For a brief discussion of the use of Alinsky's methods in Chicano organizing, see Gómez-Quiñones, *Chicano Politics,* 180.

86. Saul D. Alinsky, *Rules for Radicals: A Pragmatic Primer for Realistic Radicals* (New York: Vintage Books, 1989), 78–79.

87. Ibid., xviii–xix.

88. Ibid., 127, italics in original.

89. Ibid., 119, italics in original.

5. Grasping at the Public Airwaves

1. Streeter, *Selling the Air,* 50.

2. As Kent R. Keller notes, "Although the legal concept is circular—since a party has standing only if his interest is legally protected and his interest is legally protected only if he is afforded standing—it is the usual test for allowing or denying intervention." Keller, "The Law of Administrative Standing and the Public Right of Intervention," *Federal Communications Bar Journal* 21, no. 3 (1967): 135–36.

3. See Robert W. McChesney, *Corporate Media and the Threat to Democracy* (New York: Seven Stories, 1997), 46.

4. My summary of the WLBT case is taken from Steven Douglas Classen, "Broadcast Law and Segregation: A Social History of the WLBT-TV Case," Ph.D. diss. (University of Wisconsin, 1995).

5. These include the standing of citizen groups, shifting the burden of proof to the licensee, establishing the probative value of program monitoring, and revoking of the broadcaster's license based on failure to serve the public interest of its audience. See U.S. Commission on Civil Rights, *Window Dressing on the Set: Women and Minorities in Television* (Washington, D.C.: U.S. Government Printing Office, 1977), 61.

6. Steven Douglas Classen, "Standing on Unstable Grounds: A Reexamination of the WLBT-TV Case," *Critical Studies in Mass Communication* 11 (1994): 73–91.

7. Ibid., 85.

8. *Office of Communication of the United Church of Christ v. FCC,* 425 F. 2d (D.C. Cir. 1969), 546–49. Quoted in Joseph A. Grundfest, *Citizen Participation in Broadcast Licensing before the FCC* (Santa Monica: Rand, 1976), 151.

9. See, e.g., the critique of the FCC as "overly cautious" in its development and implementation of an enforcement policy for equal employment opportunity and nondiscrimination, in U.S. Commission on Civil Rights, *Window Dressing on the Set: Women and Minorities in Television,* 131–32.

10. Grundfest, *Citizen Participation,* 154.

11. Form 395 was established in 1969 when the FCC adopted a formal nondiscrimination rule. The next year, the report was modified to include female employees, albeit in a way that constituted "women and minorities" as mutually exclusive groups—at the expense of minority women. Form 395 has also been criticized by media groups and federal agencies for its use of overly broad job categories that are, by and large, irrelevant to the broadcasting industry. See, e.g., the discussion throughout U.S. Commission on Civil Rights, *Window Dressing on the Set: Women and Minorities in Television;* and U.S. Commission on Civil Rights, *Window Dressing on the Set: An Update* (Washington, D.C.: U.S. Government Printing Office, 1979).

12. Quoted in Grundfest, *Citizen Participation,* 154. See also Jorge Reina Schement and Félix Frank Gutiérrez, with Oscar Gandy, Tim Haight, and M. Esteban Soriano, "The Anatomy of a License Challenge," *Journal of Communication* 27, no. 1 (Winter 1977): 89–94. For a more general discussion of the BBC, see Daniel Allan Rosen, "Mexican-Americans and the Broadcast Media: A Study of San Antonio's Bilingual Bicultural Coalition on Mass Media," master's thesis (University of Texas, 1976), esp. chap. 2 and app. K.

13. *Bilingual Bicultural Coalition on Mass Media v. FCC,* 492 F. 2d (D.C. Cir. 1974), 659. Quoted in U.S. Commission on Civil Rights, *Window Dressing on the Set: Women and Minorities in Television,* 134.

14. *Chuck Stone v. FCC,* 466 F. 2d (D.C. Cir. 1972), 332. Quoted in U.S. Commission on Civil Rights, *Window Dressing on the Set: Women and Minorities in Television,* 133.

15. Grundfest, *Citizen Participation,* 152.

16. Quoted in ibid., 119.

17. Ibid.

18. Ibid., 14–17.

19. Ibid., 14.

20. Ben Holman, "Information Memorandum for the Director, Subject: Upcoming Media Relations Activities, Community Relations Service," Oct. 9, 1967, p. 2, item 6.

21. Community Relations Service, *1968 Annual Report* (Washington, D.C.: U.S. Department of Justice, 1968), 15–17; idem, *1969 Annual Report* (Washington, D.C.: U.S. Department of Justice, 1969), 22–24; and idem, *1970 Annual Report* (Washington, D.C.: U.S. Department of Justice, 1969), 13–16. For an excellent account of CRS involvement in Chicano media reform, see Lewels, *The Uses of the Media by the Chicano Movement,* 66–94, 155–60.

22. Ibid., 155.

23. José Angel Gutiérrez, *A Gringo Manual on How to Handle Mexicans* (Crystal City, Tex.: Wintergarden Publishing House, 1974), 26–27.

24. "McGraw-Hill Sets Record for Concessions to Minorities," *Broadcasting,* May 15, 1972, 25.

25. Barry Cole and Mal Oettinger, "Petition to Deny: Heavy Artillery," in *Reluctant Regulators: The FCC and the Broadcast Audience* (Reading, Mass.: Addison-Wesley, 1978), 204–25; and Krasnow, Longley, and Terry, *The Politics of Broadcast Regulation,* 55.

26. The FCC figures for petitions to deny are: 1969 = 2, 1970 = 15, 1971 = 38, 1972 = 68, 1973 = 48, 1974 = 37, 1975 = 94, 1976 = 49, 1977 = 19, 1978 = 97, 1979 = 19, 1980 = 17. The peak years—1972, 1975, 1978—coincide with renewals in California, which has a large number of stations, and where citizen groups remained active throughout the 1970s. Krasnow, Longley, and Terry, *The Politics of Broadcast Regulation,* 80–81 n. 67.

27. Cole and Oettinger, *Reluctant Regulators,* 205.

28. "Renewal Battles in the Rockies," *Broadcasting,* Mar. 8, 1971, 34; "Signs of Changing Times in Renewals," *Broadcasting,* May 17, 1971, 34–35; "Diverse Appeals to D.C. Court," *Broadcasting,* July 3, 1972, 25; and "8 Challenged Stations Win Renewals from FCC," *Broadcasting,* Jan. 1, 1973, 6.

29. "Ethnic Dispute in San Antonio," *Broadcasting,* July 5, 1971, 49–50; "New Deal in Dallas-Fort Worth," *Broadcasting,* July 12, 1971, 33, 36 [text missing in the original]; "Open Season on Texas Stations," *Broadcasting,* Aug. 9, 1971, 19–20; "Charges Untrue, WOAI-TV Answers," *Broadcasting,* Sept. 6, 1971, 32; "6 Chicanos File Complaint with FCC Re KVOU 'Unresponsiveness' to Needs," *Variety,* Oct. 7, 1970, 37; "Inch by Inch, FCC Moves Ahead on Renewal Cases," *Broadcasting,* Nov. 13, 1972, 25; and "FCC Rejects Challenges in San Antonio, Buffalo," *Broadcasting,* Nov. 27, 1972, 8–9.

30. "Challengers Seek Station Figures," *Broadcasting,* July 26, 1971, 21–22; "Enter the Alianza in Renewal Attacks," *Broadcasting,* Aug. 23, 1971, 34–35; "Ganging Up," *Broadcasting,* Aug. 30, 1971, 7; "Minorities Gang Up in Albuquerque," *Broadcasting,* Sept. 6, 1971, 33–34; "Fifth Albuquerque Station Hit by Denial Petition," *Broadcasting,* Oct. 11, 1971, 51–52; and "Hard Bargains for KQEO too," *Broadcasting,* Nov. 29, 1971, 58, 60.

31. "D-Day Approaches for California Stations," *Broadcasting,* Nov. 1, 1971, 26–28; "Catchword in California Renewals: Minorities," *Broadcasting,* Nov. 8, 1971, 42–43; and "KEST Strikes Bargain with Citizen Group," *Broadcasting,* Mar. 13, 1972, 42.

32. "Reyes to Throw Down Gauntlet in Washington," *Broadcasting,* Apr. 24, 1972, 8, 12.

33. Grundfest, *Citizen Participation,* 63. To place the petition process into perspective, each year there were over 3,000 renewal applications filed and granted.

34. Ibid.

35. Ibid., 65. See also app. C, "Why Settlements Occur: An Economic Approach," which explains settlements as "rational optimizing behavior in a world of complicated, expensive litigation with uncertain outcomes." In other words, FCC delays and the legal precedents set by the U.S. Court of Appeals created an environment in which it was potentially more cost effective for broadcasters to settle with citizen groups.

36. Cole and Oettinger, *Reluctant Regulators,* 213–14.

37. Lewels claims that "literally hundreds of small, community media groups either formed or reoriented their goals to include media objectives." *The Uses of the Media by the Chicano Movement,* 85.

38. For a review of these settlement agreements, see ibid., 108–34.

39. Leonard Zeidenberg, "The Struggle over Broadcast Access," *Broadcasting*, Sept. 20, 1971, 35, 38.

40. "Reyes to Throw Down Gauntlet in Washington," 12.

41. Reina Schement and Gutiérrez, "The Anatomy of a License Challenge," 92.

42. Ibid., 93.

43. "An Overcrowded Winners' Circle?," *Broadcasting*, May 15, 1972, 27.

44. Lewels, *The Uses of the Media by the Chicano Movement*, 79.

45. Dr. Daniel Valdez, Metropolitan State College in Denver, who helped coordinate the first Denver conference, was also excluded. Ibid., 80–81.

46. "Time's $69-Million Sale Clears FCC," "McGraw-Hill Sets Record for Concessions to Minorities," and Lewels, *The Uses of the Media by the Chicano Movement*, 114–25.

47. "An Overcrowded Winners' Circle?"

48. As Susan Witty notes, "A painful irony is that a number of the regulators advocating deregulation were people drafted into government from, of all places, the media-reform movement. . . . Frank Lloyd, for example, was a former executive director of Citizens Communications Center. But as administrative assistant to the chairman of the FCC during the Carter Administration, he supported the commission's *laissez-faire* deregulatory philosophy." Witty, "The Citizens Movement Takes a Turn," *Channels* (June–July 1981): 71–72.

49. Mario Obledo and Robert B. Joselow, "Broadcasting: Mexican Americans and the Media," *Chicano Law Review* 1, no. 1 (Summer 1972): 85–98. A slightly different version appears as Mario Obledo, "Mexican Americans and the Media," in Mangold, *La Causa Chicana*, 6–16.

50. Even after FCC-oriented activism, the mass media would be an important component of MALDEF's Chicana Empowerment Project, which focused on the professional training and employment of women. In fact, this initiative, which was established in 1974, appears to have been more extensive than MALDEF's media activism.

51. Zeidenberg, "The Struggle over Broadcast Access," 32, 38. See also Leonard Zeidenberg, "The Struggle Over Broadcast Access (II)," *Broadcasting*, Sept. 27, 1971, 24–29. One exception to these informal measures was a multiyear effort to create a PBS station by the Rio Grande Valley Coalition on the Media in South Texas. See Antonio José Guernica, "Chicano Group to Get Its Own TV Station," *Agenda: A Journal of Hispanic Issues* 7, no. 6 (Nov.–Dec. 1977): 28–30.

52. Interestingly, that MALDEF knew about these FCC changes is indicated in a copy of an urgent memo dated July 1976 from the NOW Media Project. NOW advised members not to "get bogged down in monitoring or FCC regulation," but to invoke the regulatory process merely as a pretense to "get into the station" and start meetings with management. The memo was an addendum to an earlier "Action Plan" from May 1974 that outlined how women's groups could file petitions to deny. For a review of FCC rulemaking in this period, see Grundfest, *Citizen Participation*, 139–50.

53. Antonio José Guernica, "Cable Television . . . The Medium for Hispanics?," *Agenda: A Journal of Hispanic Issues* 7, no. 3 (May–June 1977): 25–27, 27.

54. Antonio José Guernica, "The Public Airwaves: Who Owns Them?," *Agenda: A Journal of Hispanic Issues* 7, no. 2 (Mar.–Apr. 1977): 39–40, 42.

55. Ibid., 42.

56. See William J. Drummond, "The Death of a Man in the Middle: A Requiem for Ruben Salazar," *Esquire*, Apr. 1972, 74–81; and Lewels, *The Uses of the Media by the Chicano Movement*, 86–93.

57. Reyes then took over as acting executive director, although, as Lewels concludes, "for all practical purposes the Council does not exist." Lewels, *The Uses of the Media by the Chicano Movement,* 93.

58. Ibid., 92–93.

59. I have located two issues in the MALDEF Collection: Media Action News Service, vol. 1176 (Nov. 1976), and Media Action News Service, vol. 1276 (Dec. 1976). In MALDEF Collection, M673, Box 121, Folder 9, Department of Special Collections, Stanford University.

60. I examine the National Latino Media Coalition in chapter 7.

61. Warren Weaver, *U.S. Philanthropic Foundations: Their History, Structure, Management, and Record* (New York: Harper & Row, 1967), 84.

62. Marilyn A. Lashner, "The Role of Foundations in Public Broadcasting—Part II: The Ford Foundation," *Journal of Broadcasting* 21, no. 2 (Spring 1977): 235–54, esp. 237, 250, and 254 n. 54. The quotes are from Dwight MacDonald, *The Ford Foundation* (1956), and Waldemar A. Nielsen, *The Big Foundations* (1972), both cited in Lashner's article. See also Marilyn A. Lashner, "The Role of Foundations in Public Broadcasting—Part I: Developments and Trends," *Journal of Broadcasting* 20, no. 4 (Fall 1976): 529–47.

63. Witty, "The Citizens Movement Takes a Turn," 70. Ford funded both UCC and CCC for a ten-year period, contributing 99 percent of CCC's annual budget.

64. Between 1968 and 1970, Ford allocated nearly $13 million in grants to the Mexican American community, most of it for education and "leadership development," legal rights, and free-enterprise programs to develop "brown capitalism." Ford's vice president, Mitchell Suiridoff, described the goal as one of "building the capacity of Mexican-Americans to deal with the American system, helping them achieve legal, economic, and political parity within the system." Quoted in Waldemar A. Nielsen, *The Big Foundations* (New York: Columbia University Press, 1972), 424; see also the section "The Ford Foundation and La Raza," 421–25. Ford began its program planning by gathering information on the Mexican American community through a research grant to the UCLA Mexican American Study Project in 1963. See the eventual publication, Grebler, Moore, and Guzman, *The Mexican-American People.* The report found Mexican Americans at a "social disadvantage" based on "closed local systems" as well as "institutional resistance" within the larger society; see 593–96.

65. Mitchell Suiridoff, "Recommendation for Grant/DAP Action," Oct. 24, 1980, in Siobhan Oppenheimer-Nicolau Collection, M748, Box 7, Folder 18, "MAYO/La Raza," Department of Special Collections, Stanford University.

66. Witty, "The Citizens Movement Takes a Turn," 70. Meanwhile, as Witty further notes, right-wing media groups grew in tandem with deregulation efforts. Accuracy in Media (AIM), for example, saw its budget double to over $1 million between 1980 and 1981, larger than the combined budgets of Action for Children's Television, the NOW Media Project, and the UCC Office of Communication.

67. Suiridoff, "Recommendation for Grant/DAP Action."

68. All quotations are taken from the *Congressional Record.* For a record of Gutiérrez's statements, together with González's attack, see United States of America, *Congressional Record,* 91st Cong., 1st sess., 115, pt. 7, Apr. 2–21, 1969: "Race Hate" (8590–8591), "Cause for Concern" (9058–9060), and "Foundation Responsibility" (9308–9309); 115, pt. 8, Apr. 22–May 1, 1969: "The Hate Issue" (9951–9954), "Racism in South Texas" (10522–10527), "Foundation Responsibility II" (10779–10780), and "Ford Foundation Plus San Antonio Equals Murder" (p. 11140). See also Nielsen, *The Big Foundations,* 421–22; and Alan Cranston and Alan Piper, *Foundations on Trial* (New

York: Council on Foundations, 1970). Cranston, a U.S. Senator from California, and Piper, president of the Carnegie Corporation and the Carnegie Foundation for the Advancement of Teaching, defend foundation activities that promote social change, offering a circumspect retort to González and other representatives.

69. González also claimed that Chicano groups were receiving monies from Cuba and complained about a Che Guevara poster in the MALDEF offices.

70. Interestingly, in 1974, González also voted against extending the Voting Rights Act to Mexican Americans. The one other time González led an attack from the House floor in this period involved the CBS documentary *Hunger in America* (1968), which showed a child dying of starvation in San Antonio. In the documentary, Bexar County Commissioner Albert A. Peña Jr. stated, "I would say 100,000 people are going hungry here in San Antonio." Unlike González, Peña was involved in a number of Chicano movement activities in South Texas, placing the two at odds with each other in terms of political style and strategy. But, as with the attack on MAYO, González directed his activities to major U.S. institutions vis-à-vis the regulatory arena. In the course of over one year of statements on the House floor, González eloquently voiced many of the concerns of the media reform movement, submitting a short-lived bill to amend the Communications Act of 1934 to license television networks. But that appears to be the extent of his media reform efforts. See United States of America, *Congressional Record*, 90th Cong., 2d sess., 114, pt. 14, June 19–26, 1968: "Why Must There Be Hunger?" (18472–18473); 114, pt. 17, July 17–23, 1968: "Hunger in America?" (22738–22739); 114, pt. 19, July 31– Sept. 4, 1968: "Hunger in America?" (24432–24435); 114, pt. 20, Sept. 5–16, 1968: "Hunger in America?" (26625–26626); 114, pt. 21, Sept. 17–Sept. 25, 1968: "License the Networks" (27811–27812). Also, *Congressional Record*, 91st Cong., 1st sess., 115, pt. 3, Feb. 5–21, 1969: "License the Networks" (2935–2936); 115, pt. 6, Mar. 20– Apr. 1, 1969: "Columbia Broadcasting System" (7908); 115, pt. 11, May 27–June 9, 1969: "Fraud in America" (14100–14101), "Fraud in America II" (14389–14391), "Fraud in America III" (14420–14421), "Fraud in America IV" (14984–14986), "Fraud in America V" (15069–15070); 115, pt. 12, June 10–19, 1969: "Failure at the FCC" (p. 15768); 115, pt. 13, June 20–July 1, 1969: "The Television Overlords" (p. 17887); 115, pt. 23, Oct. 21–28, 1969: "The FCC—Regulator or Regulated?" (p. 30877).

71. Ford had wanted MALDEF to relocate to Washington, D.C., as with NCLR, but the organization moved to San Francisco (NCLR's former headquarters) instead, later opening a branch office in Washington, D.C.

72. Escobar, "The Dialectics of Repression," 1513.

73. Maurilio Vigil, "The Ethnic Organization as an Instrument of Political and Social Change: MALDEF, a Case Study," *Journal of Ethnic Studies* 18, no. 1 (Spring 1990): 15–31; Karen O'Connor and Lee Epstein, "A Legal Voice for the Chicano Community: The Activities of the Mexican American Legal Defense and Education Fund, 1968–82," *Social Science Quarterly* 65, no. 2 (June 1984): 245–56; and Joe Ortega, "The Privately Funded Legal Aid Office: The MALDEF Experience," *Chicano Law Review* 1, no. 1 (Summer 1972): 80–84.

74. Escobar, "The Dialectics of Repression," 1513.

75. See Lashner, "The Role of Foundations in Public Broadcasting, II," 246.

76. Nielsen, *The Big Foundations,* 421, 425. For a leftist critique, see Rees Lloyd and Peter Montague, "Ford and La Raza: 'They Stole Our Land and Gave Us Powdered Milk,'" *Ramparts* (Sept. 1970): 10–18. See also Robert L. Allen's discussion of the Ford Foundation's domestic "neocolonialism" with respect to the militant black movement in

Black Awakening in Capitalist America: An Analytic History (New York: Doubleday and Company, 1969), 70–77. I am grateful to John Hess for pointing out Allen's book to me.

77. Nielsen, *The Big Foundations,* 422.

78. Ibid., 425.

79. Newton Minow and Craig L. Lamay, *Abandoned in the Wasteland: Children, Television, and the First Amendment* (New York: Hill and Wang, 1995), 100. In 1961, Minow was appointed FCC chairman in the wake of public debate and federal inquiry into television quiz scandals, truth-in-advertising laws, and the decline in educational and family-oriented programming. His "Vast Wasteland" speech before the National Association of Broadcasters in May 1961 galvanized reform efforts, even if, as Minow admits, the title also diverted attention from the phrase his speech addressed, "public interest." See ibid., 3–4. For a concurrent example of how media reform in this period centered on "consumers" rather than "citizens," see "Where, May We Ask, Was the FCC?," *Consumer Reports* (Jan. 1960): 9–11.

80. Minow's personal account of the creation of *Sesame Street,* for example, emphasizes the importance of institutional networks based on kinship! Ibid., 9–10.

81. Haight and Weinstein, "Changing Ideology on Television," 123.

82. Anne W. Branscomb and Maria Savage, *Broadcast Reform at the Crossroads* (Cambridge: Kalba Bowen Associates, 1978), 4.

83. See Montgomery, *Target: Prime Time,* 59–62.

84. Hall and Ikenberry, *The State,* 1–2.

85. Lewels, *The Uses of the Media by the Chicano Movement,* 1.

86. Ibid., 162–63.

87. Inflation jumped from 3.4 percent in 1972 to 8.71 percent in 1973 and 12.34 percent in 1974.

88. For a history of the formation of this dynamic in U.S. broadcasting, see Robert W. McChesney, *Telecommunications, Mass Media, and Democracy: The Battle for Control of U.S. Broadcasting, 1928–1935* (Oxford: Oxford University Press, 1994).

89. Grundfest, *Citizen Participation,* 69. The phrase "executive lunch" is taken from the address of John Schneider, president of the CBS Broadcast Group, before the Georgia Association of Broadcasters.

90. Les Brown, "Broadcasters at Convention Strike Back at Activist Critics," *New York Times,* Mar. 19, 1974; quoted in Montgomery, *Target: Prime Time,* 74.

91. Harry F. Waters, "TV: Do Minorities Rule?," *Newsweek,* June 2, 1975, 78–79.

92. U.S. Commission on Civil Rights, *Window Dressing on the Set: Women and Minorities in Television;* and U.S. Commission on Civil Rights, *Window Dressing on the Set: An Update.*

93. See Chon A. Noriega, "The Numbers Game," *Jump Cut* 39 (June 1994): 107–11. This article summarizes and comments upon my testimony before the U.S. Commission on Civil Rights in June 1993. The hearings, which dealt with minority representation on network television, were part of a multiyear study on the rise of ethnic and racial conflict in the United States.

94. See the discussion in "Reading Materials for Media Advocates," *Reporte* (Apr. 1978): 5. *Reporte* is the newsletter of the Texas Chicano Coalition on Mass Media.

95. Not even the "Domingo Nick Reyes papers, ca. 1940–1985" in the Benson Latin American Collection at the University of Texas at Austin include the NMAADC brochures. The Federal Trade Commission library, however, also has Reyes's "Testimony on Modern Advertising Practices," eight-page manuscript, Nov. 18, 1971. If, as I argue, access is paradoxical, it can also be quite expensive. The National Association of Broad-

casters (NAB) charged me fifteen dollars for a copy of Reyes's one-page statement critiquing the NAB Code in their publication *TV Code News*. See Reyes, "Anti-Defamation Committee Says Media Do Not Depict Mexican Americans Fairly," *TV Code News* 3, no. 12 (Feb. 1971): 2.

6. Training the Activists to Shoot Straight

1. Presentation by Moctesuma Esparza, Stanford University, Mar. 13, 1990.

2. Mauricio Mazón, *The Zoot-Suit Riots: The Psychology of Symbolic Annihilation* (Austin: University of Texas Press, 1984), 8. Mazón is actually writing about the zoot-suiters and the servicemen who attacked them.

3. Personal interview with Luis Garza, Los Angeles, Oct. 10, 1990.

4. Personal interview with Sylvia Morales, Los Angeles, Nov. 16, 1991.

5. Renee Tajima, "Ethno-Communications: The Film School Program That Changed the Color of Independent Filmmaking," in *The Anthology of Asian Pacific American Film and Video*, ed. Renee Tajima (New York: Third World Newsreel, 1985), 38.

6. Esparza, Morales, Ruiz, Treviño, and others make this point.

7. In this same period, the University of Southern California also initiated a special admissions program. See Treviño, "Chicano Cinema," 171. Stanford University is another film program with several Chicano film students on campus in the early 1970s. These include Richard Soto, Francisco X. Camplis, Ralph Maradiaga, and José Camacho, a Guamanian who identified himself as Chicano in the years before Pacific Islanders were considered U.S. minorities.

8. See Tajima, "Ethno-Communications"; Clyde Taylor, "The L.A. Rebellion: A Turning Point in Black Cinema," *The New American Filmmakers Series* 26 (New York: Whitney Museum of American Art, 1986); Clyde Taylor, "The L.A. Rebellion: New Spirit in American Film," *Black Film Review* 2 (1986): 2; and Ntongela Masilela, "The Los Angeles School of Black Filmmakers," in *Black American Cinema*, ed. Manthia Diawara (New York: Routledge, 1993), 107–17.

9. I am deeply indebted to Mario T. García's review of the literature on "political generations" and his application of the concept—"generally . . . applied only to national or international movements"—to specific national minorities. See García, *Mexican Americans: Leadership, Ideology, and Identity, 1930–1960* (New Haven: Yale University Press, 1989), 3–7.

10. Jack C. Ellis, *A History of Film*, 4th ed. (Boston: Allyn and Bacon, 1995), 386.

11. Personal interview with Jesús Salvador Treviño, Los Angeles, May 28, 1991.

12. Ibid. The EICC succeeded in adding a Mexican American commission within the L.A. Unified School System in order to facilitate dialogue between the Chicano community and the Board of Education.

13. Ibid.

14. Ibid.

15. Presentation by Esparza.

16. Ibid. Before that time, Racho and Esparza were undergraduates in English/dance and history, respectively.

17. Interview with Moctesuma Esparza by Armando Valdez and Tomás Ybarra-Frausto, Los Angeles, Nov. 19, 1987. According to Esparza, Taylor subsequently was denied tenure.

18. Tajima, "Ethno-Communications," 39. According to Luis Garza, the students also referred to Taylor as "Papa Doc," since he was over forty years old and thus could not be trusted. Phone conversation, Dec. 10, 1990.

19. Presentation by Esparza. Esparza had planned on returning to the history department, until he received an incomplete for a paper in which he cited progressive historians rather than his professor. He entered the film school, however, "with reservations, because I really didn't know what the heck I was going to be doing." Taylor, however, convinced him that he could be a producer, "because what producers do is they organize, originate, generate film," all skills he had acquired as an activist.

20. Tajima, "Ethno-Communications," 39.

21. See, e.g., Valerie Smith, Camille Billops, and Ada Griffin, eds., *Black Film Issue, Black American Literature Forum* 25, no. 2 (Summer 1991); Russell Leong, ed., *Moving the Image: Independent Asian Pacific American Media Arts* (Los Angeles: UCLA Asian American Studies Center and Visual Communications, 1991); and Victor Payan, "'Listen to Your Own Voice': An Interview with Native American Independent Filmmaker, Sandra Osawa," *Cine Estudiantil 97,* program guide (San Diego: Centro Cultural de la Raza, 1997), 5–6.

22. Personal interview with Garza.

23. Tajima, "Ethno-Communications," 40.

24. Ibid., 39.

25. For an overview, see Acuña, *Occupied America,* 345–50, and Mario T. García's introduction to Ruben Salazar, *Border Correspondent: Selected Writings, 1955–1970,* ed. Mario T. García (Berkeley: University of California Press, 1995), 1–5.

26. García, in Salazar, *Border Correspondent,* 33.

27. Ibid., 32.

28. Acuña, *Occupied America,* 349–52; see esp. the section "The Provocateurs."

29. See Bill Nichols, *Representing Reality: Issues and Concepts in Documentary* (Bloomington: Indiana University Press, 1991), esp. chap. 2.

30. García, in Salazar, *Border Correspondent,* 35.

31. Nichols, *Representing Reality,* 17.

32. Ibid., 16.

33. In a similar manner, *What Really Happened at the East Los Angeles Chicano Riot?* (Kevin Rafferty, c. 1971), which examines the police shooting of a Chicano youth at a demonstration on Jan. 31, 1971, uses the expository mode to undercut expository authority without becoming self-reflexive. The film uses a "voice of God" narrator who explains, "The evidence offered is impartial and you must judge where the blame lies for yourself." The narrator follows a somewhat conservative approach, distinguishing between rhetorical radicals and the moderates, but also between these youth and their families. Through slow motion, freeze frame, and sound effects, the narration becomes increasingly pitched, until the narrator drops his "voice of God" delivery and cries out, "What does this mean? . . . Look at them! These people have absolutely no respect for the law." As the events leading up to the shooting are repeated, the narrator voices a frantic litany against Chicano youth from a "law and order" perspective that conflates ostensibly "white" viewers *cum* citizens with the police under attack: "You've got a gun and you've gotta use it. And that's just what they're gonna do." The narrator then returns to a calm voice-of-God delivery: "And that's just what they do. Watch." Then comes the shooting, interspersed with negative shots and nondocumentary footage used to express the subjective state of a mortally wounded Chicano youth. As the dead youth is carried away, the narrator concludes: "So, it is most important to see here that the fundamental right of every American to live in freedom has been defended." What is most interesting about the film is that it exposes the complicity between voice-of-God exposition and a viewer vested in law and order, public property, and racial privilege—the white citizen. But the film's irony does not produce a semantic reversal per se, since the critique

nonetheless stems from expository narration that, per dramatic irony, addresses a privileged audience about another person who is the subject of that irony. In other words, the film never offers an alternative point of view aligned with Chicanos, remaining bounded by the very subjectivity it critiques. To that extent, the film provides a counterpart to *Requiem-29*, which addresses the Chicano demonstrators, and not the body politic assumed by this film.

34. Nichols, *Representing Reality*, 67.

35. Tajima, "Ethno-Communications," 41.

36. Ibid.

37. The early Chicana feminist literature placed an emphasis on defining an active and substantive role both within the movement and in redefining its central issues. In placing women's issues and female agency within the context of Chicano civil rights, Chicana feminists argued for the importance of race *and* gender, drawing attention to their own structural absence in the gap between Chicanismo and white feminism. See Sylvia Delgado, "Chicana: The Forgotten Woman," *Regeneración* 2, no. 1 (1971): 2–4; Francisca Flores, "Comisión feminil mexicana," *Regeneración* 2, no. 1 (1971): 6–8; Mirta Vidal, *Chicanas Speak Out: Women, New Voice of La Raza* (New York: Pathfinder, 1971); Gracia Molina de Pick, "Reflexiones sobre el Feminismo y la Raza," *La Luz* 1, no. 4 (Aug. 1972): 58; Anita Espinosa-Larsen, "Machismo: Another View," *La Luz* 1, no. 4 (Aug. 1972): 59; Jennie V. Chavez, "Women of the Mexican-American Movement," *Mademoiselle*, Apr. 1972, 82, 150–52; Francisca Flores, "Equality," *Regeneración* 2, no. 3 (1973): 4–5; Linda Aguilar, "Unequal Opportunity and the Chicana," *Civil Rights Digest* (Spring 1973): 31–33.

38. See, e.g., Sandra Osawa's accounts in Payan, "Listen to Your Own Voice."

39. Interview with Esparza by Valdez and Ybarra-Frausto.

40. For an overview, see Alma M. García, "The Development of Chicana Feminist Discourse, 1970–1980," *Gender and Society* 3, no. 2 (June 1989): 217–38.

41. Patricia Zavella, "Feminist Insider Dilemmas," 56–57.

42. Personal interview with Morales.

43. Charles Burnett and Ben Caldwell also make this point in Renee Tajima and Tracey Willard, "Nothing Lights a Fire like a Dream Deferred," *The Independent* (Nov. 1984): 20.

44. See Leong, *Moving the Image*.

45. See, e.g., the interview with Sandra Osawa, who went on to produce the first Native American television series in 1975. Payan, "Listen to Your Own Voice."

46. See the report and order, rule [73.658 (k)], and comments in Federal Communications Commission Reports, *Decisions and Reports of the Federal Communications Commission of the United States*, May 29–July 17, 1970, vol. 23, 2d ser. (Washington, D.C.: United States Government Printing Office, 1971), 382–429, esp. 402.

47. Personal interview with Garza.

48. Personal interview with Morales. Morales worked as the cameraperson, experimenting with cinematography during location shoots. In the episode on Native Americans, for example, she began shots with close-ups on a subject's eye or mouth, then pulled back to reveal the face. These shots were used as a montage for a poem read by a Native American woman in Topanga Canyon. *Unidos* was perhaps the first Chicano public affairs show to move away from a strict talk show format, producing short documentary segments.

49. Personal interview with Garza. The show shared its time slot with a Black program, *I Am Somebody*, airing at 7:00 P.M. on alternate Saturdays. Thirty-nine episodes were broadcast between 1972 and 1973.

50. Ibid.

51. Ibid. The argument often given for such actions was that the show would generate lawsuits.

52. Ibid.

53. See FCC 73.658 (k) in United States of America, *Code of Federal Regulations* 47 Telecommunication, pts. 70–79, rev. as of Oct. 1, 1975 (Washington, D.C.: United States Government Printing Office, 1975), 256–57.

54. Streeter, *Selling the Air,* 172.

55. Luis Valdez and Roberto Rubalcava, reprinted in Luis Valdez and Stan Steiner, eds., *Aztlán: An Anthology of Mexican American Literature* (New York: Alfred A. Knopf, 1972): 215–16.

56. See Valdez's essays and narrative poem on *teatro,* politics, and spirituality—"Notes on Chicano Theatre," "The Actos," and "Pensamiento Serpentino: A Chicano Approach to the Theatre of Reality"—in *Luis Valdez, Early Works* (Houston: Arte Público, 1990), 6–13, 168–99.

57. For a more detailed account of the *acto, mito,* and *corrido* in El Teatro Campesino, see Yvonne Yarbro-Bejarano, "From *Acto* to *Mito:* A Critical Appraisal of the Teatro Campesino," in *Modern Chicano Writers: A Collection of Critical Essays,* ed. Joseph Sommers and Tomás Ybarra-Frausto (Englewood Cliffs, N.J.: Prentice-Hall, 1979), 176–85. See also Guillermo E. Hernández's chapter on Valdez's use of satire in the *actos* in *Chicano Satire: A Study in Literary Culture* (Austin: University of Texas Press, 1991), 31–51.

58. In addition to Valdez's work, several other *teatro* pieces were adapted for television broadcast in the 1970s: an episode of *¡Ahora!* featuring a performance by Los Mascarones, *Somos Uno* (1973), and *Guadalupe* (1976). Valdez's feature film *Zoot Suit* (1981) also uses *teatro* as a cost-cutting device in order to compensate for the small budget.

59. In summer 1974, pursuant to its earlier settlement agreement, McGraw-Hill Broadcasting signed a contract with El Teatro Campesino's Pixan Films. Treviño served as writer, producer, and director of the first project, *Amor Chicano,* which McGraw-Hill shelved just prior to its completion. The contract with Pixan Films was canceled. See two-page document, Amanecer Film Associates, n.d., distributed in *Media Action News Service,* vol. 1276 (Dec. 1976), unpaginated. MALDEF Collection, M673, Box 121, Folder 9, Department of Special Collections, Stanford University. In 1975, Treviño moved to Massachusetts to become the executive producer of *Infinity Factory,* while Ruiz returned to Los Angeles to become the executive director of the Latino Consortium at KCET.

60. See Luis Valdez, *"Zoot Suit" and Other Plays* (Houston: Arte Público, 1992). For considerations of Valdez's feature-length work in film and television, see Rosa Linda Fregoso, "Intertextuality and Cultural Identity in *Zoot Suit* (1981) and *La Bamba* (1987)," in *The Bronze Screen,* 21–48; Christine List, "Mythic Proportions: Creating *Raza* Heros in *Zoot Suit* and *La Bamba,*" in *Chicano Images: Refiguring Ethnicity in Mainstream Film* (New York: Garland, 1996), 59–81; and Kathleen Newman, "Nation and Virgin as Great Performances in El Teatro Campesino's *La Pastorela: A Shepherds' Tale* (1991)," *Jump Cut* 38 (June 1993): 87–91.

61. Yolanda Broyles-González, *El Teatro Campesino: Theater in the Chicano Movement* (Austin: University of Texas Press, 1994).

62. For scholarship on Aztlán and its role in Chicano thought, see Rudolfo A. Anaya and Francisco Lomelí, eds., *Aztlán: Essays on the Chicano Homeland* (Albuquerque: Academia/El Norte Publications, 1989).

63. Ernesto Laclau, "Universalism, Particularism, and the Question of Identity," *Oct.* 61 (Summer 1992): 90.

64. The closing *mito* includes a musical performance by Daniel Valdez of "América de los Indios" (America of the Indians).

65. Sid Hix, cartoon with Frito Bandito character, *Broadcasting,* Mar. 23, 1970, 80.

66. See Valdez, "Los Vendidos," in *Luis Valdez, Early Works,* 40–52. For a concurrent and strikingly similar parody of the Mexican American as political commodity, see Steve Gonzales, "The Advertisement," *El Grito* 1, no. 1 (Fall 1967): 12–13. Guillermo Hernández argues that *Los Vendidos* resembles the Greek satire *Philosophies for Sale* (A.D. 120?), which Valdez may have read while studying drama in college. Hernandez, *Chicano Satire,* 38–41.

67. For an overview of Chicano *teatro* and *carpa* as well as an account of the *rasquache* aesthetic, see Nicolás Kanellos, "Folklore in Chicano Theater and Chicano Theater as Folklore," in *The Chicano Experience,* ed. Stanley A. West and June Macklin (Boulder: Westview, 1979), 165–89. See also Broyles-González, *El Teatro Campesino,* and Jorge A. Huerta, *Chicano Theater: Themes and Forms* (Ypsilanti, Mich.: Bilingual Press/Editorial Bilingüe, 1982).

68. The conflation of mother, wife, and the Virgin in Mexican culture has been written about extensively. For a review of this material, together with an excellent discussion of gender archetypes and stereotypes in contemporary Mexican cinema, see Charles Ramírez Berg, *Cinema of Solitude: A Critical Study of Mexican Film, 1967–1983* (Austin: University of Texas Press, 1992). Joanne Hershfield applies this work to the classical period in *Mexican Cinema/Mexican Woman, 1940–1950* (Tucson: University of Arizona Press, 1996). Drawing upon feminist theory, Rosa Linda Fregoso examines the cinematic representation of the Chicana mother by Luis Valdez in "The Mother Motif in *La Bamba* and *Boulevard Nights,*" in *Building with Our Hands: New Directions in Chicana Studies,* ed. Adela de la Torre and Beatríz M. Pesquera (Berkeley: University of California Press, 1993), 130–45.

69. Mircea Eliade, *Myth and Reality* (New York: Harper & Row Publishers, 1963), 18. Quoted in Michael Pina, "The Archaic, Historical and Mythicized Dimensions of Aztlán," in Anaya and Lomelí, *Aztlán: Essays on the Chicano Homeland,* 18.

70. *Ibid.,* 28–29.

71. Adrienne Rich, "Driving into the Wreck," *The Fact of a Doorframe: Poems Selected and New, 1950–1984* (New York: W. W. Norton, 1984), 164.

72. Interestingly, Laura Martin argues that *Zoot Suit* gives the perception of a high degree of "foreign language usage" but is not bilingual "from a purely linguistic point of view." Instead, the film uses slang, gesture, and pronunciation to give cultural differences the patina of linguistic difference, when in fact, the text is entirely intelligible to a monolingual English-speaking audience. See Martin, "Language Form and Language Function in *Zoot Suit* and *The Border:* A Contribution to the Analysis of the Role of Foreign Language in Film," *Studies in Latin American Popular Culture* 3 (1984): 57–69.

73. For a historical overview, see Chávez, *The Lost Land.* As he demonstrates, the object of the "lost lands" differs according to historical period and region, whether Mexico, Spain, or Aztlán.

74. The "Plan Espiritual de Aztlán" is reprinted in Anaya and Lomelí, *Aztlán: Essays on the Chicano Homeland,* 1–5.

75. Alurista, "Myth, Identity, and Struggle in Three Chicano Novels: Aztlán . . . Anaya, Méndez, and Acosta," in *Missions in Conflict: Essays on U.S.-Mexican Relations and Chicano Culture,* ed. Renate Barbeleben et al. (Tübingen: Gunter Narr Verlag, 1986); reprinted in Anaya and Lomelí, *Aztlán: Essays on the Chicano Homeland,* 219–29.

76. Rudolfo Anaya, *Heart of Aztlán* (Berkeley: Editorial Justa Publications, 1976), 131.

77. In Anaya and Lomelí, *Aztlán: Essays on the Chicano Homeland,* 2.

7. "Our Own Institutions"

1. Felix Gutiérrez, "Civil Rights Media Hearings," Southwest Network: Chicano Media Clearinghouse, distributed in Media Action News Service, vol. 1276 (Dec. 1976), unpaginated. MALDEF Collection, M673, Box 121, Folder 9, Department of Special Collections, Stanford University.

2. David Morales, "Media in El Paso," Committee for the Develompent of Mass Communications, distributed in Media Action News Service, Volume 1176 (November 1976), np. MALDEF Collection, M673, Box 121, Folder 9, Department of Special Collections, Stanford University.

3. "Because of the establishment's need to control media and the Committee's determination to control the media for the people, confrontations were inevitable. Since 1975, over ten members of the Committee have been unjustly convicted of crimes ranging from drug charges to arson." Ibid.

4. Morales recounts the committee's efforts to implement the Doubleday agreement. See also Lewels, *The Uses of the Media by the Chicano Movement,* 130–34.

5. Morales, "Media in El Paso."

6. José Antonio Parra, "Bilingual Programming for Latinos: The Media's Missing Link?," *PTR: Public Telecommunications Review* 4, no. 4 (July–Aug. 1976): 18.

7. Ibid., 14; Antonio José Guernica, "The Development of the National Latino Media Coalition," *Agenda: A Journal of Hispanic Issues* 7, no. 4 (July–Aug. 1976): 31; and Antonio José Guernica, "Chicano Production Companies: Projecting Reality, Opening the Doors," *Agenda: A Journal of Hispanic Issues* 8, no. 1 (Jan.–Feb. 1978): 12–15.

8. Quoted in Barbara Zheutlin and David Talbot, "Jesús Salvador Treviño," in *Creative Differences: Profiles of Hollywood Dissidents* (Boston: South End, 1978), 345–46. The authors were members of the Socialist Media Group in Los Angeles (1974–77), which sought a "grand vision—of Hollywood employees, independent media producers, and media activists working together for social change" (xii).

9. Marshall McLuhan, "The Medium Is the Message," in *Understanding Media: The Extensions of Man* (Cambridge: MIT Press, 1994), 7–21.

10. Treviño, "The Media Is the Mistake," five-page manuscript, 5. Treviño Collection, Box 13, Folder 4. Marginal notes indicate it was later published in the *Eastside Sun* (Apr. 1970).

11. Ibid., 4.

12. Ibid., 5.

13. Treviño, "Mexican American and Mass Media," three-page document, c. 1970. Treviño Collection, M634, Box 13, Folder 1.

14. Treviño, "The Need for More Spanish American Affairs Programs," two-page document, presented to the General Assembly of the Public Broadcast Service Public Affairs Workshop, Sept. 24–25, 1972, in Atlanta, Ga.; and Treviño and José Luis Ruiz, "Hispanics and CPB: In Quest of National Programming," seven-page document, presented by Carlos Penichet before the members of the board of the Corporation for Public Broadcasting, Oct. 17, 1979. Treviño Collection, M634, Box 13, Folders 10 and 11.

15. Treviño and Ruiz, "Hispanics and Public Broadcasting: A History of Neglect," ten-page document, presented at the Rockefeller Seminar on Independent Television

Makers and Public Communications Policy, New York City, June 1979. Treviño Collection, M634, Box 13, Folder 11.

16. Treviño, "The Media Is the Mistake."

17. Treviño, "The Roar of a Mighty River," four-page document, presented at the Annual General Assembly of the Texas Catholic Conference, San Antonio, Tex., Sept. 24, 1974. Treviño Collection, M634, Box 13, Folder 10.

18. See the report, "400 Media Activists Meet at Alternative Cinema Conference," *Jump Cut* 21 (Nov. 1979): 31–38.

19. Treviño, "Commentarios de un Cineasta Chicano," three-page document, presented at UNAM/CUEC, Mexico City, Aug. 12, 1974; and Treviño, "El Desarrollo del Cine Chicano," six-page document, presented at the Comité de Cineastas de América Latina, Havana, Cuba, June 18, 1978. Treviño Collection, M634, Box 13, Folders 10 and 11.

20. Jesús Salvador Treviño, "Lights, Camera, Action," *Hispanic* (Aug. 1992): 76.

21. Quoted in Guernica, "Chicano Production Companies," 13.

22. Jesús Salvador Treviño, interview by Francisco X. Camplis, no date (circa 1974), p. 3. Transcript in Treviño Collection, M634, Box 13, Folder 10, Department of Special Collections, Stanford University.

23. Carnegie Commission on Educational Television, *Public Television: A Program for Action* (New York: Harper & Row, 1967), 1.

24. See Patricia Aufderheide, "Public Television and the Public Sphere," *Critical Studies in Mass Communication* 8 (1991): 168–83.

25. For more on the history of public television in the United States, see Robert K. Avery and Robert Pepper, "The Evolution of the CPB-PBS relationship, 1970–1973," *PTR: Public Telecommunications Review* 4, no. 5 (Sept.–Oct. 1976): 6–17; idem, "An Institutional History of Public Broadcasting," *Journal of Communication* 30, no. 3 (Summer 1980): 126–38; Robert Pepper, "The Interconnection Connection: The Formation of PBS," *PTR: Public Telecommunications Review* 4, no. 1 (Jan.–Feb. 1976): 6–26; Willard D. Rowland Jr., "Continuing Crisis in Public Broadcasting: A History of Disenfranchisement," *Journal of Broadcasting and Electronic Media* 30, no. 3 (Summer 1986): 251–74; John Witherspoon and Roselle Kovitz, *The History of Public Broadcasting* (Washington, D.C.: Corporation for Public Broadcasting, 1987), a report originally published in *Current;* William Hoynes, *Public Television for Sale: Media, the Market, and the Public Sphere* (Boulder: Westview, 1994); and B. J. Bullert, *Public Television: Politics and the Battle over Documentary Film* (New Brunswick: Rutgers University Press, 1997).

26. Nicholas A. Valenzuela, *Media Habits and Attitudes of Mexican-Americans: Surveys in Austin and San Antonio* (Austin: Center for Communication Research at the University of Texas, June 1973); Frederick Williams, Nicholas A. Valenzuela, and Pamela Knight, *Prediction of Mexican-Americans' Communication Habits and Attitudes* (Austin: Center for Communication Research, University of Texas, June 1973); and Nicholas A. Valenzuela, *Public Television and the Mexican-American Audience in the Southwest*, CPB/OCR Report 214 (Washington, D.C.: Corporation for Public Broadcasting, Office of Communication Research, 1974).

27. *Affirmative Action Plan* (Washington, D.C.: Corporation for Public Broadcasting, 1975). Two years later, however, Congress took CPB to task for its continued poor record of minority and female employment. See "Authorizations Tied to Improved EEO Efforts," *CPB Report: The Newsletter of the Corporation for Public Broadcasting* 8, no. 9 (May 2, 1977): 1; "Public Broadcasting Authorization Process," *CPB Report* 8, no. 9 (May 2, 1977): 2; "Capitol Hill Tells CPB to Shape Up Minority Records or Money May Be Difficult to Get," *Broadcasting,* Feb. 14, 1977, 58.

28. José García Torres, "José García Torres & Realidades," interview by Aurora Flores and Lillian Jiménez, *Centro de Estudios Puertorriqueños Bulletin* 2, no. 8 (Spring 1990): 31–43.

29. "Latinos and CPB: In Quest of National Programming," *Chicano Cinema Newsletter* 1, no. 6 (Aug. 1979): 2–3. CPB policy formally recognized the minority consortia in 1980.

30. "ESAA Funding of Bilingual Programming," *PTR: Public Telecommunications Review* 4, no. 4 (July–Aug. 1976): 25. See also Eric Wentworth, "Bilingual TV Funds Resumed Cautiously," *Washington Post,* July 3, 1973.

31. Gerald Astor, *Minorities and the Media,* A Ford Foundation Report, Nov. 1974.

32. KCET acknowledged this fact in the timeline that accompanied a series of articles celebrating its tenth anniversary in 1974, although to my knowledge it has not done so since. The articles themselves do not acknowledge issues of racial diversity as part of the station's history. See James L. Loper, Art Seidenbaum, and Cecil Smith, "The KCET Story: Reminiscences of the First Ten Years," *Gambit* [program guide, KCET/Channel 28] (Oct. 1974): 20–24. The timeline is published on pp. 26–29. In addition to the awards received by the series, the timeline states that in Oct. 1968, "KCET emerges as national production center with national broadcast of *Canción de la Raza.*"

33. The Ford Foundation and the Carnegie Corporation were the other major supporters of *Sesame Street.*

34. For a general critique of children's programming, see Minow and Lamay, *Abandoned in the Wasteland.*

35. Aida Nydia Barrera, "Multiculturalism before Its Time: The Making of *Carrascolendas,*" Ph.D. diss. (University of Texas, 1992), 140–41.

36. Moctesuma Esparza, among other producers, makes this point with respect to the emergence of Chicano *filmmakers* within the industry. Interview with Esparza by Valdez and Ybarra-Frausto.

37. From their positions on these series, Esparza went on to form his own company in 1974, and Treviño traveled to Mexico to direct his first feature film, *Raíces de Sangre* (Roots of Blood, 1976). While at *Villa Alegre,* Esparza set up a Chicano trainee program. Participants included Bobby Paramo, who would afterwards work with Treviño on the public affairs series *Acción Chicano,* and Esperanza Vásquez, who then joined Esparza's company, directing the Academy Award–nominated film *Agueda Martinez: Our People, Our Country* (1977).

38. Barrera produced 220 half-hour programs between 1970 and 1976, receiving $5,854,809 in competitively awarded grants from the U.S. Office of Education. According to Barrera, "[p]ortions of the series are still in reruns in 1992, with licensed and pirated transmissions extending to southern Canada and areas of Latin America." Barrera, "Multiculturalism before Its Time," 1.

39. For more on *Carrascolendas,* see Barrera, "Multiculturalism before Its Time"; idem, "Carrascolendas," *PTR: Public Telecommunications Review* 4, no. 4 (July–Aug. 1976): 20–24; Frederick Williams and Geraldine Van Wart, *Carrascolendas: Bilingual Education through Television* (New York: Praeger Publishers, 1974); Monty Carlis Stanford, "On Predicting the Effects of a Bilingual Children's Educational Television Program," Ph.D. diss. (University of Texas, 1973). For a critique of the series that signals a backlash against bilingual education programming and Barrera's emphasis on affective concerns, see Sally Bedell, "A Generation without Cultural Hangups," *TV Guide,* May 21, 1977, 37–40.

40. Michel Foucault, "Nietzsche, Genealogy, History," in *Language, Counter-*

Memory, Practice: Selected Essays and Interviews, ed. Donald F. Bouchard, trans. Donald F. Bouchard and Sherry Simon (Ithaca: Cornell University Press, 1977), 142–43.

41. Barrera, "Multiculturalism before Its Time," 336–39.

42. Astor, *Minorities and the Media,* 6.

43. "Feedback for Mexican Americans," program guide, KCET/Channel 28 (July 1968): 4; "'Canción de la Raza/Song of the People,'" program guide, KCET/Channel 28 (Oct. 1968): 2–4; Ed Moreno, "'Canción de la Raza,'" program guide, KCET/Channel 28 (Jan. 1969): 6–7; and "'Canción de la Raza': A Song of Success," program guide, KCET/Channel 28 (Mar. 1969): 6–7.

44. Astor, *Minorities and the Media,* 6, and Wes Marshall et al., *Fiesta: Minority Television Programming* (Tucson: University of Arizona Press, 1974), app. A (Canción de la Raza), 101–2.

45. On *¡Ahora!,* see "Inside Channel 28: '¡Ahora!,'" program guide, KCET/Channel 28 (May 1969): 10; "'¡Ahora!,'" program guide, KCET/Channel 28 (Aug. 1969): 6–7; "'¡Ahora!,'" program guide, KCET/Channel 28 (Sept. 1969): 2–3; Art Flores, "The '¡Ahora!' Synthesis," program guide, KCET/Channel 28 (Feb. 1970): 14–15; and Chon A. Noriega, "Imagined Borders: Locating Chicano Cinema in America/América," in *The Ethnic Eye: Latino Media Arts,* ed. Chon A. Noriega and Ana M. López (Minneapolis: University of Minnesota Press, 1996), 9–11. On *Periódico,* see Frank Duane, "A People and a Program," in *Broadcasting and Social Action: A Handbook for Station Executives* (Washington, D.C.: National Association of Educational Broadcasters, 1969), 33–35. On *Fiesta,* see Marshall et al., *Fiesta: Minority Television Programming;* E. B. Eiselein and Wes Marshall, "'Fiesta'—An Experiment in Minority Audience Research and Programming," *Educational Television* (Feb. 1971): 11–15; and E. B. Eiselein and Wes Marshall, "Mexican-American Television: Applied Anthropology and Public Television," *Human Organization* 35, no. 2 (Summer 1976): 147–56.

46. Astor, *Minorities and the Media,* 30.

47. E. B. Eiselein, "Television and the Mexican-American," *PTR: Public Telecommunications Review* 2, no. 1 (Feb. 1974): 18.

48. For a discussion of Fordism and the shift to flexible accumulation since the 1970s, see David Harvey, *The Condition of Postmodernity: An Enquiry into the Origins of Cultural Change* (Cambridge: Blackwell, 1990), chaps. 8–9.

49. Ibid., 138–39.

50. See the opening paragraphs of "'Canción de la Raza,'" program guide, KCET/Channel 28 (Oct. 1968), which quotes from the grant proposal to the Ford Foundation. The proposal—like the Ford initiative itself—alludes to the Kerner Commission report.

51. Astor, *Minorities and the Media,* 26.

52. Treviño, "Chicano Cinema Overview," 40.

53. See "400 Media Activists Meet at Alternative Cinema Conference"; "Alternative Cinema Conference," *Chicano Cinema Newsletter* 1, no. 3 (May 1979): 1; and Jesús Salvador Treviño, "Alternative Cinema Conference: Optimism, Realistic Expectations," *Chicano Cinema Newsletter* 1, no. 4 (June 1979): 1. The event did result in ongoing connections between *Jump Cut* editors and Chicano filmmakers. Treviño and others later contributed articles to *Jump Cut,* while its coeditor, John Hess, wrote various pieces on Latin American cinema for *Cine Acción News* throughout the 1980s.

54. Carlos Morton, "Why There Are No Chicano Filmmakers: Plática de José Luis Seda y Antonio Ogaz," *Caracol* 2, no. 11 (July 1976): 18–19, 5, 16; Umberto Rivera, "Film Notes," *Chismearte* 1, no. 2 (Winter–Spring 1977): 20–24; Marcelo Epstein, "Film and Industry," *Chismearte* 1, no. 2 (Winter–Spring 1977): 25; Ron Arias, "Getting on the Set," *Nuestro: The Magazine for Latinos* 1, no. 7 (Oct. 1977): 18–21; "Stage

and Screen: Struggles behind the Scenes," *Nuestro: The Magazine for Latinos* 3, no. 3 (Apr. 1979): 19–20; "Feature Section on Chicano Films," guest ed. Jesús Salvador Treviño, *Caminos* 3, no. 10 (Nov. 1982): 6–20.

55. "Cine Chicano Primer Acercamiento," *La Opinión,* Nov. 16, 1980, cultural supplement.

56. In addition to programming information, the festival catalogs include essays, often providing early critical work on issues related to the films and filmmakers. Other annual festivals include Cine Estudiantil in San Diego (established in 1994, renamed Cine in 1998), Cine Sol Latino Film Festival in Harlingen, Tex. (established in 1993), the East Los Angeles Chicano Film Festival (established in 1995), and the Los Angeles International Latino Film Festival (established in 1997). See Ray Santisteban, "Notes on the Hows and Whys of Latino Film Festivals," *AHA! Hispanic Art News* 167 (July–Aug. 1998): 12; and Ethan van Thillo, "A Guide to Understanding Chicano Cinema and Organizing a Chicano Film Festival," senior thesis, Latin American Studies, University of California, Santa Cruz, Winter 1992. For an early overview of Chicano film festivals, see Yolanda Broyles, "Chicano Film Festivals: An Examination," in Keller, *Chicano Cinema,* 116–20.

57. In addition to its festival catalogs, Cine Acción publishes *Cine Acción News* and *CineWorks: A Latino Media Resource Guide,* a directory of members' films and videos.

58. The exception seems to be university-based exhibitions, which build upon a Chicano studies and student group constituency.

59. William Gallo, "Chicano Filmmakers Strike Vivid Spark of Life," *Rocky Mountain News,* Jan. 18, 1980. This shift was complete by the late 1980s, as filmmakers rejected an "ethnic" label as artists and placed their Chicano-themed work in an "American" or "universal" context. Thus, in 1987, Luis Valdez explained, "I want to be part of the mainstream—as myself." See the interview, "An Artist Who Has Blended Art and Politics," *El Tecolote* (San Francisco Mission District), Oct. 1987, 9 ff.

60. Gallo, "Chicano Filmmakers."

61. Personal interview with Treviño, Los Angeles, May 28, 1991.

62. Jesús Salvador Treviño, "The Mural That Whitewash Could Not Destroy," *Nuestro* (Feb. 1978): 50, 52.

63. "Soledad: Inside California's Reform Center," *Gambit* [program guide, KCET/Channel 28] (Mar. 1971): 12.

64. Jesús Salvador Treviño, "Chicano Filmic Art," KCET News (press release), July 24, 1972, 2 pages; "'Yo Soy Chicano': Past and Present Mingle in this Dramatic New Portrayal of the Chicano Experience," *Gambit* [program guide, KCET/Channel 28] (Aug. 1972): 4; Luis Valdez, "'Yo Soy Chicano': An Appreciation," *Gambit* [program guide, KCET/Channel 28] (Aug. 1972): 5; Gregg Kilday, "The Chicano: His Past and Present," *Los Angeles Times,* Aug. 10, 1972, ; Cecil Smith, "'Yo Soy' Captures the Chicano Soul," *Los Angeles Times,* Aug. 17, 1972; and Alejandro Morales, "Expanding the Meaning of Chicano Cinema: Yo Soy Chicano, Raíces de Sangre, Seguín," in Keller, *Chicano Cinema,* 121–37.

65. "América de los Indios," *Gambit* [program guide, KCET/Channel 28] (Sept. 1972): 6.

66. Jesús Salvador Treviño, letter and report to William G. Harley, May 23, 1972, Treviño Collection, M634, Box 13, Folder 10, Department of Special Collections, Stanford University. Related correspondence involving Harley and to the CBP are also in this folder.

67. Treviño, "The Need for More Spanish American Affairs Programs."

68. Treviño, "Comentarios de un Cineasta Chicano."

69. Personal interview with Treviño; "New Mexican-American Series Debuts,"

Gambit [program guide, KCET/Channel 28] (Dec. 1972): 7; and Frank del Olmo, "'Acción Chicano,'" *Gambit* [program guide, KCET/Channel 28] (Nov. 1973): 28–29.

In Spanish, adjectives usually conform to the gender of the noun. Thus, the correct title would be *Acción Chicana.* Treviño, however, "purposely changed it to Chicano," since "I basically, at that time, thought that Chicana would read that it was a show only for women, and I wanted to make it clear that this was for the whole community." That there would have been such confusion owes more to decreased Spanish-language maintenance within the Chicano generation than to sexism alone. In fact, Treviño himself was not fluent in Spanish at the time.

Treviño's concern was not unfounded. For example, *La Causa Chicana: The Movement for Justice* (1972) is often listed in early bibliographies as a book about Chicanas, when, in fact, it deals with the Chicano movement as a whole. Perhaps, if one never opened the book, the fact that it had a "white" woman as editor (Margaret M. Mangold) and was published by the Family Service Association of America might also lead one to think the book was somehow a feminist tract.

70. Personal interview with Treviño.

71. Páramo came to *Acción Chicano* as an undergraduate student at California State University–Los Angeles through a media training program sponsored by the bilingual children's program *Villa Alegre,* then produced by Esparza. Fifteen Latinos were trained at USC and Loyola University, and then given "on the job" training at a local station. Bobby Páramo, "Cerco Blanco, the Balloon Man, and Fighting City Hall: On Being a Chicano Filmmaker," *Metamorfosis* 3, no. 2 (1980–81): 77–82.

72. García Torres, who is quoting Frederick Douglass, became executive director of *Realidades.* In addition to the series, the protest group demanded Puerto Rican representation on the WNET board of directors, resulting in the appointment of Luis Alvarez. García Torres, "José García Torres & Realidades." See also Lillian Jiménez, "From the Margin to the Center: Puerto Rican Cinema in New York," *Centro de Estudios Puertorriqueños Bulletin* 2, no. 8 (Spring 1990): 28–43; and Antonio José Guernica, "Las Realidades de Raquel Ortiz: An Interview with a Latina Television Producer," *Agenda: A Journal of Hispanic Issues* 7, no. 4 (July–Aug. 1976): 40–41.

73. Personal interview with Antonio Parra, San Antonio, Sept. 27, 1992.

74. Since then, CPB has not funded a national Latino-produced series beyond the pilot episode. The list is compiled from Treviño, "Chicano Cinema"; Páramo, "On Being a Chicano Filmmaker"; and my own viewing of episodes from the series.

75. "Latinos and CPB: In Quest of National Programming," *Chicano Cinema Newsletter* 1, no. 6 (Aug. 1979): 2. For the expanded version presented to the CPB Board of Directors, see Treviño and Ruiz, "Hispanics and CPB."

76. Ibid.

77. Ibid.

78. Parra, "Bilingual Programming for Latinos," quote from 17. The material on the consortium's "scheduling nightmare" is drawn from my personal interview with José Luis Ruiz, Los Angeles, Apr. 23, 1993.

79. "Answers to Questions Frequently Asked about the Latino Consortium," two-page document, in MALDEF Collection, M673, Box 121, Folder 5, Special Collections, Stanford University. While the document is undated, references in the text suggest that it was written around the start of the second year of operation.

80. Ruiz, who had been producer of *Unidos* (KABC) and *Impacto* (KNBC), had proposed a similar concept for the five ABC-owned and -operated stations in 1971. Parra, "Bilingual Programming for Latinos," 16; and personal interview with José Luis Ruiz.

81. Personal interview with José Luis Ruiz.

82. Ibid.

83. The figure comes from a fact sheet for the Latino Consortium in a press kit for the second half of the first season of *Vistas,* dated Apr. 22, 1987. In contrast, Ruiz describes the "peak" period of the late 1980s as one involving 26 producing stations and 160 member stations, with about 35 hours per year in syndicated programming. Given the use of satellite feed, it is possible that there would be a disparity between member stations and the actual number of stations that carried consortium programming. Ibid.

84. Quoted in "Latinos and CPB."

85. Hoynes, *Public Television For Sale,* 105.

86. Ibid., 94.

87. Personal interview with José Luis Ruiz.

88. Ibid.

89. See Guernica, "The Development of the National Latino Media Coalition"; and "National Latino Media Coalition (NLMC): A Progress Report," *Reporte* 1, no. 1 (Feb. 1977): 5–6.

90. Quoted in Guernica, "The Development of the National Latino Media Coalition," 30.

91. Personal interview with Jesús Salvador Treviño.

92. "Latino Coalition Resigns from CPB Advisory Council," *Access* 44 (Oct. 26, 1976): 3. For information on congressional pressure on CPB, see note 27.

93. Treviño's *La Historia* series was loosely based on the earlier "La Raza History" segments produced for *¡Ahora!* in 1970. For scripts of "La Raza History" and materials related to the *La Historia* proposal, see Treviño Collection, M634, Boxes 1–5, Department of Special Collections, Stanford University.

94. Treviño and Ruiz, "Hispanics and Public Broadcasting." See also Treviño's account and funding information in his article "Latinos and Public Broadcasting," 65.

95. Treviño and Ruiz, "Hispanics and Public Broadcasting," 5–6.

96. José Luis Ruiz, ed., *Media and the Humanities,* Proceedings of the Hispanic Southwest Regional Conference, Dec. 4–7, 1980, San Diego, Calif.

97. Since these films were intended for theatrical release, I consider them at greater length as part of another book on Chicano media and public exhibition. For excellent production histories of *The Ballad of Gregorio Cortez* (1983), *El Norte* (1983), and *Stand and Deliver* (1988), see David Rosen, *Off-Hollywood: The Making and Marketing of Independent Films* (New York: Grove Weidenfeld, 1990). Severo Pérez and Paul Espinosa's . . . *and the Earth Did Not Swallow Him* (1994) is the most recent feature film to have been funded through NEH.

98. In addition to Cine-Aztlán and Cine Acción, the Los Angeles–based Emancipation Arts (established 1978) represented a multiracial and feminist nonprofit corporation that included coalition member David Sandoval. See the newsletter, *Emancipation Arts* (Spring 1980), which includes their manifesto, "Toward a Multinational Film Movement," and an account of their feature-length documentary project, *Valley of Tears.*

99. Chicano Cinema Coalition press statements: Mar. 23, 1979, and Nov. 15, 1979. In addition to a detailed, step-by-step list of reasons the coalition objected to the films, the television movies were cited as "acts of psychological violence against the Latino community," a phrase the press quoted often.

100. "CCC Meets AFI," *Chicano Cinema Newsletter* 1, no. 2 (Feb. 1979): 2.

101. "The Los Angeles Chicano Cinema Coalition: Statement of Purpose," *Chicano Cinema Newsletter* 1, no. 2 (Feb. 1979): 8.

102. Ibid. See also Jason Johansen, "Notes on Chicano Cinema," *Chicano Cinema Newsletter* 1, no. 4 (June 1979): 6–8.

103. Cine-Aztlán, "Ya Basta con Yankee Imperialist Documentaries," *La Raza Film Bibliography* (Santa Barbara: Cine-Aztlán, 1974), 20–25; and Francisco X. Camplis, "Towards the Development of a Raza Cinema," in *Perspectives on Chicano Education,* ed. Tobias Gonzales and Sandra Gonzales (Stanford: Chicano Fellows/Stanford University, 1975), 155–73. I cite from the excerpted version of Camplis's manifesto, which appears in *Tin Tan Magazine* 2, no. 5 (June 1977): 5–7. These two manifestos, along with the one by Jason Johansen, are reprinted in Noriega, *Chicanos and Film.* Subsequent citations of these three manifestos will be in the text itself. For a related statement from an influential Chicano poet and visual artist, see José Montoya's presentation to the First Annual Chicano Film Series at Stanford University in Jan. 1979: "Thoughts on La Cultural: The Media, Con Safos, and Survival," *Caracol* 5, no. 9 (May 1979): 6–8, 19.

104. Mario Barrera, Carlos Muñoz, Jr., and Charles Ornelas, "The Barrio as Internal Colony," *Urban Affairs Annual Reviews* 6 (1972): 465–98, reprinted in *La Causa Política: A Chicano Politics Reader,* ed. F. Chris Garcia (Notre Dame: University of Notre Dame Press, 1974), 281–301; and Acuña, *Occupied America.*

105. Barrera, Muñoz, and Ornelas, " The Barrio as Internal Colony," in Garcia, *La Causa Politica,* 289. By the mid-1970s, Chicano scholars were reevaluating and critiquing the internal colony model and its role in the university and the community. Some scholars looked to either an increased class analysis or a return to a traditional colonial model. For a recent critique of the legal basis of the internal colony model, see Tomás Almaguer, "Ideological Distortions in Recent Chicano Historiography: The Internal Model and Chicano Historical Interpretation," *Aztlán: A Journal of Chicano Studies* 18, no. 1 (Spring 1987): 7–28.

106. Translations of these manifestos appeared in the Summer 1970 and Winter 1970–71 issues of *Cinéaste.* See also Michael Chanan, ed., *Twenty-five Years of the New Latin American Cinema* (London: British Film Institute and Channel Four Television, 1983).

107. As children, however, these same filmmakers were part of the last Chicano generation to attend movie theaters showing the "classic" cinema of both Mexico and the United States.

108. It is not surprising, then, that these manifestos were written by university students allied with independent producers: Camplis at Stanford University, Johansen at the University of California, Los Angeles, and Cine-Aztlán members at the University of California, Santa Barbara. In fact, Camplis and Johansen were MFA students in film production.

109. José E. Limón, *Mexican Ballads, Chicano Epic: History, Social Dramas and Poetic Persuasions,* SCCR Working Paper Series no. 14 (Stanford: Stanford Center for Chicano Research, 1986).

110. For collected press coverage and position statement, see Gang Exploitation Film Committee, *A Reader and Information Packet on the "Gang Exploitation Films"* (Monterey Park, Calif.: East Los Angeles College M.E.Ch.A., 1979). See also Daniel G. Solorzano, "Teaching and Social Change: Reflections on a Freirian Approach in a College Classroom," *Teaching Sociology* 17 (Apr. 1989): 218–25.

111. "Declaración del Comité de Cineasta de America Latina," *Cine Cubano* 8, no. 3 (1977–78): 45–46. Translation mine. The declaration was translated by Ralph Cook and reprinted in *Cinéaste* 9, no. 1 (Fall 1978): 54. Cook inserts references to the Chicano movement. The original text, however, refers to the Chicano "community," and not the "movement," whose militant phase had already come to an end.

112. For press accounts of Chicano participation in the festival, see Patricia Aufderheide, "Latins, Exiles, U.S. Chicanos Attend Havana's Film Fest," *Variety,* Dec. 19, 1979;

and Clyde Taylor, "Special Report—Cuba: A Festival," *Chamba Notes: A Media Newsletter* (Summer 1980): 1–3. Essays by Treviño and Johansen, along with a filmography by Héctor Garza, were later translated and published in a collection documenting the New Latin American Cinema, *Hojas de Cine: Testimonios y Documentos del Nuevo Cine Latinoamericano* (México: Fundación del Nuevo Cinema Latinoamericano, 1986).

113. Personal interview with Treviño.

114. Eduardo Diaz, "Chicano Film Festivals," unpublished paper, Aug. 1990, 7. Cited with permission of the author.

115. Personal interview with Graciela I. Sánchez, San Antonio, Sept. 29, 1992. Enrique Berumén from Los Angeles entered the program in Jan. 1988, staying for six months.

116. Coco Fusco's brief historical trajectory for New Latin American Cinema speaks to Chicano cinema as well: "Times have changed, and manifestos have given way to deeper reflection and commentary, the signs of a movement in the process of assessing itself. More recent films are generally less sweeping, and often less polemical, but the finest of them continue to combine aesthetic innovation and social commitment." In *Reviewing Histories: Selections from New Latin American Cinema*, ed. Coco Fusco (Buffalo: Hallwalls Contemporary Arts Center, 1987), 4. For critical accounts of New Latin American Cinema in relation to its earlier manifestos, see Paul Willemen, "The Third Cinema Question: Notes and Reflections," *Framework* 34 (1987): 4–38; Ana M. López, "An 'Other' History: The New Latin American Cinema," in *Resisting Images: Essays on Cinema and History*, ed. Robert Sklar and Charles Musser (Philadelphia: Temple University Press, 1990), 308–30; Patricia Aufderheide, "Latin American Cinema and the Rhetoric of Cultural Nationalism: Controversies at Havana in 1987 and 1989," *Quarterly Review of Film and Video* 12, no. 4 (1991): 61–76; B. Ruby Rich, "Another View of New Latin American Cinema," *Iris: A Journal of Theory on Sound and Image* no. 13 (Summer 1991): 5–28; Catherine Davies, "Modernity, Masculinity, and Imperfect Cinema in Cuba," *Screen* 38, no. 4 (Winter 1997): 345–59; and Michael Chanan, "The Changing Geography of Third Cinema," *Screen* 38, no. 4 (Winter 1997): 372–88. Manifestos and key critical works are anthologized in Michael T. Martin, ed., *New Latin American Cinema*, vol. 1, *Theory, Practices, and Transcontinental Articulations* (Detroit: Wayne State University Press, 1997). Volume 2 provides historical accounts of various national cinemas, blurring the boundary between the eponymous film movement and contemporary industrial and independent cinemas. For close textual analysis of major works, see Julianne Burton, ed., *The Social Documentary in Latin America* (Pittsburgh: University of Pittsburgh Press, 1990), and Zuzana M. Pick, *New Latin American Cinema: A Continental Project* (Austin: University of Texas Press, 1993).

8. This Is Not a Border

1. The FCC's chairman, Mark S. Fowler, laid out the rationale for pursuing deregulation in an article coauthored with Daniel L. Brenner, legal assistant to the chairman: "A Marketplace Approach to Broadcast Regulation," *Texas Law Review* 60 (1982): 207–57. The closing sections of the article suggest, however, that "the Commission can make some provision for programs that might not find their way on the air through market mechanisms" (252). While leaving the issue open, this apparent concession engages in two maneuvers that support an overall marketplace approach: it redirects all "trusteeship obligations" to public television while also subordinating the operation of the public broadcast system to the same marketplace approach (thereby ensuring its failure); and, it allows the authors to suggest that Congress either ratify such a mission or return the frequencies to "the rigors of the marketplace" (256). For insightful critiques of deregula-

tion, see Horwitz, *The Irony of Regulatory Reform;* Vincent Mosco, "The Mythology of Telecommunications Deregulation," *Journal of Communication* 40, no. 1 (Winter 1990): 36–49; and Duncan H. Brown, "The Academy's Response to the Call for a Marketplace Approach to Broadcast Regulation," *Critical Studies in Mass Communication* 11 (1994): 257–73.

2. Robert W. McChesney, *Corporate Media and the Threat to Democracy* (New York: Seven Stories Press, 1997), 44. I am greatly indebted to McChesney's argument in this section. For recent critical work on global media, see Edward S. Herman and Robert W. McChesney, *The Global Media: The New Missionaries of Corporate Capitalism* (London: Cassell, 1997); Annabelle Sreberny-Mohammadi et al., eds., *Media in Global Context: A Reader* (London: Arnold, 1997); and Armand Mattelart, *Mapping World Communication: War, Progress, Culture,* trans. Susan Emanuel and James A. Cohen (Minneapolis: University of Minnesota Press, 1994 [1991]). The classic text on the concentration of corporate ownership of news and entertainment media is Ben H. Bagdikian, *The Media Monopoly,* 5th ed. (Boston: Beacon, 1997). For policy-oriented approaches, see Brian Kahin and Ernest Wilson, eds., *National Information Infrastructure Initiatives: Vision and Policy Design* (Cambridge: MIT Press, 1997), and Brian Kahin and Charles Nesson, eds., *Borders in Cyberspace: Information Policy and the Global Information Infrastructure* (Cambridge: MIT Press, 1997).

3. Anderson, *Imagined Communities,* 43, 37.

4. Ibid., 7.

5. Herman and McChesney, *The Global Media,* 133.

6. Valentine spoke as part of a panel on television at "Hollywood: A Design for Living," 47th International Design Conference in Aspen (IDCA), June 5–8, 1997; available through the IDCA on audiotape no. 18. I was also on the panel, and this section incorporates and advances my response.

7. Streeter, *Selling the Air,* 287.

8. Herman and McChesney, *The Global Media,* 111.

9. For an excellent critical overview of the social construction of the Hispanic market in the 1990s, see América Rodríguez, "Racialization, Language, and Class in the Construction and Sale of the Hispanic Audience," in *Reflexiones 1997: New Directions in Mexican American Studies,* ed. Neil Foley (Austin: CMAS Books, 1998), 29–51.

10. See Stuart Miller, "Hispanics Conspicuous in Census, But Missing in Prime," *Variety,* Oct. 7, 1991, 4, 37; and Greg Braxton and Jan Breslauer, "Casting the Spotlight on TV's Brownout," *Los Angeles Times,* Mar. 5, 1995, Calendar section, 8–9, 76–77. More critical articles appeared in independent film publications, e.g., Katharine Stalter, "Latinos in Television," *Film and Video* (July 1993): 70–78.

11. See her remarks in David Robb, "Doors Creaking Open to Latinos," *Hollywood Reporter,* Dec. 30, 1993–Jan. 2, 1994, 1, 6, 18; also Guy Garcia, "Tropical Tycoon: Nely Galán—Television Is Finally Targeting the Huge Latino Viewership, and She's Leading the Charge," *New York Times Magazine,* Dec. 11, 1994; Braxton and Breslauer, "Casting the Spotlight on TV's Brownout"; and Jill Stewart, "Whoa, Nely!," *Buzz* (June–July 1995): 80–83, 116.

12. Spanish-language programs first appeared on local television stations in South Texas as early as 1951, followed by the first Spanish-language television station in San Antonio four years later. From the 1960s through the 1980s, Spanish-language television in the United States centered on three networks that repackaged *telenovelas* and other programs produced in Latin America: Spanish International Network, renamed Univisión in 1987 (1961–); Galavisión (1979–), Univisión's cable network; and Telemundo (1986–). See Harry F. Waters, "The New Voice of America," *Newsweek,* June 12, 1989,

54–58; Kathleen Murray, "Banging the Drums as Spanish TV Comes of Age," *New York Times,* Apr. 10, 1994; Alex Avila, "Trading Punches: Spanish-Language Television Pounds the Competition in the Fight for Hispanic Advertising Dollars," *Hispanic* (Jan.–Feb. 1997): 39–40, 42, 44; Tony Cantu, "The Adventures of Super Latino," interview with Henry Cisneros, *Hispanic* (Apr. 1997): 18–20, 22, 24; Elia Esparza, "The Telemundo Takover: Can a Corporate Coup Save the Embattled Network?," *Hispanic* (Jan.–Feb. 1998): 19, 22, 24; James F. Smith, "Two Mexican Networks in Pitched Battle for Markets," *Los Angeles Times,* Aug. 23, 1998; and Kevin Baxter, "Spanish-Language Networks Seek Wider Niche," *Los Angeles Times,* Sept. 21, 1998. For a recent overview of Spanish-language television, see Federico A. Subervi-Vélez et al., "Mass Communication and Hispanics," in *Handbook of Hispanic Cultures in the United States: Sociology,* ed. Félix Padilla (Houston: Arte Público, 1994), 334–50. For an insightful analysis of the cultural and economic forces shaping the nightly news on Spanish-language television, see América Rodríguez, "Objectivity and Ethnicity in the Production of the *Noticiero Univisión,*" *Critical Studies in Mass Communication* 13 (1996): 59–81.

13. "Nielsen Launches Spanish Ratings," *Variety,* Oct. 26, 1992, 26.

14. Hernan de Beky, "Spanish TV Needs to Open Up," *Los Angeles Times,* Mar. 24, 1995. Later in this chapter, I address the more recent Latino media reform efforts directed at Spanish-language television.

15. See, e.g., Christy Haubegger, "TV Shows and Advertisers Are Overlooking the Latino Market," *Los Angeles Times,* June 29, 1998; Marla Matzer, "Ads Not Reaching Latinos, Publisher Says," *Los Angeles Times,* July 23, 1998; and Paul Farhi, "FCC Probes Discrimination Charges Against Advertisers," *Los Angeles Times,* Aug. 21, 1998.

16. Claudia Puig, "New Focus for Telemundo," *Los Angeles Times,* June 3, 1995; Lee Marguiles, "National Survey Shows Most Latino Listeners Are Bilingual," *Los Angeles Times,* Nov. 8, 1997; Yvette C. Doss, "A Spanish-Language TV Network Tries Bilingualism," *Los Angeles Times,* Nov. 11, 1997; Elia Esparza, "Must Sí TV: Galavisión and Producer Jeff Valdez Go Bilingual," *Hispanic* (May 1998): 20–27; and Baxter, "Spanish-Language Networks Seek Wider Niche."

17. Victor Mejia, "Sony Introduces Telemundo's New Management," *Hispanic* (Oct. 1998): 16.

18. Kevin Baxter, "As Telemundo Turns," *Los Angeles Times,* Dec. 20, 1998, Calendar section; and "Prophecy Fulfilled," *Hispanic* (Dec. 1998): 14.

19. On ITVS, see Patricia Aufderheide, "Public Television and the Public Sphere," *Critical Studies in Mass Communication* 8 (1991): 168–83; and Armando Valdez, "A Framework for Multicultural Programming: Considerations on Independent Productions and Public Television," a concept paper for the Independent Television Service, Feb. 1991. On subsequent policy issues prior to the Telecommunications Act of 1996, see Jeffrey Chester and Kathryn Montgomery, "Media in Transition: Independents and the Future of Television," *NVR Reports* no. 10 (Nov. 1992); *The Future of Communications Policy in the New Technological Environment,* proceedings of sessions held in June and Nov. 1992 by Grantmakers in Film, Television, and Video, an affinity group of the Council on Foundations; and Armando Valdez, "The Development of a National Information Infrastructure and its Implications for Latinos," *CLPP Policy Profile* 2, no. 3 (1995).

20. Chester and Montgomery, "Media in Transition," 3. See also the coverage in *The Independent,* the publication of the Association of Independent Video and Filmmakers.

21. While the mainstream press rarely considered "public interest" issues, there were a few exceptions. See Jube Shiver Jr., "Digital TV May Squelch Minority-Owned Stations," *Los Angeles Times,* June 10, 1998.

22. Francis D. Fisher, "What the Coming Telecommunications Infrastructure Could Mean to Our Family," *Aspen Institute Quarterly* 5, no. 1 (Winter 1993): 121–41.

23. Ibid., 125. Fisher's "want" list for the Gonzales family also includes a keyboard.

24. Denise Gellene, "In Their Own Images: TV Ad Seeks to Broaden the Public's View of Latinos," *Los Angeles Times*, Apr. 2, 1998.

25. In pointed contrast, the former MALDEF director Mario Obledo re-emerged in the same period, threatening to burn down a billboard calling California the "Illegal Immigration State" and to launch a boycott against Taco Bell for its Chihuahua-fronted television ads. The billboard message was removed. Sometimes atavism is the best alternative to an entrenched paradigm. David Reyes, "Seasoned Activist's Passions Burn Bright Again," *Los Angeles Times,* Aug. 2, 1998.

26. Given the focus on institutions, I do not examine many independent productions for this period. One notable example of such work is Carlos Avila's four-part dramatic series *Foto-Novelas* (1997). The episodes include "Seeing Through Walls," "In the Mirror," "Mangas," and "The Fix." Avila served as executive producer and director of three episodes. A. P. Gonzalez directed "Mangas." The series, which uses the fotonovela as a stylistic format for social narratives with "magical real" elements, has been funded for additional episodes.

27. Michel de Certeau, *The Writing of History,* trans. Tom Conley (New York: Columbia University Press, 1988 [1975]), 5.

28. This section is adapted from a longer essay summarizing my testimony before the U.S. Commission on Civil Rights in June 1993. See Chon A. Noriega, "The Numbers Game," *Jump Cut* 39 (June 1994): 107–11.

29. Jesús Salvador Treviño, "Latinos and Public Broadcasting," 65. See other similar essays by Treviño: "Latinos are Imprisoned by TV's Color Barrier, Too," *Los Angeles Times,* June 15, 1992; and "Lights, Camera, Action," *Hispanic* (Aug. 1992): 76. The Directors Guild of America, Writers Guild of America, and Screen Actors Guild release annual reports on minority employment. The one area where there has been significant improvement over the past three decades is in acting roles for television commercials. See also S. Robert Lichter and Daniel R. Amundson, "Distorted Reality: Hispanic Characters in TV Entertainment," Center for Media and Public Affairs, Sept. 1, 1994.

30. Frank L. Schick and Renee Schick, eds., *Statistical Handbook on U.S. Hispanics* (Phoenix: Onyx, 1991).

31. As the U.S. Commission on Civil Rights noted in its 1977 report, "The presentation of minorities and women in a representative and realistic manner has been impeded by an assumption that do to so would diminish television's use as a medium whose programming is designed primarily to attract the largest possible audience." Despite the apparent critique of this assumption, the report offered no direct response or refutation. U.S. Commission on Civil Rights, *Window Dressing on the Set,* 148.

32. Daniel Cerone, "TV Heats Up the Leftovers: Unaired Episodes on Summer Lineup," *Los Angeles Times,* June 10, 1992; and Steve Coe, "Networks Test Development Alternatives," *Broadcasting,* Mar. 9, 1992, 21.

33. Henri Lefebvre, *The Production of Space,* trans. Donald Nicholson-Smith (Oxford: Blackwell, 1991), 27–29.

34. Personal interview with Alex Nogales, Los Angeles, Sept. 18, 1995.

35. Ibid.; personal interview with Esther Renteria, Los Angeles, Aug. 22, 1995; and personal interview with Armando Durón, Los Angeles, Sept. 18, 1995.

36. Personal interview with Renteria.

37. Coalition members have included Comisión Femenil, Congreso Para Pueblos Unidos, Hermandad Mexicana Nacional, Hispanic Urban Planners Association, L.A. County Chicano Employees Association, Latin Business Association, Latin Business and Professional Association, League of United Latin American Citizens, Mexican American Bar Association, Mexican American Correctional Association, Mexican American Grocer's Association, Mexican American Political Association, Mexican American Legal Defense and Education Fund, National Hispanic Leadership Conference, National G.I. Forum, Personnel Management Association of Aztlán, and United Latino Artists of Los Angeles. Media-related groups have included Alliance of Hispanic Media Professionals, Hispanic Academy of Media Arts and Sciences, Hispanic Public Relations Association, and Nosotros.

38. The phrase "incredible strength" is from Nogales. This point is reiterated by Durón and Renteria. Alinsky, *Rules for Radicals,* 127; emphasis in the original.

39. Barry Cole and Mal Oettinger, "Petition to Deny," in *Reluctant Regulators,* 204–25; and Krasnow, Longley, and Terry, *The Politics of Broadcast Regulation,* 55.

40. Personal interview with Renteria.

41. Thomas K. Van Amburg, vice president and general manager, KCBS-TV, letter to John E. Huerta, National Hispanic Media Coalition, Mar. 31, 1987.

42. Unfortunately, the coalition expends a significant amount of time in "educating" incoming station managers and news directors who often have little understanding of the Los Angeles area. As Renteria explains, "I call them all migrant workers because they go from station to station, city to city, and they are never there too long." Personal interview with Renteria.

43. These include the National Puerto Rican Forum in New York and the Spanish American League Against Discrimination (SALAD) in Miami.

44. The National Puerto Rican Forum, G.I. Forum, and Telemundo also filed petitions, arguing that the transfer would reduce U.S. production and Latino employment. My account derives from my interviews with Durón, Renteria, and Nogales, as well as from coalition documents related to the Telemundo agreement.

45. For Spanish-language press coverage of these events, see Jaime Olivares, "Piden Aclaraciones a Telemundo: Coalición Nacional Hispana Desea Discutir Problemas Surgidos en KVEA," *La Opinión,* May 11, 1989; Clara Inés Potes, "Levin da Su Versión sobre Cambios en el Equipo Noticioso de Canal 52," *La Opinión,* June 1, 1989; Clara Inés Potes, "Grupos Mexicoamericanos Protestan Cambios en Equipo Noticioso de Canal 52," *La Opinión,* June 6, 1989; Rosa María Villalpando, "Grupos Mexicoamericanos Acusan al Canal 52 de Desdeñar a Su Auditorio," *La Opinión,* June 15, 1989; Bob Navarro, "Mi Experiencia en KVEA TV," *La Opinión,* June 16, 1989; and Rosa María Villalpando, "Gerente del Canal 34 Achaca a la Prensa Versión de 'Cubanización,' de la T.V.," *La Opinión,* June 21, 1989. For English-language press coverage of these events, see Victor Valle, "Ethnic Fight Heats Up at Latino Station," *Los Angeles Times,* May 19, 1989; idem, "KVEA Shakeup Fuels Debate at Latino Station," *Los Angeles Times,* June 2, 1989; idem, "Shake-Up at Latino Station Sparks Protest," *Los Angeles Times,* June 6, 1989; and idem, "Community Coalition Threats Compromise KVEA's Future," *Los Angeles Times,* June 30, 1989.

46. See editor Sergio Muñoz's three-part series "¿La TV en Español Sufre un Proceso de Cubanización?," *La Opinión,* May 10, 1989; "Miami y Los Angeles, Dos Ciudades Incomparables," *La Opinión,* May 11, 1989; and "Crónica de un Despido Anunciado," *La Opinión,* June 9, 1989.

47. For a recent discussion of Miami as a nexus for Latin American and U.S. Latino

entertainment, see Kevin Baxter, "Latin America Looks to Miami, Not Hollywood, for Music, Film," *Los Angeles Times,* Aug. 26, 1998.

48. See Frank del Olmo, "El Mito de la Unidad Hispana," *La Opinión,* May 29, 1989; idem, "La Diversidad Latina y el Mito de la Unidad," *La Opinión,* June 11, 1989, sec. 1, 5; and idem, "TV Dispute Sheds Light on the 'Hispanic' Myth," *Los Angeles Times,* May 29, 1989.

49. Kathleen O'Steen, "White Male Pens Still Busiest: Study Finds H'wood Lags in Hiring Minority, Female Writers," *Variety,* June 15, 1993, 1, 42; Jim Benson, "NHMC Fights B'Casters: Claims Hispanics Underemployed at TV Stations," *Variety,* June 15, 1993, 5, 43; Kathleen O'Steen, "TV Distorts Minorities, Study Finds," *Variety,* June 16, 1993, 1, 40; "Face of Prime Time TV Is Still White," *Variety,* June 21, 1993, 4; Kathleen O'Steen, "Guild Study Finds TV Bias," *Variety,* June 28, 1993, 37; David Robb, "WGAW: Minorities 'Typecast': Modest Gains Said Overshadowed by 'Little If Any Access,'" *Hollywood Reporter,* June 15, 1993, 1, 12, 14; David Robb, "Kids TV Gets Worst Marks on Minority Images," *Hollywood Reporter,* June 16, 1993, 1, 8, 33; Terry Pristin, "'Substantial Barriers' to Minority Writers, Survey Finds," *Los Angeles Times,* June 15, 1993; Daniel Cerone, "TV Not Representative of Society, Study Finds," *Los Angeles Times,* June 16, 1993; Greg Braxton, "Networks, Studios Won't Discuss Minority Reports," *Los Angeles Times,* June 17, 1993; Greg Braxton, "TV Executives Give Mixed Report on Minority Hiring," *Los Angeles Times,* June 18, 1993; Greg Braxton, "TV Stations Have Muted Response to Investigation," *Los Angeles Times,* Mar. 18, 1994; and Greg Braxton, "U.S. to Examine Hiring of Minorities in Entertainment," *Los Angeles Times,* Feb. 22, 1996. See also reports on an ill-fated training program by one network: Greg Braxton, "KCBS to Establish Minority Employee Panel," *Los Angeles Times,* Mar. 19, 1994; Migdia Chinea-Varela, "Platform: Second-Class Writers," *Los Angeles Times,* Oct. 20, 1994; and Shauna Snow, "Morning Report: Latino Training Program Dropped," *Los Angeles Times,* May 2, 1995.

50. Lichter and Amundson, "Distorted Reality." For press coverage, see Rick Du Brow, "Portrayals of Latinos on TV Regressing," *Los Angeles Times,* Sept. 7, 1994; Claudia Puig, "Study No Surprise to Latinos," *Los Angeles Times,* Sept. 8, 1994; Rick Du Brow, "Latino Roles Still 'Mired in Stereotypes,'" *Los Angeles Times,* Oct. 1, 1994; Miluka Rivera, "When Will TV Reflect Latino Audience?," *Los Angeles Times,* Dec. 12, 1994; Greg Braxton, "Latinos on TV: Mixed Findings, Progress," *Los Angeles Times,* Apr. 16, 1996; Del Zamora, "Where Are the Latinos in Films, TV?," *Los Angeles Times,* May 20, 1996; and Miluka Rivera, "Film and TV Perpetuate Invisibility," *Hispanic* (June 1996): 12–13.

51. Greg Braxton, "Latinos to Press for Boycott of ABC-TV," *Los Angeles Times,* Jan. 13, 1995; Greg Braxton, "Latinos Protest at ABC Stations," *Los Angeles Times,* Apr. 27, 1995; Shauna Snow, "Morning Report: ABC Versus Latinos," *Los Angeles Times,* May 9, 1995; and Greg Braxton, "Cancellations Upset Minority Groups," *Los Angeles Times,* May 17, 1995. See also Braxton and Breslauer, "Casting the Spotlight on TV's Brownout," and Yvette C. Doss, "Network TV: Latinos Need Not Apply," *Frontera* 1, no. 2 (1996): 20–21, 43.

During this period, the coalition also became involved in protests against radio talk show host Howard Stern after his disparaging remarks about the late Selena, convincing about fifteen sponsors to drop the program. Stern eventually issued a public apology in Spanish. Personal interview with Nogales; and Jerry Crowe, "Latinos to Stern: Apology Is Not Accepted," *Los Angeles Times,* Apr. 11, 1995.

52. Shauna Snow, "Morning Report: For Latino Writers," *Los Angeles Times,* June 13, 1995.

53. "Hispanic Org Mulls Protest," *Variety*, Aug. 3, 1995, 4; Shauna Snow, "Morning Report: KCAL Protest," *Los Angeles Times*, Aug. 3, 1996.

54. Greg Braxton, "Latino-Based Sitcom Seen as Partial Win," *Los Angeles Times*, May 22, 1996.

55. Shauna Snow, "Morning Report: Boycotting ABC, Disney," *Los Angeles Times*, Apr. 25, 1997; and Jill Leovy, "Latino Group to Launch Disney Boycott," *Los Angeles Times*, Apr. 24, 1997; Greg Braxton, "Molina Joins in Protest over Alleged Disney Discrimination," *Los Angeles Times*, June 27, 1997; Shauna Snow, "Morning Report: Mickey's Defense," *Los Angeles Times*, June 28, 1997; and Shauna Snow, "Morning Report: Latinos and Disney," *Los Angeles Times*, July 26, 1997.

56. The National Council of La Raza paid more than $500,000 for the time slot but retained the advertising revenue, which came from the Ford Motor Company, the Coca-Cola Company, and General Motors, among others. Greg Braxton, "Latinos Split over Disney's Motivations," *Los Angeles Times*, Dec. 13, 1997.

57. The FCC responded with a plan to increase recruitment of minorities and women applicants but could no longer require goals in terms of actual hiring. "FCC Urges New Rules for Broadcaster Hiring," *Los Angeles Times*, Nov. 20, 1998.

58. Ethan B. Kapstein, "Back to Basics," *Los Angeles Times*. See also Horwitz, *The Irony of Regulatory Reform*, 11–12.

59. Personal interview with Nogales.

60. *Who Will Sing the Songs?* (1990), written by William Landsford and directed by Bob Morones, and *Chavez Ravine* (1992), written and directed by Norberto Barba.

61. *Mission Dolores* (1989), written by Norberto Barba and directed by José Ludlow.

62. *Always Roses* (1989), written by George Figueroa and directed by Luis Avalos; *I'll Be Home For Christmas* (1990), written and directed by Robert Diaz LeRoy; *How Else Am I Supposed to Know I'm Still Alive?* (1991), written by Evelina Fernández and directed by José Luis Valenzuela; *Tanto Tiempo* (1991), written and directed by Cheryl Quintana Leder; *Breaking Pan with Sol* (1992), written and directed by Nancy de los Santos.

63. See Ramón Favela, "*Entrance Is Not Acceptance*: A Conceptual Installation by Richard Lou and Robert Sanchez," in Marilu Knode and Anne Ayres, *Third Newport Biennial: Mapping Histories*, exhibition catalog (Newport Beach: Newport Harbor Art Museum, 1991), 50–56.

64. Roberto Rodríguez, "Media Report," *Hispanic Link Weekly Report*, June 4, 1990, 8.

65. Personal interview with José Luis Ruiz, Los Angeles, Apr. 23, 1993.

66. Sources cited in *Final Report and Recommendations of the Task Force on National Minority Programming*, sponsored by the National Asian American Telecommunications Association, submitted Dec. 15, 1989, 1.

67. Aufderheide, "Public Television and the Public Sphere," 170.

68. Ibid. The National Asian American Telecommunications Association coordinated efforts among the consortia to develop an implementation strategy. See its *Final Report and Recommendations*, and Don Adams and Arlene Goldbard, "Cultural Diversity in Public Broadcasting," prepared for the National Asian American Telecommunications Association, Oct. 19, 1989.

69. Armando Valdez, "A Study of Multicultural Content in Selected Public Television Series," commissioned by the National Latino Communications Center, June 1990. I drafted the initial study in 1991; NLCC prepared an "proposal outline" dated Nov. 10, 1992 and received a seed grant from ARCO Foundation. KCET donated more than

400 Latino program tapes. By 1997, the archive holdings included over 5,000 videotapes and 200 reels of film (including the KMEX-TV collection), research materials and transcripts related to *Chicano!*, and an index of Latino-themed photographs in public and private collections in the United States (includes photocopy reproductions and use fee information). Based on an inventory by Pocha Peña, Archive Coordinator, Jan.–July 1997.

70. José Luis Ruiz in *NLCC Video Collection* (1997): 2, and José Luis Ruiz, "Future of NLCC: New Directions," *NLCC News* (Fall 1996): 1.

71. The second catalog, *1998 Video Collection,* more than doubled in size to thirty pages and included a digitally restored version of *Requiem-29* (1971). See also Ken Campo, "NLCC Launches Distribution Division," *NLCC News* (Fall 1996): 3.

72. Funds for educational and community outreach materials were raised in part through the first-ever telethon held by a PBS station for a single production. KCET devoted eleven and a half hours to it on Sunday, Sept. 10, 1995, resulting in $100,000 in pledges. Judith Michaelson, "KCET Breaks With History to Fund 'Chicano!' Series," *Los Angeles Times,* Sept. 9, 1995; and Shauna Snow, "Morning Report: Telethon Results," *Los Angeles Times,* Sept. 12, 1995.

73. See reports on the series in *NLCC Newsletter* 1 (Fall 1992) and *NLCC Newsletter* 2 (Spring 1993); *!Chicano! TV Series Newsletter* 1, no. 1 (Summer 1992); *Chicano! History of the Mexican American Civil Rights Movement* 1 (Feb. 1996); and *Chicano! History of the Mexican American Civil Rights Movement* 2 (Mar. 1996). Judith Michaelson, "The Chicano Rallying Cry," *Los Angeles Times,* Apr. 7, 1996, Calendar section, 6, 70–71; R. Hunter Garcia, "'Chicano!,'" *Hollywood Reporter,* Apr. 12–14, 1996, 16, 33; and Howard Rosenberg, "Eyes on the 'Chicano!' Prize," *Los Angeles Times,* Apr. 12, 1996.

74. Michaelson, "The Chicano Rallying Cry," 6.

75. Corporation for Public Broadcasting, *Reaching Common Ground: Public Broadcasting's Services to Minority Groups and Other Groups,* Report to the 103d Congress and the American People Pursuant to Pub.L. 100–626, July 1, 1994.

76. Corporation for Public Broadcasting Office of Inspector General, *Operation Audit of the National Latino Communications Center,* audit report no. 98–02, Mar. 31, 1998; and Kevin Baxter, "Groups Voice Concern Over Funding for Latino Programming," *Los Angeles Times,* Jan. 30, 1999.

77. Greg Braxton, "Latino Public TV Program Developer Shuts Its Doors," *Los Angeles Times,* Mar. 13, 1998; Karen Everhart Bedford, "Out of Cash and under Scrutiny, Latino Center Closes," *Current,* Mar. 16, 1998; Karen Everhart Bedford, "CPB Finds Fault in Latino Consortium Spending Practices," *Current,* May 4, 1998. See José Luis Ruiz's response in Monica Rivas, "NLCC Out of Cash—Shuts Down Operations," *Nosotros News,* 1998 collector's ed., 51.

78. Letter to Sandie Pedlow, Senior Program Officer, Corporation for Public Broadcasting, from Coalition for Latino Programming on Public Broadcasting, Sept. 29, 1998.

79. Open letter from Latino Producers Ad Hoc Committee, Nov. 13, 1998. I was a signatory to this letter.

80. Shauna Snow, "Morning Report," *Los Angeles Times,* Nov. 17, 1998; Karen Everhart Bedford, "Olmos Will Head Interim Latino TV Grantmaking," *Current,* Nov. 23, 1998; and Greg Braxton, "Olmos-Led Group to Help Develop Latino TV Projects," *Los Angeles Times,* Nov. 18, 1998.

81. Letter to Edward James Olmos from Coalition for Latino Programming on Public Broadcasting and Latino Producers Ad Hoc Committee, Dec. 27, 1998; and Baxter, "Groups Voice Concern Over Funding for Latino Programming." I was a member of

the planning committee organizing the national conference and related activities, which took place June 3–6, 1999, in San Francisco.

82. Liz Kotz, "Unofficial Stories: Documentaries by Latinas and Latin American Women," *Centro de Estudios Puertorriqueños Bulletin* 2, no. 8 (Spring 1990): 59–69.

83. Personal interview with Lourdes Portillo, Albuquerque, Dec. 5, 1991.

84. Rosa Linda Fregoso, "La Quinceañera of Chicana Counter Aesthetics," *Centro de Estudios Puertorriqueños Bulletin* 3, no. 1 (Winter 1990–91): 89.

85. Luz Castillo and Liz Kotz, "Note from the Directors," in *Women of the Americas Film and Video Festival* (catalog), Oct. 19–23, 1988, 2.

86. For an insightful review of the *encuentro,* see Rosa Linda Fregoso, "Close Encuentro of a First Kind: The Cruzando Fronteras Conference," *Independent* 14, no. 4 (May 1991): 13–16. The proceedings have recently been published in Norma Iglesias and Rosa Linda Fregoso, eds., *Miradas de Mujer: A Bi-Lingual Anthology of Mexicana-Chicana-Latina Cinema* (Davis: Chicana/Latina Research Center at the University of California, Davis; Colegio de la Frontera Norte, 1998).

87. Rosa Linda Fregoso, "Chicana Film Practices: Confronting the 'Many-Headed Demon of Oppression," in Noriega, *Chicanos and Film,* 170.

88. Lourdes Portillo, "On Chicanas and Filmmaking: A Commentary," in *Chicana (W)rites on Word and Film,* ed. María Herrera-Sobek and Helena María Viramontes (Berkeley: Third Woman, 1995), 279–82.

89. Personal interview with Portillo.

90. Unlike soap operas, *telenovelas* are not open ended but are designed to run a certain number of episodes (usually several hundred). Ana M. López, "The Melodrama in Latin America: Films, Telenovelas and the Currency of a Popular Form," *Wide Angle* 7, no. 3 (1985): 8.

91. Ibid., 10.

92. Ibid., 9.

93. For a general discussion of Latino AIDS media, see Catherine Saalfield and Ray Navarro, "Not Just Black and White: AIDS Media and People of Color," *Independent* (July 1989): 18–23; reprinted in *Centro de Estudios Puertorriqueños Bulletin* 2, no. 8 (Spring 1990): 70–78; and Alexandra Juhasz, *AIDS TV: Identity, Community, and Alternative Video* (Durham, N.C.: Duke University Press, 1995).

94. While the late 1970s saw increased awareness of the pan-American dimension of immigration from Mexico and of gender politics within the Chicano-Latino community, these remain hot issues. When the film was shown at the Whitney Museum in Jan. 1991, one Chicano viewer stood up and complained that the film was not about the Chicano movement (the subject of the film series). By the end of the film, however, he realized that, in the broadest sense, it was, and applauded the film with the phrase "viva la raza" ("long live the Latino people").

95. Fregoso, *The Bronze Screen,* 97–98.

96. See Fregoso's extended reading of the film in *The Bronze Screen,* 96–105.

97. Personal interview with Portillo.

98. See Kathleen Newman, "Steadfast Love and Subversive Acts: The Politics of *La Ofrenda: The Days of the Dead,*" *Spectator* 13, no. 1 (Fall 1992): 98–109; and Fregoso, *The Bronze Screen,* 110–18.

99. For an insightful close reading of the film, see Rosa Linda Fregoso, "Sacando los Trapos al Sol (Airing Dirty Laundry) in Lourdes Portillo's Melodocumentary, *The Devil Never Sleeps,*" in *Redirecting the Gaze: Gender, Theory, and Cinema in the Third World,* ed. Diana Robin and Ira Jaffe (Albany: State University Press of New York, 1990), 307–29.

Epilogue

1. I consider several of these videomakers in my essay "Talking Heads, Body Politic: The Plural Self of Chicano Video," in *Resolutions: Contemporary Video Practices,* ed. Michael Renov and Erika Suderburg (Minneapolis: University of Minnesota Press, 1996), 207–28.

2. For a more comprehensive list, see my editor's commentary in *Aztlán: A Journal of Chicano Studies* 23, no. 2 (Fall 1998): 1–9.

3. Fregoso, "Chicana Film Practices: Confronting the 'Many-Headed Demon of Oppression,'" in Noriega, *Chicanos and Film,* 169–70.

4. José Montoya of the Sacramento-based art collective Royal Chicano Air Force (RCAF) made these same points at the First Annual Chicano Film Series, Stanford University, Calif., Jan. 10–12, 1979. See José Montoya, "Thoughts on la Cultural: The Media, Con Safos, and Survival," *Caracol* 5, no. 9 (May 1979): 6–8, 19.

5. From Greek poet Archilochus. In his well-known essay "The Hedgehog and the Fox," Isaiah Berlin reads the distinction as one between eclectic and systemic thought, or what he calls "centrifugal" and "centripetal." Berlin divagates on these two styles of thought as a way of understanding various writers (Tolstoy in particular) but loses sight of the power differential between these two animals that is conjured up by this line from Archilochus. What each knows is determined by the power it has relative to the other. Isaiah Berlin, "The Hedgehog and the Fox: An Essay on Tolstoy's View of History," in *The Proper Study of Mankind: An Anthology of Essays* (New York: Farrar, Straus, and Giroux, 1997), 436–98.

6. E. P. Thompson, *The Making of the English Working Class* (New York: Vintage Books, 1966), 9.

Filmography

TV Programs

1968–70. *Canción de la Raza* (KCET-TV), dramatic series.
1969–70. *¡Ahora!* (KCET-TV), public affairs.
1970–74. *Impacto* (KNBC-TV), public affairs.
1970–71. *Unidos* (KABC-TV), public affairs.
1972–73. *Reflecciones* (KABC-TV), public affairs.
1972–74. *Acción Chicano* (KCET-TV), public affairs.
1972–73. *The Siesta Is Over* (KNXT-TV, now KCBS-TV), public affairs.
1973. *Bienvenidos* (KNXT-TV, now KCBS-TV), public affairs.

Documentaries

1969. *I Am Joaquin*. Luis Valdez and El Teatro Campesino.
1969. *La Raza Nueva*. Jesús Salvador Treviño.
1969. *Ya Basta!* Jesús Salvador Treviño.
1970. *Los Mascarones*. Jesús Salvador Treviño; episode of *¡Ahora!* (KCET-TV).
1971. *América Tropical*. Jesús Salvador Treviño.
1971. *Nosotros Venceremos/We Will Overcome*. United Farm Workers Service Center.
1971. *Requiem-29*. David Garcia.
1972. *Cinco Vidas*. José Luis Ruiz and Moctesuma Esparza.
1972. *La Raza Unida*. Jesús Salvador Treviño.
1972. *Yo Soy Chicano*. Jesús Salvador Treviño.
1973. *A la Brava: Prison and Beyond*. Ricardo Soto.
1973. *Carnalitos*. Bobby Páramo.
1973. *Sí, Se Puede*. Rick Tejada-Flores.
1974. *Cristal*. Severo Pérez.
1975. *De Colores*. Jay Ojeda.
1975. *Garment Workers*. Susan Racho.
1975. *The Unwanted*. José Luis Ruiz.
1976. *La Onda Chicana*. Efraín Gutiérrez.
1977. *Agueda Martinez: Our People, Our Country*. Esperanza Vásquez.
1979. *Chicana*. Sylvia Morales.
1981. *El Teatro Campesino*. Humberto Rivera.
1981. *Port of Entry*. Nancy de los Santos.

1983. *Ballad of an Unsung Hero.* Isaac Artenstein and Paul Espinosa.
1983. *Barrio Murals.* Paul Venema.
1983. *Low 'n Slow: The Art of Lowriding.* Rick Tejada-Flores.
1984. *Rag Top Ralph.* Juan Garza.
1985. *Vayan con Dios.* Sylvia Morales.
1985. *The Lemon Grove Incident.* Paul Espinosa.
1985. *Yo Soy.* Jesús Salvador Treviño.
1986. *Las Madres: The Mothers of Plaza de Mayo.* Susana Muñoz and Lourdes Portillo.
1986. *Santeros.* Ray Telles.
1986. *When You Think of Mexico: Commercial Images of Mexico.* Yolanda Lopez.
1987. *El Corrido de Juan Chacon.* Beverly Sanchez-Padilla.
1988. *After Joaquin: The Crusade for Justice.* Daniel Salazar.
1988. *Chicano Park.* Marilyn Mulford and Mario Barrera.
1988. *No Porque lo Diga Fidel Castro.* Graciela Sanchez.
1988. *La Ofrenda: The Days of the Dead.* Lourdes Portillo.
1989. *Mbamba.* Olivia Chumacero.
1989. *Uneasy Neighbors.* Paul Espinosa.
1990. *Friday Night under the Stars.* Rick Leal.
1990. *The New Tijuana.* Paul Espinosa.
1990. *Twenty Years . . . y Que?* Nancy de los Santos.
1990. *Una Lucha por Mi Pueblo.* Federico Antonio Reade.
1991. *Faith Even to the Fire.* Sylvia Morales.
1991. *Los Mineros.* Hector Galán and Paul Espinosa.
1993. *Cholo Joto.* Augie Robles.
1993. *De Mujer a Mujer.* Beverly Sanchez-Padilla.
1994. *El Diablo Nunca Duerme/The Devil Never Sleeps.* Lourdes Portillo.
1994. *¡Vive 16!* Valentin Aguirre and Augie Robles.
1996. *Chicano! The History of the Mexican American Civil Rights Movement.* Four-part documentary series. Executive producer: José Luis Ruiz. Series producer: Hector Galán. Segment producers: Robert Cozens, Hector Galán, Sylvia Morales, Mylene Moreno, and Susan Racho.
1996. *The Fight in the Fields: César Chávez and the Farmworkers Struggles.* Ray Telles and Rick Tejada-Flores.
1997. *Fear and Learning at Hoover Elementary.* Laura Angélica Simón.

Short or Video Narrative

1972. *Los Vendidos: The Sellouts.* Luis Valdez.
1976. *El Corrido.* Luis Valdez.
1976. *Guadalupe.* José Luis Ruiz.
1979. *Después del Terremoto/After the Earthquake.* Lourdes Portillo and Nina Serrano.
1981. *Seguin.* Jesús Salvador Treviño.
1985. *Esperanza.* Sylvia Morales.
1985. *Tormenta.* Juan Garza.
1987. *Corridos! Tales of Passion and Revolution.* Luis Valdez.
1987. *Esperanza.* Graciela Sanchez.
1987. *Ojos Que No Ven.* José Gutiérrez-Gómez and José Vergelín.
1987. *The Royal Family.* Juan Garza.
1987. *Who Gets to Water the Grass?* Luis Meza.
1988. *Face to Face with AIDS.* Socorro Valdez.

1989. *Albert Pastor's First Video Project.* Juan Garza.

1989. *Dreams of Flying.* Severo Pérez.

1989. *Mi Casa.* Edgar Bravo.

1989. *Mi Hermano.* Edgar Bravo.

1989. *Mission Dolores.* Norberto Barba and José Ludlow.

1989. *Vida.* Lourdes Portillo.

1990. *Always Roses.* Luis Avalos and George Figueroa.

1990. *Between Friends.* Severo Pérez.

1990. *Distant Water.* Carlos Avila.

1990. *I'll Be Home for Christmas.* Robert Diaz LeRoy.

1990. *The Trouble with Tonia.* Juan Garza.

1990. *Who Will Sing the Songs?* Bob Morones.

1991. *The Bike.* Gary Soto.

1991. *The Detour.* Joseph Tovares and Raul Tovares.

1991. *La Pastorela: The Shepherds' Tale.* Luis Valdez.

1992. *Bedheads.* Robert Rodriguez.

1992. *Breaking Pan with Sol.* Nancy de los Santos.

1992. *Chavez Ravine.* Norberto Barba.

1992. *The Pool Party.* Gary Soto.

1992. *Tanto Tiempo.* Cheryl Quintana Leader.

1993. *La Carpa.* Carlos Avila.

1993. *How Else Am I Supposed to Know I'm Still Alive?* Evelina Fernández and José Luis
      Valenzuela.

1994. *The Ballad of Tina Juarez.* Juan A. Uribe.

1994. *Cruel.* Desi Del Valle.

1995. *El Corrido de Cherry Creek.* Gwylym Cano.

1995. *Mi Pollo Loco.* Andrew Durham, Rico Martinez, and Victor Vargas.

1996. *The Party Line.* Marlo Barrera.

1996. *Pretty Vacant.* Jim Mendiola.

1997. *Foto-Novelas.* Four-part dramatic series: "Seeing through Walls," "In the Mirror,"
      "Mangas," "The Fix." Executive producer: Carlos Avila. Episode directors: Car-
      los Avila and A. P. Gonzalez.

1997. *I.N.F.I.T.D. [I'll Not Fall Into the Devil].* Aldo Velasco.

Experimental

1966. *My Trip in a '52 Ford.* Ernie Palomino.

1968. *Mozo: An Introduction into the Duality of Orbital Indecision.* Severo Pérez.

1973. *Tabla Rosa.* Esperanza Vásquez.

1974. *Ghost Town (1974).* Willie Varela.

1975. *Becky's Eye.* Willie Varela.

1975. *Cruel Profit.* Harry Gamboa Jr. (destroyed).

1975–78. *No Movies* (misc.). Harry Gamboa Jr. and Asco.

1977. *April 1977.* Willie Varela.

1978. *Entelequia.* Juan Salazar.

1978. *Mi Hermano, Mi Hambre.* Gustavo Vazquez.

1980. *Stan and Jane Brakhage.* Willie Varela.

1982. *Night Vigil.* Betty Maldonado.

1982. *Recuerdos de Flores Muertas.* Willie Varela.

1983. *Imperfecto.* Harry Gamboa Jr.

1983. *Insultan*. Harry Gamboa Jr.
1984. *Agent Ex*. Harry Gamboa Jr.
1984. *Baby Kake*. Harry Gamboa Jr.
1984. *Blanx*. Harry Gamboa Jr.
1984. *Vaporz*. Harry Gamboa Jr.
1985. *Fearless Leader*. Willie Varela.
1985. *In Progress*. Willie Varela.
1985. *Juntos en la Vida, Unidos en la Muerte*. Willie Varela.
1987. *No Supper*. Harry Gamboa Jr.
1988. *Border Crossing, Versions One & Two*. Willie Varela.
1989. *Anima*. France Salomé España.
1989. *Making Is Choosing: A Fragmented Life: A Broken Line: A Series of Observations*. Willie Varela.
1989. *Replies of the Night*. Sandra P. Hahn.
1990. *Cronica de un Ser*. S. M. Peña.
1990. *The Idea We Live In*. Pilar Rodriguez.
1990. *Reaffirmation*. Willie Varela.
1991. *Border Brujo*. Isaac Artenstein.
1991. *El Espejo*. Frances Salomé España.
1991. *A History of Violence*. Danny G. Acosta.
1991. *L.A. Merge*. Harry Gamboa Jr.
1991. *Mujeria: The Olmeca Rap*. Osa Hidalgo de la Riva.
1991. *Slipping Between*. Sandra P. Hahn.
1992. *A Lost Man*. Willie Varela.
1992. *Columbus on Trial*. Lourdes Portillo.
1992. *El Mundo L.A.: Humberto Sandoval, Actor*. Harry Gamboa Jr.
1993. *L.A. Familia*. Harry Gamboa Jr.
1993. *Thanksgiving Day*. Willie Varela.
1994. *Border Swings/Vaivenes fronterizos*. Berta Jottar.
1994. *Fire Ants for Nothing*. Harry Gamboa Jr.
1994. *Loner with a Gun*. Harry Gamboa Jr.
1995. *Straight, No Chaser*. Eugene Rodriguez.
1996. *The Body*. Laura Aguilar.
1996. *Depression*. Laura Aguilar.
1996. *Knife*. Laura Aguilar.
1996. *In Saturn*. Willie Varela.
1997. *St. Francis of Aztlán*. Ramón García and Rita González.

Feature Films

1976. *Please Don't Bury Me Alive/Por Favor, ¡No Me Entierren Vivo!* Efraín Gutiérrez.
1977. *Raíces de Sangre* (Mexico). Jesús Salvador Treviño.
1978. *Amor Chicano Es para Siempre/Chicano Love Is Forever*. Efraín Gutiérrez.
1978. *Only Once in a Lifetime*. Alejandro Grattan and Moctesuma Esparza.
1979. *Run, Tecato, Run*. Efraín Gutiérrez.
1981. *Zoot Suit*. Luis Valdez.
1983. *The Ballad of Gregorio Cortez*. Robert Young and Moctesuma Esparza.
1983. *El Norte*. Gregory Nava.
1984. *Heartbreaker*. Frank Zuniga.
1987. *La Bamba*. Luis Valdez.

1987. *Born in East L.A.* Richard "Cheech" Marin.

1988. *Break of Dawn.* Isaac Artenstein.

1988. *Stand and Deliver.* Ramon Menendez.

1991. *Kiss Me a Killer.* Marcus de Leon.

1992. *American Me.* Edward James Olmos.

1992. *El Mariachi.* Robert Rodriguez.

1992 and 1994. *River Bottom.* Robert Diaz LeRoy.

1994. *. . . and the Earth Did Not Swallow Him.* Severo Pérez and Paul Espinosa.

1994. *A Million to Juan.* Paul Rodriguez.

1995. *Follow Me Home.* Peter Bratt.

1995. *My Family/Mi Familia.* Gregory Nava.

1995. *Painflower.* Fred Garcia.

1996. *The Big Squeeze.* Marcus de Leon.

1996. *Staccato Purr of the Exhaust.* Luis M. Meza.

1997. *Selena.* Gregory Nava and Moctesuma Esparza.

Bibliography

Books

Acosta, Oscar Zeta. *The Revolt of the Cockroach People*. New York: Vintage Books, 1989.

Acuña, Rodolfo. *Occupied America: A History of Chicanos*. 3d ed. New York: Harper Collins, 1988.

Alinsky, Saul D. *Rules for Radicals: A Pragmatic Primer for Realistic Radicals*. New York: Vintage Books, 1989.

Allen, Robert L. *Black Awakening in Capitalist America: An Analytic History*. New York: Doubleday, 1969.

Allport, Gordon. *The Nature of Prejudice*. Cambridge: Addison-Wesley, 1954.

Almaguer, Tomás. *Racial Fault Lines: The Historical Origins of White Supremacy in California*. Berkeley: University of California Press, 1994.

Anaya, Rudolfo A. *Heart of Aztlán*. Berkeley: Editorial Justa Publications, 1976.

————, and Francisco Lomelí, eds. *Aztlán: Essays on the Chicano Homeland*. Albuquerque: Academia/El Norte Publications, 1989.

Anderson, Benedict. *Imagined Communities: Reflections on the Origin and Spread of Nationalism*. 2d ed. New York: Verso, 1991.

Anderson, Christopher. *Hollywood TV: The Studio System in the Fifties*. Austin: University of Texas Press, 1994.

Anzaldúa, Gloria. *Borderlands/La Frontera: The New Mestiza*. San Francisco: Spinsters/ Aunt Lute, 1987.

Arendt, Hannah. *The Human Condition*. Chicago: University of Chicago Press, 1958.

Arnheim, Rudolf. *Film Essays and Criticism*. Translated by Brenda Bentheim. Madison: University of Wisconsin Press, 1977.

Bagdikian, Ben H. *The Media Monopoly*. 5th ed. Boston: Beacon Press, 1997.

Balio, Tino, ed. *Hollywood in the Age of Television*. Boston: Unwin Hyman, 1990.

Barbeleben, Renate, et al., eds. *Missions in Conflict: Essays on U.S.-Mexican Relations and Chicano Culture*. Tübingen: Gunter Narr Verlag, 1986.

Barrera, Mario. *Race and Class in the Southwest: A Theory of Racial Inequality*. Notre Dame: University of Notre Dame Press, 1979.

————. *Beyond Aztlán: Ethnic Autonomy in Comparative Perspective*. Notre Dame: University of Notre Dame Press, 1988.

Berg, Charles Ramírez. *Cinema of Solitude: A Critical Study of Mexican Film, 1967– 1983*. Austin: University of Texas Press, 1992.

Berlin, Isaiah. *The Proper Study of Mankind: An Anthology of Essays*. New York: Farrar, Straus, and Giroux, 1997.

Berumen, Frank Javier Garcia. *The Chicano/Hispanic Image in American Film*. New York: Vantage, 1995.

Boddy, William. *Fifties Television: The Industry and its Critics*. Champaign: University of Illinois Press, 1990.

Branscomb, Anne W., and Maria Savage. *Broadcast Reform at the Crossroads*. Cambridge: Kalba Bowen Associates, 1978.

Broyles-González, Yolanda. *El Teatro Campesino: Theater in the Chicano Movement*. Austin: University of Texas Press, 1994.

Bruce-Novoa, Juan. *Chicano Poetry: A Response to Chaos*. Austin: University of Texas Press, 1982.

———. *Retrospace: Collected Essays on Chicano Literature*. Houston: Arte Público, 1990.

Bullert, B. J. *Public Television: Politics and the Battle over Documentary Film*. New Brunswick: Rutgers University Press, 1997.

Burton, Julianne, ed. *The Social Documentary in Latin America*. Pittsburgh: University of Pittsburgh Press, 1990.

Calavita, Kitty. *Inside the State: The Bracero Program, Immigration, and the I.N.S*. New York: Routledge, 1992.

Caldwell, John Thornton. *Televisuality: Style, Crisis, and Authority in American Television*. New Brunswick: Rutgers University Press, 1995.

Candelaria, Cordelia. *Chicano Poetry: A Critical Introduction*. Westport: Greenwood, 1986.

Chanan, Michael, ed. *Twenty-Five Years of the New Latin American Cinema*. London: British Film Institute and Channel Four Television, 1983.

———. *The Cuban Image: Cinema and Cultural Politics in Cuba*. London: BFI Publishing, 1985.

Chávez, John R. *The Lost Land: The Chicano Image of the Southwest*. Albuquerque: University of New Mexico Press, 1984.

Cole, Barry, and Mal Oettinger. *Reluctant Regulators: The FCC and the Broadcast Audience*. Reading, Mass.: Addison-Wesley, 1978. 204–25.

de Certeau, Michel. *The Writing of History*. Translated by Tom Conley. New York: Columbia University Press, 1988.

de Lauretis, Teresa. *Alice Doesn't: Feminism, Semiotic, Cinema*. Bloomington: Indiana University Press, 1984.

Eliade, Mircea. *Myth and Reality*. New York: Harper & Row, 1963.

Ellis, Jack C. *A History of Film*. 4th ed. Boston: Allyn and Bacon, 1995.

Fish, Stanley E. *Is There a Text in This Class? The Authority of Interpretive Communities*. Cambridge: Harvard University Press, 1980.

Foucault, Michel. *Language, Counter-Memory, Practice: Selected Essays and Interviews*. Edited by Donald F. Bouchard. Translated by Donald F. Bouchard and Sherry Simon. Ithaca: Cornell University Press, 1977.

———. *The History of Sexuality*. Vol. 1: *An Introduction*. Translated by Robert Hurley. New York: Vintage Books, 1978.

Freeman, Jo. *The Politics of Women's Liberation: A Case Study of an Emerging Social Movement and Its Relation to the Policy Process*. New York: David McKay, 1975.

Fregoso, Rosa Linda. *The Bronze Screen: Chicana and Chicano Film Practices*. Minneapolis: University of Minnesota Press, 1993.

Friedman, Lester D., ed. *Unspeakable Images: Ethnicity and the American Cinema*. Urbana: University of Illinois Press, 1991.

Fusco, Coco, ed. *Reviewing Histories: Selections from New Latin American Cinema.* Buffalo: Hallwalls Contemporary Art Center, 1987.

Gamboa Jr., Harry. *Urban Exile: Collected Writings of Harry Gamboa Jr.* Edited by Chon A. Noriega. Minneapolis: University of Minnesota Press, 1998.

García, Mario T. *Mexican Americans: Leadership, Ideology and Identity, 1930–1960.* New Haven: Yale University Press, 1989.

———. *Memories of Chicano History: The Life and Narrative of Bert Corona.* Berkeley: University of California Press, 1994.

Ginzburg, Carlo. *Clues, Myths, and the Historical Method.* Translated by John Tedeschi and Anne Tedeschi. Baltimore: Johns Hopkins University Press, 1989.

Girard, René. *Violence and the Sacred.* Translated by Patrick Gregory. Baltimore: Johns Hopkins University Press, 1977.

Goldman, Shifra M., and Tomás Ybarra-Frausto. *Arte Chicano: A Comprehensive Annotated Bibliography of Chicano Art, 1965–1981.* Berkeley: University of California, Chicano Studies Library Publications Unit, 1985.

Gómez-Peña, Guillermo. *Warrior for Gringostroika: Essays, Performance Texts, and Poetry.* Saint Paul: Graywolf Press, 1993.

———. *The New World Border: Prophecies, Poems, and Loqueras for the End of the Century.* San Francisco: City Lights, 1996.

———, and Jeff Kelley, eds. *The Border Art Workshop: A Documentation of Five Years of Interdisciplinary Art Projects Dealing with U.S.-Mexico Border Issues, 1984– 1989.* New York: Artists Space; La Jolla: Museum of Contemporary Art, 1989.

Gómez-Quiñones, Juan. *Chicano Politics: Reality and Promises, 1940–1990.* Albuquerque: University of New Mexico Press, 1990.

Grebler, Leo, Joan W. Moore, and Ralph C. Guzman. *The Mexican-American People: The Nation's Second Largest Minority.* New York: Free Press, 1970.

Griswold del Castillo, Richard, Teresa McKenna, and Yvonne Yarbro-Bejarano, eds. *Chicano Art: Resistance and Affirmation, 1965–1985.* Los Angeles: UCLA Wight Art Gallery, 1991.

Grundfest, Joseph A. *Citizen Participation in Broadcast Licensing before the FCC.* Santa Monica: Rand, 1976.

Gutiérrez, David G. *Walls and Mirrors: Mexican Americans, Mexican Immigrants, and the Politics of Ethnicity.* Berkeley: University of California Press, 1995.

Gutiérrez-Jones, Carl. *Rethinking the Borderlands: Between Chicano Culture and Legal Discourse.* Berkeley: University of California Press, 1995.

Habermas, Jürgen. *The Structural Transformation of the Public Sphere: An Inquiry into a Category of Bourgeois Society.* Translated by Thomas Burger. Cambridge: MIT Press, 1989.

Hall, John A., and G. John Ikenberry. *The State.* Minneapolis: University of Minnesota Press, 1989.

Hammerback, John C., Richard J. Jensen, and José Angel Gutiérrez. *A War of Words: Chicano Protest in the 1960s and 1970s.* Westport, Conn.: Greenwood, 1985.

Harvey, David. *The Condition of Postmodernity: An Enquiry into the Origins of Cultural Change.* Cambridge: Blackwell, 1990.

Herman, Edward S., and Robert W. McChesney. *The Global Media: The New Missionaries of Corporate Capitalism.* London: Cassell, 1997.

Hernández, Guillermo E. *Chicano Satire: A Study in Literary Culture.* Austin: University of Texas Press, 1991.

Hershfield, Joanne. *Mexican Cinema/Mexican Woman, 1940–1950.* Tucson: University of Arizona Press, 1996.

Hilmes, Michele. *Hollywood and Broadcasting: From Radio to Cable.* Champaign: University of Illinois Press, 1990.

Hobsbawm, E. J., and Terence Ranger, eds. *The Invention of Tradition.* Cambridge: Cambridge University Press, 1983.

Horwitz, Robert Britt. *The Irony of Regulatory Reform: The Deregulation of American Telecommunications.* New York: Oxford University Press, 1989.

Hoynes, William. *Public Television for Sale: Media, the Market, and the Public Sphere.* Boulder: Westview, 1994.

Huerta, Jorge A. *Chicano Theater: Themes and Forms.* Ypsilanti, Mich.: Bilingual Press/ Editorial Bilingüe, 1982.

Huston, Aletha C., et. al. *Big World, Small Screen: The Role of Television in American Society.* Lincoln: University of Nebraska Press, 1992.

Iglesias, Norma. *La Visión de la Frontera a Través del Cine Mexicano.* Tijuana, Baja California: Centro de Estudios Fronterizos del Norte de Mexico, 1985.

————. *Entre Yerba, Polvo, y Plomo: Lo Fronterizo Visto por el Cine Mexicano.* Tijuana, Baja California: El Colegio del la Frontera Norte, 1991.

————, and Rosa Linda Fregoso, eds. *Miradas de Mujer: A Bi-Lingual Anthology of Mexicana-Chicana-Latina Cinema.* Davis: Chicana/Latina Research Center at the University of California, Davis, and Tijuana, Baja California: Colegio de la Frontera Norte, 1998.

James, David E. *Allegories of Cinema: American Film in the Sixties.* Princeton: Princeton University Press, 1989.

Jasper, James M. *The Art of Moral Protest: Culture, Biography, and Creativity in Social Movements.* Chicago: University of Chicago Press, 1997.

Jessop, Bob. *State Theory: Putting Capitalist States in Their Place.* University Park: Pennsylvania State University Press, 1990.

Johnston, Hank, and Bert Klandermans, eds. *Social Movements and Culture.* Minneapolis: University of Minnesota Press, 1995.

Juhasz, Alexandra. *AIDS TV: Identity, Community, and Alternative Video.* Durham, N.C.: Duke University Press, 1995.

Kahin, Brian, and Ernest Wilson, eds. *National Information Infrastructure Initiatives: Vision and Policy Design.* Cambridge: MIT Press, 1997.

Kahin, Brian, and Charles Nesson, eds. *Borders in Cyberspace: Information Policy and the Global Information Infrastructure.* Cambridge: MIT Press, 1997.

Keller, Gary D., ed. *Chicano Cinema: Research, Reviews, and Resources.* Binghamton, N.Y.: Bilingual Review/Press, 1985.

————. *Hispanics and United States Film: An Overview and Handbook.* Tempe: Bilingual Press, 1994.

King, John, Ana M. López, and Manuel Alvarado, eds. *Mediating Two Worlds: Cinematic Encounters in the Americas.* London: British Film Institute, 1993.

Krasnow, Erwin G., Lawrence D. Longley, and Herbert A. Terry. *The Politics of Broadcast Regulation.* 3d ed. New York: St. Martin's, 1982.

Lefebvre, Henri. *The Production of Space.* Translated by Donald Nicholson-Smith. Oxford: Blackwell, 1991.

Leong, Russell, ed. *Moving the Image: Independent Asian Pacific American Media Arts.* Los Angeles: UCLA Asian American Studies Center, 1991.

Lewels, Francisco J., Jr. *The Uses of the Media by the Chicano Movement: A Study in Minority Access.* New York: Praeger Publishers, 1974.

Liebman, Nina C. *Living Room Lectures: The Fifties Family in Film and Television.* Austin: University of Texas Press, 1995.

Limón, José E. *Mexican Ballads, Chicano Poems: History and Influence in Mexican-American Social Poetry*. Berkeley: University of California Press, 1992.

Lipsitz, George. *Time Passages: Collective Memory and American Popular Culture*. Minneapolis: University of Minnesota Press, 1990.

List, Christine. *Chicano Images: Refiguring Ethnicity in Mainstream Film*. New York: Garland, 1996.

Ludwig, Ed, and James Santibañez, eds. *The Chicanos: Mexican American Voices*. Baltimore: Penguin Books, 1971.

Mackenzie, Angus. *Secrets: The CIA's War at Home*. Berkeley: University of California Press, 1997.

Maciel, David R. *El Bandolero, el Pocho, y la Raza: Imágenes Cinematográficas del Chicano*. Cuadernos de Cuadernos, no. 5. México, D.F.: Universidad Nacional Autónoma de México, 1994.

Mangold, Margaret M., ed. *La Causa Chicana: The Movement for Justice*. New York: Family Service Association of America, 1972.

Martin, Michael T., ed. *New Latin American Cinema*. Vol. 1: *Theory, Practices, and Transcontinental Articulations*. Detroit: Wayne State University Press, 1997.

Mattelart, Armand. *Mapping World Communication: War, Progress, Culture*. Translated by Susan Emanuel and James A. Cohen. Minneapolis: University of Minnesota Press, 1994.

Mazón, Mauricio. *The Zoot Suit Riots: The Psychology of Symbolic Annihilation*. Austin: University of Texas Press, 1984.

McChesney, Robert W. *Telecommunications, Mass Media, and Democracy: The Battle for Control of U.S. Broadcasting, 1928–1935*. Oxford: Oxford University Press, 1994.

———. *Corporate Media and the Threat to Democracy*. New York: Seven Stories Press, 1997.

McLuhan, Marshall. *Understanding Media: The Extensions of Man*. Cambridge: MIT Press, 1994.

Meier, Matt S., and Feliciano Ribera. *Mexican Americans/American Mexicans: From Conquistadors to Chicanos*. Rev. ed. New York: Hill and Wang, 1993.

Michaelsen, Scott, and David E. Johnson, eds. *Border Theory: The Limits of Cultural Politics*. Minneapolis: University of Minnesota Press, 1997.

Minow, Newton, and Craig L. Lamay. *Abandoned in the Wasteland: Children, Television, and the First Amendment*. New York: Hill and Wang, 1995.

Montgomery, Kathryn C. *Target: Prime Time: Advocacy Groups and the Struggle over Entertainment Television*. New York: Oxford University Press, 1989.

Moraga, Cherríe. *Loving in the War Years: Lo Que Nunca Pasó por Sus Labios*. Boston: South End, 1983.

———. *The Last Generation: Prose and Poetry*. Boston: South End, 1993.

———, and Gloria Anzaldúa, eds. *This Bridge Called My Back: Writings by Radical Women of Color*. 2d ed. New York: Kitchen Table Press, 1983.

Muñoz, Carlos, Jr. *Youth, Identity, Power: The Chicano Movement*. New York: Verso, 1989.

Negt, Oskar, and Alexander Kluge. *Public Sphere and Experience: Toward an Analysis of the Bourgeois and Proletarian Public Sphere*. Translated by Peter Labanyi, Jamie Owen Daniel, and Assenka Oksiloff. Minneapolis: University of Minnesota Press, 1993.

Nichols, Bill. *Representing Reality: Issues and Concepts in Documentary*. Bloomington: Indiana University Press, 1991.

Nielsen, Waldemar A. *The Big Foundations*. New York: Columbia University Press, 1972.

Noriega, Chon A., ed. *Chicanos and Film: Representation and Resistance*. Minneapolis: University of Minnesota Press, 1992.

————, and Ana M. López, eds. *The Ethnic Eye: Latino Media Arts*. Minneapolis: University of Minnesota Press, 1996.

Ortego, Philip, ed. *The Chicano Literary World: 1974*. Las Vegas: New Mexico Highlands University Press, 1975.

Paredes, Américo. *"With a Pistol in His Hand": A Border Ballad and Its Hero*. Austin: University of Texas Press, 1958.

Paz, Octavio. *The Labyrinth of Solitude*. Translated by Lysander Kemp. New York: Grove Weidenfeld, 1985.

Pérez-Torres, Rafael. *Movements in Chicano Poetry: Against Myths, against Margins*. Cambridge: Cambridge University Press, 1995.

Pettit, Arthur G. *Images of the Mexican American in Fiction and Film*. College Station, Tex.: Texas A&M University Press, 1980.

Pick, Zuzana M. *New Latin American Cinema: A Continental Project*. Austin: University of Texas Press, 1993.

Rich, Adrienne. *The Fact of a Doorframe: Poems Selected and New, 1950–1984*. New York: W.W. Norton, 1984.

Rodriguez, Richard. *Hunger of Memory: The Education of Richard Rodriguez*. New York: Bantam Books, 1982.

Romo, Ricardo. *East Los Angeles: A History of a Barrio*. Austin: University of Texas Press, 1983.

Rosaldo, Renato. *Culture and Truth: The Remaking of Social Analysis*. Boston: Beacon, 1989.

Rosales, F. Arturo. *Chicano! The History of the Mexican American Civil Rights Movement*. Los Angeles: Arte Público, 1996.

Rosen, David. *Off-Hollywood: The Making and Marketing of Independent Films*. Commissioned by the Sundance Institute and Independent Film Project. New York: Grove Weidenfeld, 1990.

Rowbotham, Sheila. *Woman's Consciousness, Man's World*. Harmondsworth: Penguin Books, 1973.

Runes, Dagobert D. *The Dictionary of Philosophy*. 16th ed. New York: Philosophical Library, 1960.

Salazar, Ruben. *Border Correspondent: Selected Writings, 1955–1970*. Edited by Mario T. García. Berkeley: University of California Press, 1995.

Saldívar, José David. *The Dialectics of Our America: Genealogy, Cultural Critique, and Literary History*. Durham, N.C.: Duke University Press, 1991.

Saldívar, Ramón. *Chicano Narrative: The Dialetics of Difference*. Madison: The University of Wisconsin Press, 1990.

Sánchez, George J. *Becoming Mexican American: Ethnicity, Culture and Identity in Chicano Los Angeles, 1900–1945*. New York: Oxford University Press, 1993.

Sayres, Sohnya, et al., eds. *The 60s without Apology*. Minneapolis: University of Minnesota Press, 1984.

Schick, Frank L., and Renee Schick, eds. *Statistical Handbook on U.S. Hispanics*. Phoenix: Onyx, 1991.

Skrentny, John David. *The Ironies of Affirmative Action: Politics, Culture, and Justice in America*. Chicago: University of Chicago Press, 1996.

Slotkin, Richard. *Gunfighter Nation: The Myth of the Frontier in Twentieth-Century America*. New York: HarperPerennial, 1992.

Smith, Christian. *Resisting Reagan: The U.S. Central American Peace Movement.* Chicago: University of Chicago Press, 1996.

Sommers, Joseph, and Tomás Ybarra-Frausto, eds. *Modern Chicano Writers: A Collection of Critical Essays.* Englewood Cliffs, N.J.: Prentice-Hall, 1979.

Sperling Cockcroft, Eva, and Holly Barnet-Sánchez, eds. *Signs from the Heart: California Chicano Murals.* Venice, Calif.: Social and Public Art Resource Center, 1990.

Spigel, Lynn. *Make Room for TV: Television and the Family Ideal in Postwar America.* Chicago: University of Chicago Press, 1992.

Sreberny-Mohammadi, Annabelle, et al., eds. *Media in Global Context: A Reader.* London: Arnold, 1997.

Streeter, Thomas. *Selling the Air: A Critique of the Policy of Commercial Broadcasting in the United States.* Chicago: University of Chicago Press, 1996.

Tarrow, Sidney. *Power in Movement: Social Movements, Collective Action, and Politics.* Cambridge: Cambridge University Press, 1994.

Thompson, E. P. *The Making of the English Working Class.* New York: Vintage Books, 1966.

Toledo, Teresa. *10 Años del Nuevo Cine Latinoamericano.* Madrid: Verdoux, S.L., 1990.

Vasconcelos, José. *The Cosmic Race: A Bilingual Edition.* Translated by Didier T. Jaén. Baltimore: Johns Hopkins University Press, 1997.

Weaver, Warren. *U.S. Philanthropic Foundations: Their History, Structure, Management, and Record.* New York: Harper & Row, 1967.

Wilson, Michael. *Salt of the Earth.* Edited by Deborah Silverton Rosenfelt. Old Westbury, N.Y.: Feminist Press, 1978.

Woll, Allen L., and Randall M. Miller. *Ethnic and Racial Images in American Film and Television: Historical Essays and Bibliography.* New York: Garland, 1987.

Women of the Americas Film and Video Festival. Catalog. Oct. 19–23, 1988. San Francisco: Cine Acción, 1988.

Zheutlin, Barbara, and David Talbot. *Creative Differences: Profiles of Hollywood Dissidents.* Boston: South End, 1978.

Articles

Almaguer, Tomás. "Ideological Distortions in Recent Chicano Historiography: The Internal Model and Chicano Historical Interpretation." *Aztlán: A Journal of Chicano Studies* 18, no. 1 (Spring 1987): 7–28.

Aufderheide, Patricia. "Latin American Cinema and the Rhetoric of Cultural Nationalism: Controversies at Havana in 1987 and 1989." *Quarterly Review of Film and Video* 12, no. 4 (1991): 61–76.

———. "Public Television and the Public Sphere." *Critical Studies in Mass Communication* 8 (1991): 168–83.

Avery, Robert K., and Robert Pepper. "The Evolution of the CPB-PBS Relationship, 1970–1973." *PTR: Public Telecommunications Review* 4, no. 5 (Sept.–Oct. 1976): 6–17.

———. "An Institutional History of Public Broadcasting," *Journal of Communication* 30, no. 3 (Summer 1980): 126–38.

Barrera, Mario, Carlos Muñoz, and Charles Ornelas. "The Barrio as Internal Colony." *Urban Affairs Annual Reviews* 6 (1972): 465–498. Reprinted in *La Causa Política: A Chicano Politics Reader,* edited by F. Chris García. Notre Dame: University of Notre Dame Press, 1974. 281–301.

Berg, Charles Ramírez. "Images and Counterimages of the Hispanic in Hollywood." *Tonantzin* 6, no. 1 (Nov. 1988): 12–13.

———. "Immigrants, Aliens, and Extraterrestrials: Science Fiction's Alien 'Other' as (among Other Things) New Hispanic Imagery." *CineAction!* 18 (Fall 1989): 3–17.

———. "Stereotyping in Films in General and of Hispanics in Particular." *Howard Journal of Communications* 2, no. 3 (Summer 1990): 286–300.

Briegel, Kaye. "The Development of Mexican-American Organizations." In *The Mexican-Americans: An Awakening Minority,* edited by Manuel P. Servín. Beverly Hills: Glencoe, 1970. 160–78.

Brown, Duncan H. "The Academy's Response to the Call for a Marketplace Approach to Broadcast Regulation." *Critical Studies in Mass Communication* 11 (1994): 257–73.

Broyles-Gonzalez, Yolanda. "Women in El Teatro Campesino: '¿Apoco Estaba Molacha la Virgen de Guadalupe?'" In *Chicana Voices: Intersections of Class, Race and Gender,* National Association for Chicano Studies. Austin: CMAS [Center for Mexican American Studies, University of Texas] Publications, 1986. 162–87.

———. "What Price 'Mainstream'? Luis Valdez' Corridos on Stage and Film." *Cultural Studies* 4, no. 3 (Oct. 1990): 281–93.

Bruce-Novoa, Juan. "The Hollywood Americano in Mexico." In *Mexico and the United States: Intercultural Relations in the Humanities,* edited by Juanita Luna Lawhn et al. San Antonio: San Antonio College, 1984. 19–34.

———. "Canonical and Non-Canonical Texts." *Americas Review* 14, no. 3–4 (Fall–Winter 1986): 119–35.

Burton, Julianne. "Marginal Cinemas and Mainstream Critical Theory." *Screen* 26, no. 3 (1985): 2–21.

Candelaria, Cordelia. "La Malinche, Feminist Prototype." *Frontiers* 5, no. 2 (1980): 1–6.

———. "Film Portrayals of la Mujer Hispana." *Agenda: A Journal of Hispanic Issues* 11, no. 3 (May–June 1981): 32–36.

———. "Social Equity in Film Criticism." In *Chicano Images in Film,* edited by Don Cardenas and Suzanne Schneider. Denver: Denver International Film Festival, 1981. Reprinted in Keller, *Chicano Cinema,* 64–70. An earlier version appears as "Perspectives on Social Equity in Film Criticism: With a Look at Images of Chicanas in Film," in *Media and the Humanities,* edited by José Luis Ruiz. Proceedings of the Hispanic Southwest Media Conference, Dec. 4–7, 1980, San Diego, Calif. Unpaginated.

Chabram, Angie. "Chicano Critical Discourse: An Emerging Cultural Practice." *Aztlán: A Journal of Chicano Studies* 18, no. 2 (Fall 1987): 45–90.

Chanan, Michael. "The Changing Geography of Third Cinema." *Screen* 38, no. 4 (Winter 1997): 372–88.

Classen, Steven Douglas. "Standing on Unstable Grounds: A Reexamination of the WLBT-TV Case." *Critical Studies in Mass Communication* 11 (1994): 73–91.

Cortés, Carlos E. *"The Greaser's Revenge* to *Boulevard Nights:* The Mass Media Curriculum on Chicanos." In *History, Culture, and Society: Chicano Studies in the 1980s,* National Association for Chicano Studies. Ypsilanti, Mich.: Bilingual Press/Editorial Bilingue, 1983. 125–40.

———. "The History of Ethnic Images: The Search for a Methodology." *MELUS [Journal of Multi-Ethnic Literature of the United States]* 11, no. 3 (1984): 63–77.

Davies, Catherine. "Modernity, Masculinity, and Imperfect Cinema in Cuba." *Screen* 38, no. 4 (Winter 1997): 345–59.

de la Garza, Rudolph O. "'And Then There Were Some . . .': Chicanos as National Political Actors, 1967–1980." *Aztlan: A Journal of Chicano Studies* 15, no. 1 (Spring 1984): 1–23.

————, and Rowena Rivera. "The Socio-Political World of the Chicano: A Comparative Analysis of Social Scientific and Literary Perspectives." In *Minority Language and Literature: Retrospective and Perspective,* edited by Dexter Fisher. New York: Modern Language Association, 1977. 50–51.

Díaz, Eduardo. "Latino Cinema in the U.S." In *Latin American Visions: Catalogue,* edited by Pat Aufderheide. Philadelphia: Neighborhood Film/Video Project of International House of Philadelphia, 1989. 46–47.

Escobar, Edward J. "The Dialetics of Repression: The Los Angeles Police Department and the Chicano Movement, 1968–1971." *Journal of American History* 79, no. 4 (Mar. 1993): 1483–1514.

Favela, Ramón. "*Entrance Is Not Acceptance:* A Conceptual Installation by Richard Lou and Robert Sanchez." In *Third Newport Biennial: Mapping Histories.* Newport Beach: Newport Harbor Art Museum, 1991. 50–56.

Fisher, Francis D. "What the Coming Telecommunications Infrastructure Could Mean to Our Family." *Aspen Institute Quarterly* 5, no. 1 (Winter 1993): 121–41.

Flores, Juan, and George Yudice. "Living Borders/Buscando America: Languages of Latino Self-Formation." *Social Text: Theory/Culture/Ideology* no. 24 (1990): 57–84.

Fraser, Nancy. "Rethinking the Public Sphere: A Contribution to the Critique of Actually Existing Democracy." In *The Phantom Public Sphere,* edited by Bruce Robbins. Minneapolis: University of Minnesota Press, 1993. 1–32.

Fregoso, Rosa Linda. "La Quinceañera of Chicana Counter Aesthetics." *Centro de Estudios Puertorriqueños Bulletin* 3, no. 1 (Winter 1990–91): 87–91.

————. "Close Encuentro of a First Kind: The Cruzando Fronteras Conference." *Independent* 14, no. 4 (May 1991): 13–16.

————. "The Mother Motif in *La Bamba* and *Boulevard Nights.*" In *Building With Our Hands: New Directions in Chicana Scholarship,* edited by Beatriz M. Pesquera and Adela Ala Torre. Los Angeles: University of California Press, 1993. 130–45.

————. "Sacando los trapos al sol (Airing Dirty Laundry) in Lourdes Portillo's Melodocumentary, *The Devil Never Sleeps.*" In *Redirecting the Gaze: Gender, Theory, and Cinema in the Third World,* edited by Diana Robin and Ira Jaffe. Albany: State University Press of New York, 1990. 307–29.

Fuentes, Víctor. "Luis Valdez: de Delano a Hollywood." *Xalmán* 2 (1979): 7–8.

————. "Luis Valdez, Hollywood, y Tezcatlipoca." *Chiricu* 5, no. 2 (1988): 35–39.

Fusco, Coco. "Fantasies of Oppositionality: Reflections on Recent Conferences in Boston and New York." *Screen* 29 (Autumn 1988): 80–93.

————. "Ethnicity, Politics and Poetics: Latinos and Media Art." In *Illuminating Video: An Essential Guide to Video Art,* edited by Doug Hall and Sally Jo Fifer. New York: Aperture/BAVC, 1990. 304–16.

García, Alma M. "The Development of Chicana Feminist Discourse, 1970–1980." *Gender and Society* 3, no. 2 (June 1989): 217–38.

Gómez-Peña, Guillermo. "The Multicultural Paradigm: An Open Letter to the National Arts Community." *High Performance* 12, no. 3 (Fall 1989): 18–27.

————. "Death on the Border: A Eulogy to Border Art." *High Performance* 14, no. 1 (Spring 1991): 8–9.

Greenberg, Bradley S., and Pilar Baptista-Fernandez. "Hispanic-Americans: The New Minority on Television." In *Life on Television: Content Analysis of U.S. TV Drama,* edited by Bradley S. Greenberg. Norwood, N.J.: Ablex, 1980. 3–12.

Gutiérrez, Armando, and Herbert Hirsch. "The Militant Challenge to the American Ethos: 'Chicanos' and 'Mexican Americans.'" *Social Science Quarterly* 53, no. 4 (Mar. 1973): 830–45.

Gutiérrez, Félix. "Advertising and the Growth of Minority Markets and Media." *Journal of Communication Inquiry* 14, no. 1 (Winter 1990): 6–16.

Gutiérrez, Ramón. "Community, Patriarchy, and Individualism: The Politics of Chicano History and the Dream of Equality." *American Quarterly* 45, no. 1 (Mar. 1993): 44–72.

Haight, Timothy R., and Laurie R. Weinstein. "Changing Ideology on Television by Changing Telecommunications Policy: Notes on a Contradictory Situation." In *Communication and Social Structure: Critical Studies in Mass Media Research,* edited by Emile G. McAnany, Jorge Schnitman, and Noreene Janus. New York: Praeger Publishers, 1981. 110–44.

Iglesias, Norma. "El Desarrollo del Cine Fronterizo: Análisis de los Últimos Tres Sexenios." In *Frontera Norte: Chicanos, Pachucos, y Cholos,* edited by Hernández Palacíos and Juan Manuel Sandoval. México, D.F.: Ancien Régime, 1989. 501–24.

Jenkins, J. Craig. "Social Movements, Political Representation, and the State: An Agenda and Comparative Framework." In *The Politics of Social Protest: Comparative Perspectives on States and Social Movements,* edited by J. Craig Jenkins and Bert Klandermans. Minneapolis: University of Minnesota Press, 1995. 14–35.

Jiménez, Lillian. "From the Margin to the Center: Puerto Rican Cinema in New York." *Centro de Estudios Puertorriqueños Bulletin* 2, no. 8 (Spring 1990): 28–43.

Kanellos, Nicolás. "Folklore in Chicano Theater and Chicano Theater in Folklore." In *The Chicano Experience,* edited by Stanley A. West and June Macklin. Boulder: Westview, 1979. 165–89.

Keller, Kent R. "The Law of Administrative Standing and the Public Right of Intervention." *Federal Communications Bar Journal* 21, no. 3 (1967): 134–61.

Kotz, Liz. "Unofficial Stories: Documentaries by Latinas and Latin American Women." *Centro de Estudios Puertorriqueños Bulletin* 2, no. 8 (Spring 1990): 58–69.

Laclau, Ernesto. "Universalism, Particularism, and the Question of Identity." *October* 61 (Summer 1992): 83–90.

Lamb, Blaine P. "The Convenient Villain: The Early Cinema Views the Mexican-American." *Journal of the West* 14, no. 4 (Oct. 1975): 75–81.

Lashner, Marilyn A. "The Role of Foundation in Public Broadcasting, Part I: Developments and Trends." *Journal of Broadcasting* 20, no. 4 (Fall 1976): 529–47.

———. "The Role of Foundation in Public Broadcasting, Part II: The Ford Foundation." *Journal of Broadcasting* 21, no. 2 (Spring 1977): 235–54.

Lewels, Francisco J. "Racism in the Media: Perpetuating the Stereotype." *Agenda: A Journal of Hispanic Issues* 8, no. 1 (1978): 4–6.

Limón, José E. "Stereotyping and Chicano Resistance: An Historical Dimension." *Aztlan: International Journal of Chicano Studies Research* 4, no. 2 (Fall 1973): 257–70. Reprinted in Noriega, *Chicanos and Film.* 3–17.

———. "The Folk Performance of 'Chicano' and the Cultural Limits of Political Ideology." In *And Other Neighborly Names: Social Process and Cultural Image in Texas Folklore,* edited by Richard Bauman and Roger D. Abrahams. Austin: University of Texas Press, 1981. 197–225.

———. *Mexican Ballads, Chicano Epic: History, Social Dramas and Poetic Persuasions.* SCCR Working Paper Series no. 14. Stanford: Stanford Center for Chicano Research, 1986.

———. *The Return of the Mexican Ballad: Américo Paredes and His Anthropological Text as Persuasive Political Performance.* SCCR Working Paper Series no. 16. Stanford: Stanford Center for Chicano Research, 1986.

List, Christine. "El Norte: Ideology and Immigration." *Jump Cut* 34 (Mar. 1989): 27–31.

Lloyd, Rees, and Peter Montague. "Ford and La Raza: 'They Stole Our Land and Gave Us Powdered Milk.'" *Ramparts* (Sept. 1970): 10–18.

López, Ana M. "The Melodrama in Latin America: Films, Telenovelas, and the Currency of a Popular Form." *Wide Angle* 7, no. 3 (1985): 9.

———. "An 'Other' History: The New Latin American Cinema." In *Resisting Images: Essays on Cinema and History,* edited by Robert Sklar and Charles Musser. Philadelphia: Temple University Press, 1990. 308–30.

———. "Setting Up the Stage: A Decade of Latin American Film Scholarship." *Quarterly Review of Film and Video* 13, no. 1–3 (1991): 239–60.

———. "Are All Latins from Manhattan?: Hollywood, Ethnography, and Cultural Colonialism." In *Unspeakable Images: Ethnicity and the American Cinema,* edited by Lester D. Friedman. Urbana: University of Illinois Press, 1991. 404–24.

Macias, Reynaldo, and Roberto Cabello Argondoñia. "Media Research and the Chicano." *Latin Quarter* 1, no. 2 (Oct. 1974): 14–18.

Maciel, David R. "Braceros, Mojados, and Alambristas: Mexican Immigration to the United States in Contemporary Cinema." *Hispanic Journal of Behavioral Sciences* 8, no. 4 (1986): 369–85.

———. "The Celluloid Frontier: The U.S.-Mexico Border in Contemporary Cinema, 1970–1988." *Renato Rosaldo Lecture Series,* Monograph 5, ser. 1987–88 (1989): 1–34.

———. "Cine Chicano: Proceso y Florecimiento, Primera Parte." *Dicine* 32 (Jan. 1990): 16–17.

———. "Cine Chicano: Proceso y Florecimiento, Segunda Parte." *Dicine* 33 (Mar. 1990): 16–17.

———. "Cine Chicano: Proceso y Florecimiento, Tercera Parte." *Dicine* 34 (May 1990): 13–16.

———. "Cine Chicano: Proceso y Florecimiento, Cuarta Parte." *Dicine* 35 (July 1990): 12–13.

Martin, Laura. "Language Form and Language Function in *Zoot Suit* and *The Border:* A Contribution to the Analysis of the Role of Foreign Language in Film." *Studies in Latin American Popular Culture* 3 (1984): 57–69.

Martínez, Eliud. "*I Am Joaquin* as Poem and Film: Two Modes of Chicano Expression." *Journal of Popular Culture* 13, no. 3 (Spring 1980): 505–15.

Martínez, Manuel L. "'With Imperious Eye': Kerouac, Burroughs, and Ginsberg on the Road in South America." *Aztlán: A Journal of Chicano Studies* 23, no. 1 (Spring 1998): 33–53.

Masilela, Ntongela. "The Los Angeles School of Black Filmmakers." In *Black American Cinema,* edited by Manthia Diawara. New York: Routledge, 1993. 107–17.

McComb, Don. Introduction. Special issue, *Minority Images in Advertising. Journal of Communication Inquiry* 14, no. 1 (Winter 1990): 3–5.

Mosco, Vincent. "Toward a Theory of the State and Telecommunications Policy." *Journal of Communication* 38, no. 1 (Winter 1988): 107–24.

———. "The Mythology of Telecommunications Deregulation." *Journal of Communication* 40, no. 1 (Winter 1990): 36–49.

Newman, Kathleen. "Steadfast Love and Subversive Acts: The Politics of *La Ofrenda: The Days of the Dead.*" *Spectator* 13, no. 1 (Fall 1992): 98–109.

———. "Nation and Virgin as Great Performances in El Teatro Campesino's *La Pastorela: A Shepherds' Tale* (1991)." *Jump Cut* 38 (June 1993): 87–91.

Noriega, Chon A. "Chicano Cinema and the Horizon of Expectations: A Discursive

Analysis of Recent Film Reviews in the Mainstream, Alternative and Hispanic Press." *Aztlán: A Journal of Chicano Studies* 19, no. 2 (Fall 1988–90): 1–32.

———. "Citizen Chicano: The Trials and Titillations of Ethnicity in the American Cinema, 1935–1962." *Social Research: An International Quarterly of the Social Sciences* 58, no. 2 (Summer 1991): 413–38.

———. "El Hilo Latino: Representation, Identity, and National Culture." *Jump Cut* 38 (June 1993): 45–50.

———. "The Numbers Game." *Jump Cut* 39 (June 1994): 107–11.

———. "'Waas Sappening?': Narrative Structure and Iconography in *Born in East L.A.*" *Studies in Latin American Popular Culture* 14 (1995): 107–28.

———. "Talking Heads, Body Politic: The Plural Self of Chicano Experimental Video." In *Resolutions: Contemporary Video Practices,* edited by Michael Renov and Erika Suderburg. Minneapolis: University of Minnesota Press, 1995. 207–28.

———. "The Aztlán Film Institute's Top 100 List." *Aztlán: A Journal of Chicano Studies* 23, no. 2 (Fall 1998): 1–9.

O'Connor, Karen, and Lee Epstein. "A Legal Voice for the Chicano Community: The Activities of the Mexican American Legal Defense and Education Fund, 1968–82." *Social Science Quarterly* 65, no. 2 (June 1984): 245–56.

Ortega, Joe. "The Privately Funded Legal Aid Office: The MALDEF Experience." *Chicano Law Review* 1, no. 1 (Summer 1972): 80–84.

Pepper, Robert. "The Interconnection Connection: The Formation of PBS." *PTR: Public Telecommunications Review* 4, no. 1 (Jan.–Feb. 1976): 6–26.

Powers, Lloyd D. "Chicano Rhetoric: Some Basic Concepts." *Southern Speech Communication Journal* 38 (Summer 1973): 340–46.

Pratt, Mary Louise. "'Yo Soy La Malinche': Chicana Writers and the Poetics of Ethnonationalism." *Callaloo* 16, no. 4 (1993): 859–73.

Rich, B. Ruby. "Another View of New Latin American Cinema." *IRIS: A Journal of Theory on Image and Sound* no. 13 (Summer 1991): 5–28. [Special issue on Latin American cinema.]

Rodríguez, América. "Objectivity and Ethnicity in the Production of the *Noticiero Univisión.*" *Critical Studies in Mass Communication* 13 (1996): 59–81.

———. "Racialization, Language, and Class in the Construction and Sale of the Hispanic Audience." In *Reflexiones 1997: New Directions in Mexican American Studies,* edited by Neil Foley. Austin: CMAS Books, 1998. 29–51.

Rosen, David, and Nancy Sher. "Independent Features: Foundation Support for Narrative Films." *Benton Foundation Bulletin* 4 (May 1990).

Rowland, William D., Jr. "The Illusion of Fulfillment: The Broadcast Reform Movement." *Journalism Monographs* 79 (Dec. 1982): 1–41.

———. "Continuing Crisis in Public Broadcasting: A History of Disenfranchisement." *Journal of Broadcasting and Electronic Media* 30, no. 3 (Summer 1986): 251–74.

Saalfield, Catherine, and Ray Navarro. "Not Just Black and White: AIDS Media and People of Color." *Centro de Estudios Puertorriqueños Bulletin* 2, no. 8 (Spring 1990): 70–78.

Saragoza, Alex M. "Recent Chicano Historiography: An Interpretive Essay." *Aztlán: A Journal of Chicano Studies* 19, no. 1 (Spring 1988–90): 1–78. An earlier version appears in *Ethnic Affairs* 1, no. 1 (Fall 1987): 24–62.

Schement, Jorge Reina, and Félix Frank Gutiérrez, with Oscar Gandy, Tim Haight, and M. Esteban Soriano. "The Anatomy of a License Challenge." *Journal of Communication* 27, no. 1 (Winter 1977): 89–94.

Sedano, Michael Victor. "Chicanismo: A Rhetorical Analysis of Themes and Images of

Selected Poetry from the Chicano Movement." *Western Journal of Speech Communication* 44 (Summer 1980): 177–90.

Solorzano, Daniel G. "Teaching and Social Change: Reflections on a Freirian Approach in a College Classroom." *Teaching Sociology* 17 (Apr. 1989): 218–25.

Subervi-Vélez, Federico A., et al. "Mass Communication and Hispanics." In *Handbook of Hispanic Cultures in the United States: Sociology,* edited by Félix Padilla. Houston: Arte Público, 1994. 334–50.

Tajima, Renee. "Ethno-Communications: The Film School Program That Changed the Color of Independent Filmmaking." In *The Anthology of Asian Pacific American Film and Video,* edited by Renee Tajima. New York: Third World Newsreel, 1985. 38–42.

———, and Tracey Willard. "Nothing Lights a Fire like a Dream Deferred." *Independent* (Nov. 1984): 18–21.

Taylor, Clyde. "The L.A. Rebellion: A Turning Point in Black Cinema." *The New American Filmmakers Series* 26. New York: Whitney Museum of American Art, 1986.

———. "The L.A. Rebellion: New Spirit in American Film." *Black Film Review* 2 (1986): 2.

Ulmer, Gregory. "The Puncept in Grammatology." In *On Puns,* edited by Jonathan Culler. Oxford: Blackwell, 1988. 164–89.

Vigil, Maurilio. "The Ethnic Organization as an Instrument of Political and Social Change: MALDEF, a Case Study." *Journal of Ethnic Studies* 18, no. 1 (Spring 1990): 15–31.

Whitney, John. "Image Making in the Land of Fantasy." *Agenda: A Journal of Hispanic Issues* 8, no. 1 (Jan.-Feb. 1978): 7–11.

Willeman, Paul. "The Third Cinema Question." *Framework* 34 (1987): 4–38.

Yarbro-Bejarano, Yvonne. "From *Acto* to *Mito*: A Critical Appraisal of the Teatro Campesino." In Sommers and Tomás Ybarra-Frausto, *Modern Chicano Writers: A Collection of Critical Essays.* Englewood Cliffs, N.J.: Prentice-Hall, 1979. 176–85.

Ybarra-Frausto, Tomás. "The Chicano Movement and the Emergence of a Chicano Poetic Consciousness." *New Scholar* 6 (1977): 81–109.

———. "The Chicano Alternative Film Movement: Interview." *Centro de Estudios Puertorriqueños Bulletin* 2, no. 8 (Spring 1990): 44–47.

———. "Rasquachismo: A Chicano Sensibility." In *Chicano Art: Resistance and Affirmation, 1965–1985,* edited by Richard Griswold del Castillo, Teresa McKenna, and Yvonne Yarbro Bejarano. Los Angeles: Wight Art Gallery/UCLA, 1991. 155–62.

Zavella, Patricia. "Feminist Insider Dilemmas: Constructing Ethnic Identity with 'Chicana' Informants." *Frontiers* 13, no. 3 (1993): 53–76.

Theses and Dissertations

Barrera, Aida Nydia. "Multiculturalism before Its Time: The Making of *Carrascolendas*." Ph.D. diss., University of Texas, 1992.

Classen, Steven Douglas. "Broadcast Law and Segregation: A Social History of the WLBT-TV Case." Ph.D. diss., University of Wisconsin, 1995.

Kosiba-Vargas, S. Zaneta. "Harry Gamboa and Asco: The Emergence and Development of a Chicano Art Group, 1971–1987." Ph.D. diss., University of Michigan, 1988.

List, Christine. "Chicano Images: Strategies for Ethnic Self-Representation in Mainstream Cinema." Ph.D. diss., Northwestern University, 1991.

Rosen, Daniel Allan. "Mexican-Americans and the Broadcast Media: A Study of San Antonio's Bilingual Bicultural Coalition on Mass Media." Master's thesis. University of Texas, 1976.

Stanford, Monty Carlis. "On Predicting the Effects of a Bilingual Children's Educational Television Program." Ph.D. diss., University of Texas, 1973.
van Thillo, Ethan. "A Guide to Understanding Chicano Cinema and Organizing a Chicano Film Festival." Senior thesis, University of California, Santa Cruz, 1992.

Primary Sources

Books and Pamphlets

Cardenas, Don, and Suzanne Schneider, eds. *Chicano Images in Film*. Denver: Denver International Film Festival, 1981.
Cine-Aztlán. *La Raza Film Bibliography*. Santa Barbara: Cine-Aztlán, 1974.
Cranston, Alan, and Alan Piper. *Foundations on Trial*. New York: Council on Foundations, 1970.
Gang Exploitation Film Committee. *A Reader and Information Packet on the "Gang Exploitation Films."* Monterey Park, Calif.: East Los Angeles College M.E.Ch.A., 1979.
Gonzales, Rodolfo "Corky." *I Am Joaquin*. New York: Bantam Books, 1972.
Gutiérrez, José Angel. *A Gringo Manual on How to Handle Mexicans*. Crystal City, Tex.: Wintergarden, 1974.
Hojas de Cine: Testimonios y Documentos del Nuevo Cine Latinoamericano. México: Fundación del Nuevo Cinema Latinoamericano, 1986.
Johnson, Nicholas. *How to Talk Back to Your Television Set*. Boston: Little, Brown, 1969.
Marshall, Wes, et al. *Fiesta: Minority Television Programming*. Tucson: University of Arizona Press, 1974.
Rendon, Armando B. *Chicano Manifesto*. New York: Macmillan, 1971.
———, and Domingo Nick Reyes. *Chicanos and the Mass Media*. Washington, D.C.: National Mexican-American Anti-Defamation Committee, 1971.
Ruiz, José Luis, ed. *Media and the Humanities*. Proceedings of the Hispanic Southwest Regional Conference, San Diego, Calif. Dec. 4–7, 1980.
Valdez, Luis. *Pensamiento Serpentino: A Chicano Approach to the Theater of Reality*. San Juan Bautista, Calif.: Cucaracha Publications, 1973.
———. *Luis Valdez, Early Works*. Houston: Arte Público, 1990.
———. *"Zoot Suit" and Other Plays*. Houston: Arte Público, 1992.
———, and Stan Steiner, eds. *Aztlán: An Anthology of Mexican American Literature*. New York: Alfred A. Knopf, 1972.
Vidal, Mirta. *Chicanas Speak Out: Women, New Voice of La Raza*. New York: Pathfinder, 1971.
Williams, Frederick, and Geraldine Van Wart. *Carrascolendas: Bilingual Education through Television*. New York: Praeger Publishers, 1974.

Articles

Aceves Madrid, Vincente. "The Controversy Surrounding NBC's 'Chico and the Man.'" *Latin Quarter* 1, no. 2 (Oct. 1974): 5–7.
Aguilar, Linda. "Unequal Opportunity and the Chicana." *Civil Rights Digest* (Spring 1973): 31–33.
"¡Ahora!" Program guide, KCET/Channel 28, 6, no. 8 (Aug. 1969): 6–7.
"¡Ahora!" Program guide, KCET/Channel 28, 6, no. 9 (Sept. 1969): 2–3.
Alinsky, Marvin. "The Mexican-Americans Make Themselves Heard." *Reporter*, Feb. 9, 1967, 45–48.
"Alternative Cinema Conference." *Chicano Cinema Newsletter* 1, no. 3 (May 1979): 1.
"América de los Indios." *Gambit* [program guide, KCET/Channel 28] (Sept. 1972): 6.

"An Overcrowded Winners' Circle?" *Broadcasting,* May 15, 1972, 27.

"Andrade Jailed on Bomb Charge." *Los Angeles Herald-Examiner,* July 11, 1972.

"Andrade Hearing Is Set." *Los Angeles Herald-Examiner,* July 13, 1972.

"Anti-Defamation Group Fights Ads Using Spanish Name Stereotypes." *Advertising Age,* Sept. 30, 1968, 94.

Arias, Ron. "Getting on the Set." *Nuestro: The Magazine for Latinos* 1, no. 7 (Oct. 1977): 18–21.

"As We See It." *TV Guide,* Oct. 5, 1968, 5.

Aufderheide, Patricia. "Latins, Exiles, U.S. Chicanos Attend Havana's Film Fest." *Variety,* Dec. 19, 1979.

"Authorizations Tied to Improved EEO Efforts." *CPB Report: The Newsletter of the Corporation for Public Broadcasting* 8, no. 9 (May 2, 1977): 1.

Avila, Alex. "Trading Punches: Spanish-Language Television Pounds the Competition in the Fight for Hispanic Advertising Dollars." *Hispanic* (Jan.–Feb. 1997): 39–40, 42, 44.

"Ban the Bandito?" *Newsweek,* Dec. 22, 1969, 82, 86.

Barrera, Aida. "Carrascolendas." *PTR: Public Telecommunications Review* 4, no. 4 (July–Aug. 1976): 20–24.

Barrios, Gregg. "Efraín Gutiérrez y el Nuevo Cine Chicano." *La Opinión,* Aug. 18, 1985, La Comunidad, 3.

———. "And the Earth Did Not Swallow This Film Project." *Los Angeles Times,* Mar. 10, 1994.

Baxter, Kevin. "Latin America Looks to Miami, Not Hollywood, for Music, Film." *Los Angeles Times,* Aug., 26, 1998.

———. "Spanish-Language Networks Seek Wider Niche." *Los Angeles Times,* Sept. 21, 1998.

———. "As Telemundo Turns." *Los Angeles Times,* Dec. 20, 1998, Calendar section.

———. "Groups Voice Concern over Funding for Latino Programming." *Los Angeles Times,* Jan. 30, 1999.

Bedell, Sally. "A Generation without Cultural Hangups." *TV Guide,* May 21, 1977: 37–40.

Bedford, Karen Everhart. "Out of Cash and under Scrutiny, Latino Center Closes." *Current,* Mar. 16, 1998.

———. "CPB Finds Fault in Latino Consortium Spending Practices." *Current,* May 4, 1998.

———. "Olmos Will Head Interim Latino TV Grantmaking." *Current,* Nov. 23, 1998.

Benavidez, Max. "Latino Dada: Savage Satire from Harry Gamboa Jr." *L.A. Weekly,* May 16–22, 1986, unpaginated.

Benson, Jim. "NHMC Fights B'Casters: Claims Hispanics Underemployed at TV Stations." *Variety,* June 15, 1993, 5, 43.

"Bill Dana Defends 'Jellow Pages' Spots." *Advertising Age,* Sept. 30, 1968, 94.

Braxton, Greg. "Networks, Studios Won't Discuss Minority Reports." *Los Angeles Times,* June 17, 1993.

———. "TV Executives Give Mixed Report on Minority Hiring." *Los Angeles Times,* June 18, 1993, B1, B4.

———. "TV Stations Have Muted Response to Investigation." *Los Angeles Times,* Mar. 18, 1994.

———. "KCBS to Establish Minority Employee Panel." *Los Angeles Times,* Mar. 19, 1994.

———. "Latinos to Press for Boycott of ABC-TV." *Los Angeles Times,* Jan. 13, 1995.

————. "Latinos Protest at ABC Stations." *Los Angeles Times* Apr. 27, 1995.

————. "Cancellations Upset Minority Groups." *Los Angeles Times,* May 17, 1995.

————. "U.S. to Examine Hiring of Minorities in Entertainment." *Los Angeles Times,* Feb. 22, 1996.

————. "Latinos on TV: Mixed Findings, Progress." *Los Angeles Times,* Apr. 16, 1996.

————. "Latino-Based Sitcom Seen as Partial Win." *Los Angeles Times,* May 22, 1996.

————. "Molina Joins in Protest over Alleged Disney Discrimination." *Los Angeles Times,* June 27, 1997.

————. "Latinos Split over Disney's Motivations." *Los Angeles Times,* Dec. 13, 1997.

————. "Latino Public TV Program Developer Shuts Its Doors." *Los Angeles Times,* Mar. 13, 1998.

————. "Olmos-Led Group to Help Develop Latino TV Projects." *Los Angeles Times,* Nov. 18, 1998.

————, and Jan Breslauer. "Casting the Spotlight on TV's Brownout." *Los Angeles Times,* Mar. 5, 1995, Calendar.

Brinsley, John H. "Chico and the Man." Letter to the editor. *Los Angeles Times,* Nov. 18, 1974.

Brown, Les. "Broadcasters at Convention Strike Back at Activist Critics." *New York Times,* Mar. 19, 1974.

Burke, Vincent J. "Film and TV Minority Job Plan in Effect." *Los Angeles Times,* Apr. 1, 1970. Reprinted as "New Movie, TV Plan Bans Job Bias," *Washington Post,* Apr. 1, 1970.

Camplis, Francisco X. "Towards the Development of a Raza Cinema." In *Perspectives on Chicano Education,* edited by Tobias Gonzales and Sandra Gonzales. Stanford: Chicano Fellows/Stanford University, 1975. 155–73. Reprinted in Noriega, *Chicanos and Film,* 284–302. An excerpted version appears in *Tin Tan* 2, no. 5 (June 1977): 5–7.

Campo, Ken. "NLCC Launches Distribution Division." *NLCC News* (Fall 1996): 3.

"'Canción de la Raza/Song of the People.'" Program guide, KCET/Channel 28, 5, no. 10 (Oct. 1968): 2–4.

"'Canción de la Raza': A Song of Success." Program guide, KCET/Channel 28, 6, no. 3 (Mar. 1969): 6–7.

Cantu, Tony. "The Adventures of Super Latino." Interview with Henry Cisneros. *Hispanic* (Apr. 1997): 18–20, 22, 24.

"Capitol Hill Tells CPB to Shape Up Minority Records or Money May Be Difficult to Get." *Broadcasting,* Feb. 14, 1977, 58.

"Catchword in California Renewals: Minorities." *Broadcasting,* Nov. 8, 1971, 42–43.

"CCC Meets AFI." *Chicano Cinema Newsletter* 1, no. 2 (Feb. 1979): 2.

Cerone, Daniel. "TV Heats Up the Leftovers: Unaired Episodes on Summer Lineup." *Los Angeles Times,* June 10, 1992.

————. "TV Not Representative of Society, Study Finds." *Los Angeles Times,* June 16, 1993.

"Challengers Seek Station Figures." *Broadcasting,* July 26, 1971, 21–22.

"Charges Untrue, WOAI-TV Answers." *Broadcasting,* Sept. 6, 1971, 32.

Chavez, Jennie V. "Women of the Mexican-American Movement." *Mademoiselle,* Apr. 1972, 82, 150–52.

"Chicanos List 'Grievances,' Issue Ultimatum to Px, TV." *Daily Variety,* Oct. 9, 1970, 1, 6.

"Chicanos' Question: What about Us?" *Broadcasting,* June 28, 1971, 23.

Chinea-Varela, Migdia. "Platform: Second-Class Writers." *Los Angeles Times,* Oct. 20, 1994.

"Coast One of Richest Spanish Markets." *Broadcasting,* Sept. 19, 1966, 77–83.
Coe, Steve. "Networks Test Development Alternatives." *Broadcasting,* Mar. 9, 1992, 21.
"Crowd Outside Awards Was Scant but Very Enthusiastic." *Daily Variety,* Apr. 15, 1969, 17.
Crowe, Jerry. "Latinos to Stern: Apology Is Not Accepted." *Los Angeles Times,* Apr. 11, 1995.
"D-Day Approaches for California Stations." *Broadcasting,* Nov. 1, 1971, 26–28.
de Beky, Hernan. "Spanish TV Needs to Open Up." *Los Angeles Times,* Mar. 24, 1995.
"Declaración del Comité de Cineasta de América Latina." *Cine Cubano* 8, no. 3 (1977–78): 45–46. Reprinted in *Cinéaste* 9, no. 1 (Fall 1978): 54. Translated by Ralph Cook.
Delaney, Paul. "Major Moviemakers Agree to a Fair-Hiring Plan." *New York Times,* Apr. 1, 1970.
Delgado, Sylvia. "Chicana: The Forgotten Woman." *Regeneración* 2, no. 1 (1971): 2–4.
del Olmo, Frank. "Acción Chicano." *Gambit* [program guide, KCET/Channel 28] 10, no. 11 (Nov. 1973): 28–29.
———. "El Mito de la Unidad Hispana." *La Opinión,* May 29, 1989.
———. "TV Dispute Sheds Light on the 'Hispanic' Myth." *Los Angeles Times,* May 29, 1989.
———. "La Diversidad Latina y el Mito de la Unidad." *La Opinión,* June 11, 1989.
"Diverse Appeals to D.C. Court." *Broadcasting,* July 3, 1972, 25.
Doss, Yvette C. "Network TV: Latinos Need Not Apply." *Frontera* 1, no. 2 (1996): 20–21, 43.
———. "A Spanish-Language TV Network Tries Bilingualism." *Los Angeles Times,* Nov. 11, 1997.
Drummond, William J. "The Death of a Man in the Middle: A Requiem for Ruben Salazar." *Esquire,* Apr. 1972, 74–81.
Duane, Frank. "A People and a Program." In *Broadcasting and Social Action: A Handbook for Station Executives.* Washington, D.C.: National Association of Educational Broadcasters, 1969. 33–35.
Du Brow, Rick. "Portrayals of Latinos on TV Regressing." *Los Angeles Times,* Sept. 7, 1994.
———. "Latino Roles Still 'Mired in Stereotypes.'" *Los Angeles Times,* Oct. 1, 1994.
Edwards, Bill. "Chicanos Picket Academy Awards." *Daily Variety,* Apr. 8, 1970, 1, 8.
"8 Challenged Stations Win Renewals from FCC." *Broadcasting,* Jan. 1, 1973, 6.
Eiselein, E. B., and Wes Marshall. "'Fiesta': An Experiment in Minority Audience Research and Programming." *Educational Television* (Feb. 1971): 11–15.
———. "Mexican-American Television: Applied Anthropology and Public Television." *Human Organization* 35, no. 2 (Summer 1976): 147–56.
Eiselein, E. B. "Television and the Mexican-American." *PTR: Public Telecommunications Review* 2, no. 1 (Feb. 1974): 13–18.
"El Mexicano through the Eyes of the Gavacho." *La Raza* 1, no. 4 (June 1971): 23–24.
"Enter the Alianza in Renewal Attacks." *Broadcasting,* Aug. 23, 1971, 34–35.
Epstein, Marcelo. "Film and Industry." *Chismearte* 1, no. 2 (Winter–Spring 1977): 25.
"ESAA Funding of Bilingual Programming." *PTR: Public Telecommunications Review,* 4, no. 4 (July–Aug. 1976): 25.
Esparza, Elia. "The Telemundo Takeover: Can a Corporate Coup Save the Embattled Network?" *Hispanic* (Jan.–Feb. 1998): 19, 22, 24.
———. "Must Sí TV: Galavisión and Producer Jeff Valdez Go Bilingual." *Hispanic* (May 1998): 20–27.

Espinosa-Larsen, Anita. "Machismo: Another View." *La Luz* 1, no. 4 (Aug. 1972): 59.

"Ethnic Dispute in San Antonio." *Broadcasting,* July 5, 1971, 49–50.

"Ethnic Groups Seek Ban of Slurs on TV." *New York Times,* July 15, 1968.

"Face of Prime Time TV Is Still White." *Variety,* June 21, 1993, 4.

Farhi, Paul. "FCC Probes Discrimination Charges against Advertisers." *Los Angeles Times,* Aug. 21, 1998.

Farr, William. "Militant Chicano Faces Three Felony Charges in Bomb Cases." *Los Angeles Times,* July 12, 1972.

"FCC Crackdown on Job Bias." *Daily Variety,* Aug. 2, 1972.

"FCC Rejects Challenges in San Antonio, Buffalo." *Broadcasting,* Nov. 27, 1972, 8–9.

"FCC Urges New Rules for Broadcaster Hiring," *Los Angeles Times,* Nov. 20, 1998.

"Feedback for Mexican Americans." Program guide, KCET/Channel 28, 5, no. 7 (July 1968): 4.

"Fifth Albuquerque Station Hit by Denial Petition." *Broadcasting,* Oct. 11, 1971, 51–52.

"Film Guilds Air Needs of Chicanos." *Los Angeles Times,* Oct. 16, 1970.

"Film Guilds Vow Aid for Chicano Image." *New York Times,* Aug. 28, 1970.

"Film Studios Flunk Hiring Quiz; Send Untutored, Don't Know 'Voices.'" *Daily Variety,* Mar. 19, 1969, 17.

Flores, Art. "The '¡Ahora!' Synthesis." Program guide, KCET/Channel 28, 7, no. 2 (Feb. 1970): 14–15.

Flores, Francisca. "Comisión Feminil Mexicana." *Regeneración* 2, no. 1 (1971): 6–8.

———. "Equality." *Regeneración* 2, no. 3 (1973): 4–5.

"400 Media Activists Meet at Alternative Cinema Conference." *Jump Cut* 21 (Nov. 1979): 31–38.

Fowler, Mark S., and Daniel L. Brenner. "A Marketplace Approach to Broadcast Regulation." *Texas Law Review* 60 (1982): 207–57.

"Frito Bandito Is Still Around." Editorial. *Advertising Age,* Jan. 11, 1971, 10. Reprinted in *Regeneración* 1, no. 9 (1970): 20.

Gallo, William. "Chicano Filmmakers Strike Vivid Spark of Life." *Rocky Mountain News,* Jan. 18, 1980.

Gamboa Jr., Harry. "Silver Screening the Barrio." *Equal Opportunity Forum* 6. no. 1 (Nov. 1978): 6–7.

———. "Harry Gamboa Jr.: No Movie Maker." Interview by Marisela Norte. *El Tecolote* (San Francisco Mission District), n.d. [c. 1983]: 3 ff.

"Ganging Up." *Broadcasting,* Aug. 30, 1971, 7.

Garcia, Guy. "Tropical Tycoon: Nely Galán—Television is Finally Targeting the Huge Latino Viewership, and She's Leading the Charge." *New York Times Magazine,* Dec. 11, 1994.

García, Margaret. "A Review of the 4th Annual Chicano Film Festival" *De Colores* 5, no. 1–2 (1980): 133–35.

Garcia, R. Hunter "'Chicano!'" *Hollywood Reporter,* Apr. 12–14, 1996, 16, 33.

García Torres, José. "José García Torres and *Realidades.*" Interview by Aurora Flores and Lillian Jiménez. *Centro de Estudios Puertorriqueños Bulletin* 2, no. 8 (Spring 1990): 31–43.

Garza, Sabino, Efraín Gutiérrez, and Juan Garza. "Película." *Caracol* (Nov. 1974): 8–10.

Gellene, Denise. "In Their Own Images: TV Ad Seeks to Broaden the Public's View of Latinos." *Los Angeles Times,* Apr. 2, 1998.

Gonzales, Rodolfo "Corky." "Chicano Nationalism: The Key to Unity for la Raza." *Militant,* Mar. 30, 1970.

Gonzales, Steve. "The Advertisement." *El Grito* 1, no. 1 (Fall 1967): 12–13.

Guernica, Antonio José. "Las Realidades de Raquel Ortiz: An Interview with a Latina Television Producer." *Agenda: A Journal of Hispanic Issues* 7, no. 4 (July–Aug. 1976): 40–41.

———. "The Development of the National Latino Media Coalition." *Agenda: A Journal of Hispanic Issues* 7, no. 4 (July–Aug. 1976): 29–31.

———. "The Public Airwaves: Who Owns Them?" *Agenda: A Journal of Hispanic Issues* 7, no. 2 (Mar.–Apr., 1977): 39–40, 42.

———. "Cable Television: The Medium for Hispanics?" *Agenda: A Journal of Hispanic Issues* 7, no. 3 (May–June 1977): 25–27.

———. "Chicano Group to Get Its Own TV Station." *Agenda: A Journal of Hispanic Issues* 7, no. 6 (Nov.–Dec. 1977): 28–30.

———. "Chicano Production Companies: Projecting Reality, Opening the Doors." *Agenda: A Journal of Hispanic Issues* 8, no. 1 (Jan.–Feb. 1978): 12–15.

"Half the Latin Market Is in Southwest." *Broadcasting,* Sept. 19, 1966, 74–77.

"Hard Bargains for KQEO Too." *Broadcasting,* Nov. 29, 1971, 58, 60.

Haubegger, Christy. "TV Shows and Advertisers Are Overlooking the Latino Market." *Los Angeles Times,* June 29, 1998.

"Hispanic Org Mulls Protest." *Variety,* Aug. 3, 1995, 4.

Hix, Sid. Cartoon with Frito Bandito character. *Broadcasting,* Mar. 23, 1970, 80.

"I Am Joaquin." *La Raza,* Sept. 16, 1967, 4.

"Inch by Inch, FCC Moves Ahead on Renewal Cases." *Broadcasting,* Nov. 13, 1972, 25.

"Inside Channel 28: '¡Ahora!'" Program guide, KCET/Channel 28, 6, no. 5 (May 1969): 10.

Johansen, Jason C. "Notes on Chicano Cinema." *Chicano Cinema Newsletter* 1, no. 4 (June 1979): 6–8. Reprinted in *La Opinión,* Nov. 16, 1980, cultural supplement, 3–4; *Jump Cut* 23 (Oct. 1980): 9–10; and Noriega, *Chicanos and Film,* 303–7.

———. "El Cine Chicano: Una Breve Reseña." In *Hojas de Cine: Testimonios y Documentos del Nuevo Cine Latinoamericano.* Fundación del Nuevo Cine Latinoamericano. México: n.p., 1986. Unpaginated.

Jones, Jack. "U.S. Board to Ask Suit Charging Film Job Bias." *Los Angeles Times,* Mar. 14, 1969.

"Justicia, Nosotros Iron Out Differences for Bowl Bash." *Daily Variety,* Aug. 6, 1971, 19.

"Justicia Now Moves against NBC-TV." *Broadcasting,* Aug. 2, 1971, 38.

"Justicia o Muerte." *La Raza* 1, no. 8 (Apr. 1972): 14.

Kaufman, Dave. "2-Mil. Mexicans Can't Be Conned, Says Martell; Also-Angry Negro Actors Copping Latin Roles." *Daily Variety,* Sept. 25, 1968, 17.

———. "Mexamericans Prep Boycott despite AMPTP." *Daily Variety,* Sept. 27, 1968, 1, 6.

———. "U.S. Equal Opportunity Commission Puts Network TV Coast Execs on Hot Seat Re Jobs for Minorities." *Daily Variety,* Mar. 19, 1969, 78.

———. "EEOC Brushed Off One IA Union: Costumers Local 20% Minorities." *Daily Variety,* Mar. 20, 1969, 1, 8.

———. "'Chico' Associate Producer Andrade Unhappy over Show's Chicano Image." *Daily Variety,* Sept. 19, 1974, 7.

"KEST Strikes Bargain with Citizen Group." *Broadcasting,* Mar. 13, 1972, 42.

Kilday, Gregg. "The Chicano: His Past and Present." *Los Angeles Times,* Aug. 10, 1972.

"Latino Coalition Resigns from CPB Advisory Council." *Access* 44 (Oct. 26, 1976): 3.

"Latinos and CPB: In Quest of National Programming." *Chicano Cinema Newsletter* 1, no. 6 (Aug. 1979): 2–3.

Lenti, Paul. "Broad U.S. Presence at Havana's New Latino Fest." *Variety,* Dec. 23, 1987, 5.

Leovy, Jill. "Latino Group to Launch Disney Boycott." *Los Angeles Times,* Apr. 24, 1997.

Levine, Frank. "Spanish-Lingo Broadcasting Booms, with Visions of a 'Fourth Network,' but Barrios Still to Be Hurdled." *Daily Variety,* Aug. 9, 1972, 35.

Loper, James L., Art Seidenbaum, and Cecil Smith. "The KCET Story: Reminiscences of the First Ten Years." *Gambit* [program guide, KCET/Channel 28] (Oct. 1974): 20–24.

López Oliva, M. "Proyección Chicana en *Raíces de Sangre.*" *Cine Cubano* 100 (1981): 75–80.

"The Los Angeles Chicano Cinema Coalition: Statement of Purpose." *Chicano Cinema Newsletter* 1, no. 2 (Feb. 1979): 8.

Los Angeles Hispanic Urban Center. "Under Fire: Chico and the Man." *Los Angeles Times,* Sept. 30, 1974.

Marguilies, Lee, ed. "The Proliferation of Pressure Groups in Primetime." *Emmy* 3, no. 3 (Summer 1981): A1–32.

———. "National Survey Shows Most Latino Listeners Are Bilingual." *Los Angeles Times,* Nov. 8, 1997.

Martinez, Max. "¡No Me Entierren Vivo!/Please Don't Bury Me Alive!" *Caracol* (May 1976): 15.

Martinez, Thomas M. "Advertising and Racism: The Case of the Mexican-American." *El Grito* 2, no. 4 (Summer 1969): 3–13; Reprinted as "How Advertisers Promote Racism." *Civil Rights Digest* 2, no. 4 (Fall 1969): 5–11; and "The Profit of Advertising: Racism." *La Raza* 1, no. 4 (June 1971): 27–31.

———, and José Peralez. "Chicanos and the Motion Picture Industry." *La Raza* 1, no. 5 (1971): 60–64.

Matzer, Marla. "Ads Not Reaching Latinos, Publisher Says." *Los Angeles Times,* July 23, 1998.

"McGraw-Hill Sets Record for Concessions to Minorities." *Broadcasting,* May 15, 1972, 25–27.

Mejia, Victor. "Sony Introduces Telemundo's New Management." *Hispanic* (Oct. 1998): 16.

"Mexican-Americans Assail Commercials." *New York Times,* Dec. 10, 1969.

"Mexican-Americans Seek New Film, TV Image." *Los Angeles Herald-Examiner,* Oct. 10, 1970.

"Mexican Outlets Beam to States." *Broadcasting,* Sept. 19, 1966, 83–84.

"Mexicans' Defenders Err." Editorial. *Advertising Age,* Mar. 16, 1970, 24.

Michaelson, Judith. "KCET Breaks With History to Fund 'Chicano!' Series." *Los Angeles Times,* Sept. 9, 1995.

———. "The Chicano Rallying Cry." *Los Angeles Times,* Apr. 7, 1996. Calendar.

"'Midnight Cowboy' Gets Oscar; Wayne and Maggie Smith Win." *New York Times,* Apr. 8, 1970.

Miller, Stuart. "Hispanics Conspicuous in Census, But Missing in Prime." *Variety,* Oct. 7, 1991, 4, 37.

"Million Dollar Four Acquitted: Courts Admit to Bias Against Chicanos in Jury Selection." *La Raza* 1, no. 11 (July 1973): 32–33.

"Minorities Gang Up in Albuquerque." *Broadcasting,* Sept. 6, 1971, 33–34.

Molina de Pick, Gracia. "Reflexiones Sobre el Feminismo y la Raza." *La Luz* 1, no. 4 (Aug. 1972): 58.

Montoya, José. "Thoughts on la cultural: The Media, Con Safos, and Survival." *Caracol* 5, no. 9 (May 1979): 6–8, 19.

Morales, Sylvia. "Filming a Chicana Documentary." *Somos* 2, no. 5 (June 1979): 42–45. Reprinted in Noriega, *Chicanos and Film,* 308–11.

Moreno, Ed. "Canción de la Raza." Program guide, KCET/Channel 28, 6, no. 1 (Jan. 1969): 6–7.

———. "The Spanish Language Market: Promises, Premises, and Possibilities." In *Broadcasting and Social Action: A Handbook for Station Executives.* Washington, D.C.: National Association of Educational Broadcasters, 1969. 41–45.

Morton, Carlos. "Why There Are No Chicano Filmmakers: Plática de José Luis Seda y Antonio Ogaz." *Caracol* 2, no. 11 (July 1976): 18–19, 5, 16.

Muñoz, Sergio, ed. "Cine Chicano Primer Acercamiento" In *La Opinión,* Nov. 16, 1980, cultural supplement [special section on Chicano cinema].

———. "¿La TV en Español Sufre un Proceso de Cubanización?" *La Opinión,* May 10, 1989.

———. "Miami y Los Angeles, Dos Ciudades Incomparables." *La Opinión,* May 11, 1989.

———. "Crónica de un Despido Anunciado." *La Opinión,* June 9, 1989.

Murray, Kathleen. "Banging the Drums as Spanish TV Comes of Age." *New York Times,* Apr. 10, 1994.

"The Name's Familiar: Ed Moreno." *Gambit* [program guide, KCET/Channel 28] 10, no. 12 (Dec. 1973): 34.

"National Latino Media Coalition (NLMC): A Progress Report." *Reporte.* Newsletter of the Texas Chicano Coalition on Mass Media. 1, no. 1 (Feb. 1977): 5–6.

Navarro, Bob. "Mi Experiencia en KVEA TV." *La Opinión,* June 16, 1989.

Navarro, Ray. " 'Eso, Me Está Pasando.' " *Tonantzin* 7, no. 1 (Jan.–Feb. 1990): 17. Reprinted in Noriega, *Chicanos and Film,* 312–15.

"NBC Answers Chicano Beefs on Portrayals." *Daily Variety,* Aug. 4, 1971, 2.

"New Deal in Dallas–Fort Worth." *Broadcasting* July 12, 1971, 33, 36. [Text missing in the original.]

"New Mexican-American Series Debuts." *Gambit* [program guide, KCET/Channel 28] 9, no. 12 (Dec. 1972): 7.

"Nielsen Launches Spanish Ratings." *Variety,* Oct. 26, 1992: 26.

Nuiry, Octavio E., and Alex Avila. "Hall of Shame." *Hispanic* (July 1996): 30–31.

Obledo, Mario G. "Mexican Americans and the Media." In *La Causa Chicana: The Movement for Justice,* edited by Margaret M. Mangold. New York: Family Service Association of America, 1972. 6–16.

———, and Robert B. Joselow. "Broadcasting: Mexican-Americans and the Media." *Chicano Law Review* 1, no. 1 (Summer 1972): 85–98.

Olivares, Jaime. "Piden Aclaraciones a Telemundo: Coalición Nacional Hispana Desea Discutir Problemas Surgidos en KVEA." *La Opinión,* May 11, 1989.

"Open Season on Texas Stations." *Broadcasting,* Aug. 9, 1971, 19–20.

Ordoñez, Elizabeth J. "La Imagen de la Mujer en el Nuevo Cine Chicano." *Caracol* 5, no. 2 (Oct. 1978): 12–13.

O'Steen, Kathleen. "White Male Pens Still Busiest: Study Finds H'wood Lags in Hiring Minority, Female Writers." *Variety,* June 15, 1993, 1, 42.

———. "TV Distorts Minorities, Study Finds." *Variety,* June 16, 1993, 1, 40.

———. "Guild Study Finds TV Bias." *Variety,* June 28, 1993, 37.

Páramo, Bobby. "*Cerco Blanco, The Balloon Man,* and *Fighting City Hall:* On Being a Chicano Filmmaker." *Metamorfosis* 3, no. 2 (1980–81): 77–82.

Parra, José Antonio. "Bilingual Programming for Latinos: The Media's Missing Link?" *PTR: Public Telecommunications Review* 4, no. 4 (July–Aug. 1976): 14–18.

Payan, Victor. " 'Listen to Your Own Voice': An Interview with Native American Independent Filmmaker, Sandra Osawa." In *Cine Estudiantil 97.* San Diego: Centro Cultural de la Raza, 1997. 5–6.

Peña-Sarmiento, Sandra. "Pocha Manifesto #1." *Jump Cut* 39 (June 1994): 105–6.

Portillo, Lourdes. "On Chicanas and Filmmaking: A Commentary." In *Chicana (W)rites on Word and Film,* edited by María Herrera-Sobek and Helena María Viramontes. Berkeley: Third Woman Press, 1995. 279–82.

Potes, Clara Inés. "Levin da Su Versión sobre Cambios en el Equipo Noticioso de Canal 52." *La Opinión,* June 1, 1989.

———. "Grupos Mexicoamericanos Protestan Cambios en Equipo Noticioso de Canal 52." *La Opinión,* June 6, 1989.

Pristin, Terry. "'Substantial Barriers' to Minority Writers, Survey Finds." *Los Angeles Times,* June 15, 1993.

"Prophecy Fulfilled," *Hispanic* (Dec. 1998): 14.

"Public Broadcasting Authorization Process." *CPB Report: The Newsletter of the Corporation for Public Broadcasting* 8, no. 9 (May 2, 1977): 2.

Puig, Claudia. "Latino Writers Form Group to Fight Stereotypes." *Los Angeles Times,* Aug. 10, 1989.

———. "Study No Surprise to Latinos." *Los Angeles Times,* Sept. 8, 1994.

———. "New Focus for Telemundo." *Los Angeles Times,* June 3, 1995.

Raspberry, William. "How About Frito Amigo?" *Washington Post,* June 2, 1971.

———. "Who's the Real Bandito?" *Washington Post,* June 7, 1971.

"Rated X: Racist Films." *La Raza* 1, no. 7 (Jan. 1972): 57.

Reed, Roy. "Movies Face U.S. Suits on Hiring Bias." *New York Times,* Mar. 14, 1969.

"Renewal Battles in the Rockies." *Broadcasting,* Mar. 8, 1971.

Reyes, David. "Seasoned Activist's Passions Burn Bright Again." *Los Angeles Times,* Aug. 2, 1998.

Reyes, Domingo Nick. "Anti-Defamation Committee Says Media Do Not Depict Mexican Americans Fairly." *TV Code News* 3, no. 12 (Feb. 1971): 2.

"Reyes to Throw Down Gauntlet in Washington." *Broadcasting,* Apr. 24, 1972, 8, 12.

Rivas, Monica. "NLCC Out of Cash—Shuts Down Operations." *Nosotros News* (1998 collector's edition): 51.

Rivera, Miluka. "When Will TV Reflect Latino Audience?" *Los Angeles Times,* Dec. 12, 1994.

———. "Film and TV Perpetuate Invisibility." *Hispanic* (June 1996): 12–13.

Rivera, Umberto. "Film Notes." *Chismearte* 1, no. 2 (Winter–Spring 1977): 20–24.

Robb, David. "WGAW: Minorities 'Typecast': Modest Gains Said Overshadowed by 'Little If Any Access.'" *Hollywood Reporter,* June 15, 1993, 1, 12, 14.

———. "Kids TV Gets Worst Marks on Minority Images." *Hollywood Reporter,* June 16, 1993, 1, 8, 33.

———. "Doors Creaking Open to Latinos." *Hollywood Reporter,* Dec. 30, 1993–Jan. 2, 1994, 1, 6, 18.

Rodriguez, Roberto. "Media Report." *Hispanic Link Weekly Report* (June 4, 1990): 8.

Rosenberg, Howard. "Eyes on the 'Chicano!' Prize." *Los Angeles Times,* Apr. 12, 1996.

Royko, Mike. "Mexicans Fix Admen's Clock." *Chicago Daily News,* June 9, 1970.

Ruiz, José Luis. "Future of NLCC: New Directions." *NLCC News* (Fall 1996): 1.

Saenz, Rita, one of three personal statements in "Toward One Nation, Indivisible; or, 'Getting It Together Again.'" *Gambit* [program guide, KCET/Channel 28] 7, no. 8 (Aug. 1970): 7.

Salazar, Ruben. "Gilbert Roland Raps Films Portraying Mexicans as Foolish." *Los Angeles Times,* Mar. 14, 1969.

———. "Chicanos Would Find Identity before Coalition with Blacks." *Los Angeles Times,* Feb. 20, 1970. Reprinted in Salazar, *Border Correspondent,* 239–41.

"San Antonio Bell Unit Criticized for 'Jellow Pages' Ads." *Advertising Age,* Aug. 5, 1968, 4.

Sanders, Steve. "Two National Hispanic Media Organizations File for Divorce." *Hollywood Reporter,* Jan. 19, 1989, 3, 50.

Santisteban, Ray. "Notes on the Hows and Whys of Latino Film Festivals." *AHA! Hispanic Art News* 167 (July–Aug. 1998): 12.

Shiver Jr., Jube. "Digital TV May Squelch Minority-Owned Stations." *Los Angeles Times,* June 10, 1998.

"Signs of Changing Times in Renewals." *Broadcasting,* May 17, 1971, 34–35.

"6 Chicanos File Complaint with FCC re KVOU 'Unresponsiveness' to Needs." *Daily Variety,* Oct. 7, 1970, 37.

"$610,000,000 Suit: The National Mexican American Anti-Defamation Committee." *La Raza* 1, no. 4 (June 1971): 26.

Smith, Cecil. "'Yo Soy' Captures the Chicano Soul." *Los Angeles Times,* Aug. 17, 1972.

———. "Chico and the Man: A Hit in Spite of the Controversy." *Los Angeles Times,* Nov. 10, 1974, TV Times.

Smith, James F. "Two Mexican Networks in Pitched Battle for Markets." *Los Angeles Times,* Aug. 23, 1998.

Snow, Shauna. "Morning Report: Latino Training Program Dropped." *Los Angeles Times,* May 2, 1995.

———. "Morning Report: ABC Versus Latinos." *Los Angeles Times,* May 9, 1995.

———. "Morning Report: For Latino Writers." *Los Angeles Times,* June 13, 1995.

———. "Morning Report: KCAL Protest." *Los Angeles Times,* Aug. 3, 1996.

———. "Morning Report: Boycotting ABC, Disney." *Los Angeles Times,* Apr. 25, 1997.

———. "Morning Report: Mickey's Defense." *Los Angeles Times,* June 28, 1997.

———. "Morning Report: Latinos and Disney." *Los Angeles Times,* July 26, 1997.

———. "Morning Report: Telethon Results." *Los Angeles Times,* Sept. 12, 1995.

———. "Morning Report." *Los Angeles Times,* Nov. 17, 1998.

"Spanish Americans Hit 'Derogatory' Stereotypes in Ads." *Advertising Age,* May 19, 1969, 112.

"Spanish Market: Undersold, Undervalued." *Broadcasting,* Sept. 19, 1966, 67–68, 70.

"Stage and Screen: Struggles Behind the Scenes." *Nuestro: The Magazine for Latinos* 3, no. 3 (Apr. 1979): 19–20.

Stalter, Katharine. "Latinos in Television." *Film and Video* (July 1993): 70–78.

Stewart, Jill. "Whoa, Nely!" *Buzz* (June–July 1995): 80–83, 116.

Taylor, Clyde. "Special Report—Cuba: A Festival." *Chamba Notes: A Media Newsletter* (Summer 1980): 1–3.

Tebble, John. "Newest TV Boom: Spanish-Language Stations." *Saturday Review,* June 8, 1968, 70–71.

Thackery, Ted, Jr. "John Wayne and Maggie Smith; 'Midnight Cowboy' Top Picture." *Los Angeles Times,* Apr. 8, 1970.

Thomas, Kevin. "'The Earth' Revolves around a Moving Spiritual Odyssey." *Los Angeles Times,* May 5, 1994.

"Time to Answer Frito Bandito? Mexican-American Groups to Seek Fairness Ruling on Frito-Lay Commercials." *Broadcasting,* Dec. 15, 1969, 37, 40.

"Time's $69-Million Sale Clears FCC." *Broadcasting,* Mar. 13, 1972, 32.

"'Tio Taco is Dead.'" *Newsweek,* June 29, 1970, 22–28.

Torres, Luis R. "Hollywood and the Homeboys: The Studios Discover Barrio Gangs." *Nuestro* 3, no. 3 (Apr. 1979): 27–30.

———. "Distortions in Celluloid: Hispanics and Film." *Agenda: A Journal of Hispanic Issues* 11, no. 3 (May–June 1981): 37–40.

———. "The Chicano Image in Film." *Caminos* 3, no. 10 (Nov. 1982): 8–11 ff.

Treviño, Jesús Salvador. "Jesús S. Treviño Habla para Cine Cubano: Entrevista." *Cine Cubano* 83 (1977–1978): 11–16.

———. "The Mural That Whitewash Could Not Destroy." *Nuestro* (Feb. 1978): 50, 52.

———. "Mirando Hacia America Latina: Entrevista." *Cine Cubano* 94 (1979): 5–10.

———. "Alternative Cinema Conference: Optimism, Realistic Expectations." *Chicano Cinema Newsletter* 1, no. 4 (June 1979): 1.

———. "Cinéma Chicano aux États-Unis." In *Les Cinémas de l'Amérique Latine*, edited by Guy Hennebelle and Alfonso Gumucio-Dagron. Paris: Nouvelles Éditions Pierre Lherminier, 1981. 493–99.

———. "Chicano Cinema." *New Scholar* 8 (1982): 167–80.

———, ed. "Feature Section on Chicano Films." *Caminos* 3, no. 10 (Nov. 1982): 6–20.

———. "Latinos and Public Broadcasting: The 2% Factor." *Jump Cut* 28 (1983): 65.

———. "Presencia del Cine Chicano." In *A Traves de la Frontera*. Mexico, D.F.: Centro de Estudios Económicos y Sociales del Tercer Mundo, A.C., and Instituto de Investigaciones Estéticas de la U.N.A.M., Aug. 1983. 194–201.

———. "Chicano Cinema Overview." *Areíto* 37 (1984): 40–43.

———. "Latino Portrayals in Film and Television." *Jump Cut* 30 (Mar. 1985): 14–16.

———. "El Desarrollo del Cine Chicano." In *Hojas de Cine: Testimonios y Documentos del Nuevo Cine Latinoamericano*, edited by Fundación del Nuevo Cine Latinoamericano. México, 1986. Unpaginated.

———. "Latinos Are Imprisoned by TV's Color Barrier, Too." *Los Angeles Times*, June 15, 1992.

———. "Lights, Camera, Action." *Hispanic* (Aug. 1992): 76.

"12,000 Potential Chicano Employes." *Broadcasting*, Aug. 30, 1971, 26.

"U.S. Latins on the March." *Newsweek*, May 23, 1966, 32–36.

Valdez, Luis. "'Yo Soy Chicano': An Appreciation." *Gambit* [program guide, KCET/Channel 28] 9, no. 8 (Aug. 1972): 5.

———. Interview. "An Artist Who Has Blended Art and Politics." *El Tecolote* (Oct. 1987): 9 ff.

Valle, Victor. "Ethnic Fight Heats Up at Latino Station." *Los Angeles Times*, May 19, 1989.

———. "KVEA Shakeup Fuels Debate at Latino Station." *Los Angeles Times*, June 2, 1989.

———. "Shake-Up at Latino Station Sparks Protest." *Los Angeles Times*, June 6, 1989.

———. "Community Coalition Threats Compromise KVEA's Future." *Los Angeles Times*, June 30, 1989.

Vasquez, Richard. "Jose Jimenez 'Dies'—and Pride Lives." *Los Angeles Times*, Apr. 5, 1970.

———. "Chicano Protest on Movie Image Backed by Guild." *Los Angeles Times*, Aug. 27, 1970.

Vasquez, Victor. "More on 'Chicano and the Man.'" *Latin Quarter* (Jan.–Feb. 1975): 13–15.

———. "Who's behind Chico and the Man?" Interview with James Komack. KPFK, 1975. 61 minutes. Pacifica Radio Archive, North Hollywood, Calif.

Vega, Patricia. "Chicanos 90." *La Jornada* (Mexico, D.F.), Feb. 9, 1990, 33.

———. "El Movimiento Chicano Tiene Una Meta: Poner Su Cultura en el Centro de EU." *La Jornada* (Mexico, D.F.), Feb. 11, 1990, 29.

Villalpando, Rosa María. "Grupos Mexicoamericanos Acusan al Canal 52 de Desdeñar a Su Auditorio." *La Opinión,* June 15, 1989.
———. "Gerente del Canal 34 Achaca a la Prensa Versión de 'Cubanización,' de la T.V." *La Opinión,* June 21, 1989.
Waters, Harry F. "Hot Hungarican." *Newsweek,* Nov. 11, 1974, 74–75.
———. "TV: Do Minorities Rule?" *Newsweek,* June 2, 1975, 78–79.
———. "The New Voice of America." *Newsweek,* June 12, 1989, 54–58.
Wentworth, Eric. "Bilingual TV Funds Resumed Cautiously." *Washington Post,* July 3, 1973.
"Where, May We Ask, Was the FCC?" *Consumer Reports,* Jan. 1960, 9–11.
Witty, Susan. "The Citizens Movement Takes a Turn." *Channels* (June–July 1981): 68–73.
"'Yo Soy Chicano': Past and Present Mingle in this Dramatic New Portrayal of the Chicano Experience." *Gambit* [program guide, KCET/Channel 28] 9, no. 8 (Aug. 1972): 4.
Zamora, Del. "Where Are the Latinos in Films, TV?" *Los Angeles Times,* May 20, 1996.
Zeidenberg, Leonard. "The Struggle over Broadcast Access." *Broadcasting,* Sept. 20, 1971, 32–43.
———. "The Struggle Over Broadcast Access (II)." *Broadcasting,* Sept. 27, 1971, 24–29.

Media Reports

Adams, Don, and Arlene Goldbard. *Cultural Diversity in Public Broadcasting.* A discussion paper prepared for the National Asian American Telecommunications Association. Oct. 19, 1989.
Affirmative Action Plan. Washington, D.C.: Corporation for Public Broadcasting, 1975.
Astor, Gerald. *Minorities and the Media.* A Ford Foundation Report. Nov. 1974.
Carnegie Commission on Educational Television. *Public Television: A Program for Action.* New York: Harper & Row, 1967.
Chester, Jeffrey, and Kathryn Montgomery. "Media in Transition: Independents and the Future of Television." *NVR Reports* no. 10 (Nov. 1992).
Final Report and Recommendations of the Task Force on National Minority Programming. Sponsored by the National Asian American Telecommunications Association, with the cooperation of the Latino Consortium and the Native American Public Broadcasting Consortium. Funded by a grant from the Corporation for Public Broadcasting. Submitted Dec. 15, 1989.
The Future of Communications Policy in the New Technological Environment. Proceedings of sessions held in June and Nov. 1992 by Grantmakers in Film, Television, and Video, an affinity group of the Council on Foundations.
Lichter, S. Robert, and Daniel R. Amundson. "Distorted Reality: Hispanic Characters in TV Entertainment." Center for Media and Public Affairs. Funded by a grant from the National Council of La Raza. Sept. 1, 1994.
Valdez, Armando. "A Study of Multicultural Content in Selected Public Television Series." Study commissioned by the National Latino Communications Center. June 1990.
———. "A Framework for Multicultural Programming: Considerations on Independent Productions and Public Television." Concept paper for the Independent Television Service (ITVS). Feb. 1991.
———. "The Development of a National Information Infrastructure and its Implications for Latinos." *CLPP Policy Profile* 2, no. 3 (1995).
Valenzuela, Nicholas A. *Media Habits and Attitudes of Mexican-Americans: Surveys in Austin and San Antonio.* Austin: Center for Communication Research at the University of Texas, June 1973.

Valenzuela, Nicholas A. *Public Television and the Mexican-American Audience in the Southwest.* CPB/OCR Report 214. Washington, D.C.: Corporation for Public Broadcasting, Office of Communication Research, Jan. 1974.

Williams, Frederick, Nicholas A. Valenzuela, and Pamela Knight. *Prediction of Mexican-Americans' Communication Habits and Attitudes.* Austin: Center for Communication Research, University of Texas, June 1973.

Witherspoon, John, and Roselle Kovitz. *The History of Public Broadcasting.* Washington, D.C.: Corporation for Public Broadcasting, 1987. Report originally published in *Current.*

Press Releases and Newsletters

Chicano Cinema Coalition. "*Boulevard Nights* Statement." Press release (Mar. 23, 1979).

———. "Statement on *Act of Violence* and *Streets of L.A.*" Press release (Nov. 15, 1979).

Chicano Cinema Newsletter 1, no. 1 (Dec. 1978). Newsletter of the Chicano Cinema Coalition, Los Angeles.

Chicano Cinema Newsletter 2, no. 4 (Apr. 1980). Newsletter of the Chicano Cinema Coalition, Los Angeles.

Chicano! TV Series Newsletter 1, no. 1 (Summer 1992). Newsletter from the National Latino Communications Center.

Chicano! History of the Mexican American Civil Rights Movement no. 1 (Feb. 1996) and no. 2 (Mar. 1996). Newsletter from the National Latino Communications Center.

Cine Acción News 1, no. 1 (Apr. 1984–present). Newsletter of Cine Acción, a national Latino media arts center based in San Francisco.

Emancipation Arts (Spring 1980). Newsletter for Emancipation Arts, Inc., a multiracial production company in Los Angeles.

"'L.A. Collective' to Cover La Raza Unida Party." Press release (draft; n.d.). 2 pages. KCET-TV, Los Angeles.

"La Raza Unida." Press release (n.d.). 1 page. KCET-TV, Los Angeles.

NLCC Newsletter no. 1 (Fall 1992). Newsletter of the National Latino Communications Center.

NLCC Newsletter no. 2 (Spring 1993). Newsletter of the National Latino Communications Center.

Reporte (Apr. 1978). Newsletter of the Texas Chicano Coalition on Mass Media.

"'El Teatro Campesino' Showcased on KNBC Ethnic Special." Press release. KNBC Press and Publicity (Nov. 29, 1972). 2 pages.

Tierra Newsletter (May 1992), KPBS-TV, San Diego State University; Press package for *. . . and the Earth Did Not Swallow Him,* KPBS-TV, San Diego State University (n.d., c. 1995).

Treviño, Jesús Salvador. "Chicano Filmic Art." KCET News. Press release for *Yo Soy Chicano* (July 24, 1972).

Government Publications

California Advisory Committee to the U.S. Commission on Civil Rights. *Behind the Scenes: Equal Opportunity on the Motion Picture Industry.* Washington, D.C.: U.S. Government Printing Office, 1978.

Community Relations Service. *1968 Annual Report.* Washington, D.C.: U.S. Department of Justice, 1968.

———. *1969 Annual Report.* Washington, D.C.: U.S. Department of Justice, 1969.

———. *1970 Annual Report.* Washington, D.C.: U.S. Department of Justice, 1970.

Corporation for Public Broadcasting. *Reaching Common Ground: Public Broadcasting's*

Services to Minority Groups and Other Groups. A Report to the 103d Congress and the American People Pursuant to Pub. L. 100–626. July 1, 1994.

Corporation for Public Broadcasting Office of Inspector General. *Operation Audit of the National Latino Communications Center.* Audit report no. 98–02. Mar. 31, 1998.

Federal Communications Commission. *Decisions and Reports of the Federal Communications Commission of the United States.* May 29–July 17, 1970. Vol. 23. 2d ser. Washington, D.C.: U.S. Government Printing Office, 1971.

Report of the National Advisory Commission on Civil Disorders. Otto Kerner, Chairman. New York: Bantam Books, 1968.

United States of America, *Code of Federal Regulations* 47 Telecommunication, Parts 70–79, revised as of Oct. 1, 1975. Washington, D.C.: U.S. Government Printing Office, 1975.

United States of America, *Congressional Record,* Proceedings and Debates of the 90th Congress, 2d sess. Vol. 114, part 14, June 19–26, 1968.

Rep. Henry B. González: "Why Must There Be Hunger?" (18472–18473); vol. 114, part 17, July 17–23, 1968: "Hunger in America?" (22738–22739); vol. 114, part 19, July 31–Sept. 4, 1968: "Hunger in America?" (24432–24435); vol. 114, part 20, Sept. 5–16, 1968: "Hunger in America?" (26625–26626); vol. 114, part 21, Sept. 17–25, 1968: "License the Networks" (27811–27812).

United States of America, *Congressional Record,* Proceedings and Debates of the 91st Congress, 1st sess. Vol. 115, part 3, Feb. 5–21, 1969.

Rep. Henry B. González: "License the Networks" (2935–2936); vol. 115, part 6, Mar. 20–Apr. 1, 1969: "Columbia Broadcasting System" (7908); vol. 115, part 7, Apr. 2–21, 1969: "Race Hate" (8590–8591), "Cause for Concern" (9058–9060), and "Foundation Responsibility" (9308–9309); vol. 115, part 8, Apr. 22–May 1, 1969: "The Hate Issue" (9951–9954), "Racism in South Texas" (10522–10527), "Foundation Responsibility II" (10779–10780), and "Ford Foundation Plus San Antonio Equals Murder" (11140); vol. 115, part 11, May 27–June 9, 1969: "Fraud in America" (14100–14101), "Fraud in America II" (14389–14391), "Fraud in America III" (14420–14421), "Fraud in America IV" (14984–14986), "Fraud in America V" (15069–15070); vol. 115, part 12, June 10–19, 1969: "Failure at the FCC" (15768); vol. 115, part 13, June 20–July 1, 1969: "The Television Overlords" (17887); vol. 115, part 23, Oct. 21–28, 1969: "The FCC: Regulator or Regulated?" (30877).

U.S. Congress, Senate Committee of the Judiciary, *Extent of Subversion in the "New Left": Testimony of Robert J.Thoms,* Hearings before the Subcommittee to Investigate the Administration of the Internal Security Act and Other Internal Security Laws, part 1, Jan. 20, 1970. Washington, D.C.: U.S. Government Printing Office, 1970.

U.S. Congress, Senate Select Committee on Equal Educational Opportunity, "Effect of Television on Equal Educational Opportunity," July 30, 1970, *Hearings on Equal Educational Opportunity,* part 2—Equality of Educational Opportunity: An Introduction—Continued, 91st Congress, 1st sess., 1970. Washington, D.C.: U.S. Government Printing Office, 1970. 928A–928BM.

U.S. Congress, House Subcommittee on Communications and Power, *Films and Broadcasts Demeaning Ethnic, Racial, or Religious Groups,* hearings held Sept. 21, 1970. Washington, D.C.: U.S. Government Printing Office, 1970.

U.S. Congress, House Subcommittee on Communications and Power, *Films and Broadcasts Demeaning Ethnic, Racial, or Religious Groups: 1971,* hearings held Apr. 27–28, 1971. Washington, D.C.: U.S. Government Printing Office, 1971.

U.S. Commission on Civil Rights. *Window Dressing on the Set: Women and Minorities in Television.* Washington, D.C.: U.S. Government Printing Office. Aug. 1977.
————. *Window Dressing on the Set: An Update.* Washington, D.C.: U.S. Government Printing Office, Jan. 1979.
U.S. Equal Employment Opportunity Commission. *First Annual Report.* Submitted to the House of Representatives. Washington, D.C.: U.S. Government Printing Office, 1967.
————. *Second Annual Report.* Submitted to the House of Representatives. Washington, D.C.: U.S. Government Printing Office, 1968.
————. *Hearings on Utilization of Minority and Women Workers in Certain Major Industries.* Mar. 12–14, 1969, Los Angeles, Calif. Washington, D.C.: U.S. Government Printing Office, 1969.
U.S. General Accounting Office. *The Equal Employment Opportunity Commission Has Made Limited Progress in Eliminating Employment Discrimination.* Report to the Congress. Washington, D.C.: U.S. Government Printing Office, 1976.

Archival Holdings

Laura Aguilar Papers. Department of Special Collections, Stanford University, Stanford, Calif.
Harry Gamboa Jr. Papers. Department of Special Collections, Stanford University, Stanford, Calif.
Efraín Gutiérrez Papers. Department of Special Collections, Stanford University, Stanford, Calif.
Mexican American Legal Defense and Education Fund Papers, Department of Special Collections, Stanford University, Stanford, Calif.
Ernesto R. Palomino Papers. California Ethnic and Multicultural Archives, Donald Davidson Library, University of California, Santa Barbara.
Domingo Nick Reyes Papers. The Benson Latin American Collection at the University of Texas at Austin.
Domingo Nick Reyes. "Testimony on Modern Advertising Practices." Eight-page manuscript (Nov. 18, 1971). Federal Trade Commission Library.
Siobhan Oppenheimer-Nicolau Papers, Department of Special Collections, Stanford University, Stanford, Calif.
Jesús Salvador Treviño Papers. Department of Special Collections, Stanford University, Stanford, Calif.
Willie Varela Papers, Department of Special Collections, Stanford University Libraries, Stanford, Calif.

Unpublished Sources

Holman, Ben. Information Memorandum for the Director. Subject: Upcoming Media Relations Activities. Community Relations Service (Oct. 9, 1967).
Letter to Edward James Olmos, from Coalition for Latino Programming on Public Broadcasting and Latino Producers Ad Hoc Committee (Dec. 27, 1998).
Letter to Sandie Pedlow, Senior Program Officer, Corporation for Public Broadcasting, from Coalition for Latino Programming on Public Broadcasting (Sept. 29, 1998).
Open letter from Latino Producers Ad Hoc Committee (Nov. 13, 1998).
Treviño, Jesús Salvador, and José Luis Ruíz. "Hispanics and Public Broadcasting: A History of Neglect." Paper prepared for the Rockefeller Seminar on Independent Television Makers and Public Communications Policy, a Seminar-Conference to Promote Telecommunications for Diversity in the 1980s (June 1979).

Interviews by the Author

Artenstein, Isaac. Stanford, Calif. (Mar. 8, 1990).
Camplis, Francisco X. Daly City, Calif. (Feb. 28, 1990).
Diaz, Eduardo. San Antonio, Tex. (Sept. 28, 1992).
Diaz LeRoy, Robert. Wells College, N.Y. (Aug. 12, 1993).
Durón, Armando. Los Angeles, Calif. (Sept. 18, 1995).
España, Frances Salomé. Los Angeles, Calif. (May 27, 1991).
Esparza, Moctesuma. Stanford, Calif. (Mar. 13, 1990).
Espinosa, Paul. San Diego, Calif. (Mar. 19, 1993).
Gamboa Jr., Harry. Los Angeles, Calif. (May 27, 1991).
Garza, Luis. Los Angeles, Calif. (Oct. 10, 1990).
Gronk. San Francisco, Calif. (Aug. 4, 1991).
Gutiérrez, Efraín. Los Angeles, Calif. (Apr. 16, 1997, and July 20, 1997).
Hahn, Sandra P. Los Angeles, Calif. (May 27, 1991).
Marin, Richard "Cheech." Malibu, Calif. (Oct. 16, 1990).
Morales, Sylvia. Los Angeles, Calif. (Nov. 16, 1991).
Moreno, Eduardo. Los Angeles, Calif. (May 29, 1991).
Nieves-Cruz, Yvette. San Antonio, Tex. (Sept. 29, 1992).
Nogales, Alex. Los Angeles, Calif. (Sept. 18, 1995).
Olmos, Edward James. New York, N.Y. (Apr. 5, 1992).
Parra, Antonio. San Antonio, Tex. (Sept. 27, 1992).
Pérez, Severo. San Antonio, Tex. (Feb. 3, 1990). Interview by author and Lillian Jiménez.
Portillo, Lourdes. Albuquerque, N.M. (Dec. 5, 1991).
Renteria, Esther. Los Angeles, Calif. (Aug. 22, 1995).
Ruiz, José Luis. Los Angeles, Calif. (Feb. 22, 1990 [telephone], and Apr. 23, 1993).
Sanchez, Graciela. San Antonio, Tex. (Sept. 29, 1992).
Treviño, Jesús Salvador. Los Angeles, Calif. (May 28, 1991).
Varela, Willie. El Paso, Tex. (June 28, 1991 [telephone]), and San Antonio, Tex. (July 12, 1991).
Young, Robert M. Los Angeles, Calif. (Apr. 21, 1990).

Index

Chon A. Noriega is associate professor of film and television at the University of California, Los Angeles. He has written on avant-garde and popular cinemas, visual art, alterity and media, and television in such journals as *Art Journal, Daedalus, Social Research,* and *Wide Angle.* In addition to curating exhibitions at the Whitney Museum of American Art, the Mexican Museum (San Francisco), and the American Museum of the Moving Image, among others, he produced and wrote the documentary *Revelations: Hispanic Art of Evanescence.* He is the editor of *Aztlán: A Journal of Chicano Studies* and six books, including *Chicanos and Film: Representation and Resistance* (Minnesota, 1992), *Urban Exile: Collected Writings of Harry Gamboa Jr.* (Minnesota, 1998), and *Visible Nations: Latin American Cinema and Video* (Minnesota, 2000).